MY GENERATION

FOR DENNY CORDELL AND BILL GRAHAM

MY GENERATION

ROCK'N'ROLL REMEMBERED
AN IMPERFECT HISTORY

EDITORS

Antony Farrell, Vivienne Guinness
and Julian Lloyd

ASSISTANT EDITORS

Brendan Barrington

Faith O'Grady

THE LILLIPUT PRESS

First published in 1996 by
THE LILLIPUT PRESS LTD
4, Rosemount Terrace, Arbour Hill,
Dublin 7, Ireland.

CIP record for this title
is available from
The British Library

ISBN 1 874675 5 11

Design by Mary Guinan
Illustrations by Ron Wood
Typeset in Optima display and 10pt on 12 Goudy
Printed in Dublin by
βetaprint of Clonshaugh

'Hearing him for the first time was like bursting out of jail.'
Bob Dylan on Elvis Presley

CONTENTS

EDITORS' PREFACE

THIS BOOK HAD ITS ORIGINS in Loughcrew, County Meath, one late spring evening in 1994. My stepbrother Charlie Naper and I started naming our favourite albums and unravelled a past signposted by its music, leading to the garden of the late sixties and early seventies. An important point of departure was *The Heart of Rock and Soul: The 1001 Greatest Singles Ever Made* (1989) by Dave Marsh (rock bibliography is still in its infancy: Greil Marcus, Nick Kent and Hugo Williams are other reliable guides). I elaborated on the idea with the poet-publisher Peter Fallon, enlisted my co-editors Julian Lloyd and Vivienne Guinness, and the journey began.

My *Generation* is an act of aural repossession. We asked for 'notes towards an autobiography through sound', inviting contributors to select ten albums of classic, formative rock – a broad church that housed jazz, blues, soul, folk, country, reggae, punk. The memories elicited speak for a generation coming of age in a world in radical transition.

The responses, as they came, were generous and unqualified. First in was John Stephenson, by fax: 'What a glorious idea! Thank you for the invitation, which so caught my fancy that I sat down immediately and churned it out. I haven't enjoyed myself so much in ages.' Ian Whitcomb, an early icon from Trinity College days, came next. (In May 1965 *Trinity News* reported that Whitcomb's 'You Turn Me On', recorded at the Eamonn Andrews Studios, had reached number 3 on the West Coast of America, topped by the Rolling Stones with '(I Can't Get No) Satisfaction' and the Byrds' 'Mr Tambourine Man'. The paper noted that he was scheduled to appear at the Trinity Ball, 'where we hope to get a pre-view of this song, especially as it has been banned by Radio Eireann for being "erotic" '.) Aisling Foster, Elgy Gillespie and Frank Mc Guinness followed, setting a seal on the enterprise, and through friendship and propinquity we gathered in a rich haul of over seventy contributors, all of them broadly Irish by birth, residence or association.

We had a few refusals. Among politicians, Mary Banotti 'spent the 60s in the United States marching and not listening to a great deal of music'. One prominent novelist responded, 'I'm afraid my days of Bob Dylan impersonations are no more now than a warm, pink smudge of embarrassment in my memory.

Besides, I never think of it as *my* generation, but *theirs* ...'. An eminent poet declined saying that he was 'a case of total burn-out. I *feel you* will understand'. A columnist stated she never 'had money for albums.' Ronan O'Rahilly, founder of Radio Caroline and grandson of The '1916' O'Rahilly, nearly came on board. We courted Lynn Geldof assiduously but failed, despite a shared affection for Billy Fury.

As bodies swayed to music, editorial rules were bent. Aisling Foster wrote:

How serious is that 'no more than one singer or group, no best-of compilations'? One of the first titles I thought of was *The Rock Machine Turns You On* – surely everyone's most-played mid-60s album? – and a compilation. What about the Motown compilations which came out at the same time as the (generally dire) individual albums – or most especially the Atlantic label *Solid Gold Soul* volume 1 and on, the absolute mother's milk of Ireland's long romance with black American soul music?

Jeananne Crowley, Mick Hanly, Kevin Myers, Colm Tóibín, Kathleen Williamson and others proceeded to fly the editorial net, magnificently.

The shards, narratives and vinyl dreams that go to form *My Generation* reveal an era in outline. Ireland's intimate scale lends coherence to material dense with cross-reference and shared experience. While international rock music fed our elemental hungers and asserted itself as a lingua franca during the sixties, singles gave way to albums and the 'rock industry' became a part of corporate culture, smoothing away the individualism from which it developed. Irish rock itself came into its own during the seventies by using an idiom drawn from traditional sources and fired by the energy and excitement at large in the global village.

There was a world out there, stirring beneath our feet. At Haight-Ashbury an alternative society momentarily pitched its tents, Ken Kesey and Timothy Leary its avatars, *The Psychedelic Experience: A Manual based on the Tibetan Book of the Dead* its guide to the underworld; from it some of us returned, bearing *The Whole Earth Catalog* and new ways of seeing. In Carnaby Street and later at Bow Street Magistrates Court, wizard of Oz Richard Neville waved his magic wand, announced a sexual revolution and earned our gratitude. Radicalized Maoist students moved along the Boulevard Saint-Michel, overturning governments. More somberly, a movement begun at Burntollet culminated in Derry's Bloody Sunday, the burning of the British Embassy in Dublin's St Stephen's Green and the end of Stormont. Those *were* the days – our pied pipers playing us through, these pages their memorial.

The precise nature of some contributions to *My Generation* contrasts with the baroque discursiveness of others. Space permitting, the players 'speak for themselves'. The result is a wonderful landscape in which as readers and editors we are privileged to find ourselves. The last contribution in was from that quintessential rock correspondent, BP Fallon. Having begun with his brother Peter, the circle was complete.

[AF]

THIS IS A BOOK WITH A SOUNDTRACK. As an unashamed groupie, albeit rather a grown-up one now, I loved the singer as much as the song, so it was no hardship to gather many of the musicians' contributions on tape (designated on the page). Marianne Faithfull quoted to me David Bowie's maxim that 'writing about music is like dancing about architecture', but overcame her own reservations with some lucid and evocative recollections. Her remark, though, did make me wonder how the many gifted writers who have contributed to this work would fare if asked to make a record about their favourite books.

The going got delightfully tough in the case of Ronnie Wood: after a long and happy night I felt we had some resonant material on tape. The transcription was one of the most hilariously dadaistic documents imaginable ('Got my mojo working' came out as 'Got my mother working'). Something had obviously gone wrong. I listened to the tape again. The truth was that snatches of conversation in euphoric late-night code, interspersed with pregnant pauses – some of considerable length – and cackles of laughter do not make good copy. We had another bash. It wasn't quite such a riot, but we were able to make a proper record of Ronnie's friendships and memories, going back to the dawn of British R&B, the crucial influence of which on 1960s music cannot be underestimated.

Both Denny Cordell and Bill Graham died while writing their entries. It is impossible to think of two people who loved music more or who more completely embodied the sense of adventure that is expressed in rock 'n' roll and all its many roots and branches.

[JL]

And, for the record, here are the editors' selections:

Aftermath	The Rolling Stones
Ballad of Easy Rider,	The Byrds
Family Entertainment	Family
Abbey Road	The Beatles
New Morning	Bob Dylan
Moondance	Van Morrison
Who's Next	The Who
Every Picture Tells a Story	Rod Stewart
Harvest	Neil Young
Me and Bobby McGee	Kris Kristofferson
Good Old Boys	Randy Newman
Cohen Live	Leonard Cohen

[AF]

Jerry Lee Lewis	Jerry Lee Lewis
Mr Tambourine Man	The Byrds
Rubber Soul	The Beatles
Blonde on Blonde	Bob Dylan
Bitches Brew	Miles Davis
Are You Experienced?	Jimi Hendrix
Blue	Joni Mitchell
Solo Music	Philip Glass
New Boots and Panties!!	Ian Dury
Broken English	Marianne Faithfull

[VG]

Upside Your Head	Jimmy Reed
Five Live Yardbirds	The Yardbirds
Them	Them
The Rolling Stones	The Rolling Stones
Blonde on Blonde	Bob Dylan
The Genius of Ray Charles	Ray Charles
New Boots and Panties!!	Ian Dury
Mink de Ville	Willie de Ville
King of the Tenors	Ben Webster
The Harder They Come	(Soundtrack: Various Artists)
The Sun Sessions	Elvis Presley
Another Saturday Night, Louisiana Jukebox Hits	

[JL]

MY GENERATION

DERMOT BOLGER

MARTHA

I found the box of old albums,
Blew dust off a disused needle,

Tom Waits began to sing 'Martha'.
Once again I was twenty-four,

The pull of hash and tobacco,
Cheap white wine at my elbow

At the window of your bedsit
In the dust-filled August light,

A needle bobbing over warped vinyl
One final time before we stroll

Down to bars where friends gather.
Decks to be shuffled, numbers rolled,

Blankets bagged on some dawnlit floor.
Our lives are just waiting to occur

As we linger in the infinity it takes
For the voice of Tom Waits to fade.

TIM BOOTH

THERE HAS ALWAYS BEEN MUSIC: my mother playing the piano while I beat my head in time against the bars of the play-pen; the wireless in the early fifties with programmes like 'Music While You Work'. Daa, de daa, de daa, deee daa da … 'brought to you today by Geraldo and his Orchestra' – earworm signature tune followed by 'How Much is that Doggie in the Window?' and 'The Deadwood Stage is a-Comin'' on over the Hill' – all blown relentlessly from the old valve radio by a wind they called 'Maria'. Terrible *straight* music.

In boarding-school, after lights-out, hit-parade fodder leaked furtively from Luxembourg 208, but that wasn't the real thing either. You needed to hear the Everly Brothers, and Carl Perkins, boys like that, who could really *do it*. But what you got was the Kingston Trio, and Helen Shapiro, geeks, so the only thing to do was to go out and buy something for yourself. But what to buy? It had to be something to really impress your peers. After all, you had just mastered B7th on the six-quid guitar your mother gave you for your fourteenth birthday and you saw yourself as somehow akin to the young Beethoven, brimming with musical talent. So, maybe it should be jazz. That ought to knock 'em dead. But no. Too many notes, too hard to listen to, and there was no way any of you could actually play it. God alone knows what kind of chords were in there. Take five? Take a hike, Dave. Stick to the easy stuff – 'Livin' Doll', 'All Shook Up'. Tricky shit like that. Learn the chords, and get the Terylene slacks taken in.

Then, in 1962, your callow student ears heard something at a friend's place – 'What in the name of God is that?' Lonesome high voices on a bed of guitars. No electricity, but somehow earthy. The white-trash roots of rock'n'roll. Music that you could take and fuse with black R&B. Stuff that people out there were already taking and fusing … as you would soon learn. Appalachian mountain music, with harmony singing so tight that, like the closely fitted stones of those fabled Andean temples, you couldn't get a knife-blade between the elements.

The New Lost City Ramblers. Mono, but sounding sweet on my mother's new hi-fi – a state-of-the-art Pye Black Box, with little built-in speakers on each side of the unit – maybe not rock'n'roll, but the pure stuff all the same. They had these *sounds*: fiddles, mandolins, banjos, put the hair up on the back of my neck, just like the Everlys could, that vibrato in the vocals, a desperate yearning in the voices, like some kind of pre-electric poor-boy Buddy Holly singing harmonies with himself. But the girls didn't like it, so it was back to the popular stuff: 'Why mustah bee-eee a te-e-enaaaaggger in luuuve?'

5

That Ramblers album got a lot of play. I don't have it anymore, but there were songs like 'Mighty Mississippi', 'She Tickled Me', and 'All the Good Times', as well as rags and breakdowns, that I learned, and subsequently attempted in places like The Pike, a late-night club in Herbert Lane, where in 1964 a young American, Andy Leader, with a big Martin guitar that he could fingerpick, had a song that I could not believe. Written by this newcomer called Bob Dylan. I'd never heard a song like that before. It sounded like the way things actually were. Andy taught me the picking style and the chords, and there I was. 'Don't think twice, it's all right.'

I got the Dylan albums as they came out, grew my hair a bit and practised hard – both the guitar and the attitude. But I was also listening to other music: John Hammond Junior's first album, entitled *John Hammond* – produced by his father John Hammond Senior, the man who had first discovered Dylan – spoke to my condition. Black R&B, but a white boy singing it: numbers like 'You Can't Judge a Book by the Cover' and 'Who Do You Love?', all played by an electric band that could make the music flow, stretching it out, hitting the bio-rhythm. I've still got that album.

Then the word went out: Dylan was coming to Dublin. So there I was, in the fifth row as his band took the stage, an all-electric outfit with a stereo-sound system. Jesus! A guitar each side on the speakers, and Garth Hudson's Hammond, swirly and iridescent in the mix, like oil on water. The audience hated it, hated this movement forward, disgracing themselves yet again, but I had my innocent mind well and truly blown that night. When *Blonde on Blonde* came out, I was the first in the shop. An electric album, almost better than the concert. List-ening to it today I move back through time, to that flat on Waterloo Road, taste those tastes, smell those smells. 'Nobody feels any pain ...'

'You heard this?' somebody said, and this weirdness came out of the radiogram speaker – in glorious monorama naturally – 'Come a little closer to my breast and I'll tell you that you really are the one I love the best, and you don't have to worry about any of the rest, 'cause everything's fine right now.' Which it undoubtedly was: Incredible String Band's first, eponymous album, hit with a huge impact, and like some vast extraterrestrial object whacking in from Tau Cetii, it blew our safe little musical world into a different orbit. Williamson, Heron and Palmer weren't American, they were Scots, and their way of playing was completely new. The words and music came from their background, pioneered by them, out there on some strange frontier, each song exploring the parameters of their personal world, forging music that felt like it came from a tradition, from the source, even though it was fresh out of the mould. Music that made the mundane suddenly exotic, and allowed the everyday events of our lives take on a fantastical spin. Inspiring stuff. If they could do it, then maybe we could as well.

In Edinburgh, people followed a different drummer, so when I returned to Dublin I had a copy of *Disraeli Gears*, Cream's second album, with its tacky Martin Sharp cover that still managed to say it all, and *those sounds*. Oh, the glorious pretension of the whole thing, a sort of quasi-yuppie rhetoric born ahead of its time: 'Tales of Brave Ulysses', my arse. Those voices quivering together, guitar cutting through a ground-zero onslaught of drums and bass. Clapton, Bruce, and some whangdoodle drummer called Ginger Baker doing stuff that shouldn't be allowed. Sound waves whacking out from battered speakers like an F15 kicking in its afterburners – by now we had a crude stereo system in the house in Sandymount: 'Do do do, do doo do. I feel free.'

Which I did, until in 1968, on the barricades somewhere, somebody put on an album called *Music from Big Pink* by the Band. That put a halt to our tango! These guys were serious, and who's that drummer? After the rococo bombast of Cream, this outfit was lean and dangerous, hard-edge. Nothing stated unless it was needed. Supposedly a début album, but you could tell from the music that these boys had been out there forever. Originally the Hawks, backing Ronnie Hawkins, and then Dylan's first real band, these were veterans, seasoned campaigners, men who had paid their dues and could still smile about it. Their music had the lonely yearning of Appalachian music on the one hand and the power of rock'n'roll on the other – a fusion that went into your head and down your spine, little tantric fingers jacking in on-line, exactly there, at the heart of the matter. 'I pulled in to Nazareth, I was feelin' about half past dead ...' Getting that song down, trying out those long harmonies: 'Annnnnnnnnnnnnd you put the load right on me ...'

Then somebody, that same nameless somebody, did put the load right on me, with yet another album on the turntable. Side two, track one, something called 'Ice'. Out-there stuff, warped stuff, full of seductive mind-enhancing sounds that not only spoke to my condition, but danced an off-centre hallucinogenic watusi *with* that condition. The album was *Clear* by Spirit, produced by Lou Adler in 1969, and its jazzy overtones breathed a sophistication that was very different from the Band, yet in its own way just as authentic. Ed Cassidy, their drummer, was the stepfather of guitarist Randy California. Ed sounded like he had been taught by Gene Krupa: he didn't exactly swing, but somehow fit right in with the younger musicians. A good steadying influence. They produced a body of work, and maybe *The Twelve Dreams of Dr Sardonicus* is a better album, but *Clear* was the first one I heard. There was also at that time a green VW beetle with *Clear* on the eight-track, and Johanna at the wheel, and these three facts enhance my recollection: 'I said too much business is wrong for you baby.' Track six, side two also offered the opinion that there was 'New Dope in Town', and there was, in not inconsiderable amounts.

The town was London in 1972, Van Morrison on the stereo. The album was *Saint Dominic's Preview*. Every track just right for the times and their interconnected leisure activities. In from Hampstead Heath of an autumn evening, pockets and cortex full of a certain mushroom, and Van the Man telling us that it was 'Almost Independence Day' while the Moogs of Bernie Krause and Mark Naftalin boomed and swooped behind the mix, as if the spiralling double helix of our own DNA had somehow escaped from our genes and replicated itself deep in the grooves of the vinyl. 'As we gaze out on, as we gaze out on ... St. Dominic's Preview.' Nobody knew what the words meant exactly, but it didn't matter. They represented something that seemed profound, a way to go, a way to be, with the synapses firing on all four million cylinders, and John McFee's steel guitar stringing silvery phrases across the melody like neural power-lines. We knew the precise location of St. Dominic's Preview.

Back in Ireland, the real Bill Graham, for reasons that escape me, laid an album on me – *In My Own Time*, by an American singer called Karen Dalton. I had never heard of her before, nor have I since. Maybe something happened to her, but should you ever come across any of her work, buy it. Suffice to say that the record was produced by Harvey Brooks, and the backing musicians include such luminaries as Amos Garrett and Gregg Thomas.

Singing like Billie Holiday on meta-steroids, Dalton – who seems to come from a folk background – also plays twelve-string guitar and banjo. The album kicks off with Dino Valenti's 'Something on Your Mind', then slips into 'When a Man Loves a Woman', followed by Paul Butterfield's 'In My Own Dream'. Dalton's voice, phrasing like an alto sax, weaves through the superb ensemble players. Then comes the pearl. Something called 'Katie Cruel', the antithesis of everything that went before. Just banjo, voice, and the beautiful fiddle of Bobby Notkoff. Short and sweet. She resumes, back where she started, with Holland-Dozier-Holland's standard 'How Sweet It Is'. Side two kicks off with Richard Manuel's epic 'In a Station', and like side one, a surprise lurks here as well, but you will have to discover this for yourself.

I've had the album for over twenty years. It's worn and scratchy now, but I have never heard anything like it before or since. Eat your heart out Björk. 'Here I am where I must be, where I would be I cannot.'

During those twenty years I had been listening to Frank Zappa, album after album, each one even better or even worse than the last, depending on your viewpoint. In 1979 he released *Joe's Garage, Act I*, a wholesome piece of fun in the form of a morality play (according to the liner notes). Along with the usual superb musicianship, warped humour, blatant in-your-face sexuality and iconoclastic shadow-boxing, the album contains the classic 'Joe's Garage'. A rags-to-riches tale of your average beat combo in pursuit of fame, their playing ability slowly creeping up the quality scale – showband to four-chord naff to slick – while the lyrics unfold, Zappa displaying a bizarre yet comprehensive understanding of the music business. It should be compulsory listening at music schools everywhere, along with the wonderful 'Why Does It Hurt When I Pee?', a lampoon of the bombastic pomp-rock Meatloaf archetype.

Zappa is no longer with us, but everybody should give him a listen at least once. He's the musical equivalent of reading Thomas Pynchon. 'Oh those Catholic girls, with their tiny moustaches ...'

It happened again last year – somebody, that famous somebody, put on a CD, and my attention was grabbed. Guitars, sparkling and slashing, Jesse Ed Davis-style, fluid bass and drums, swampy organ chords and some type of native chanting going down. What's this? Somebody speaking the lyrics now ... whatever happened to singing for chrissake? No, hold on. This is good ... the business, the full shilling. A big resonant dramatic voice with a Yankee curl to the vowels: lyrics that are full of righteous anger, full of poetry, full of love. Songs with titles like 'See the Woman', 'Raptor', 'Shadow over Sisterland', hard-muscled committed ideas, taking no prisoners, the whole structure of the concept held in place by a hefty foundation of rock'n'roll, underpinned and reinforced by a layering of Native-American traditional vocals and drumming, from which the words soar up gracefully, implacably, to form music of great power and honesty, compelling you to listen:

> Welcome to graffiti land
> All the rides are in your head
> The ticket is what is thought
> And what is said.

From 'Rant and Roll', the first track on *Johnny Damas and Me* by John Trudell.

Says it all really.

PAUL BRADY

FAMILY STYLE
THE VAUGHAN BROTHERS

Among the last recordings by Stevie Ray Vaughan before his untimely death. Here, he and his brother Jimmy play the kind of music that must have been heard in bars throughout Texas from the late forties on. In a former incarnation I must have been a barfly in Texas because this music is a language I spoke fluently ... before I even heard it. Essential listening.

MALAGASY GUITAR
D'GARY

Real name Ernest Randrianasolo, D'Gary is from the Bara tribal group of southern Madagascar. Hearing this record for the first time, I again felt this strange feeling of coming home. D'Gary's guitar-playing is the most stunning thing I have ever heard. The music he plays and sings seems like the source of almost every type of music in existence. Here are Caribbean, Andalusian, Indian, European classical/church harmony, blues and Celtic rhythms all cascading riotously together, and not in a conscious New Age concoction. This music has been there forever. Not for the faint-hearted, but hugely rewarding and continuously so.

DIRTY MIND
PRINCE

From 1980, this is Prince in his classic early pop days before the funk-rock took over. Nothing wrong with his funk, but here he seemed more into straight-ahead songs and stripped-down dynamite. Incest, head, and doing it all night: what more could a body want? Nobody should have this much talent.

TRADITIONAL IRISH UNACCOMPANIED SINGING
DARACH Ó CATHÁIN

Originally released in Ireland on the Gael Linn label in the early sixties, these are some of the greatest-ever recordings of pure Gaelic 'Sean Nós' singing. Darach Ó Catháin was born in Leitir Mór in Connemara and became recognized as probably the best Connemara singer of his time. A hard life 'working, drinking and making music' in Leeds only served to make his voice all the richer. To hear him 'open up' a song still devastates me. Anyone who doubts the legend that Connemara people are descended from the Moors of North Africa and southern Spain should listen to this record. *Dia Leat a Dhara*, up there wherever you are!

PIRATES
RICKIE LEE JONES

From 1981, this record was Jones's follow-up to her hit début album (featuring 'Chuck E's in Love') and was already showing the dark side which came to dominate all her later albums. Rarely is darkness so sublime as this. All her street characters – Eddie, Zero, Bird, Cuntfinger Louie, Woody and Dutch – seem like the only people really alive as long as this record plays. Check out 'Skeletons', which is number one on my list of songs I wish I'd written.

ALL TIME GREATS
ELVIS PRESLEY

After all the attitude, hype, movies, excess, fantasy, myths and legends, what remains is that Elvis was simply an incredible singer. Instinct and talent shoot through every phrase of every line of every song, no matter what mood he was trying to convey. 'Jailhouse Rock' to 'Wooden Heart'? Who else can show such balls alongside such tenderness and vulnerability?

THE BOTHY BAND
THE BOTHY BAND

Fasten your seat-belts! Dónal Lunny has been at the centre of energy in Irish music for so long now, it's easy to forget the shock that greeted the unveiling of the Bothy Band, his inspired post-Planxty creation of the seventies. More so than the Chieftains, who were too orchestral and lacking in the engine-room department, the Bothy Band ran on high-octane all night. When Tommy Peoples, Matt Molloy and Paddy Keenan tore off with Tríona Ní Dhomhnaill and her brother, Mícheál, with Dónal stoking up the fire behind, people just started to giggle helplessly with excitement. Everything that happens in Irish music today owes something to this record.

GRACELAND
PAUL SIMON

This was a record struck by lightning. The inspiration to seek out the music of Soweto, as yet unheard on the world stage, and marry it with his own laconic poetry, gave Paul Simon one of the brightest moments in his career. To introduce a sound combination, ethnic and totally new, and make it appeal to the mainstream in a world of market research and playlist consultants, was a sweet triumph. A classic from day one, not least for the huge Roy Halley sound production.

BOP TILL YOU DROP
RY COODER

Was this the first-ever digitally recorded album? 'Pop' album certainly. That's what we all thought in Dublin in 1979. We passed it around and listened to it as if it were something from another planet. Musically it hit us almost like *Graceland* did years later – a totally new sonic and attitudinal approach to sixties soul, sampled at fifty thousand times a second and recorded as numbers. Far out, man!

GIVE IT UP
BONNIE RAITT

I found this record when I was kipping on Chuck Neighbors' floor in New York in 1972 or thereabouts. The Johnstons, an Irish folk group I was a member of, had just supported Bonnie Raitt at Tufts University, Boston, and this record was hot at the time. Little did I know that twenty years later she would record some of my songs and call her album *Luck of the Draw* after one of them. This was the coolest record of that summer. It still is pretty cool. Any sound that comes out of that girl's mouth is okay by me.

PHILIP CASEY

SGT. PEPPER'S LONELY HEARTS CLUB BAND
THE BEATLES

Rediscovering the date of this record, June 1967, is disconcerting, because the event I associate with it happened a year and a half before. This will be the case with a few more of my songs of experience, I have to confess.

I was in bed in Cappagh Hospital, beside the ward gramophone. It was a lovely mahogany set, with rich speakers, and it found its way into my novel *The Fabulists*, thirty years later, as belonging to Tess's parents. One or two beds up from me was Paddy Doyle, since famous as author of *The God Squad*. Paddy later owned an almost identical machine. I had thought of the Beatles as a yeh yeh band, and so was startled to hear the rich, opening chords, a sound that remains vivid as a sensual shock. Perhaps this is why I associate it with the following.

In orthopaedic hospitals, apart from after operations, very few people are actually sick, and so teenage patients get up to ordinary teenage things, and in those days many patients spent years at a time in hospital. There were a few experimentation hotspots, the notorious one being behind the Congress Altar (I'm not sure if the nuns were aware how aptly it was named), which was the original Eucharistic Congress Altar on O'Connell Bridge in 1932, later rebuilt in Cappagh. Another hotspot was the linen room. One nurse took exception to my sojourns there, which were mostly with a beautiful colleague of hers, to whom I will be forever grateful, and never lost an opportunity to disapprove of my behaviour, which was innocent enough, if high-spirited. On Christmas Eve, those of us who could walk or go in wheelchairs were ordered to midnight Mass. The off-duty nurses were there too, in all their white-gloved splendour, and afterwards, when we were safely in bed, they returned to the ward with their mistletoe. One by one they kissed us, and I was beginning to feel very pleasant indeed, when I noticed the disapproving one was taking her turn. I expected a chaste peck, but for the first time in my life I got the length of a woman's tongue down my throat. I remember you, and your name, very well, Nurse X, but our secret is safe.

It's wonderful to be here, it's certainly a thrill. You're such a lovely audience, we'd like to take you home with us, we'd love to take you home.

AMERICAN PIE
DON MCLEAN

From about 1972 until he married Eileen Mulrooney in 1974, I shared a flat with Paddy Doyle in Ranelagh. Soon it became the norm to have a party every Saturday night. The evening might begin in Toner's of Baggot Street, or the Chariot Inn, or T. Humphrey's (Thumphrey's as we called it) in Ranelagh. On a pay-packet of £8 a week, I paid tax, £5 as my share of my rent, bought food, clothing and transport, and had enough to get pie-eyed at the weekend. A pint was nineteen new pence. By 1974 I had a job as an 'animal technician' in the Medical Research Council labs in Trinity, which brought me up to £19 a week, though I wasn't much better off. At one time there was a hard core of friends who made it to our parties most weekends: Jim Greeley, Maura Smith, Eucharia Morrissey, Eamonn Dawson, Carmel O'Rourke if she was off-duty, Dave Stokes, Mervyn Gilbert when he came to live next door, Siodhbhra Larkin when she wasn't somewhere exotic, and Eileen Stokes, who always seemed to appear magically with a plastic basin when I'd had just too much. And Tony Corbett, who would have us in kinks with one of his Donald Duck routines, or describing two small breadcrumbs ganging up on a big breadcrumb. One night our landlord, an enormous Kerryman, arrived with twenty-four bags of fish and chips. On another, Eamonn Dawson arrived from work just before closing time, gasping for a pint. 'You'll get one if you take my wheelchair down to Thumphrey's,' Paddy told him. 'But whatever you do, don't get out of the chair.' Dave Stokes wheeled him down, and sure enough, the closing-time crowd parted like the waters of the Red Sea, and Eamonn got his pint. Most of us had long hair, and I had thick ginger sideburns. Paddy lay on the floor, accompanying himself on guitar, and as we got mellower we all joined in, although Paddy was the only one who knew all the words: Buddy Holly, the Beatles, Cliff Richard's 'Travelling Light', 'The Butcher Boy', 'Scarlet Ribbon', 'The Banks of the Ohio'. But what really got us going, perhaps because it was so long that you had time to get into the mood, was 'American Pie', and around about the maudlin hour, 'Vincent'.

Starry, starry night ...

ABRAXAS
SANTANA

I don't remember much about this one except myriad parties, smoke haze and dawns in Ranelagh or Rathmines. I didn't inhale, despite an hallucinatory memory of waking up in an enormous room beside a young woman I had never seen before, in the midst of what seemed like dozens of sleeping bodies (all of us fully dressed) – but I didn't know about passive smoking then. As I remember it, Bob Marley was big, but so were Santana, and I preferred Santana.

You're a Black Magic Woman, you're a Black Magic Woman ...

IRISH TOUR '74
RORY GALLAGHER

One of my few claims to musical fame is that Rory Gallagher's guitar once glanced off my head as he ran from the dressing-room to the stage in the National Stadium. The trouble is I have no idea when this was, despite enquiries – even on the Internet (by the way, for Gallagher admirers with Internet access *cf.* htpp://www.wmd.de/~grupe). My brother Peter and our old pal Mick Considine remember seeing him in the Carlton Cinema on his Irish Tour '74, which is when I thought I had seen him in the Stadium. I first heard Rory Gallagher on the radio when he was with Taste and I was about nineteen, with greats like 'Blister on the Moon' and 'Born on the Wrong Side of Time', which are songs I still love. But the one I've always liked best is 'Too Much Alcohol'.

> *91%. Better make it 92. 93%, 94, that'll do. 95, 96, 97%, 98*
> *– Bartender that's 99! Make it 100%. 100%. 100%. Wanna try some?*
> *Wanna try some? 100%. And I won't feel a thing at all.*

HAPPY TO MEET, SORRY TO PART
HORSLIPS

When we were in secondary school, Martin Armstrong was noted for two things: his brains, and his neatness. College put an end to the neatness. I didn't see him for a number of years, until we worked together on an experiment in community radio organized by Paul Funge's Gorey Arts Centre and Festival, the logo of which was the Dancing Man. Martin was brilliant at radio, a natural, and I remember working all night with him editing tapes and compiling material. I could only marvel.

Many bands, including U2 and, famously, the Virgin Prunes, came to the Gorey Arts Festival, but the night I cherish was the first Horslips concert. The Arts Centre was really a shed, used as a store for Funge's drapery shop during the year, and it was unaccustomed to booming bass and pumped-up volume, which must have been heard all over Gorey. By the end we were dancing in the aisles, and Paul Funge's father appeared in a vain attempt to stop the mayhem. Martin died a few years back, but he is forever etched on my memory as dancing with total abandon that summer's evening, the apotheosis of the Dancing Man.

> *The best and straightest arrow is the one that will range out of the archer's view.*

GOAT'S HEAD SOUP
THE ROLLING STONES

On leaving Ireland in 1974 to live in Spain, I was carrying the residue of an unrequited love, which is an ideal way to begin a voluntary exile. About twenty friends had all said they would come with me on my planned trip to a Gypsy Festival in Andalucia, but they were sceptical that Tony Corbett would be among them. In the event, Tony was the only one to venture forth.

15

We got a lift from Le Havre to Paris with Eileen Mulrooney's brother and his friend. We found a café, and talked about what we would do, as we still had-n't decided exactly where we were going. My unrequited love was at me, so I went over to the jukebox and picked out 'Angie' by the Rolling Stones. Outside, a pneumatic drill was hammering away in the heat.

On the platform Tony and I tossed a coin: Barcelona or Madrid, and Barcelona won. In our naiveté, we hadn't booked a seat, and so we stood all the way to Port Bou, an overnight journey. Somewhere around four in the morning we met a Spaniard, a man of about twenty-seven, who spoke perfect English and told us a lot about Spain. I didn't know anything about Catalonia, or the Basque country, or that Spain was anything other than one big homogeneous beach, with gypsies who lived mostly in the south and had a festival. As we were pulling into Port Bou, he took me aside and asked me if I would do him a favour. When I enquired as to what that might be, he said he wanted me to bring in a book for him. I coughed hard when I saw the title, *Techniques of Guerrilla Warfare*, and said that as this would my first time in Spain, I wanted to get in – and more to the point, I would like to get out if I so desired. He shrugged, not in the least offended or perturbed. When I saw the Spanish customs, with the frontier police armed to the teeth, I feared the worst. He put his bag on the table, and the *Techniques of Guerrilla Warfare* on top of his bag. The customs officer put the book on the table, and gave his bag an exhaustive search before putting the *Techniques of Guerrilla Warfare* back on top of the bag and waving him on.

Angie, oh Angie, ain't it good to be alive.

TUBULAR BELLS
MIKE OLDFIELD

When Tony Corbett and I arrived in Barcelona, we lived for a number of months in a *pension* opposite what was then Estación de Francia, and discovered a great bar next door in the Hotel Park. This was full of wonderful characters, behind and in front of the bar, and within six weeks we had been to two weddings. We had very good friends among the staff, and as soon as they had finished work at 3 a.m. they brought us everywhere. This was how I discovered the Guardia Civil, or *grises* (greys), very nasty customers with whom we had several run-ins but sur-vived unscratched because we were foreigners. One night we were returning from a bar with our Hotel Park friends at 5 a.m., on our way to get *churros* (pas-try dipped in hot chocolate) at Parque Ciudadela, when I decided to raise a toast with my glass of rum to one of the *grises*, whose sub-machine gun was pointed somewhere between my heart and forehead. *Salut, y forsa al ganut!* (Good health, and strength to your member!), I greeted him. Fortunately, he realized I was a stupid *extranjero*, as Franco was still very much alive and Catalan was most def-initely banned, but my friends almost had a collective heart attack.

Adjacent to this government building was a very large restaurant, and one night in the small hours Tony and I found ourselves in there as guests of the owner's son. He had arranged several speakers around the walls; it looked wonderful with the chairs stacked upside-down on the tables. We sat in the centre and he put *Tubular Bells* on the turntable. It is forty-eight minutes and fifty seconds I will never forget.

PEARL
JANIS JOPLIN

Janis Joplin is my favourite singer, and her 'Mercedes-Benz' is one of the few songs I ever learned. I sang it at my party the night before the Pope came to Ireland. Mad at my friends (who I had taken to be atheistic or at least agnostic) who were either coming to my party early to get up to see the Pope, or coming late to go directly from my party to the Phoenix Park, I got rather drunk, convinced I was the only one left with any integrity.

But fortune smiled. I like to think it was my passionate singing of 'Mercedes-Benz', but whatever it was, a beautiful Irish-Australian with the sexiest antipodean accent you ever heard took a fancy to me, and I fell deeply in love, a state I remained in for a number of years, and indeed, although Philomena is now happily married with two beautiful children in Sydney, we still keep in touch. We had the house to ourselves the next morning, and over a late fry breakfast we watched the Pope on TV.

To hell with integrity. I was so happy I'd have spent my holidays in Castelgondofo without blinking, and in the end we walked down to Christ Church to join the throng waving at John Paul II (although I drew the line at waving at the cardinals) as he sped past in the Papal bus. I owed him. It was the least I could do.

O Lord, won't you buy me a Mercedes-Benz?

NASHVILLE SKYLINE
BOB DYLAN

When I was about fifteen, at the height of the ballad boom, I used to sing around the parish halls with my brother John. John had a prodigious memory for song lyrics but I could not remember a line. However, I used to stand at an angle to John, and read his lips, and in this way I muddled through until we were separated one night when all the performers got on stage to sing the National Anthem, and I was exposed as unpatriotic, not to mention a fraud.

Many years later I thought of this at parties thrown by my friends, Dave and Emer. These parties reminded me of our hooleys in Beechwood Avenue – except that Emer prepared wonderful food instead of chips – in that everyone talked to each other, and the night ended in song, usually led by Dave on the guitar, with his endless Beatles and Dylan repertoire. When I discovered that I could read Dave's lips in much the same way that I had read John's, we became something of a team, to the extent that we sang at a friend's wedding, which shows I have nerves of steel or a hard neck, or both. Somehow I reckon our best duet was

Dylan's 'Girl of the North Country', especially as it stands out as the song I nearly learned.

> *I'm a-wonderin' if she remembers me at all. Many times I've often prayed*
> *In the darkness of my night. In the brightness of my day.*

I'M YOUR MAN
LEONARD COHEN

For my fortieth birthday Ulrike gave me a holiday in Berlin. I had been there while the Wall was still up, and had been in the East. It was strange driving back and forth with Ulrike in 1990, not knowing whether we were in the East or West. We visited Brecht's grave. The window of an old-fashioned tobacco shop that I remembered from before was now full of baubles from the Far East. There were posters for strip joints. An East Berlin speciality, a dessert, was no longer on the menu at a restaurant.

> *First we take Manhattan, then we take Berlin.*

At that time, Ulrike was studying philosophy, and was part of a study group, all women. I was invited on a picnic with them, along with the boyfriend of one of the others. At first I was reluctant. 'What would I have to say to Seven Female Philosophers?' I asked Ulrike. We set off in two cars for a picnic on the banks of the Oder, passing through East Berlin which still boasted a giant red-stone statue of Lenin, out past the already rusting factories and dilapidated apartment blocks (I'm still convinced that Communism fell for want of a tin of paint). The East German countryside was a revelation. We passed through beautiful old towns, preserved as they had been for hundreds of years – but what impressed me most, as a countryman, were the grasses and wild flowers.

The most significant thing about that trip, however, was the gossip. I have never heard, before or since, such red hot, XXXXX gossip and, for my benefit, it was all in English. We arrived at the Oder, which marks the border between Germany and Poland, in brilliant sunshine, and as we sat on the riverbank one of the women leaned over to me and said, 'Well, Philip, a picnic with Seven Female Philosophers is not so bad, eh?' I could only agree.

We went for a walk afterwards and had I not been told I would never have seen that the water was heavily polluted. We broke into small groups, and as the sun was setting, I looked back to see that as the light held them, the smog-filled air made our companions seem as if they were breaking into fuzzy pieces. Darkness fell as we drove home, and a wild boar leapt out in front of us. We drove along a tree-lined road, which I had seen in a dream fifteen years before, exactly like that, the headlights illuminating the row of white trunks.

> *I'm guided by a signal in the heavens.*
> *I'm guided by the birthmark on my skin.*
> *I'm guided by the beauty of our weapons.*
> *First we take Manhattan, then we take Berlin.*

LAR CASSIDY

MY LOVE OF SERIOUS MUSIC began when I was twelve years old, in 1962. Until then I had been listening to fifties rock'n'roll on the radio and on singles. Somehow, my friend John Cullen, who was two years older than me, obtained a copy of a budget record album of the great Chicago blues bands, for which I gave him a ten-shilling note. The album contained a selection of classics of fifties and early sixties Chicago blues, including a 'live' version of 'Got My Mojo Workin' by Muddy Waters, 'First Time I Met the Blues' by Buddy Guy, and other tracks by great musicians such as the harmonica player Little Walter. Its impact was profound and I started to listen to more blues music.

Shortly thereafter, the London blues movement got underway and had a significant following among pop audiences. These British bands – including John Mayall and the Bluesbreakers, early Rolling Stones, Eric Clapton with the Yardbirds, Alexis Korner and Long John Baldry – included many adherents of the Chicago blues style. Because they sold a lot of records, the popular music press in Britain gave them extensive coverage in which they stated how devoted to Chicago blues they were. Reading about how B.B. King influenced Eric Clapton, or how Big Bill Broonzy shaped the style of Alexis Korner, reinforced my own growing interest.

Following this grounding in blues, my interest in jazz grew through the rather simple, popular 'soul' jazz played by the Ramsey Lewis Trio in the sixties. In particular I remember buying two 'live' albums by this group, *Hang On, Ramsey!* and *The In Crowd*, in the mid-sixties. They provided the bridge for me from blues into jazz. Because my first interest in jazz was piano/bass/drums trio, I was led on to buy an Oscar Peterson album, *Night Train*, which Verve brought out in 1962. When I put this record on the turntable I found myself floundering between two river banks. On the left bank, which I comprehended somewhat, was the twelve-bar blues form I was learning to play on the piano. On the right was the much more sophisticated harmonic and rhythmic world of modern jazz. *Night Train* has a number of classic jazz tunes in the blues form like 'Bag's Groove', 'C-Jam Blues' and 'Things Ain't What They Used to Be', which receive bracing and technically perfect performances from the Oscar Peterson Trio. The group boasted Oscar himself on piano, Ray Brown on bass and Ed Thigpen on drums, and over three months I struggled to come to terms with the more elastic, complex spaces of their approach to the blues.

I was encouraged in my explorations by a schoolfriend, Dave MacHale.

We both attended junior school in Willow Park and senior school in Blackrock College. Dave became a professional rock and jazz musician on leaving school. He plays piano, electronic keyboards, alto saxophone and flute, and has been the musical director of the Boomtown Rats, among others, during his career. Dave's mother was a fine pianist who could play much of the classical repertoire and was also a mistress of the traditional solo jazz piano style, in particular that of Fats Waller. As a result Dave was a precocious jazz musician with advanced tastes when he was fourteen years old.

Throughout our years in Blackrock, Dave kept stretching my taste, introducing me to Art Blakey after I had absorbed Oscar Peterson. After that, he let me hear what 'Cannonball' Adderley was doing, particularly with his hit single 'Mercy, Mercy, Mercy', written by Joe Zawinul and featuring very early jazz electric piano by the composer. I also listened with delight to the masters of bebop when I picked up a budget album on a visit to Derry with my father. This collection included 'Perdido' as performed by the Charlie Parker-Dizzy Gillespie Quintet from the *Live at Massey Hall* album (1953), with a trumpet solo by Dizzy that is an artistic achievement to stand beside the greatest of twentieth-century Western classical music.

The broadcaster Gay Byrne was a good friend of my father's and he suggested I should take jazz piano lessons from Tony Drennan. In the mid-sixties, Ireland possessed two masters of the traditional jazz piano, Tony Drennan and Professor Peter O'Brien, who remain great exponents today of this immensely demanding, difficult, joyful piano music. I had the great fortune to attend lessons with Tony Drennan from 1966 to 1970. He is a master of Harlem stride piano, of boogie, but perhaps above all, of the 'swing' piano style exemplified by Teddy Wilson and that great genius, Art Tatum. When we finished the lesson, Tony would play records. Among the riches he let me hear were the original 78s of the 'boogie-woogie' masters Albert Ammons, Meade 'Lux' Lewis and Pete Johnson, who recorded between 1930 and 1941.

Dave MacHale also introduced me to the free jazz of Ornette Coleman. The jump to atonality and a more lateral conception of music-making was encapsulated for me on *The Empty Foxhole*, on which Ornette's son Denardo, then twelve years old, played drums. Dave also played me an album by Archie Shepp, through whose work one could hear the protests of African-Americans in the sixties. The raucous and uninhibited atonality of free jazz became an exciting musical parallel to the riots and rebellions taking place in American cities in this period.

In 1968, the international year of protest, I arrived in Trinity College, Dublin to study English, philosophy and history, and I quickly made a friend of the poet and publisher Peter Fallon of the Gallery Press. I was now a confirmed jazz and blues listener and I enjoyed playing piano. In secondary school, Dave MacHale and I had stayed apart from the general mass enthusiasm for rock music. We were conscious that rock musicians often earned money out of all proportion to their talent while dedicated jazz artists like Ornette Coleman and

Louis Stewart had meagre returns. Stewart, a guitarist, then lived in Dublin and was an inspiration to musicians and listeners in Ireland. He spent most of his time between 1970 and 1972 touring Britain with the great British tenor saxophonist Tubby Hayes.

The serious and intense world of modern jazz was radically altered from 1967 onwards. It had been operating within two movements, namely bop, which has chromatic harmony, and free jazz, which is characterized by atonality. To these now were added jazz-rock or electric jazz, and neo-tonal jazz or worldbeat. These two new traditions became the new jazz of the period 1967 to 1975. As Frank Tirro states in *Jazz: A History* (1993), 'The soul-wrenching cries of free jazz, the tortuous path of advanced bebop, and all those cerebral forms of music that seemed to have led jazz to artistic heights and financial bankruptcy were dispossessed, at least temporarily, in favour of fun and the search for a people's music.'

The first harbinger of jazz-rock was contained in *Bitches Brew* (1969), a double album by Miles Davis. I recall experiencing it as a difficult music with which it took some months to come to terms. The electric and electronic instruments heretofore played by rock musicians were brought into jazz, including the electric piano, synthesizer, and bass guitar. Miles Davis amplified his trumpet. Two keyboards or more were used. The new sonorities involved an exploration of the rock vernacular. The tracks on *Bitches Brew* last for whole sides of a vinyl album and have a compendious, brooding, open-ended quality.

The next shock was the arrival of *The Inner Mounting Flame* (1971) by the Mahavishnu Orchestra, a quintet of virtuoso musicians led by Mahavishnu John McLaughlin, the British electric guitarist. The band used Indian music as a glue to conjoin jazz and rock. We were delighted that Rick Laird, from Dun Laoghaire, was their bass guitarist. Over a summer working in New York City my friend Brendan Frawley rang up McLaughlin and informed him that we knew Louis Stewart and were anxious to drive up to Massachussetts to see the band at the open-air Tanglewood Festival. To the delight of us all, including my then girlfriend, Clodagh O'Reilly, and Michael Moore, McLaughlin kindly set aside tickets for us and we saw the band perform in perfect stereo, in which the sound picture was visually matched to the position of the band on stage. The Mahavishnu Orchestra was a type of supersonic seventies version of the Django Reinhardt thirties group, the Quintet of the Hot Club of France.

Nineteen seventy-one also brought the welcome emergence of a band that was to be a fixture until its demise in 1986, the innovative Weather Report. Their 1972 album *I Sing the Body Electric* represented a compendium of particularly startling developments. Most of this material was found documented at greater length in the double album *Live in Tokyo*. Weather Report, led by Joe Zawinul (keyboards) and Wayne Shorter (saxes) were pioneers in many areas. They were leaders in the field of synthesizer, with Joe Zawinul giving orchestral body to the band's lines. They invented a new tapestry-like form of improvisation wherein different band members followed each other in a species of conversation.

From 1971 until 1986, their yearly albums were awaited with eager anticipation all over the world, particularly by musicians.

The pianistic genius of Chick Corea was deployed in all its superb brilliance in his band, Return to Forever. He became the first great master of the electric piano on their first two albums, *Return to Forever* (1971) and *Light as a Feather* (1972). These two albums of Latin-slanted pieces also introduced a second genius, double bassist Stanley Clarke, who became an inventive rival to Miroslav Vitous, Weather Report's bassist. Return to Forever then mutated and became an aggressive jazz-rock band with Stanley Clarke proving to be a challenging virtuoso on the bass guitar. On the third album, *Hymn of the Seventh Galaxy* (1973), the quartet, which also included Bill Connors on guitar and Lenny White III on drums and percussion, played the first successful suite for a small jazz-rock band. Indeed, *Hymn of the Seventh Galaxy* is one of the first jazz concept albums.

Working in New York City as a cleaner during the summer of 1973, I saw Weather Report and Return to Forever at Philharmonic Hall in Lincoln Center during the Newport-New York Jazz Festival. Weather Report were disappointing because they did not get the right sound balance. Return to Forever were magnificent, however, playing the full suite 'Hymn of the Seventh Galaxy', with Corea's electric piano glittering with crystalline clarity above the surging electric mix.

The seventies also provided a new avenue of development for the solo jazz piano, and this was the most important period on the instrument since the thirties. Chick Corea released *Piano Improvisations Vols 1* and *2* in 1971 on E.C.M., a label that set extremely high standards for jazz records. In 1993 E.C.M. issued its five hundredth album, appropriately from the great Norwegian saxophonist Jan Garbarek. E.C.M. also released *Facing You* by Keith Jarrett, who became the most important solo jazz pianist since the death of Art Tatum in 1956. *The Köln Concert* (1975), a double album, and *Solo Concerts* (1973), a triple album, became very influential.

Also in the early seventies, the tradition of modal jazz was carried forward by my favourite player of the period, McCoy Tyner and his Quartet. He had been John Coltrane's pianist and reinvigorated the modal style of Coltrane with his intense, muscular and spiritual piano. On our second night in New York City in 1973 we went to the Village Vanguard, one of the shrines of jazz music. The McCoy Tyner Quartet was in full cry. Their sound is captured on *Enlightenment*, a soaring double album recorded at the Montreux Jazz Festival two weeks later.

The new jazz of the early seventies was also embodied in important extended works. Just as Duke Ellington's work *Black Brown and Beige* summed up many trends and ideas within traditional jazz, so *Escalator Over the Hill* (1971), a jazz oratorio by Carla Bley, and *Metropolis* (1973) and *Citadel/Room 315* (1975) by Mike Westbrook, were among the period's greatest works for big band. *Escalator over the Hill* (1971) is a type of oratorio into which Bley gathered many of the different confluences that jazz players were interested in at the time.

Indian sounds govern the tracks, led by the trumpeter Don Cherry. John McLaughlin plays searing electric guitar showing the strong influence of the sitar, and he is accompanied by the original master of the bass guitar, Jack Bruce.

Westbrook was the major composer of jazz-extended works at a time when British jazz was living through an artistic golden age, on which we eavesdropped over BBC Radio. Like Carla Bley in the U.S., he had the scope and greatness of spirit to provide structures for jazz-rock players, free-jazz players and bop players. In *Citadel/315*, in particular, he was brilliantly served by the baritone saxophonist John Surman.

It was a time of enormous change and excitement as jazz exploded and took on rock music, electric instruments and musics from cultures around the world. The discoveries of that period remain constantly audible in the new jazz of the nineties, as is evident from today's figures on the cutting edge like Joe Lovano, Bill Frisell and Steve Coleman. By the mid-seventies jazz had become a world-music tradition in itself and was no longer the exclusive property of Americans in general or African-Americans in particular. It had become an art music for all of humanity.

PAUL CHARLES

ASTRAL WEEKS
VAN MORRISON

I can remember catching a tube in 1968 from Wimbledon to Piccadilly Circus, on one of my rare trips 'up the West End', to see Terry Reid play at the Marquee Club in Wardour Street. For whatever reason, he didn't show and so I visited Musicland for a browse.

I happened upon *Astral Weeks*. It was an import copy, more expensive than the coins in my pockets. So I paid a deposit, returned to Wimbledon, made up the money with a little help from my friends, and tubed it to Musicland to claim my prize. And what a prize. I spent every minute awake that weekend listening to this beautiful work.

This is probably the album I have listened to most in my life. It is still a treasure over a quarter of a century later. I worked with Van for about six years and saw all of his concerts during that period. On the rare occasions Van performed 'Madame George' or 'Ballerina', you could sense the audience taking a deep collective breath of anticipation on hearing the opening chords.

I have no idea whatsoever why *Astral Weeks* has that power. It's not simply that it might be better than anything else ever recorded ... it's a different language, made all the more remarkable when you hear the early versions of some of the titles on *The Bang Sessions*. Van clearly had a vision, and if *The Bang Sessions* are anything to go by, he obviously had to fight hard to realize his vision. Thank your God, whomever she may be, he did.

ELEVEN KINDS OF LONELINESS
TANITA TIKARAM

Tanita Tikaram is one of my favourite songwriters and she stretches herself as a writer on this album beyond anything I might have dreamed of on first seeing her at the Mean Fiddler on 16 December 1987. Certainly a night that changed my life.

Drawing on her childhood influences, the Beatles and Phil Spector, Tanita infuses these songs with her own unique style. She lets the songs dictate the direction and the colour of the production rather than dovetailing the songs into the sound of an album. The result preserves the old-fashioned tradition of a great album: variety, magic colours, inspired performances, unforgettable melodies, stimulating lyrics, delivered in one of the most listenable voices around today.

I DON'T BELIEVE YOU
DON WILLIAMS

It seems that there has always been a Don Williams muse in my life. You know what I mean: a deep brown voice singing autumn music. Before Don Williams, it would have been Jim Reeves and lately it's been Randy Travis – all singers with an honest delivery, singing warm simple songs.

I particularly like Don Williams singing the songs of Bob McDill (another of my favourite songwriters), and you are always guaranteed at least one, sometimes as many as three, McDill songs on Don's discs. Perhaps he could pen a song from a short Don Williams story a tour-manager friend of mine recently told me.

Don Williams was apparently touring Europe with this same tour manager. The entourage had just checked into their hotel in yet another European capital when Mr Williams summoned the tour manager to his room to sort out a problem. A few seconds later the tour manager entered the artist's room to discover the gentleman reclining on his bed, trademark cowboy hat and boots evident. Everything seemed fine to the tour manager as he surveyed the room. The problem? Mr Williams couldn't see his TV. On close inspection the tour manager worked out that the artist's view was being obscured by his very own famous boots. He suggested Mr Williams move his feet a short distance to the right. 'Nope, they're perfectly fine where they are, sir. Why don't you move the TV a little to the left!' came the reply.

All together now, 'You're my friend ...'

FOR EVERYMAN
JACKSON BROWNE

I do not remember how I first picked up on Jackson Browne – it was either David Crosby or Joni Mitchell mentioning him in an interview.

Jackson Browne, his first album on Elektra (released at a time when it was worth checking out an artist's music because of the label, notably Warner Bros., Elektra and Reprise, with Island keeping up the UK end), was a classic and I loved it. I was totally hooked and could hardly wait for the release of his next album, a buzz rarely experienced these days.

I remember the first time listening to *For Everyman*, the way 'Take it Easy' segued into 'Our Lady of the Well'. I love things like that. This album was and still is a delight. No waste, no skimping, a true artist using all the known colours to paint visual pictures with his words and music. He is aided and abetted beautifully here by David Lindley on guitars, electric fiddle and very loud clothes, and Jim Keltner, the master of the skins.

THE FREEWHEELIN' BOB DYLAN
BOB DYLAN

What could I possibly say about the person who wrote:

Like a Rolling Stone
Mr Tambourine Man
I Want You
She Belongs to Me
Tangled Up in Blue
Positively Fourth Street
It's All Over Now, Baby Blue
Sad-Eyed Lady of the Lowlands
The Death of Emmett Till
Blowin' in the Wind
Masters of War
Girl of the North Country
A Hard Rain's A-Gonna Fall
Don't Think Twice, It's All Right
Corrina, Corrina
I Shall Be Released
The Times They Are A-Changin'
Boots of Spanish Leather
All I Really Want to Do
To Ramona
My Back Pages
I Don't Believe You
It Ain't Me, Babe
Ballad in Plain D
Maggie's Farm
Love Minus Zero/No Limit
Gates of Eden
It's Alright, Ma (I'm Only Bleeding)
It Takes a Lot to Laugh, It Takes a Train to Cry
From a Buick 6
Queen Jane Approximately
Highway 61 Revisited
Desolation Row
Just Like a Woman
Absolutely Sweet Marie
All Along the Watchtower
I Pity the Poor Immigrant
John Wesley Harding
The Ballad of Frankie Lee and Judas Priest
Lay Lady Lay

I Threw It All Away
Tonight I'll be Staying Here with You
If Not for You
Forever Young
Billy
Knocking on Heaven's Door
This Wheel's on Fire
If You See Her Say Hello
Slow Train
Isis

These songs were the soundtrack of my growing up in Ireland and moving to London. Dylan is one of the few artists they'll still be talking about in a hundred years' time.

RAIN DOGS
TOM WAITS

The agent goes shopping for the artist and finds the artist!

Tom Waits was an artist I had tried unsuccessfully to represent as an agent for several years during the late seventies and early eighties. I had spoken with various managers who, in turn, would become various ex-managers. Every time I visited Los Angeles I would meet with someone about the possibility of representing Tom Waits.

I had just about given up hope when, while browsing in Tower Records on Sunset, I spied the promo material for *One from the Heart*.

The answer to my request for a copy of the same was greeted with, 'Oh, we're sorry, sir, we've just sold the last copy.' The shop assistant dropped to a conspiratorial whisper as she continued, 'In fact, I sold it to Tom Waits himself and he's standing ... don't look now! ... just behind you.' She smiled, awkwardly gesturing with her eyes and nose to my left.

I 'casually' browsed my way in his direction, and when I was close enough to make eye contact, introduced myself. 'Hi, I'm Paul Charles from Asgard in London, and I've been trying to work with you for several years.' (You have to make your point quickly.) He and his wife, Kathleen, had heard of my efforts and were very friendly, so we repaired to a nearby recreational area for tea and I became their agent for concert work everywhere outside North America and Canada. That's how easy it was!

The first tour I did with Tom was a treat. With Tom Waits not only do you book the show but you also help put it together and stage it each night. My job was to make the 'rain' fall at the appropriate times and figure out how to make a bright light shine on Tom's face from inside his top hat. The former we perfected on the third night of the tour and the latter took until the last night to work out.

The musical basis for that tour was the album *Rain Dogs*. On this album Tom Waits re-invented the singer-songwriter genre. He came up with a complete new lyrical and musical language.

REVOLVER
THE BEATLES

So here is the deal: pick a Beatles album, any Beatles album, and it will be my favourite Beatles album. Until this split second I would have chosen *Abbey Road*. But I've just listened to *Revolver* and today it wins by a short head – not Ringo's, probably George's. It has to be *Revolver* because it is the pivotal album of their career. With it they took a left turn off the road from being another great act onto the one marked 'Stratosphere'.

OTIS BLUE
OTIS REDDING

I managed a group, my first, when I was about fourteen or fifteen. They were called Blues by Five and performed about 70 per cent of the material on this album. The singer was a chap called Paddy Shaw, Magherafelt's answer to Otis Redding. (In the North in those days most acts were the North's answer to so and so.) Anyway Paddy Shaw did have a soulful gift and was a fine chap to boot.

I would include *Otis Blue* in any top ten if only for 'My Girl' or 'I've Been Loving You Too Long'. I'm full of envy for artists who can interpret another writer's songs as their own and Otis sells me on 'his' girl every single time I listen.

Sadly I never saw Otis Redding perform live. There is, however, a video with Otis and his band performing live on *Ready, Steady, Go!*, and even on TV his magnetism shines through. Every pore of his body is oozing music ... he just can't stop. Otis looked so joyous as he sang, incredible when you consider he probably performed on at least three other occasions that same day. (Check out some of the tour dates from those sixties tours – an agent's dream and an artist's nightmare.)

On *Otis Blue* you have the feeling that most of it is live, with one, or at most, two take recordings – a special time captured in a small studio in America nearly thirty years ago which is still bringing untold joy today.

BRYTER LAYTER
NICK DRAKE

I'm not sure how great one can feel about enjoying someone so obviously in pain. This is an exquisite but, at the same time, unsettling album. I bought it the week it was released knowing nothing at all about Nick Drake. Island Records was recommendation enough. *Bryter Layter* is Nick Drake at his peak. When he sings 'One of These Things First' you have the overwhelming feeling he would prefer to be any of the list of things other than himself.

The story going around London was that Nick Drake was so shy that when he completed work on one of his albums (I don't know which one), he took it into Island Records and left the tapes with the receptionist. You can hear this loneliness in the words and music on this flawless work. Perhaps he was dealing with his demons successfully through his music. He committed suicide a few years later, leaving three powerful albums as a testament to his short life.

Please listen to this artist, especially to *Bryter Layter*.

CLOSE TO YOU
THE CARPENTERS

I've been trying to find a way of delaying this final choice. There are so many albums I have left out which have been important in my life. I've thought of the Roches, the Blue Nile, Ray Davies, Mary Margaret O'Hara, Crosby, Stills and Nash (the first one), Nat King Cole, Rickie Lee Jones, Neil Young (*Everybody Knows This Is Nowhere*), Elvis (Presley and Costello), Hank Williams, Ray Charles, Patsy Cline, the Traveling Wilburys, John Lee Hooker, Rockpile – but, and again it's a big BUT, I will spin the Carpenters, *Close to You*.

I think the Carpenters worked very successfully on one of the Beatles' secrets: 'Make it great but keep it simple. Never clever, Trevor.' At the time this record was released there was not a lot of new music around that I could get into, so it was a pleasure to discover how wonderful this album was.

I was managing a group from Belfast called Fruupp around the time of its release. Fruupp were the group who made Thurles famous way before the Fleadh put the town in the spotlight again. When Fruupp were taking ammm ... sorry I meant listening to Led Zep, Trapeze, Blodwin Pig, Grinodolog, I was taking solace in Van, the Beatles, and the Carpenters.

Karen Carpenter could have sung the proverbial telephone directory, but I would have loved to have heard her record in a more contemporary setting. I saw the Carpenters once at the London Palladium and was astounded by her amazing voice – full of soul but still technically perfect. She was a damned fine drummer to boot.

DENNY CORDELL

I GREW UP IN RIO DE JANEIRO and from the age of twelve there seemed to be a party almost every Saturday night. The bigger parties usually had a Brazilian quartet playing foxtrots, quicksteps, sambas, cha-chas, and the odd waltz, but at the occasional teen parties we danced to records.

I remember very clearly going to a party, in about 1956, at Suzanne Landis's place. She was the daughter of the U.S. naval attaché in Rio and we all danced to American records, anything from Frank Sinatra and Ray Coniff, to the Platters, Pat Boone and the Ink Spots. Suddenly a record came on that electrified me. It was a 45 of Lloyd Price singing 'Lawdy Miss Clawdy', and all the older kids jumped up and started jiving and when the record finished it came on again, and again and again. It played about six times in a row and at the finish everyone flopped down exhausted – and I was hooked.

Suzanne told me there was an LP of Lloyd Price to be had from the P.X. stores and in a couple of weeks I scraped up enough cash and she got me the record. It completely flipped me out, and I played it all day long, week in, week out.

A few months later I was in the back of my stepfather's car going somewhere for Sunday lunch when a record came on the radio that paralyzed me. On the one hand I was flipping on the sound, on the other hand I was terrified that my stepfather (who forbade the playing of Lloyd Price in his hearing) would turn the radio off before I could find out who it was. Mercifully it made it through with the DJ telling me in Portuguese that it was '*Ooh Evish Prezley contandeo a gouja hockeen to Nyechi*'. That was it! At first I could only find an EP of Elvis singing but what had caught my eye was his first album, *Elvis Presley*, on Brazilian RCA, and I soon became the proud owner of both records.

These completely changed my life and, among other things, my hairstyle. (My housemaster's report from my first term at Cranleigh School, England, said it was 'a pity such a manly boy affects such an effeminate hairstyle'.) I arrived at Cranleigh in 1957 armed with my three LPs and soon found a small handful of like-minded rockers, but it was during a school outbreak of measles that I discovered Fats Domino blaring out of the quarantine ward. A boy called Robin Whitcomb was the proud owner and our friendship was cast. 'Ain't That a Shame', 'Blueberry Hill', 'Yes, It's Me and I'm in Love Again' and 'Whole Lotta Lovin'' were absolutely the business, as far as we were concerned.

Through Robin I met his brother Ian 'You Turn Me On' Whitcomb, who has a mindblowing collection of records, and through him I learned about American music from Dixieland jazz through boogie-woogie, Fats Waller, Louis Jordan, Memphis Slim, Jerry Lee Lewis, Ray Charles, up to Thelonius Monk. The two records that stayed with me, and that I still completely love today, were *Ray Charles Live* and Thelonius Monk's *Blue Monk*.

MARY COUGHLAN

WHEN I WAS THIRTEEN I went to see Rory Gallagher. I wasn't allowed, but I climbed out the window. He was playing at this ballroom in Galway. Then my boyfriend bought me the record for my birthday. I just thought Rory Gallagher was brilliant. Then I met a girl who actually lived beside him in Cork and she became my friend for a while. That album lasted a good few years. I used to play it constantly.

The same fella bought me the *Easy Rider* album because we'd seen the movie and I loved it. My father used to shout at me to turn it down. I had one of those red-and-white Dansette record-players. I used to sneak into the sitting-room and turn it on really low and pretend to do my homework and have my hand on the on/off button. There was 'Take the Weight Off Me' and the 'Ballad of Easy Rider'. The whole thing was great. I didn't know the bands, it didn't make much sense to me. I liked it. In retrospect, it became a very important film, but at the time, I didn't know that. I was growing up that summer and I was a bit of a rebel. I was wearing enormous flares, tie-dye shirts and becoming a hippie.

My uncle Kenneth and his brother fought over who was king: Elvis or the Beatles. In America, Kenneth discovered Blood, Sweat and Tears and Chicago and brought back thirty LPs. He spent all his money on albums. We'd just listen to the stuff all the time. I'd escape into it. I had a little radio under my pillow at night and would listen to Radio Luxembourg. 'You Make Me So Very Happy' – I'd listen to that all the time. I'm trying to do a version of it at the moment. There are some songs you'll never forget. Crappy ones like 'Fox on the Run' and 'Young Girl' and 'Blackberry Way'.

My uncle Gay was the Elvis fan. He wore the hair and he used to get the *Elvis Fortnightly* magazine. He was in the fan club. There were a couple of guys on the street who were much older than I was. They all wore winkle-pickers. They had the flick hair. They were called Teddy Boys and all they listened to was Elvis. They were so different. Gay going off on his bicycle with his albums down to his friends' houses. That's all he did. He went to college and was a beatnik. He has probably one of the biggest record collections in Ireland. He'd send away and go shopping for records in Dublin. It's been his life since he was about sixteen. He's now a teacher in Ennis and is married with a family.

Kenneth started getting into the Stones and I remember the *High Tide, Green Grass* album. I think that was the first one he bought. I'd just hang around their house listening to their music. They were cool students and I was still going to school, which I hated. I'd come straight home and go over there. My granny kept students as well and they'd all lounge around the sitting-room listening.

I thought Mick Jagger was ugly. There was a programme which we'd all been talking about for weeks at school on TV with Cream and the Stones. My father and my uncles wouldn't let me watch it. They really thought it was the devil's music. My grandparents went ape when they heard their music. I'll never forget missing that programme.

I used to love George Harrison. His pictures were all over my wall. I thought he was gorgeous. I really thought the strong singing done in the Beatles was by John Lennon, but I was disappointed to find it was all Paul McCartney.

I had a boyfriend called Froggy at the time and he had just discovered Van Morrison. 'St Dominic's Preview' is the first song of his I heard. I was about six-teen, and I remember Froggy turning up just before Christmas with Astral Weeks. I would just sit and listen constantly to 'Madame George'. Van used to send me into a particular mood. That was when I started getting into where music could take you. The rest of it was fun, but this you'd just get lost in it. The emotions make you cry. I've never played with him, but I must ask him one of these days. I used to love the way he could improvise and get into the thing in 'Listen to the Lion'. 'Warm Love' is a happy one. I was doing acid at the time and wanted to leave home. I was looking for something. Then I did leave home, and went to London after my Leaving Cert, and that was more acid and sitting around rooms listening to Van and Bob Dylan.

That summer in London I saw Lady Sings the Blues, the Billie Holiday, Diana Ross thing. She was singing her heart out, and so I got my hands on all the Billie Holiday albums. For a period of about two years I used to listen to nothing else. I used to go in and out of moods, and I found listening to Van and Billie Holiday very cathartic.

The first time I sang was ten years ago. I actually got up with a jazz band on Sunday mornings in Salthill and did 'Lover Man' and 'San Francisco Bay Blues' and a couple of standards that they knew. I played with another band on Wednesday nights in Galway. I was also singing traditional songs at the time in sessions because I liked Dolores Keane and I used to sing 'The Blacksmith' and 'January Snows'. I went to see Gay Woods' band and I'd sing one of those songs at a session. Still do. I found that those Irish songs were the same as Billie Holiday was singing. Irish blues.

I met Tom Waits once in London in the Mean Fiddler and fuckin' nearly dropped dead. He was like Van Morrison only in another direction. He was off his head, loopy, great .... He takes chances with his arrangements. He has done really safe, ordinary, sentimental stuff too, but the other wacky stuff is great.

Frank Sinatra – I hate the fucker. He was a tortured old soul, trying to get through. Some of his songs are real throwaway tracks, but a few are incredible. Billie Holiday did that as well, I think. She didn't sing like ordinary jazz singers at the time. Her voice was more like an instrument. Sinatra led the whole orchestra. They followed him. It is so effortless, it certainly seems that way.

I just bought a double album, *The Reprise Years*. 'A Quarter to Three' is on it, which is the piano/drinking song. 'I'm a Fool to Love You' – you know that one? It's incredible. I think that's when he's going through that thing with Ava Gardner. It comes across. You can hear in people's voices where they've been. You can tell the difference between when Billie Holiday is out of it and when she's not. And him, as well. I didn't think that until a few years ago about Frank Sinatra. I had never really listened.

JEANANNE CROWLEY

POST-ADOLESCENT STRESS DISORDER is a serious affliction. Like post-traumatic stress only no amount of ECT can cure it. Years after the event I continue to manifest the effects of something that happened long long time ago, only the music didn't bloody die but went on and on and now it's achieved the status of 'Classic Rock' because you can hardly admit to having been severely damaged by pop music can you? The stuff seeped in through every open pore. Anyone who had a heart would turn a whiter shade of pale for everything I failed to become thanks to being hooked on the kind of romantic tosh that just was not available in my Granny's day. She had a serious life and a wind-up gramophone. I'm from the first generation with its very own backing track and my emotional life veers towards the mawkish and sentimental. If there's one word that sums up the spirit in which I live it must be *yearning*.

It starts off innocently enough to the sound of 'Little children you'd better not tell on me' as the babysitter lets her boyfriend in and you're told to go upstairs so they can snog on the sofa. Thus early on you yearn to be a babysitter yourself so you can do the same. Then in the car on the way back from Mass your Mammy tells your Daddy to turn the radio off because 'The young ones, darlin' we're the young ones' is being played and she's afraid it will put ideas into our young heads. And you yearn to know just what those ideas are. So next time you listen closely: 'And young ones shouldn't be afraid/To live, love while the flame is strong because we may not be the young ones very long.' Imagine it. My mother was actively concerned about rampant sexual innuendo in a Cliff Richard song when even a ten-year-old could have told her he was harmless. Driving a double-decker bus to Greece with Una Stubbs in tow and the Shadows as singalong chaperones is not exactly a trip to the wilder shores of rock. Mind you I probably yearned a bit for even that amount of freedom but no, I had to go to Kilkee *en famille* instead.

It was known as Limerick-Sur-La-Mer, and the local flea-pit used to re-run the Elvis flicks nightly so we soon knew all the words to 'Jailhouse Rock' but we didn't reckon Presley. For some reason he was perceived as a bit naff. Maybe because 'Wooden Heart' and 'Love Me Tender' were the sort of songs the mother's help ('you mustn't call her a maid darling') used to sing around the house. Cissy wore big skirts and white stilettos and screamed when Billy Fury sang 'Don't leave me half-way to paradise' on *Ready, Steady, Go!*, which struck me even then as a little excessive. In Kilkee Bill Whelan put *Bookends* on his record-player – 'Can you imagine us years from today, sharing a park bench quietly … how terribly strange to be seventy' – which was how I found out about Paul Simon, and then Bill played me 'MacArthur Park' and said Jimmy Webb wrote it and wasn't it the best thing I'd ever heard and that even though his parents wanted him to go to college and do Law he was going to be a musician come hell or high water and didn't he do just that and years later didn't Jimmy Webb turn up at the opening night of 'Riverdance' at Radio City Music Hall to praise him to the skies.

And that's a perfect example. While chaps like Whelan were out achieving I was still stuck in yearning mode which I ought to have grown out of. But unfortunately some of us don't ever grow up and out of things; we just grow older and I blame pop music. As Nick Hornby says in *High Fidelity*:

The unhappiest people I know romantically speaking are the ones who like pop music the most; and I don't know whether pop music has caused this unhappiness but I do know that they've been listening to the sad songs longer than they've been living the unhappy lives.

At boarding-school we listened to Radio Luxembourg with our transistors under our pillows. Jimmy Saville even had an 'under-the-bedclothes-club' so we wouldn't feel left out of the swinging sixties just because we weren't quite old enough to join in yet. Anna Carey wrote to him and he wrote straight back! We knew it was only because she sent him a photo. Anna had Protestant hair and she hitched up her school skirt to show off her legs. The cigar-chomping DJ obviously knew a good thing when he saw it and invited her over to be on *Top of the Pops* during the summer holidays. The class seethed with envy. The letter I got from Mícheál MacLiammóir was only in the ha'penny place compared with that excitement. Like Ebony Eyes, Prod Hair obviously got you places and we all firmly believed Anna would end up running away from school to become one of Pan's People and there wasn't a damn thing any of us could do about it.

There were lots of Protestants at home in Malahide. In fact as a kid the only reason I knew I must be Catholic was because we had Catechism lessons while the lucky Prods sang hymns downstairs. In our teens a crowd of us formed a gang, our HQ a hut in Roger Doyle's back garden where we had parties with the lights out. I yearned for breasts like Sandra's or Boyer's 'cause then maybe I could go with someone instead of having to change the singles on the Dansette. Roger's lips met mine to the sound of something like 'That Boy isn't good for you, though he may want you too-oo-oo-oo-oo-oo-oo', not passionate, mind, just a pair of apprentice adolescents getting off with each other to see what kissing felt like.

With The Beatles was the first album I ever owned. A present from my stupid parents who said the Beatles were only a flash in the pan and wouldn't last. I used to stare at the black-and-white cover and yearn to be John Lennon. Pocket money being in short supply we mostly bought singles, not albums. Cilla, Sandi, Dusty, Manfred Mann, the Troggs and Herman's Hermits. Well I exaggerate: no one would have been caught dead listening to Peter Noone. The Who definitely and Georgie Fame and Alan Price, of course. I knew he left the Animals and that another Animal had discovered Jimi Hendrix and brought him to England where for a while he thrived. Snippets of info but nothing that could be construed as a body of knowledge even though so much of my time was spent listening to the stuff. Roger could play 'The House of the Rising Sun' on the piano but really he preferred Dave Brubeck and I think the first album he ever bought was *Take Five*. I loved Ray Davies, he of the letterbox mouth and those ace lyrics, and I knew who Jimmy Page and Jeff Beck were and that the Yardbirds were good but by the time they metamorphosed into Led Zeppelin we were into a bit of metamorphosing ourselves. Funnily enough I don't remember being big into the Rolling Stones.

Sgt. Pepper might have been seminal in terms of 'aeolian clusters' and all but the one Beatles LP I remember us listening to most respectfully was the White Album. Ankle socks and tennis shoes, ponytails and school jumpers, swimming at High Rock and necking with the lights off. Last of the innocents, no one launching into adolescence after us would ever have such a simple easy time and the sad thing is I didn't even properly appreciate it.

Emotionally inarticulate, sexually naive but still yearning I found myself in Paris where the men had clean fingernails and smelled of *Eau Sauvage*. 'All over the world people are sad tonight/There's someone like me watching the sun's fadin' light.' Françoise Hardy had Protestant hair too and even though I had breasts by then I thought they were too small and my bottom too big for the kind of life I wanted. Besides, my upbringing hadn't included lessons on becoming a *femme fatale* so I took the soft option and went home to university instead.

'Anyone who wants to know where the teeny-bopper's contribution to the UCD radical movement got her blue plastic boots will be pleased to know they are still available at Tylers of Henry Street.' Despite the routine slagging those were the days and the friends I made then are still with me and at last I had a boyfriend though I hadn't a clue what to do with him. I had no training in normal behaviour. Listening over and over to hundreds of songs about heartbreak and rejection and pain and loss had subconsciously prepared me for nothing but the worst. He lived near Palmerstown Park and I had a flat on Pembroke Road. The house belonged to my grandmother and I shared with my cousin who was at Trinity. Her legs went on forever and a skinny lad from Kerry called Dick was in love with her. Whatever the lads might have boasted to the contrary, us girls were all virgins. In O'Dwyers one night Pat Kenny said all us Freshers may well have arrived at college *intacta* but we certainly weren't going to leave it that way. Huh. I decided then and there to prove him wrong. Of course now I could expound at length on the sociological reasons why my legs remained firmly crossed but then all I could do was bloody yearn on. The Mamas and the Papas had me yearning to be a psychedelic hippie and trail around San Francisco, the Beach Boys encouraged visions of becoming a pre-*Baywatch* babe and all that Tamla-Motown stuff made me wish I was black. Vicarious living all of it and seriously damaging to the mental health.

In the flat, which was always freezing, Carly Simon, Joni Mitchell, Carole King and Judy Collins provided background sound and I had *The Female Eunuch* in hardback. Peter Fallon cracked up when he saw it but I seem to remember Kevin Myers, who was keen to relieve me of my burdensome maidenhead, being marginally impressed.

Cousin Helena liked the Carpenters – 'We've only just begun ... white lace and promises ... A kiss for luck and we're on our way ...'. I preferred Dionne Warwick – 'If you see me walking down the street and I start to cry each time we meet ...Walk on by ... walk oooonnn by' – because I sort of knew before Helena did that whatever happened it would probably all end in tears anyway. Once I let Myers unzip my paisley-print tent-dress and I still wonder if it was only the mortification of having a woolly vest on underneath that prevented me letting him go any further. Entirely honourable, he said no he didn't love me, he only fancied me but wouldn't that do? We were sober too. No booze and no drugs either. Yeah I stepped over people at parties smoking dope and had the odd glass of wine but yearning was the only vice I allowed myself and pity 'tis pity it took such a hold. Years later a shy guy from my English tutorial told me on a plane somewhere that the lads had decided that of all the girls in class I was definitely the one who did. 'We all reckoned you'd look on it as something artistic', he said almost wistfully. If only, I thought to myself, while happily accepting the undue compliment all the same.

Me and Kathy Gilfillan worked the odd evening in a night-club wearing puce velvet hot-pants, serving steaks to men who didn't much want to eat but wanted badly to get laid. We couldn't oblige as we were both, in a manner of speaking, spoken for. She was going out with Paul, and by then I was stepping out with Michael Colgan, who was even madder about theatre than he was about me. I've still only to hear the opening bars of 'Grapevine' to be back there with him dancing the night away to Marvin Gaye – a happy break from all that yearning, and entirely welcome. I lost my virginity eventually in the vicinity of Holland Park with one of those guys who sat soulfully on a stool in the National Stadium playing acoustic guitar and singing songs about being heartbroken for life at the age of twenty-four. Not quite Colin Blunstone, but close. Sadly the yearning continued – for what I'm not sure. All I know for certain is that the bloody music is to blame.

PETER CUNNINGHAM

ROCK TO ME WAS A ROUND STICK OF SUGAR with a stripe through it that they said was bad for my teeth. (They were right.)

I did hear of Tommy Steele, but only at first from an uncle who advised me gravely that Steele in Russian was Lenin, that a Tommy was a Brit, and that the only way to stop what would inevitably happen was to circle the beds and not to fire our rosary beads until we saw the reds of their eyes.

I grew up near the sea. A place called the Boat Cove was a hang-out for the hard men where mere satellites like myself could look over shoulders and through legs at the photographs culled from sailors' magazines. They did savage things at night to my lonely imagination. One afternoon on someone's tranny I heard: 'At only sixteen years of age, the so-called pop idol, Miss Helen Shapiro, will this year earn more money than the Prime Minister.' I was actually halfway down slimy stone steps on my way to deep water. 'Don't treat me like a child' beat out over the sea, as six of us, skinny, malfeasant and rancid with hormones, swam out into the bay and the voice of the sixteen-year-old millionairess followed us. I would have swum to Wales there and then if I thought there was half a chance of Helen being there to meet me. She came across a bridge of music with the unforgettable watermark of physical accessibility and my innocence went out on the tide.

•

Although Dad said that when he had seen *West Side Story* on the London stage he had cried, we all suspected there must have been other, contributing circumstances. If he had been talking about Ricky Nelson I would have understood. 'Mary Lou' was and will always be written and sung for an English girl, called, well, Mary Lou. She had a blonde ponytail and priceless knowledge of how people in France kissed. The fact that it included more than the lips, that the tongue was involved, came like a thunderbolt – something like the discovery by man of fire, I imagine.

Mary Lou was much in demand at Christmas parties where games in which people hid in pairs in darkened rooms suddenly became the vogue. The French, it seemed, did this a lot. There was a very specific technique to French kissing and many of the players did not master it. Mary Lou tasted of aniseed – a French drink – and anyone who drew her company benefited greatly from their indenture. One Christmas night, as the rain beat down on a skylight above us, she promised me she would soon elaborate even further on the habits of the French. Alas, fate being what it is, Mary Lou's father was posted elsewhere and the best French lesson I was ever likely to have dissolved like a puff from a Gitane. 'Hello Mary Lou, Goodbye Heart' still stirs up the ruins of my ransacked and tearful soul.

•

I don't recall much about the U.S. blockade of Cuba, except that Chris Montez sang 'Let's Dance' right through it.

•

I was working in a meat factory in Willesden Junction where my job was to inject brine into dead pigs when I first heard Dylan. It was like one day he had not existed and the next you couldn't wake up without him. Like sex.

The advice 'Don't think twice, it's alright' was particularly apt. His harmonica sounded at first like a wasp caught in a jam jar, but his message was the free flight of human liberty. 'I ain't gonna work on Maggie's farm no more' was sung late at night with 'Maggie's Farm' changed to 'Wall's Meats'. When Bob sang, 'I ain't gonna work for Maggie's brother no more!' the hated faces of time-keepers and foremen swam up from the bottom of our Watney's tankards.

Dylan was so good he blotted out the sun, and everything else. We went home at night to Swiss Cottage, on the dark side of the road, with giggly English girls who loved the line, 'It's a shame the way she makes me scrub the floo-or.' We curled up with our funny cigarettes and someone took out a guitar and we drifted through the great British summer like poppy seeds.

We never did much talkin' anyway.

•

I'm still not sure whether or not I like Donovan, but I am grateful to him. At a time when most of my friends were into 'Norwegian Wood' from the Beatles' *Rubber Soul* LP, I was still struggling with 'Mellow Yellow'. It seemed to have just the right element of conceit about it. I took to singing it to folk at bus stops at times when I might reasonably have been assumed to be at study or otherwise engaged. Since eccentricity is often confused with intellectual ability, 'Mellow Yellow' was a harmless smokescreen in which to hide my dysfunctions of the time, and for this if nothing else I am grateful.

•

Paris, 1968, wasn't just a case of 'There's Going to Be a Revolution'. There was one. I worked shifts at Pizza de Cyclopi (the eye was the oven – just like the medium was the message) and in my free time hung around in a joint called Le Petit Bar, a cobblestone's throw from Place St Michel. Centimes went into Tilt machines or a jukebox where to play anything other than 'Revolution' could get you into trouble with Danny the Red.

Both sides of Boulevard St Michel were lined twenty-four hours a day with Black Marias, stuffed sardine-can-like with 'flics'. The bastards had also lined the right bank of the Seine as they thought we were going to make a move on the Elysée Palace. I say 'we'. This was everybody's revolution. Word of looming battle drifted into Le Petit Bar, at which time cognacs were put up on the house and out we went, squinting for the enemy.

Cops like to enforce the fact that they're in charge and so there were crazy rules like you couldn't cross the street. This led to tension. The cobblestones were remarkably big when you prised them out of the sand where they'd been embedded since Napoleon's time. Each set was twice the size of a pound of butter and hard to throw. Sometimes the 'flics' threw them back, which was unwise, since they were returning us our ammunition.

Dad, a businessman, was coming to town. I took the day off and, en route to meet him, went to grab a few beers and throw granite at French policemen. Then I crossed the road to catch the Metro to Avenue George V, a gross miscalculation. The first truncheon blow knocked two teeth out, the second concussed me – changed my constitution. The inside of a French paddywagon in June is very warm and smells of urine. They let me out that night when I pleaded Irish, and so I turned up twelve hours late to meet Dad.

I told him I had fallen off a train. Dad seemed anxious to be off. News bulletins said Paris was on fire and Dad had business in Munich. He gave me twenty dollars and said he'd be in touch. 'You'd want to watch yourself here,' he warned with touching sincerity. 'They say there's going to be a revolution.'

Nice one, Dad.

•

I met this girl called Cindy at lunchtime in a bar on Broadway during the first Nixon Administration. It must have been on a weekend because Monday to Friday I went to work down the old West Side Highway, at six every morning, with a moonlighting cabbie from the Bronx.

She said, 'It's Cin for short,' with a knowing look and I reckoned the old three lemons in a row had come up in my window. At that exact moment Don McLean broke out 'American Pie' from the jukebox in the corner. It was an electrifying moment assisted by the incomparable vista of sin – that's what she'd said, hadn't she? I kind of guessed what a Chevy was; a levy, I had no idea. We drank whiskey and rye though, me and Cin, boy did we what. She wore her hair in a black bob and her deep, black and possibly Italian eyes swam with opportunities.

There's a very neat drummer in that song. I know this because we both remarked it dozens of times.

'Neat drummer.'

'Neat, yuh.'

It may well have been the neat drummer that led us to feed quarters to the jukebox the afternoon long in the cause of this, at the time, epic ballad.

The day ended with a fight in the furniture department of Macy's. We had adjourned there on Cin's insistence. She needed to buy something called a tub chair, she maintained.

'Oh my Gawd, I'm as sick as a dog,' Cin wailed as our cab bumped downtown.

Crawling from an elevator on to the relevant floor, who was waiting but Don himself, and that neat drummer, blasting out 'American Pie' over the soft furnishings. Cin and I hurled ourselves into it and when some killjoy came and told us that the store was now closed, Cin lurched to her tub chair – a white, glossy thing like a pig – and scrawled with a marker on its back, 'Who wanta this lode a shitz?'

That's when there was the fight.

•

Mungo Jerry was shuffling out 'In the Summertime' in Cassis, a town outside Marseilles, at a time when neither the terms mortgage nor matrimony had any real meaning. The song brought out the hunting instinct. It helped if you rode a big, chrome bike and wore shades, but even smashed on the hard, black-curranty rocks of Cassis it was difficult to have anything but women, but women on your mind.

•

Although there were those who thought that John had let the side down by teaming up with Yoko, the poet in him overcame everything in the end. You needed special equipment to hear some of the lyrics, including Yoko's orgasm, which made everyone envious, when they had the time.

Long years had passed since the days of the revolution, many more since Helen Shapiro had transformed my outlook on life and Mary Lou had shown me the exciting possibilities in saliva. The only things we wrote now in furniture stores were cheques. Where had the time come from before, we wondered? How did we manage to do so little for so long? Time was money, they said, and since they had been right about other things, we listened. Clever time-planners allowed you to plot your course into the future, schedule meetings a year ahead whilst at the same time making sure that the telephone was always answered before the second ring. I wore braces, the type that hold up your trousers. I acquired a potbelly and flew a lot to cities for meetings with similar people. Now there was no time. Not even time to panic that my existence was a sham.

Then one morning, late for a plane, wondering if that chest pain was meaningful, I heard the man sing, 'Life is what happens to you whilst you're busy doing other things.'

In that soft accent that had made the Mersey as famous as the Nile.

Hearing him sing it again all these years on I just know he had understood it all exactly. Which takes some of the sting out of what happened so soon afterwards. It seemed we had both gone the distance together. His poetry had changed his life.

It changed mine.

P.J. CURTIS

THE BOTHY BAND

This band represented to me the flowering and blossoming of all the energies that had been unleashed in Ireland in the early seventies with bands like Planxty and Dé Danann. I'd been in the RAF for five years and scuffed around after that as a salesman, a gardener, a roadsweeper. I was also in two bands – a rock'n'roll one and a blues one. When I came back to Dublin, I joined the Bothy Band as their road manager. I was on the road with them for three years and was everything to them: nursemaid, midwife, babysitter, you name it. I ended up being their soundman as well.

The Bothy Band sound is difficult to describe. It was absolutely new. It welded the firepower of traditional music at its very best with the trio Matt Molloy, Tommy Peoples and Paddy Keenan, against the contemporary rhythms that were being laid down by Dónal Lunny and Mícheál and Tríona Ní Dhomhnaill. It opened a lot of people's ears to Irish music. Touring was phenomenal, and it released unchecked excitement. It also gave me my first grounding in record production at the feet of the two great masters – Dónal Lunny and Mícheál Ó Domhnaill. It was when Irish musicians stood up and said, 'We're not just a bunch of culchies who play music in smoky pubs. We can deliver like a rock band, right?' It was exciting and dangerous.

THE 'CHIRPING' CRICKETS
THE CRICKETS

I wanted to choose Elvis's Sun records because Elvis was the man who really pinned my ears to the gatepost. I first heard him at the age of eleven, I think. It was a hard choice to make to drop him in favour of the Crickets. Elvis made me want to get a guitar, which I did in 1956, but Buddy Holly made me lust after an electric one. Buddy played a Fender Stratocaster. He was the first ever to be seen with one this side of the Atlantic. His whole sound – electric guitar welded to drums and bass, that great voice of his, and the Crickets backing. Of course, it wasn't the Crickets, I learned later, but a backing group that had been dubbed on. I was still at school at the Christian Brothers in Ennis when I was listening to this. Prior to that I'd gained all my rock'n'roll knowledge from listening to the

American Forces Network (AFN) and I wasn't aware of anyone else around who was interested. I remember the first time I heard 'That'll Be the Day'. I had come home to my aunt's for lunch one day during September and on the radio comes Buddy Holly. My mouth just fell open and I was riveted. Some time later the first café in Ennis, Tuttles, got some Buddy Holly records in, and I spent all my hard-earned pocket money feeding the cafe's jukebox (the first in town) to hear 'Peggy Sue'. Elvis was the first music I listened to, and then along came Chuck Berry and Fats Domino and Little Richard, whose wild music I was completely blown away by. But Buddy's music was safer, and it almost made it possible that guys like me who were strumming, trying to learn that third chord, could actually get to the music and reproduce it.

THE BEST OF MUDDY WATERS
MUDDY WATERS

I went to England in 1961. I had heard the blues on the AFN in the fifties when I was still a kid, but it seemed too exotic and too dark and too inaccessible when I was still buzzing over the Everly Brothers, Buddy Holly and Jerry Lee Lewis. A friend in the air force introduced me to this new sound. I'd been aware of it but I hadn't realized the weight of it until I heard 'Hoochie Coochie Man'. It was deeper, darker. I'd also heard about Muddy Waters through Chuck Berry. I was already collecting Chuck's stuff, and he was laying down a rock'n'roll rhythm that I really adored – the guitar, the great piano in the background. He was upgrading and recreating the sound that he had access to, which was the original Chicago blues sound. He was recording at the same studio as Muddy Waters. I heard this music in the billets. One guy had this EP called (I think) *Rhythm and Blues, Volume I*. It had Howlin' Wolf, Muddy Waters, Little Walter and others on it. I became obsessed with learning about the Chicago blues and getting into the whole thing, particularly Muddy. I've listened to him all my life since then. He is the man. He had the first all-electric blues band in Chicago. He single-handedly forged the whole Chicago blues sound. I read recently that pop music is a way of extracting money from kids; he's singing something for adults. Muddy Waters played music not for fame or riches, but because his life depended on it. When Sam Phillips recorded 'Howlin' Wolf' in Memphis in 1952-3 he said, 'This is where the soul of man never dies.' The same could be said of Muddy Waters' music. This is the blues.

REVOLVER
THE BEATLES

I heard the Beatles in 1962 when they made their first single and I thought, God, this is a different sound. It sent a little shiver through me. I remember buying the single, taking it home to Ireland and in to the cousins' and saying, 'You gotta listen. These guys are going to wipe away the Shadows and all the things we've been listening to before now.' I was in a band in England at the time called Rod

Star and the Stereos. I played guitar. I even have a picture of us in 1963 at the Pavilion in Bath where the Beatles played the very next week. We were all wearing snazzy black suits and little Western ties. We were a sort of Shadows look-alike and we were also doing Buddy Holly stuff. He'd been the instigator of the four-man band – guitar, bass, drums, vocals. Then we heard *Revolver*. When the Beatles made their initial albums in 1963 and 1964 I was away in the air force in Borneo. When I came back the whole country was awash with Beatlemania and I duly got hooked into the whole thing. I also loved the Stones. The Beatles had become almost holier than thou in many respects, while the Stones were the 'bad boys' of rock. By the time *Revolver* came along in 1966 I was just out of the air force and in my drop-out stage, and I had begun to partake of certain substances; *Revolver* just opened my head. It was the first album that showed how much they had matured. Before they had been nice guys in suits, four pop mop-tops, and now they had become serious artists and songwriters exploring their own creative vein. 'Drive My Car', 'And Your Bird Can Sing', 'Tomorrow Never Knows' were all brilliant songs. I began to pay more attention to the sounds being created behind the artist. *Revolver* expanded my appreciation of the possibilities to be achieved through production. A milestone recording.

THE FREEWHEELIN' BOB DYLAN
BOB DYLAN

When I returned from Borneo everybody was talking about this folk singer, Bob Dylan. Having come from Ireland, I was no stranger to this kind of music. I grew up in a household where we played traditional music. I kind of scoffed at first because I had listened to people like Woody Guthrie and the Weavers and to a lot of acoustic music on the *Grand Ole Opry* on AFN. But Bob Dylan just started off something. It was also the first time I had heard a protest singer. When I listened to the words of 'Masters of War' and 'World War III Blues', they were obviously the work of somebody who had his head in a different space. Prior to that, bands were pretty clean-cut and we'd go onto stage wearing something like a uniform. He was just this guy who would get up there in his jeans and jacket and his postman's cap, and he had this aura of having just got off the bus, a kind of hobo chic. By 1966, when he was into his electric phase, I was beginning to live a slightly parallel life as my hair got longer and my clothes looser.

GREATEST HITS
HANK WILLIAMS

Country music was the first music I heard outside of Irish traditional music on my little steam radio. The first radio we got here in Kilnaboy was a wet-and-dry battery radio and that's how I heard AFN. It was re-broadcast from Stuttgart to AFN. So we'd get the *Grand Ole Opry* on the Thursday night following its broadcast in America the previous Saturday. The reception was good some of the time, but not in the summer. I was stunned by this music: hearing these quite alien sounds of steel guitars and the fiddle – which I could relate to as my mother played it. I didn't realize until much later that this music was an American cousin of Irish traditional music, because it had been influenced by it.

Much later on I began to hear the soul in this man's voice. I was in my twenties when I became fascinated again by the guitar sound and the way his voice was able to wrap itself around his words. It's a voice that has a crack, a cry; all great singers who can put across this emotion have this 'cry'. It comes across as being simple, as the blues often does, but if you actually peel away that layer you begin to see the great depth of it, like watching a great bridge- or chess-player. With Hank Williams what hits you first is the melody, but when you look inside, you see this man was singing the life of the downtrodden. He was singing of his life and his loves and his pain and his heart was breaking right in front of you. I think he was the original rock'n'roller; on stage he wiggled his hips. Jimmie Rodgers welded the blues and country together, but Hank brought another dimension into it. He really laid down the ground rules for rockabilly and country; we would have had no Elvis if Hank Williams had not been on this planet. His music will never die.

RAY CHARLES LIVE
RAY CHARLES

This man does not come from this planet at all. He's from the Planet Ray! There are not many artists who affect me the way Charles does. He can make me shiver and tremble and cry or shout and celebrate. His music is about the celebration of life and I see no darkness it. Ray brought his music directly from the Church and secularized it. He's an extraordinary human being, a fully-fledged, paid-up lifetime genius. His voice is like dark-brown honey with fire and all kind of spices in it. The power and range of the man and the emotions that he can evoke is astonishing. A Ray Charles scream to me is one of the most beautiful sounds I could hear. Listen to his 'Drown in My Own Tears' from the live album he recorded in Herndon Stadium in Georgia in 1958. The end, where the Raylettes are answering him, is straight out of church. He holds maybe a fifteen-second scream and it is just amazing. The record is still available.

I was back here in Ireland, in Kilnaboy, in 1959. I was fifteen and I heard 'What I'd Say'. I didn't know what I was listening to at the time. I knew it wasn't rock'n'roll or R&B, but I knew it was closer to R&B than any of the white pop singers at the time. Frankie Avalon and Bobby Vee and others were being dished out on the radio: trite, white, pop icons created in some little factory in Philadelphia. Ray was 100 per cent real. He was a man of total commitment living his art as a blind musician who was a musician to the very tips of his fingers. Every fibre in his being resounds with this power of music. He is like a lightning conductor. He can take the whole million volts of soul and rechannel it so that we mere mortals can listen and interpret.

GET YER YA-YAS OUT!
THE ROLLING STONES

This is the greatest live rock'n'roll album ever. The Stones recorded it over two nights in November 1969 in Madison Square Garden, New York. They cover Chuck Berry and Robert Johnson material, and they do their own stuff. The best version of 'Street Fightin' Man' is on this album. 'Midnight Rambler' is a classic, as is 'Love in Vain'. Mick Taylor's guitar-playing is just superb. He's playing against and with Keith. Mick had never sounded better, and they sound like a band at their peak. When I want to hear good live rock I listen to this album. I also think *Exile on Main Street* and *Let It Bleed* are classics. But to really capture what the Stones were about, before they got into the mega, overblown world tours going on forever, these guys were playing down-home rock'n'roll like very few bands were. They kept true to the roots. They laid down that Chuck Berry rhythm and they kept pounding it. It's the fuel that still drives them.

AMAZING GRACE
ARETHA FRANKLIN

She is the female Ray Charles – one of the extraordinary female vocalists of all time. I've yet to hear a voice that can do as much with a piece. *Amazing Grace* is a two-set album that she brought out with Atlantic in the early seventies, recorded live in a Baptist church in California with a congregation and choir. Her version of 'Amazing Grace', which goes on for over ten minutes, shows what a truly great artist and vocalist and technician she is. Soul, soul, soul. She does mostly gospel pieces on this album. James Cleveland was the director and he was a gospel artist in his own right. This was powerhouse stuff, no rock'n'roll could compare with it. They say rock'n'roll is from the waist down, and this is from the waist up. It's head and body stuff. It reaches out because it reaches upwards.

FORTY YEARS OF IRISH PIPING
SÉAMUS ENNIS

Patrick Sky was being touted as the next Bob Dylan, which was probably his downfall, but he made a couple of interesting albums with some bizarre and amazing songs. He was totally fascinated by Irish music and came over and became a friend of Séamus Ennis, and he made his own set of pipes and subsequently learnt how to play them. When Pat went back to America he decided to gather a lot of Séamus Ennis's stuff. Séamus had been a collector, singer, storyteller, musician, a one-man repository of Irish culture. He was a master piper. This album consists of Séamus telling some of the most surreal stories you'd ever hear. He also plays the whistle and different versions of the same tune twenty years apart. One version will show a certain technique and then later you can hear how much he has evolved. A great brain at work behind fantastic technique. This man had obviously steeped himself in the language, in the playing, in the people. He is the most completely rounded traditional musician of this century in so many ways. He plays pieces of music on this album that I would compare with the work of great artists like Charlie Parker, John Coltrane, Miles Davis, or Django Reinhardt. If I were to try to explain Irish music to people, I'd suggest they listen to the Bothy Band and Séamus Ennis for starters. His playing transcends culture, space and time.

BARRY DEVLIN

THIS IS AN OLD and irredeemably atavistic list. I make no apology. These days, I am an old and irredeemably atavistic man. Now, where did I put my *Daily Telegraph*?

PLEASE PLEASE ME, WITH THE BEATLES, A HARD DAY'S NIGHT, BEATLES FOR SALE, HELP!, RUBBER SOUL, REVOLVER, SGT. PEPPER, THE BEATLES, LET IT BE, ABBEY ROAD
THE BEATLES

OK, I know we're not supposed to nominate more than one album by the same group but the Beatles charted my life for the longest and best time, marking out my teens and early twenties, matching the moods of my growing up as if John, Paul, George and Ringo were writing and singing every song specially for me.

Which, of course, they were ...

ASTRAL WEEKS
VAN MORRISON

Falling asleep in the bedroom under the eaves in Ardboe one hot summer's night, Radio Luxembourg drifting in and out on the old Pye portable and then this honey music, drowsy and sweet and magical, seeming to go on for ever like music in a dream and gradually falling awake again. ' ... the love you love to love that loves to love the love' – the bass swooping and the strings building and by the end I was sitting up in bed wide awake like a man who had just seen a comet blaze across the sky. The comet appears in Terry Keane's page a tad too often these days but the glory of that moment lives on.

STICKY FINGERS
THE ROLLING STONES

Oh, yes indeed. Chris de Burgh was playing the door in Captain A's on Grafton Street, Horslips were doing their first nationwide tour in the Purple Tranny (Hi, Dunfanaghy!), Mick Finn and Ashtar from Mars had poppies in their hair and the glory of 'Just Another Moonlight Mile' was all around. What a year. What a summer. What a gig ...

Oh, and *Happy to Meet* was on the way ...

STAND UP
JETHRO TULL

Ian Anderson has recorded some of the most turgid music known to man (especially on his later albums – 'North Sea Oil' ... aargh!) but *Stand Up* is a compendium of majesty. 'Reasons for Waiting', 'We Used to Know', 'Look into the Sun' are simply stunning. Jim Lockhart and I used to sit in the Good Room in James's Street picking at a box of Contrast provided by Jim's father and plotting. You still won't hear a finer album of songs, light on their feet, graceful, sad and joyous by turns and adorned with some of the prettiest melodies ever played by a rock band. On the other hand, you might prefer to 'Let a man come in and do the popcorn ...'

THE JOSHUA TREE
U2

I could pick any album by the band. I'm an unashamed fan and I love them all but I'm picking this one because it was like a second childhood for me. I got to film them and America which was Outside, and best of all I got to make the video of 'I Still Haven't Found What I'm Looking For' which is my second favourite U2 song of all time (my first favourite is 'Gloria') and not just because I filmed it. *Achtung Baby* famously reinvented the band. *The Joshua Tree* did the same for me earlier, halting my decline into truculence and old age. Well, for a year anyway ...

DRIFT AWAY
DOBIE GREY

The album that was our soundtrack as we recorded *The Tain* in The Manor – the residential studio near Oxford which had just been opened by a twenty-one-year-old pup called Richard Branson. There was this little chap who used to sweep up when we left the studio. The story was that Richard Branson was letting him do some recording in return. We didn't pay him much heed because we were doing The Difficult Second Album and besides he was a very little chap with a straggly beard. Nearly invisible, actually. And then one night we all trooped in and the little chap played us his Masterwork in Progress which was called *Tubular Bells*. The rest, of course, is history.

But I remember *Drift Away*.

CAN'T BUY A THRILL
STEELY DAN

Where were you when you first heard Steely Dan? Wait, wait ... it's all coming back now. A burger van beside the Tara Towers where we used to call in for butcher's offal and lard after the gig as the sun rocketed up over Howth. Charles and Johnny and Eamon and Jim, fumbling with ketchup sachets, half listening to Tony Prince, who was a Grade A Prat and thinking 'it's Steeleye Span, idiot, why can't you talk right?', and then hearing the chords and that syncopated rolling piano and the opening words 'you've been telling me you're a genius since you were seventeen ...' and going hmmm, maybe not Maddy Prior after all. And there was more. 'Times are hard and you're afraid to pay the fee/So you find yourself somebody who can do the job for free.' We tried to lift all of their riffs but didn't really succeed. Or at least not as well as Thin Lizzy.

NUMBER ONE RECORD
BIG STAR

Every jangle band worth its salt from the Long Ryders through REM to Teenage Fanclub and the Revenants will tell you that Big Star and its crazed frontman, Alex Chilton were a Seminal Influence. The line-up changed constantly and Big Star only made two proper records, this one and *Radio City*, but Chilton and his henchman Chris Bell squabbled and fought their way to some kind of chime guitar epiphany that's never been surpassed. Then they broke up. I saw Alex Chilton long after in a club in Memphis. Drug-raddled and barefoot (Chilton, not me, I only had two Bud Lights), with a broken PA and a hunchback flugel-horn player, he was by then, clearly not a Role Model ... The Great Guitar Grunge Gods. And fifteen years before Nirvana were ever heard of.

WHEELS IN MOTION
ANY TROUBLE

Never heard of Any Trouble? Clive Gregson? Well shame on you, all fifty-eight million of you. Any Trouble were the great undiscovered band of the seventies. When it came to epigram, lesser practitioners like Elvis Costello and Billy Bragg simply paled. Songs like 'Open Fire' and 'Eastern Promise' still sound great today and Gregson's reading of 'Dawning of the Day' stands as my candidate for Most Powerful Performance By a Man Who is Not Al Green. And that's praise ... (*The Belle Album* is in my list as well. Make that two at number 6).

(WHAT'S THE STORY) MORNING GLORY?
OASIS

Plus ça change, eh, Matelots? The New Beatles are proving that guitar, bass and drums still hack it. And then some. Roll on the Champagne Supernova in the Sky. I could do with a drink and maybe some ambrosia.

And isn't this where I came in ...?

KEITH DONALD

LIVE AT CARNEGIE HALL
BENNY GOODMAN

My father had been a jazz banjo player around Belfast in the 1920s (quite an avant-garde thing to do, I've always thought) and he bought me a ukulele when I was five. My elder brother Philip used to come home from grammar school and play this Benny Goodman album. I asked my parents for something to blow instead of strum and they bought me a recorder (partly to stop me singing whilst playing ukulele, I imagine) and I taught myself to play by ear.

Later, in my twenties, I was severely injured in a car crash and Dublin's jazz musicians held a benefit night for me. I was too ill to attend and missed meeting Benny Goodman, whom Louis Stewart had brought along, so I never had a chance to thank him for being my first inspiration.

CHARLIE MARIANO
CHARLIE MARIANO

When I was just into long trousers, I was asked to join the Embankment Six, a respected Belfast jazz band who played twice a week in Sammy Housten's jazz club. One day the owner of a jazz record shop, Dougie Knight, said 'You should listen to this, son' and I came home with my first modern jazz album of Charlie Mariano (alto sax), Max Bennet (bass), John Williams (piano), and Mel Lewis (drums). I played it incessantly, saved the money from the Embankment Six and, with my mother, bought my first sax, a Conn alto. I still have the record and the alto. I bought the album on CD in New York last year and it's as good as it ever sounded.

100% PROOF
TUBBY HAYES

The Embankment Six played at the first Queen's University Arts Festival, in 1962. Top of the bill was the Tubby Hayes Quartet. I stood in the wings of the Whitla Hall, gobsmacked. I never knew until then that it was possible to play so many notes in one bar and make it lyrical, swinging and right. Soon afterwards, I used my student grant to buy a tenor sax and nearly starved for a term at Trinity. This is the best of British jazz with Tubby outstanding on sax, vibes, flute and arrangements.

THE MOZART CONCERTO K.622
GERVASE DE PAYER

In 1962 I was finishing seven years of classical clarinet tuition and was asked to perform the Mozart concerto with an orchestra in the Grosvenor Hall, Belfast. I was so nervous that my short-sighted girlfriend could see my hands shaking from her seat in the fifth row. I guess my performance could be described as functional. However, I did hear the maestro de Peyer perform it in the Ulster Hall once. During the sublime stillness of the slow movement, the back doors of the hall burst open and two teddy-boys – drape jackets, D.A. haircuts and skin-tight jeans – swaggered in. One turned to the other and in a voice louder than de Peyer's clarinet, said, 'Come on Sammy, I told ye there was no fuckin' boxing on tonight.'

MOVIN' OUT
SONNY ROLLINS

I love Sonny Rollins, for his style and tone and also for the purity of his lifestyle. He has several times in his career stopped performing in public in order to take time to reflect, read, practise and compose. On this album he plays with Kenny Dorham (trumpet), Percy Heath (bass), Art Blakey and Arthur Taylor (drums), and Thelonius Monk (piano), amongst others. It was recorded in 1954 and is still strong and fresh. The ballad 'More Than You Know' is one of my all-time favourites, with Monk and Rollins mellow and inventive.

RUM, SODOMY AND THE LASH
THE POGUES

Elvis Costello produced the Pogues on this masterpiece and did a brilliant job in capturing raw London-Irish energy. Shane MacGowan wrote five of the songs and, in the best traditions of songwriting, the words work as well on paper as they do on vinyl. The album was released just as Moving Hearts played their first farewell gig and I thought, 'Fair play to them – they're taking the high road while we have turned into a cul-de sac.' Later on I was told that the Pogues' favourite piece of music to hear in the bandwagon was the Hearts' last album, *The Storm*, and that little bit of information did this heart good.

MIDNIGHT WELL
MIDNIGHT WELL

This was recorded in 1977 and is something of a watershed in Irish folk/trad/rock music. It was also something of a personal turning point, introducing me to some great musicians and another genre of music. This line-up says it all: Dónal Lunny, Thom Moore, Janie Cribbs, Gerry O'Beirne, Ciarán Ó Braonáin, Martin O'Connor, Kevin Burke, Fran Breen, Robbie Brennan, Shaun Davey, Jolyon Jackson, Pat Farrell, Garven Gallagher, Brian Masterson, Paul Barret, Dave McAnaney, Greg Boland and myself.

THE ORIGINAL GERRY MULLIGAN QUARTET
GERRY MULLIGAN

I was president of the Trinity College, Dublin, Jazz Society in 1966/67 and was performing with other Society members one night when a tall gentleman walked in to the back of the room, carrying an odd-shaped instrument case. A few minutes later a note was handed up to me – 'Gerry Mulligan wants to know if he can sit in.' I had the honour of announcing to thirty or so people: 'Ladies and gentlemen, Gerry Mulligan.' He played every tune from then on and went with us to an impromptu party in a flat in Grove Road, Rathmines, then occupied by a student pianist from Sierra Leone, Wordsworth Jones. He stayed for hours chatting and playing some of his compositions on piano. I met Louis Stewart for the first time and went home later as high as a kite on music and people.

XIAME
XIAME

This trio consists of Jorge Degas, Michael Rodach and Andreas Weiser. Jorge is a Brazilian bass-player and singer who lives in Denmark and I first met up with him playing at a festival there. I have since played with him via an experiment conducted by Arthouse, Temple Bar, Dublin, when Jorge was in a studio in Denmark, I was in Dublin and the other musicians were in studios in Paris, New York, and Toronto. We could all see, hear and talk with each other and play connected pieces of music. Jorge is the most accomplished bass-player I know of and I look forward to playing with him again. His band Xiame are brilliant and their albums combine jazz, Brazilian rhythms and folk music.

TORONTO, MASSEY HALL, 15 MAY 1953
DIZZY GILLESPIE, CHARLIE PARKER, BUD POWELL, CHARLES MINGUS AND MAX ROACH

You could say that this live recording is a coincidence in time and place of almost all the people who redefined a musical genre. I wonder did any of the Massey Hall audience realize they were witnessing a moment in history. Every time I listen to this recording, I find something musical that affects me differently and I wonder at the mad, bad lives that musicians endured – often a succession of highs and lows, of ecstasy and tragedy relieved only in performance. When future musicologists look back at the twentieth century, they will see it as a golden age, with the genesis of jazz, blues, rock'n'roll and their offshoots. We are so lucky to have been present.

DONOVAN

THE 'CHIRPING' CRICKETS
THE CRICKETS

When I was about fourteen I used to work in a market in Hatfield. Up until that time, my tastes were dictated by living in Glasgow. Then came the mid-fifties migrations out of the industrial cities into the new towns in the south of England. Up in Glasgow people still made their own music at parties, and I listened to a lot of folk music there because I had a very strong Irish background on both parents' sides. I listened to Scottish and Irish folk songs and also the pop music of the day – Frank Sinatra, big band – but the musical jolt came when my father took me to see the movie *Rock around the Clock*, which was an extraordinary experience. I was too young to be a rocker, but four years later when I arrived in the south of England I started to listen to pop music. Then I heard Buddy Holly, who blew me out of my seat.

The curious thing is that they didn't have albums in England then. They released Buddy Holly on EP. I collected four songs at a time. It took me four EPs to get this first album, *The 'Chirping' Crickets*. I didn't realize until many years later how influential the album was for everyone else as well, the Beatles and Eric Clapton included. I didn't make the connection until later that Holly was actually a folk-style musician who played acoustic guitar in Texas. I didn't realize rockabilly owed its roots in large part to Scotland and Ireland.

Fast forward to the eighties and I'm in the Hard Rock Café in Texas with my stepson Julian (Brian Jones's son). That very night the Crickets were playing. We met them backstage and who should walk into the room but Maria Holly. It was a very emotional experience. She was the girl the songs were written about. She came straight up to us and Julian melted because he looks to that generation as a kind of extended family. He knew Maria was a very important part of history. We sat and had a wonderful evening. I never met Buddy Holly. I wish I had.

JOAN BAEZ
JOAN BAEZ

When I was fifteen I managed to get into a College of Further Education. I was about to rebel. When I checked into this college, I came slap-bang into the artistic community. There was a bunch of kids from the lower-middle class who were beatniks and who wore sloppy joes, long hair, sandals and duffel coats. We sat around on the campus and I listened to their radical views. And of course there were some kids with a guitar playing a Joan Baez song. That's when I realized Joan Baez was very important. I immediately went out and bought her record in the local eclectic record shop in St Alban's.

Joan was first. We all realize that now. She released this record, I believe, in 1960. She was obviously part of the tradition. This album had a collection of songs on it which were gathered by Francis Child, an eighteenth-century folk-song collector. He published three volumes and some of these songs had travelled over to America and become Americanized in the normal course of the Irish-Scottish migration to the New World. 'Donna, Donna' was the first song I had heard which talked about freedom, and listening to the album with its Scottish/Irish folk songs and old English ballads made me see how vibrant the folk scene was. When I heard Joan Baez I was amazed by the excitement in her voice, and this rallied people. I didn't realize she had trained as an opera singer or that she had come out of a Quaker tradition of doing good to others. A true Christian attitude. I didn't realize then that Joan had been discovered and had been offered the same deal with John Hammond at Columbia that Dylan was to be offered a few years later. (We all know that she in a way discovered Dylan with John Hammond and gave him the stage.) She decided, however, to go with a small folk label, Vanguard, instead of one of the three big labels of the time. Her mother was a wonderful person, a poet herself, and her father was a scientist, radical thinker and civil rights activist.

I was to meet Joan many years later. I had been invited by her, as Dylan had been, to play the Newport Folk Festival. When we met, she wanted to record my songs straight away. I found her to be all I had imagined she was. Radical groups all around the world rallied around her songs. I was to become spellbound by her and when I read articles by her in small folk magazines she would mention the great Woody Guthrie, which brings us on to *Bound for Glory*.

BOUND FOR GLORY
WOODY GUTHRIE

At that time, I was just about to leave home. I painted and wrote, and there was a growing restlessness in me. I can't attribute it totally to picking up the Woody Guthrie album *Bound for Glory* and hearing 'Hard Travelling', his song of the wandering he had seen and done during the thirties and forties. He was from Oklahoma and was part of a migration moving out of there because of the dust-bowl. Now at home my father, Donald Leitch, was an amateur performer of monologue and long verse poems, and he was a great fan of Robert Service, who had a Scottish background and went to the Yukon and many other places in North America working in the logging and mining camps. I had had his poems and songs read to me from an early age and was intrigued by Service and the great outdoors, and also by W.H. Davis, an English hobo who travelled on the trains. When I heard Woody Guthrie it rang lots of bells for me. I only became aware later that he has also encouraged almost every folk singer in the world. I listened to 'The Great Coolie Dam', 'Hard Travelling', 'Do Re Mi', 'Pretty Boy Floyd'. I started buying other albums. The one that impressed me the most was the first one. Then Robert Service, W.H. Auden, Woody Guthrie, and Kerouac's *On the Road* all connected to my wanderlust. I just couldn't fit in. My father was shocked because I wouldn't finish that year of college. Having picked up a few Buddhist texts, I realized that life was a journey and the songs of Woody Guthrie were a journey. Many years later I ran into Woody's son Arlo in Germany and told him a story that few people know. Just like Joan Baez, Woody had been offered a commercial job – his own midwest radio show – but they said he could-n't sing 'The Mining Disaster' and so he told them to get lost.

ALONG THE WAY
DERROLL ADAMS

In 1965, just before I was discovered, I was in touch with the American folk scene and absorbing a huge amount of folk music. I was in a folk club one night when in walks Derroll Adams who picks up his banjo and starts playing. He played in a gentle style which he called Zen Banjo. I became a disciple and start-ed hanging out with him. He was from Portland, Oregon, and had been part of the New York folk scene with Pete Seeger, Woody Guthrie and Jack Elliott. He kicked around with Alex Campbell, a rough-and-tumble Scottish travelling man, and they had all bummed around the south of France together, drinking and playing on the beaches and causing havoc in the busker's kingdom. Derroll's influence is subtle and far-reaching. Every folk singer in Europe has had person-al contact with him. At the time I was being slammed as a Dylan clone in the press. Derroll and Pete Seeger helped by accepting me in. There was a snide sort of cartoon about Dylan and me in folk magazines and some pop magazines and in all the folk clubs in Britain. They never let me play, not because I was a Dylan clone but because I was too American in my tastes. Derroll was my champion and he stood up and said, 'This young man, Donovan, is it.'

This album has an extraordinary song on it called 'The Mountain'. In fact, Derroll inspired me to write 'There Is a Mountain'. He encouraged me to con-tinue putting spiritual thoughts in popular songs because young people needed it. 'The Mountain' is about an amazing psychedelic experience that he had on a mountain. The compassion came through in the lyrics and he saw the paradise. Paradise is of course around us all the time. He's still alive in Belgium.

THE FREEWHEELIN' BOB DYLAN
BOB DYLAN

In 1964 it was impossible not to know about Bob Dylan after Joan Baez had introduced him to the world. He blew me away. I went to the Royal Festival Hall where he played in London and I listened to him outside because I couldn't afford to buy a ticket. The first impression I got was the strong Woody Guthrie connection and one song in particular I picked up on was 'Girl of the North Country'. It is one of those Child ballads whose melody he used. It was important for me to hear because I was feeling stirrings of all my traditions. I'd learned so much from Derroll Adams, Pete Seeger and Woody Guthrie but when Dylan came along it was a jolt. I was encouraged to be young and write. He was the new generation. 'Girl of the North Country' showed that traditional music was alive. 'Blowin' in the Wind' was an absolute masterpiece.

I sounded like him for about five minutes while trying out different styles. By then my repertoire was quite extensive anyway. When he arrived in Britain, Dylan was totally surprised by the response, much to the amusement of the Joan Baez camp. 'The Times They Are A-Changing' was the first single released and it was a hit. I was already two months into fame and I was happening on a grand scale. I was higher in the charts than Dylan's single in the end. Joan arrived at the Savoy, and Dylan arrived there too, and Joan decided to introduce me. But she was having a running battle with Dylan because he'd given up protest songs by now and he wouldn't go down to the march scheduled that week in Grosvenor Square in front of the U.S. embassy. We were going to march with Vanessa Redgrave as well as that curious little fellow, Marc Bolan, a folk singer at the time.

Joan was amused at the Dylan camp walking slam-bang into my controversy. Dylan treated it all very jocularly in the film *Don't Look Back*. I was accepted as a young member of the folk family and was in and out of the Savoy all the time, and I talked to him before, during and after the film.

One evening I arrived at the Savoy in my rags and tatters, not many months from sleeping on students' floors. I didn't have a house, didn't have a car. I had eight records running up the charts and money was pouring in from everywhere. I walked into the Savoy and when I called up, a man named Bobby Neuwirth answered the phone. He was a folk singer from New York, and a kind of manager with Dylan at the time. They all spoke the same way. He said, 'Hey man, come on, come on.' So I came up and he said, 'Bob is in there,' and he pointed me into this dark suite. It was a quiet night in for the man in black. It was pitch-black, except for a TV screen which showed someone ice-skating. Dylan said, 'Come in, sit down.' I didn't quite see him. My eyes became accustomed to the dark, and I'd had a joint before I came up so I was feeling quite mellow. I became aware of other figures in the room. There was silence. Nobody was saying anything. Everybody I guess had had a smoke too.

It was a night off, so there was nothing happening. And there were no questions to ask. One of the figures nearer to me leaned over and said, 'How are you, Donovan?' and the accent was unmistakable. It was John Lennon. Dylan stood up, put the light on, and it was the other three guys. They all looked at me and I looked at them. As George put it many years later, 'You were a bit out of your depth but you weren't really – you were part of it all.' So we stood up to leave at the end of the night and there I was and nothing much was said except 'Do you wanna lift?', and I went downstairs and the four of them were driving customized Mini Coopers completely tricked out with speakers and leather and black glass, and I felt that George was a bit flash, and I checked him out. He said to me later, 'You checked me out there, didn't you?' But then it would be less than a year before I would be riding around in one of those carriages, some Rolls-Royce or Jaguar. I became friends with George after that and to some extent with Paul and Ringo. In India we bonded. So Dylan accepted me with magnanimity at the height of all that craziness of comparison.

RUBBER SOUL
THE BEATLES

I fell in love with Linda Lawrence in 1965 during the second *Ready, Steady, Go!* series. I was the resident folk-singer and I used to sing songs about the road, and how tough it was for an eighteen-year-old to be sleeping rough on the beaches. It was a load of rubbish but they loved it. Linda was in the Green Room one night. She had had a two-year affair with Brian Jones and had a child by him. When I saw her across the room the earth moved. Stars started flashing. We danced and I found that she was part of a bohemian scene around Windsor. I didn't know at the time that she had been living with Brian Jones and that she was heartbroken because they had split up. I fell in love and started to court her immediately. That year I wrote 'Sunshine Superman' for her, which became number one in America in 1966. We parted temporarily in the winter of 1965, a time when I was listening to *Rubber Soul* all the time. The track 'Girl' was so obviously my Linda.

I was also smoking dope and taking LSD (it was legal in 1965) and mescaline. This album showed the Beatles' growing awareness of drugs. Dylan had already turned them on to pot. They came fully into their own on this album. It contained the beginnings of spirituality, the beginnings too of disillusionment, knowing that they had changed and could never go back. 'In My Life' is very, very moving, as is the whole album. It drove right into me because I was feeling heartbroken. Linda and I did marry many years later and we are still together. Had we married in the sixties our marriage would have been wrecked by fame.

This album continues to influence me musically. The acoustic guitars were still prominent then. The Beatles were not only influenced by Dylan's folk music, but also earlier by the Everly Brothers. 'Norwegian Wood', 'Drive My Car', 'Nowhere Man' – fourteen tracks altogether. In 1966, as fame got to them, the Beatles became more and more isolated. On their world tour, they were literally under siege from fans. It was a ridiculous life to live and they gave up very soon after that.

NINA SIMONE
NINA SIMONE

I had listened to jazz from a very early age. Although I was locked into folk-rock, I liked jazz and classical too. I realized when I did 'Sunshine Superman' that there were no barriers. There are no borders in music. It's either good or bad, well-played or not well-played, meaningful or not meaningful. And so I embraced all kinds of music. And when this album came out, I was very moved by it because it combined modern styles of jazz, folk song, spirituals. What a powerful woman, and she did it all on a very small scale, with just an upright bass. I just fell in love with the concert bass. I knew that I wanted to use that style. The way she sang 'Ne Me Quitte Pas' by Jacques Brel was astounding. I realized that there was a lot of dramatic tension in my songs that I wanted to bring out. She influenced a lot of other people, like Eric Burdon of the Animals. That's when jazz really started for me. I wrote and recorded 'Sunny Goodge Street', which was probably a first in using folk music, jazz and classical in one song. It opened up a door which Van Morrison was pleased to enter.

THE ART OF PABLO CASALS
PABLO CASALS

I think this record was recorded in 1926, and there is the atmosphere and the smell of an earlier era. This really is a period from which we have very few recordings. I played it again and again in the sixties and it was a constant influence on my own guitar work. Casals' artistry influenced how I touched the strings. My father, who travelled with me in 1967, 1968 and 1969 on enormous stadium tours in the U.S., has a story about how one night in the dressing-room Frank Zappa said, 'Mr Leitch, it's not given to many to be able to touch the strings of the guitar the way your son does.' I thank Pablo Casals for introducing me to a classical style. Nigel Kennedy, who is a good friend, could be called the Casals of today: he touches the strings in a special way.

GETZ GILBERTO
STAN GETZ AND JOAO GILBERTO

This album was recorded in 1963 in New York. It's cool jazz and a fusion of jazz, folk music, and acoustic guitar. One of Joao Gilberto's songs, 'The Girl from Ipanema', became number one in the U.S. What was extraordinary about this song was that Astrid, Jobim Gilberto's wife, was just sitting in the corner of the studio and out of the blue was asked to sing. No one thought that it was going to be a smash hit or anything. The Carter Family had done the same thing, sitting around inventing songs. I was looking for the same warm sound and feeling in my records.

CATCH A FIRE
BOB MARLEY AND THE WAILERS

This album brings us into the seventies, when the whole Jamaican scene began to influence everybody and change the world of music. I was listening to blue-beat from its early days in London. Blue-beat influenced a lot of artists like Georgie Fame and Paul McCartney ('Ob-la-di, Ob-la-da'). When I went to the island I realized that everyone was listening to the radio stations from Miami and Texas and New York. And all these influences created a sound called reggae. I went down to Negril. It was before the big tourist invasion from America when reggae really hit big. One day when we were hanging out I walked by a hut and I heard a guitar. I asked the American who was putting us up if that was a local musician and he said, 'Yeah, that's a guy called Marley.' I didn't really listen because I didn't recognize the name. Later when I picked up the album, I realized that it was him. Like Jimi Hendrix he singlehandedly moved millions of people. Although he mixed all these styles, he came out with pure folk music. The purity is a spiritual message and the sacrament is the marijuana.

I went to see him in a club in Los Angeles many years later with Linda. The manager, who I've known for years, asked us back to see him. He said that nobody was back there, which was surprising because we were in the middle of the centre of the music world. Linda and I and a lot of black people from Watts had come to hear him. The latter were rather nervous as this was a predominantly white area and racial tensions were running high.

We walked into the dressing-room and found no press, no welcome telegrams, no wine, no food, no girls, no managers. Just five guys. On the dressing-room table was no make-up, just an enormous amount of Jamaican 'ganja' in newspapers, like fish'n'chips. That was all there was in the room. And Linda and I walked into the room and introduced ourselves to Bob. And all he said was, 'Natty, Natty.' The other guys didn't say a word. Now women in their society may be different from women in our musical society; he didn't pass the sacrament to Linda, he passed it to me. And I smoked this very large Jamaican joint: leaves, seeds, twigs and everything, but I took it easy. Linda went straight up to him and picked it up off him. He gazed straight into her eyes and smiled. When we'd taken the sacrament, I really felt the purity of the music. *Catch a Fire* was the first of their albums that I loved, but all his music influences me. It is like oil, it gets everywhere and it seeps into people's lives.

THEO DORGAN

THE RAIN IS DRUMMING on the caravan roof and it's November night outside but it's warm in here and Rory Gallagher is thundering out of the record-player. Jim O'Brien's brothers live in this caravan, in the yard behind the family house and shop on Wolfe Tone Street. Tana and Paul are down in the Swan or the Pig and Whistle by the river and they don't mind that we're in here listening as long as we don't mess with anything. Jim has just started with the ESB and has bought or is buying the first of his motorbikes and he's starting to wake up, to cop on to the world, but I'm still deep in the sleepwalking of school, two years to go. Sometimes Brendan Barry's here too, and sometimes Mick Hannigan whose hair is ridiculously long for school, but somehow or other he's getting away with it. My hair is starting to grow out, like Jimi Hendrix's, or Phil Lynott's. We're very concerned with the serious business of growing your hair. It's driving our parents mad. Tana was in school with Rory. Rory went to our school. We'll be seeing him in the City Hall after Christmas. We know, because we read it in *Melody Maker* or in *NME*, that there are graffiti all over London – 'Clapton is God'. Bullshit. Nobody says it because nobody needs to, it's so obvious: Rory is God, or at least God's electric angel, and the message is that the blues plus electricity takes you there. You can't say where there is but you know it when you're there. Rory has it down hard and clear: battered Fender, check shirt, black jeans. You stand with your toes turned in and the bass goes in your spine, the drums are the ground under your feet, you lock fast and deep inside and it all comes pouring up and out in a long orgiastic pounding shuddering wail of pure beauty. What am I looking at, back there? *Taste*, or *On the Boards*. Two-tone black and orange cover, the backlit frizz of hair, Gallagher's head bent over the neat-fingered grab at the last sweet fast cluster of high notes.

•

In Brendan Barry's house. Our refuge. The house to ourselves. His father, Paddy, has a pub, is out most evenings. Older sister married, is she? Siobhán my sister's age, off out somewhere else. We sit in the small front room, playing cards. Hannigan and O'Brien. Pat Lehane, when he's not off with Theresa walking around and around our small patch of the city in the cold and night and rain, stopping for hours under streetlamps, just holding each other, speechless. When he's there we don't talk about this. When he's not there we don't mention it. We play cards. Jimmy Meaney's there usually. Hundred and ten for matches. Occasionally for threepence a game. Nobody smoking yet, nor drinking. Meaney can never remember clubs are called clubs so he calls them trallywaggles. Jesus Christ, we say. If it didn't take so much energy we'd hate the bastard. It drives us nuts. O'Brien and Barry have stereos, primitive first-generation things but it's forty watts and good enough for us. They buy the albums too. Beatles and Stones at first, then more curious and wayward stuff. As we play cards, everybody's twitching, picking a run here, a phrase there. In his head everyone's following the swoop and dip of 'Hey Jude' on the instrument or voice of his choice. 'Don't carry the world/up-on/your sho-oulder.' Sometimes the spectral echoes chime, and what's pouring out of the speakers harmonizes with the private world everybody's in, and the cards are held in mid-air and everybody comes crashing silently in on Ringo's stuttered signature change and Paul's hungback chord changes. For just a second or so, everybody looks at everybody else and there's a ghost of a smile, a nod that says it's alright, this is alright, and then we go back to the cards.

•

Those nights in out of the winter rain we were sleepwalking. When it wasn't raining we were walking. We walked that town down to a net of shiny limestone tracks. We walked and walked and in our heads each of us was Dylan on the cover of *The Freewheelin' Bob Dylan,* hands jammed into the pockets of an ancient soft-tan leather jacket, that beautiful girl's hand tucked tight and pro-prietorial under our elbows. Nobody ever said a word about this, just as nobody ever said a word when somebody lost himself in the mimeworld of picking a solo along with Rory or Keith, note for note, grimace for grimace. I have never again been for so long a time in the company of good friends with such perfect regard for each other's privacy. How viciously we might have mocked each other, bol-stered our terrified egos by turning as a pack on the unfortunate fool of the moment. Who mostly would have been me. Alright, maybe sometimes we got it up for Meaney. But apart from breaking our arses when Hannigan more or less inadvertently pinned Jimmy's foot to the ground with a garden fork we were rarely if ever cruel and now I wonder if we weren't a bit weird. So much older then, younger than that now. Dylan was how we made it alright for ourselves to be other, to be American and to dream ourselves away into drugs and sex, fast bikes and sunswept lonesome highways. Would we have been any different if we'd known how cruel he was to Joanie?

•

We know such an extraordinary amount about the musicians, or think we do. *Melody Maker* is rapidly being shifted sideways by the brasher, more knowing NME. Somewhere obscure under the puff and come-and-go of ephemeral bands, an agenda of sorts is being worked out. We're into rock music, not pop for Jesus sake, and what you listen to marks you out from the dopes. None of this is said; very little, looking back now down the narrow corridor, was ever said, you just knew. Or you didn't. Esoteric values. Insiderness. We were trying, I suppose, to approximate to something of what the musicians themselves knew, listened to, talked about among themselves. Now I think it's truly strange it never occurred to any of us to put a band together and have a go at it ourselves. But then, for whatever reasons, we were content just to know stuff.

Tana, Jim O'Brien's older brother, was, is, a very talented guitar player and singer. I couldn't figure why someone that good wouldn't have a stab at it. He'd been in school with Gallagher for Christ's sake, every Christmas when Rory came home he'd check Tana out, they'd go for a drink, maybe play a bit. He's played with a lot of the best we have, worked on a lot of albums, he has the gift but he keeps it quiet and handy and that's the way he wants it so, OK. Tana had an extraordinary collection of blues and other esoterica, and if I tried to put a word on what all those albums had in common it would be that they all had a breath of the real thing in them. Basil Bunting said, about love, 'tastes good, garlic and salt in it'. I guess that's what we were after, listening to Leadbelly or Howlin' Wolf or Sonny Terry at much the same time we were listening to Dylan's intoxicating, excruciating harmonica or to Roger McGuinn bending sweetness into a harsh and always-climbing electric guitar. There is a society of those who know, and you can join just by hearing the music. But, you have to know you're hearing it. And you have to really hear it.

•

Three memories of the Savoy. You can get to the cheap seats down the front through a tunnel that suddenly pops up in the middle of the stalls. I forget who the main act was, but the support act was Gaslight, a local band with some genuine talents but destined never to break out of Cork. We're milling through the tunnel, four or five of us, somebody's missing, and as we reach the steps the band are launching into Love's 'Seven is Seven'. We lock on the beat and come marching up and into the aisle, all the body-language signalling we know this, we know what's coming. We're shocked that anyone else in Cork has ever heard of *Da Capo*, the album they've taken this song from, but we're buzzing on the fact that we know it, and anybody watching can surely tell we know this album, we're jigging and miming in perfect synch with the band, and grinning like crazy because we know and the band knows but probably nobody else does that the guitar solo at the end is probably the most perfect and awesome, stunning and overwhelming guitar solo of all time. Pure on the beat, on the note ecstasy. We think we're great.

Another night, farther back, halfway back on the left-hand side. Peter Green's flying arrow keeps darting across the stage like a strike plane at the ridiculously tall, ridiculously long-haired Mick Fleetwood behind his tower of drums. The noise is deafening, they're working their way through the new album, *Albatross*, and we're rocking in our seats when a woman in front of us turns and says crossly, in the whining, buzz-saw drawl of the Cork middle-classes, 'Would you ever please stay quiet, I'm trying to listen to the music.' She has to shout this at the top of her voice. All I can think of, through the shock of it, is: 'What the fuck is she doing here?'

And another night. Skid Row aren't going down too well, which is strange because they're well-liked here. Suddenly the music stops, and Brush steps up to the mike, announces some darts have been thrown on stage and that's it, they're stopping the gig. We're amazed. Three, four rows from the front, we saw nothing. Later in the Pig and Whistle, the talk is that one of their roadies lobbed a few darts harmlessly on to the stage because they couldn't keep it together and they wanted to get the fuck out of there. Who knows?

•

Almost imperceptibly those of us still in school drift through the Leaving Cert. O'Brien is well on his way to becoming a qualified electrician and is driving around on a 750 Honda. Barry, also working, has another, or is it a 250? Hannigan and myself are in College, Meaney's drifted away, Lehane and Theresa have gone off to London to be doomily in love. We don't see as much of each other. In Kate Barry's flat on the corner of MacCurtain Street and Summerhill I fall into a long spell of Joni Mitchell and Crosby, Stills, Nash and Young. Neil Young is the one who gets to me, and the soundtrack to those days of dope and politics and rarely going home is *Harvest*. And I start paying more attention to the lyrics. Cohen has been floating there in the head for years but now I start listening to how the words are put together with the music. I start on the long slightly paranoid road, familiar to many, of thinking that Dylan's lyrics have an esoteric meaning peculiarly relevant to my life, that he's writing the script of what's happening to me in retrospect and prophecy. This is synaesthesia time, hearing colours, tasting the inside of a song. Getting tired of the raw electric hit, the thunder of amplified, simple music. A slow but gathering drift towards meaning over sensation. Too stupid or simple yet to realize that sensation is meaning too. Through it all are woven the lines that still haunt me, most likely always will, the high reflection of Neil Young's 'Well I dreamt I saw the silver spaceships coming ...'. There are nights still, of putting grief behind me in quiet elation, when I keep close to the windows or in winter walk outside into the frost and just stand there staring up, wondering when they'll come, and if I'll be calm when they do.

•

We're renting a chalet near Camp in County Kerry. Winter again. O'Brien sticks his head in the door of our room. 'You'd better get up. The Branch are outside, they want to talk to you.' I think he's having me on, pull back the curtains. Middle-aged countryman outside, two feet from the window, holding up a revolver in a unnatural way. 'Look, boy, I have a gun so I have.' A ferret-faced older man sticks his head around the door, trying to cop a look at Pauline in bed. Push him out in front of me. Older guy, tie outside his sweater for Jesus sake. This is fucking absurd. One minute into it and I'm breaking my arse trying not to laugh at him. Who are we, are them bikes our transport, what're we doing down around here. Round and round. Mick and Jim very calm, Jim's girlfriend Kay, big dark eyes, looks like she might lose her temper. I'm half-pissed off, half enjoying the absurdity of it. Pauline just watches, can't tell what she's thinking. Turns out some local lads, for the crack, have phoned Tralee to say a gang resembling the crowd who hit a Securicor van nearby a few days ago are staying up in the chalets. Tie-outside-jumper is badly disappointed as it becomes clear it wasn't us. When they're gone, we make breakfast, about two hours early by the hangover and body clocks, and Jim puts on an album. Steam on the windows, it's cold, rain beating the grass down outside, and over the smell of frying bacon comes the sweet redemption of that lazy man J.J. Cale: 'Magnolia, you sweet thing . . .' The colours of the warm world we knew we were born fit for. It could have been ugly; now we're laughing happily, planning revenge on the fuckers up in Mrs Ashe's, humming along to the sweet guitars. Even still, when someone puts 'Naturally' on the deck and old J.J.'s smoky leathery voice comes soothing out of the speakers I can smell the breakfast, hear the rain beating on the cedar walls, see the battered Avenger rucking away over the humpy grass with its grumpy cops and see rolling into the room and over us that sweet, warm red earth and sun-warmed porch, the impossibly laid-back Mr Cale sitting still in a bentwood chair, fingers flicking out to shape the irresistible chords, dreamy and sweet and somehow, always, true.

•

Two, three years later, 1974. Hannigan's working and living in London, in Kentish Town. Lehane and Theresa have a flat in Tufnell Park, we all meet there most Sundays. The album we play over and over is Van's *Hard Nose the Highway*. Not what you'd think of as a summer album. It's a hot hard dry summer. I'm working on the buildings out in Isleworth, living in a sordid house in Acton with an Old Etonian gone to the bad for a landlord, his crazy half-Greek girlfriend and a shifting cast of London's hippie derelicts. And Lís and myself aren't getting on too well, mostly, I guess, because I'm a lot less sussed than I think I am about what I want. So it's maybe curious that the album those dazed and muzzy days lock onto is this one. One track in particular goes around and around in the channels and loops, 'Snow in San Anselmo'. Something, maybe, to do with the bitter-sweet feel of it. Still looking west for salvation and the now, only this time, locked in a heatwave, the saving grace of the other is snow on the high sierras, or wherever the hell Van's head is as he bends and stretches for the notes of longing and regret, with his eyes screwed shut and his heart on hold. As far as I know he's never re-recorded this track, and I think I know why but what's the point of saying?

•

Strange times, six years or so when I drifted out through the gates of family, into a kind of airlocked slow-motion movie with a small, tight cast of friends. Then out the other side, into the world I've lived in ever since, the world we all live in when the truth of it strikes and stops, the realization that you really can't go home again. Except that, of course, you can. You can go home in the music. In some ways it doesn't matter what the music is or was, what matters is who you eternally are in the place that's never lost, the place where the music carries you. All it takes is a phrase that comes suddenly into your mind, a half-heard intro coming out some stranger's window, a radio playing far off in the small hours, and down comes the avalanche again, those nights and days and years. Everybody still alive, forever young.

RODDY DOYLE

STEPHEN STILLS
STEPHEN STILLS

When I was fifteen Stephen Stills was my hero. My friends were divided between Dylan and Lou Reed, but Stephen Stills was my own personal genius – largely because of his hair. I wanted hair like that, fair, split in the middle and pressed back by the wind that was always around when he was being photographed. I bought this album in Pat Egan's Sound Cellar with money my sister gave me for my birthday. It's still wonderful. With a cast of thousands singing the churchy stuff behind him, and Stills playing guitars, organ, steel drum and, of course, percussion, 'Love the One You're With' is the best opening track I've ever heard. 'If you're dow-own – and confused – and you don't remember – who you're talkin' to.' The nine songs that follow it are as good, and all very different. Love and infidelity, the gospels and poker, the rose in the fisted glove and Jose Cuervo Gold Label Tequila – Stephen Stills was a hippie with a gun, a man who loved fresh air and chemicals, a thin man who would soon be fat, playing great music with friends who would soon be dead. Stills had a great voice; he could cheer you up and scare you at the same time. He could play all those instruments listed beside his name. And he had that hair. The album is dedicated to Jimi Hendrix.

TRANSFORMER
LOU REED

A friend of mine bought *Transformer* because he liked the cover. We'd never heard of Lou Reed or the Velvet Underground or Andy Warhol. Or 'Walk on the Wild Side'. We now heard eight great songs and three outstanding ones, produced by David Bowie and Mick Ronson. We could hear Bowie singing away in the back, 'Sata-li-yite – sata-loooo – aw aw aw oh'. But it was the lyrics that grabbed us: '... shaved her legs and then he was a she – she says "Hey babe" ...'. Men that were women, women that were really men, sex in the hall, the Sugar Plum Fairy, curtains laced with diamonds dear and the coloured girls going 'Doo do doo'. Lou Reed's world was funny and unsettling. 'Swoop swoop – oh baby, rock rock.' He was the man with the strange black eyes on the cover, a woman's made-up eyes. Was he smiling or sneering? He seemed to come from the same place as Bowie but he was less silly – 'There's a star-maaaaan' – and a lot more threatening. He sang about men and women; he swapped them – it didn't seem to matter. '... plucked her eyebrows along the way ...' The songs are sweet and tricky, tough hymns of love, lullabies to perversion. We sat on the floor in Paul's front room and listened to *Transformer*. We loved it and pretended we were cool enough to understand it. Was Lou Reed a queer or what? He was – we savoured the words – a bisexual.

THE WILD, THE INNOCENT AND THE E STREET SHUFFLE
BRUCE SPRINGSTEEN

A mere sighting of the cover brings back my duffel coat, styes on three eyelids, my first pair of Levis and *Peig*. The album is absolutely packed; words, characters, instruments, voices – seven huge songs that seem to last forever. They're not just songs; they're stories. 'Spanish Johnny drove in – from the underworld last night – with bruised arms and broken rhythm and a beat-up old Buick – but dressed – just like – dynamite.' Great lines backed by beautiful piano and a guitar that made us want to cry, and told by a voice that could have been Spanish Johnny's, bruised and dressed like dynamite. Spanish Johnny, Weak-Kneed Willie, Sloppy Sue and Big-Balls Billy, Diamond Jackie and Kitty – 'Here she comes – here she comes – here she comes – here she comes'. They ran, danced and slid through the songs. They walked down Broadway. They played some pool, skipped some school, acted real cool, stayed out all night; they laughed and they died. The music is joyful and beautifully sad, honest and full of surprises. We listened, and fell in love with America. The six lads on the back cover seemed to come straight out of the songs. Vini 'Mad Dog' Lopez played drums and cornet. Clarence 'Nick' Clemons didn't play sax; he played all saxes. And the man himself, he wore a green vest and played all guitars.

REUNION – LIVE AT MADISON SQUARE GARDEN 1972
DION AND THE BELMONTS

In September 1977 I was working in a canning factory in Germany. At the end of the late shift we'd go to a bar nearby that had a jukebox. Cool. It was, however, a German jukebox; the best tracks were Abba's 'Knowing Me Knowing You', 'No Woman No Cry' by Boney M, and Kenny Rodgers singing 'Lucille', in German. Hungry for decent music, I'd go down to the local record shop and lurk. I found *Reunion* there. It didn't look promising, the ugliest album cover I'd ever seen; a very bad drawing of four smug-looking men, four Fine Gael members at a charity golf pro-am. I bought it, brought it home to Dublin and put it on. A low voice went 'Duh duh duh duh – duh duh duh', a high one went, 'Ooo – waaa – oooo' and Dion sang on top of them: 'Don't know why I love you – Don't know why I care-yere.' There was a band at the back but it was all voices, swirling and du-wa-bobbing, and the one voice, Dion di Mucci's, crying and boasting, pleading, pleading, pleading, wanting me to love him. And I did. 'A Teenager in

Love', 'No One Knows' – four men showing off, being given a second chance – 'Ruby Baby' and, best of all, 'Runaround Sue', seven glorious minutes and forty-two seconds that capture and celebrate the misery of growing up. 'She go-woes – out with other guys.' I knew her, the wagon.

MORE SONGS ABOUT BUILDINGS AND FOOD
TALKING HEADS

A guitar being scratched, crisp tingling sounds, bass to the front, over and over, a type of mutant disco. There were no multi-instrumentals here, no 'all guitars'. And the mad voice of David Byrne – 'Ohh – wohhhh' – I pictured him in the studio with a cord around his neck, pulling it and loosening it, to help him achieve just that sound. The words – when there were words – were snippets of meaning; combined they meant nothing. They were vague, childish, and unset-tling. 'As we economize – efficiency is multiplied.' The words mocked poetry. 'Stay hungry – stay hungry – move a muscle – move a muscle.' The music mocked music. I didn't know if I liked it. I didn't recognize it, until the final track, 'The Big Country'. Byrne is flying over America. 'I see the shapes – I remember from maps.' The music is warped country and western. He sees 'places to park' – by the factories and buildings – restaurants and bars – for later in the evening. On out over the countryside, he looks down and he tells us, 'I wouldn't live there if you paid me'. It wasn't America he was flying over; it was Ireland, and I was sit-ting beside him, gawking out and pointing. The green hills, the red hair, the cry of the curlew. 'I wouldn't live there – no sirree.' It was music made out of plas-tic and tarmac, music for people who travelled underground, pale, alienated, proud of it.

THE UNDERTONES
THE UNDERTONES

I saw the Undertones on the *Old Grey Whistle Test*. Feargal Sharkey was wearing a parka, and a jumper exactly like the one my mother had got me for Christmas. They played 'Get Over You', a wolf whistle followed by the best and and the fastest music I'd ever heard played by an Irish band. The album is furious and wonderful, fifteen short bursts of absolutely perfect pop. 'Family Entertainment' is a lovely little song about incest; 'The Girls Don't Like It' is introduced by the Shangri-Las' sardonic big sister – 'I don't go for him, do you?'; 'Teenage Kicks' is the best song ever written; 'Here Comes the Summer' starts with three words that define rock'n'roll – 'Ooh baby baby'. Every track is a smasher, played by young men in a hurry to get home for their dinners, and sung by Feargal Sharkey, with the voice of a Major-smoking angel – 'Jimmy Jimmy – Ohhh'. At first, they sound like the Beach Boys, without the beach or the money; the songs are bright and sunny and young. But, behind the speed and the fun, they are also dark and even cruel, songs about loners and misfits. 'And no one saw the ambulance that took little Jim away-ay.' Songs about pimples, awkwardness and the pain of not being loved. 'I need excitement – oh I need it ba-ad.' The Undertones were the best Irish band ever. I grieved when they broke up.

LIFES RICH PAGEANT
REM

For a short time in late 1986 a darkness, heaviness occupied my head. I dragged myself around, exhausted. I didn't want company, food, anything. I got through the working day, smiling, handed back homework I'd marked but hadn't corrected. At home, I'd stare for hours at the bars of the electric fire. It hadn't happened before; it scared me. There was nothing to show, nothing to tell anyone. The sound of *Lifes Rich Pageant* pulled my eyes away from the fire. It was fervent, determined music, and perfectly timed. 'I believe in coyotes – and time as an abstract.' I listened, felt the power of the songs, heard words rising through the noise. 'We are young despite the years – we are concern – we are hope despite the times.' These words seemed to mean a lot. 'Begin the Begin', 'These Days', 'Fall On Me'. Song on top of song, the music carried so much conviction and belief; it was so solid, built on a past, driving into the future. And what were the words about? Meaning disappeared under the music, and reappeared, like a whale's back, and went under again; snippets and phrases, bits of nonsense, small chunks of wisdom. 'Let's put our heads together and start a new country up.' The glimpses through the sound were enough; this was music that gloried in the world, every little thing about it, the 'bone-chains and toothpicks'. Powerful, enthusiastic, calm and just plain good, it won me.

POETIC CHAMPIONS COMPOSE
VAN MORRISON

Van Morrison stares out from the cover of this album with a look that says, 'What are you fuckin' looking at?' It's a beautiful, gentle album but Morrison's cover expression fits; it's music by a man who has found a happiness that he doesn't yet trust, a collection of love songs placed around a piece of raw, aching sadness called 'Sometimes I Feel Like a Motherless Child'. 'I forgot that love existed – troubled in my mind' – the contradictions and insecurity in those words are in the music as well. The piano and, in particular, the sax seem to be played by people sitting in corners, creating wonderful noises, by themselves; the sax is trying to get away, the strings keep bringing it back. It's a very emotional album, full of loneliness and wishing and hope. 'Sometimes I Feel Like A Motherless Child' is the perfect meeting of Ireland and America, a new country full of old pain. It's a dramatic album, a great love story – will he or won't he? Will I or won't I? By the second last track, the joy is unrestrained; Lou Reed's Coloured Girls go 'Doo-doo' and as the musicians, still playing, sneak out of the studio, a woman's voice, all humour and affection, asks, 'Did you get healed?' Yes, thank you.

BRUTAL YOUTH
ELVIS COSTELLO

It could be the intro to a Eurovision entry; a nice tinkly piano, and he starts singing, 'This is hell – this is hell'. This is Elvis Costello. This is the man who kidnaps clichés and makes them all his own. 'You're flogging a dead horse – all the way down Pony Street.' This is the man who sings and plays with an energy that denies the pessimism of many of his words, the man who has given us his best album seventeen years after the release of his first one. This is a thrilling album. Elvis doesn't sing the fifteen tracks; he occupies them. He becomes a different character for every song; a shocked brute in 'Kinder Murder' – 'She could have kept her knees together – could have kept her mouth shut' – a hurt sophisticate – 'Are you sorry – or is it still too soon to know?' – an affable bollocks. He is backed by the Attractions, one of the great bands, and Nick Lowe. Elvis manages, in the same breath, to show off and to capture moments of frailty and loneliness. 'Just look at me – I'm having the time of my life – or something quite like it.' Every song is great; I lean forward to grab every sound and word. Intelligence, compassion, bad eyesight – Elvis Costello has it all.

HIGHWAY 61 REVISITED
BOB DYLAN

The best album ever recorded, approximately. I was lying in bed. My brother was asleep in the bunk above me. I had the tape recorder resting on my chest, the earpiece stuffed into my left ear. I remember feeling giddy. 'Mama's in the factory – she ain't got no shoes.' I'd never heard anything like that before. It was brilliant, funny, loud; there was something vaguely blasphemous about it. The rhythm, the words, the harmonica. 'I am in the kitchen with the tombstone blues.' That was me there. I played it till the batteries died. I still get worked up listening to *Highway 61 Revisited*. Everything about it still excites me, song after wonderful song, image after image – 'the reincarnation of Paul Revere's horse' – the musical roughness of it, his voice, the piano in 'Ballad of a Thin Man', the way Dylan says 'enough' – 'A-nuff' – 'Just Like Tom Thumb's Blues'. Everything, even the credits – 'Bob Dylan, guitar, harmonica, piano and police car'. And there's 'Desolation Row'. 'They're selling postcards of the hanging' – the best opening line ever written. It's not a song; it's a novel, with the second last chapter told in fluent harmonica. I know all the other albums by heart, every word, beat and scratch. Not *Highway 61 Revisited*. I don't really know it yet. How could I? I've only been listening to it for twenty-two years.

JOHN DUNNE

OUR HOUSE, 7.30 P.M., THURSDAY, 6 APRIL 1995: Dolores O'Riordan keening from Aoife's room; Neil's a no-go area of wall-to-wall Nirvana; Gary rocking to Neil Young; John watching MTV; Denise in love with Mike Oldfield in the kitchen; me wandering around with a Henry Rollins album, looking for something to play it on. 10.50 p.m.: John fast asleep. The rest of us sit down together to watch *No Disco*, the lads and I arguing over who's going to tape what ...

One still Good Friday evening sometime in the early sixties, holy after kissing the Cross, I crept into the Protestant record shop and bought my first LP. Last week I bought an album by the Trash Can Sinatras. In between, I have spent thousands on records, and every one of them has added something to my life (though, now that I think of it, I'm hard pressed to find anything good in Paul Weller's *Wildwood*, *Hats* by the Blue Nile, or the Fall's *Live at the Witch Trials*).

Some of my favourite records I haven't listened to in more than twenty years. I don't need to. All I have to do is think of them and, straightaway, they're playing in my head; every beat, every note, every word as real as though I'm wearing the best headphones in the world. Others are as essential to me as love: if a week goes by without hearing them, I feel the loss and can't wait to play them again.

Some records I value for the memories they evoke; others for their purely musical highs (the nearest I ever got to the other kind was at an aromatic late-night showing of *Woodstock*), but more than any book I've ever read, more than all the films I've ever seen, music has given me a glimpse of what I call my soul.

•

It is the winter of 1973. I am in the front room of my parents' house, the lights turned off, 'The Revealing Science of God' filling every inch of darkness. I have heard this song – the word belies the scope of such a vast work of art – so often I've lost count, and each time my goose-pimples refute the *NME*'s review: '... seems to lack positive construction, just losing itself in a wash of synthetic sounds ... I only hope that Yes return to real songs ...'.

Tonight, I am shivering again and – suddenly a flash of red light and my mother's face appears around the door, inches from speakers that could deafen her. Before I can swear, she says, 'Sorry, there's someone looking for you ...'.

Fourteen years later she is on her deathbed in the same room. (When my father carried her downstairs, I didn't need to ask why.) I am beside her, trying to keep my eyes from the ledge where speakers had once stood.

I have never played 'The Revealing Science of God' since. Even thinking of it now, my mother appears before me; her face a map of bones, the lightness of her body, the darkness in her eyes bringing tears for all the times I broke her heart. *You'd crucify a saint in heaven, so you would. Crucify a saint in heaven.*

•

Sometimes, as the songs says, words are not enough. I've just crumpled my third attempt at describing the guitars on *Marquee Moon* by the New York band Television. I can tell you all you want to know about the eight songs (surreal, elliptic things, full of lines like 'Broadway looked so medieval, it seemed to flap like little pages'); I can describe the bass and drums, or Tom Verlaine's voice – brittle, neurotic, located somewhere between androgyny and Patti Smith – with no difficulty at all, but the guitars, as I say, leave me lost for words.

Apart, occasionally, from Richard Thompson, there are no discernible influences: the chord changes are utterly unconventional; the riffs and solos answerable only to their own logic. Sometimes they are as intricate as Bach, yet they make me – a middle-aged school principal – want to dance like an eejit. There's one moment – here I go, a fourth time attempting the impossible – where the notes swoop miraculously from nowhere; another where they explode in a shower of magic crystals – Stop, you're getting precious!

When *Marquee Moon* came out in 1977, the late Stewart Parker hailed it in the *Irish Times* as 'amazing' and 'revolutionary'. It is currently available on CD for less than a tenner.

•

I got married on Monday, 18 April 1977. The following night I dragged Denise to a concert in the National Stadium, Dublin. (Moralists among you can agonize over whether this was a dereliction of my conjugal duties, or a selfless act of musical devotion.)

The first *NME Book of Rock* described Roy Harper as 'England's paramount stoned freak poet' – an accolade likely to alienate all of us who never flew the freak flag, yet I have always loved his maverick imagination, his willingness to push ideas to the limit, and over the years, I've bought fourteen of his albums. I'm still not sure whether his inveterate 'fuck-the-system' is admirable or plain 'Where's the spliff, man?' silly, but there's no denying the originality and passion of his best music – qualities nowhere more apparent than on 'The Lord's Prayer', a twenty-minute track on his 1973 album *Lifemask*.

The grapevine of the time had it that Harper was dangerously ill and the song was conceived as his Last Will and Testament. He himself claimed the title was a joke. Either way, 'The Lord's Prayer' is his jaundiced view of civilization, set to music in eight sections. The only other thing I'm going to say is that

Harper's unique voice, acoustic guitar, electronics, and oblique approach to songwriting all combine with Peter Jenner's brilliant production to conjure a soundscape unlike anything you've heard before. After nearly twenty years I still haven't convinced Denise how good it is, but then, she wouldn't like Roy Harper anyway, would she?

•

I have never worn a dress, a fedora, or a one-legged leotard. I never dyed my hair orange, never sported a golden circle on my forehead or a flash of lightning on my face. I never had any time for Iggy Pop. I never tried cunnilingus on a guitar. I never spouted Nietzsche or gave a fascist salute. I did none of these, yet, for most of the seventies, David Bowie was, to misquote Van Morrison, my guru, my method, my teacher. Even today, my grey head swirls with bits and pieces of his lyrics: The Sons of the Silent Age listen to tracks by Sam Therapy and King Dice/Our weapons were the tongues of crying rage/The shrieking of nothing is killing me/Those midwives to history put on their bloody robes/Uncage the colours, unfurl the flag/Time, the sniper in the brain/I'm the twisted name on Garbo's eyes/Love descends on those defenceless/Visions of swastikas in my head, plans for everyone ... (fans will identify nine different songs).

Poets have built careers on less. And it wasn't just Bowie's lyrics: there were the stupendous chord changes of 'Cygnet Committee' and 'Life on Mars'; Mick Ronson's razor guitar on 'Moonage Daydream'; the vocal production on 'Ashes to Ashes'; the icy elegance of 'Warszawa' (which, incidentally, inspired the third movement of Philip Glass's *Low Symphony*). I could go on and on ....

And then there was Bowie's chameleon voice: a leper messiah, howling in the strobe-lit wilderness of 'Ziggy Stardust'; a sinister baritone on 'Sweet Thing'; a crooner, trembling with religious passion, on 'Word on a Wing'; a pathetic, coked-out wisp on 'Station to Station'. When, in the latter, he pleads 'Who will connect me with love?' I swear I want to put my arms around him and cry 'Jesus, David, what are you doing to yourself?'

At least six David Bowie albums mean as much to me as any recordings I've ever heard. But pride of place is occupied by *Hunky Dory*. My brother arrived home with it in 1971. That much we're sure of, but we still disagree over where he bought it. He's certain he got it in Limerick; I'm adamant it came from Alo Donegan's in the Market Square, Portlaoise. That's how much David Bowie meant to us; when we could find no more to say about the music itself, we argued over where we bought it.

I can't remember what happened in the world in 1971, but here's a picture I recall with a clarity that is luminous: darkness vying with a two-bar electric fire; *Hunky Dory* on the stereo; Tom and I seated side by side, our eyes closed; something holy passing between us. Two brothers never closer the rest of their lives.

•

How wrong can you be? When I first heard *Murmur* in 1983 I dismissed it as a load of badly recorded crap. Little did I know that over the next twelve years REM would write some of the best songs I've ever heard. The highest quota of these is in *Automatic for the People*. Has any album ever produced so many memorable singles? Think of 'Drive', 'The Sidewinder Sleeps Tonite', 'Everybody Hurts', 'Nightswimming', 'Man on the Moon'. But even better are 'Try Not to Breathe' (an old man pictures himself dead, and holds his breath in an attempt to imagine what it might be like) and 'Sweetness Follows', whose brooding approach to mortality encapsulates the intensity of writers like William Faulkner and Flannery O'Connor.

Michael Stipe is one of the great singers, but what I like most about REM is that, while none of them is a virtuoso player – you could put stickers on the frets and Peter Buck still couldn't play a solo (yet his understanding of feedback is uncanny) – collectively they write songs that, nine times out of ten, effortlessly pass my Acoustic Test. When, in the words of Leonard Cohen, it all comes down to dust, that's what songwriting is all about – if it sounds good on an acoustic guitar, it'll sound good anywhere.

•

Soul music. Who do you think of? James Brown? Aretha Franklin? Otis Redding? Al Green? Wilson Pickett? I think of Mike, Lal and Norma Waterson and their cousin John Harrison from Hull. I think of their full-throated harmonies on songs that have lived in the souls of anonymous singers for centuries; songs that are – to steal a line from Joyce – 'the eternal affirmation of the spirit of man'.

Whenever I feel the need to feel religious, I might go into an empty church; I might walk in Togher Wood; but, most of the time, I listen to *Frost and Fire* by the Watersons. First released in 1965, I bought it three years later on the recommendation of a singer from Norfolk, who told me the catalogue number and, in the same breath, 'Thanks for everything, but I'm in love with someone else.'

The album is a short collection of ritual songs – it was relentlessly pillaged by folk-rock bands in the early seventies – and, apart from a few belts of a bodhrán on 'Hal-An-Tow' (a classic welcome-in-the-summer song murdered – imagine Chuck Berry rampaging through the Cornish countryside – by the Oyster Band in the eighties), there isn't another instrument in sight.

Whenever I hear 'The Holly Bears a Berry', I am a Brueghelesque peasant trudging through snow on Christmas morning. 'Pace-Egging Song' fills me with memories of Easter I couldn't possibly have. The primitive tune of 'Souling Song' brings visions of loved ones swirling from their graves at Halloween.

I have spent nearly all my life in a small town in the Irish midlands – a far cry from mulled ale, wassail, and Morris dancing – and I've no idea why English traditional songs should move me so much. They just do. When I want that 'nearer my God to thee' feeling, it's not to any of the standard hymns that I turn:

I put on *Frost and Fire* and, for twenty-eight minutes and twenty-two seconds, I'm in seventh heaven.

•

'What do you call a Somali with buck teeth?'
'Stop it! That's not nice ...'
I FE-EL SO GOOD. I FEEL SO GOOD I'M GONNA BREAK SOMEBODY'S HEART TONIGHT ...
Jesus, that high note ...
'What is it, Gary?'
'A rake.'
'I told you to stop that!'
Brilliant change.
'I don't get it. What's a Somali?'
'Will ye listen!'
I THOUGHT SHE WAS SAYING GOOD LUCK. SHE WAS SAYING GOOD-BYE.
'That's stupid music.'
A THOUSAND LOVESICK TUNES WON'T WASH AWAY THE WOUNDS.
Definitely about Linda.
'Which is the biggest, a brontosaurus or an elephant?'
'Jesus, will ye listen!'
I SEE ANGELS ON ARIELS IN LEATHER AND CHROME SWOOPING DOWN FROM HEAVEN TO CARRY ME HOME.
Couldn't be one guitar ...
'We had no English last night.'
'We had loads.'
DON'T SIT ON MY JIMMY SHANDS, DON'T SIT ON MY JIMMY SHANDS, UNLESS YOU WANT TO WIND UP BLACK AND BLUE.
Mammy sweating at the cooker, her slipper tapping out 'The Bluebell Polka'. Will it soon be ready, Lizzie?
'Is that Irish music?'
'Scottish. Listen, the next bit's funny.'
'It's crap.'

That's me, autumn 1991, driving the kids to school, listening to *Rumour and Sigh* by Richard Thompson.

•

Route 66, the Brill Building, California, the Mississippi Delta. Add synthesizers, *cúpla focal as Gaeilge*, Philip Glass, altar boys, the Christian Brothers, and you end up with ...? A right mishmash? Music from hell? No. You'll be listening to Pierce Turner, this country's most innovative and neglected songwriter.

I first came across his work on *Absolutely and Completely*, an album he made with fellow-Wexfordman Larry Kirwan in 1977. Apart from an epic, electronic version of Ewan McColl's 'The Travelling People', the music was different but nothing special. Since then, Turner – who settled in New York in 1980 – has released four solo albums and one of them, *The Sky and the Ground*, is, I believe, the best ever made by an Irish artist.

No other music I know captures so vividly the experience of growing up in provincial Ireland in the fifties and sixties. No other Irish album encompasses, in terms of texture, such an extensive range; from the forlorn piano figure and oboe-and-string arrangement on 'The Answer', through the orchestral thunder of 'Mayhem', to the astounding mixture of Lou Reed and plainsong that is 'You Can Never Know'. Then there are the literate, resonant lyrics that shouldn't fit the notes, but do; melodies that will colonize your head, and, most of all, Pierce Turner's voice. When he sings about his childhood, I think of my own father and how 'love can't always be articulate'; when his voice soars on 'Who am I to make you want? Who am I to make you crave?' my throat wells with sorrow for the pain I've caused those who love me most.

•

There are as many ways of looking at Frank Zappa as there are – or were in 1967 – holes in Blackburn, Lancashire. (The allusion is not entirely gratuitous; the Beatles were huge Zappa fans and Paul McCartney once referred to *Sgt. Pepper* as 'our *Freak Out*'.) Here are five ways: madcap genius with a headful of doo-wop, Howlin' Wolf and Varese; long-haired weirdo old enough to have more sense; arch-cynic, scourge of rock music, Washington and hippies; juvenile scat-ologist; composer of fiendishly difficult music. But, for me, Zappa is simply the most inventive guitarist I've ever heard, and his death from cancer in 1994 left in my heart what others before me felt as an Elvis-sized hole.

Since he unleashed *Freak Out* (both the first double album and first concept album in rock history) with the Mothers of Invention in 1966, his prodigious output has varied from the sublime to the risible; the latter when he can't control his big-mouth penchant for lewdness; the former when he lets his fingers do the talking.

I play guitar myself and I'm totally in awe of what this man could do with six strings and a plectrum. Sometimes his guitar is a weapon ('Hog Heaven' has been known to send our cat squealing for cover); sometimes, as on 'Treacherous Voices', it's the most eloquent voice I have ever heard. Sometimes it's the notes he plays; sometimes it's the ones he doesn't; sometimes it's what you think he's playing. But Zappa's music is about much more than one guitar: I can mentally erase it from all his best records and still hear as much in the rhythm track as I'd ever hear on MTV, or in a whole season of classical concerts. So, Mr Milan 'The history of music is mortal, but the idiocy of the guitar is eternal' Kundera: stick *Shut Up 'N' Play Yer Guitar* in your CD player, and see how idiotic a great novelist can be.

•

Like thousands of others, I have made the pilgrimage to the EMI Studios in Abbey Road where the Beatles recorded most of their songs. And yes, I did feel something, I'm not sure what, but I imagine it wasn't a million miles from what my mother felt every time she came home from Knock in the 1950s.

I love every Beatles album, but because of its variety and, at the same time, organic unity, *Abbey Road* is the one I'd bring to that proverbial desert island. The great wonder is that it ever appeared at all: the atmosphere in the studio was so strained that, at one stage, Lennon allegedly took a swing at Linda Mc-Cartney, and there was a right schemozzle when Yoko Ono pinched one of Harrison's chocolate biscuits.

Let's ignore all that cultural legacy and aeolian cadences stuff; this is simply great music; as great today as when it was recorded in the spring and summer of 1969. When I see Gary buying his own copies of *Sgt. Pepper* and *Abbey Road*, when Aoife asks me to tape *Revolver* for her walkman, I feel … well … proud that I have fulfilled at least one of my paternal duties; I have passed on something priceless, something I hope will stay with them the rest of their lives. And what goes around comes around: from my children I have learned that there is more to Kurt Cobain than barre-chords and a stash of drugs … that the Frames are a great band … that Brett Anderson isn't just another Bowie clone … or Heather Nova another bimbo with a guitar.

Thirty-something years ago, I scorned all childish Easter Eggs and bought my first LP …

ANNE ENRIGHT

YOU'RE NEVER TOO OLD TO ROCK'N'ROLL, but can you be too young? I was a moral, solemn, pre-pubertal child when my older brother and sister deflowered the new record-player with 'Ruby Tuesday' sung by Melanie and tried to pretend to my parents that the whole enterprise was a respectable one. It was not. There was nothing respectable about it.

What you don't know is all the same. So when your older siblings start finding out about sex and (coincidentally) playing records at the same time, you just look at the sleeves and speculate. Harmless enough. The back of *Transformer*, a woman in a black corset-like thing on one side, and a man with a something down his jeans on the other. Or rather something across his jeans, like a courgette, with the end of it nearly out his pocket. Not that I knew what courgettes were either. (I saw my first one in Canada in 1980 and it was called zucchini.) Then my brother told me that the woman and the man were both Lou Reed, as if it was some kind of secret joke, and I spent weeks looking at them, trying to find the punchline.

It was a bit like geography homework really: this woman subsiding down the gathered PVC backdrop, like she had forgotten how to stand upright, and what I assumed to be a sailor on the other side, his back unnaturally arched, looking at her. Wasn't her hip-bone too low on her leg? Was that why her too-large hand was placed between men and women – that women have relatively longer legs? I knew it was. But when it came to that courgette I had no thoughts at all. When it came to the courgette, my mind was a mesmerized blank.

It is no surprise, then, that the songs were entirely without social content, they were just themselves, and they made a vicious child-like sense. He becomes she, the perfect day is (not) perfect, the slick little girl comes out of the closet like one of the undead, all is menace and peace.

My only regret is that I did not know it was funny.

Something must have filtered through in the next few months because when Frank Zappa's *Overnite Sensation* came into the house I learned all the words to 'Dynamo Hum', and sang them at school. Filthy, incomprehensible – I knew they held the key. Somewhere in there was the secret of what people actually did when they actually did It. Because music, and therefore sex, was still a family affair it was no surprise to hear 'I checked out her sister who was holding the bed, with her lips just a twitchin' and her face gone red'. And all that stuff about her drawers and thumbs and sugar plums was interesting enough. But what did they do then? What was an 'aura', as in 'Kiss my aura, Flora'? Why did he say, 'Mmm, it's real angora.' Did men have something fluffy down there?

It is impossible to remember the state of ignorance – you can not, for example, forget the taste of olives, or remember what it was like not to know the taste of olives, and the same could be said for courgettes. My first concert was Frank Zappa in Vancouver, mitching from a school fifty miles away. It was some years later but all I had learned in the meantime was how to draw the diagrams. A lot of Canadians waved their lighters in the air. Zappa did not play 'Dynamo Hum'. There was nothing filthy about it.

I did not know that we stayed the night in a brothel, I just wondered why the girl in the doorway opposite stood around like that with very little on. I did not know that the two boys I went with were beautiful, that if I had them in a brothel now, things would be a lot simpler. Neither did I know that one of them was gay, or what gay was, I just knew that the other was 'after my virginity' and that was a very serious thing. Or I knew, but I did not know that I knew.

The very brink of knowledge is not a happy place – innocence becomes an effort, a kind of misery. When I realized that I didn't know what my virginity actually was, I found I had stepped, without meaning, over to the other side. It is in this place, between knowledge and action, that the music makes real sense. The anger of knowing but not having. A couple of weeks spent listening to the Rolling Stones and you've convinced yourself you know too much to bother. It's either that or Joni Mitchell. It's either that or love. How many albums does it take to get to sex? And how much sex does it take to realize that the albums are supposed to be funny?

I was saved by Punk, the social rage of nice British children who'd lost their virginity years ago and had more important things to rant about. Punk was for girls in the way the Rolling Stones never could be. Punk was for the Little Sisters – there was nothing we didn't know about the system. There was nothing we didn't know. We were so pretty. Peaches, ice-picks, skewers, now that's a laugh. Bollox, fuck, ha ha ha. (Let's do it.)

MARIANNE FAITHFULL

🎤 MY FIRST MEMORY OF RECORDS is a record-player and lots of 78s, among them songs of Kurt Weill and Brecht, the *Threepenny Opera*, the *Alabama Song*, and so on. My mother must have brought these records with her from Vienna, and it is pretty extraordinary that such delicate records survived the war as practically everything my mother had ever owned had gone.

GIGI

The first record I ever bought (and it's very silly, but it had a tremendous effect on me) was the soundtrack of *Gigi*. I still absolutely adore it, and whenever I feel blue I put *Gigi* on, 'The Night They Invented Champagne' and all those things. I learned all the songs and took the whole thing as a sort of ethic for life. Hermione Baddesley, Lesley Caron, Louis Jordan, Maurice Chevalier: it was fabulous, and I remember thinking 'this is how I want my life to be'.

SKETCHES OF SPAIN
MILES DAVIS

I now realize this was a really weird record to buy for a fourteen-year-old. All the arrangements were done by Gil Evans and it's important because, while Miles and Gil were both musicians, they were also junkies. It was my first exposure to that kind of wonderful wildness, to where you can go in music, which was, and remains, valid.

ODETTA
ODETTA

This gives you a picture of how serious I was as a little girl. I believed deeply in all the Martin Luther King stuff: Rosa Parks on the bus in Montgomery, Alabama. Odetta was a symbol to me of this whole struggle. The cover had a picture of her, her big face, looking beautiful, with a blue tint on the black-and-white picture. This moved me a lot. I would sit by myself listening to Odetta, railing against the injustice of the world and feeling that we must all get involved. There was that terrible incident at Sharpeville, and Odetta was South African herself. I was in Reading and all this was going on a very long way away, but it affected me very much. My mother took me to see Paul Robeson, who was playing in Reading at the time, and that was also a powerful experience. I was very lucky in the sort of things I was exposed to.

BUDDY HOLLY
BUDDY HOLLY

I never really liked Elvis, I only got to like him later, but I did love Buddy Holly and the Everly Brothers. Buddy Holly is right up there to this day. I can't think of a better evening I could spend than listening to a lot of Buddy Holly. I loved the record covers and I could see the style, but when I was fourteen it seemed to be more of a boy's thing and not really relevant to how a teenage girl should dress. I didn't much like any of the girl singers that I could see or hear at the time. I thought Brenda Lee was wonderful but stylistically she wasn't at all on the same level. Buddy was really exceptional. And all the girls in the Elvis movies were pretty daft, except Ann Margaret who was rather cool. Connie Francis and Brenda Lee and all the women I could see in popular music were much too done-up.

At that time I saw *On the Waterfront* and *East of Eden*. Eva-Marie Saint, the girl in *Waterfront*, had a big effect. She hardly wore any make-up and her hair was not done, which was unusual then. She had it just tied back and was blonde, and very strong-looking, and that was an interesting role model for me. That's what I liked. Then of course there was Marlon Brando. Phew, haven't seen many boys like him since.

I have always had two lives and now at this stage I went to my first proper dance, which was not a 'nice' dance. I can well remember going with my friend Candy down to the Palais. I was very young and not allowed to go, but I bouffanted my hair and put on all the make-up. Candy had a dress – a red dress with a fringe along the bottom, which said 'I love Acker' on it. I was a Miles Davis fan, but Candy was an Acker Bilk fan. I borrowed this dress anyway and it turned out to be one of those deadly evenings where all the boys were on one side and all the girls were on the other. My mum spanked me when I got home. She was furious.

LET IT BLEED
THE ROLLING STONES

I was there when it was written, I was there when it was recorded. The whole thing is beautiful, one of the greatest. You have to listen to it to the end, you can't take it off once you've put it on.

At around the same time I was really turned on to a lot of good music by Andrew Loog Oldham, who discovered me: a lot of Phil Spector and Jack Nietsche stuff and the Beach Boys. I remember Jack playing piano on the Rolling Stones sessions, and this before I knew the Stones, but Andrew would occasionally bring me into a session because I was his new discovery. I remember so clearly meeting Jack and Phil Spector. Philip was astounding for a little girl from Reading. I didn't really understand it when I met them, but now I look back I can see they were taking a lot of speed, so much that they couldn't speak. There's a point beyond the level where you're talking all the time and go so icy that you don't say anything. They were very weird, very moody, and wore shades all the time. I'd never seen anybody wearing shades inside, and this was a very dark studio in the middle of the night. I knew that Miles Davis wore shades all the time, but I'd never actually seen anybody do it.

When Mick and Keith were mixing *Let It Bleed*, the photographer Michael Cooper, Anita Pallenberg and I were out in Los Angeles with them. Sometimes we would dress up and get very, very high on mescaline and go out to Joshua Tree. We would listen to the Band's first record, *Music from Big Pink*, all the time, over and over again. Mick and Keith were obsessed with it – it broke new territory, it was very emotional, it was rough and it was white, focussing on certain aspects of white music that had been neglected for a while. It had a historical perspective which was completely new.

SMOKEY ROBINSON AND THE MIRACLES

Looking back, quite a lot of the records I liked when I started living with Mick haven't actually stood the test of time. But one thing that Mick really turned me on to was Motown. I hadn't really thought it was very good until then, until he really showed me. He sort of played it to me, he danced it for me, he sang it to me. It was astounding and after that, of course, I completely adored Motown, particularly Smokey Robinson: 'Going to a Go-Go', 'Tracks of My Tears', 'This Girl Is Gone', 'I Second that Emotion' were all great, and 'Just a Mirage' was my absolute favourite. 'I Heard It through the Grapevine' by Marvin Gaye is one of the seminal songs. The idea of the mask that Smokey Robinson sings about – and a lot of those songs are about hiding what your true feelings are, and presenting a mask or face to the world – is fascinating.

JOHN WESLEY HARDING
BOB DYLAN

Originally I thought it would be hard to choose between *Blonde on Blonde* and *Highway 61 Revisited*, but *John Wesley Harding* is a very intense record with a different kind of energy. When I got it, it was clear that things weren't going to work out for me and that I was heading for a bumpy road. Not just me, but the whole fucking planet, the whole of the sixties, the whole of everything I was part of. But *John Wesley Harding* was the music of the apocalypse. The Vietnam War was escalating, the whole thing was getting worse, and I could see that 'the movement', whatever it was, wasn't going well. I was having a very hard time; this album was expressing that, my own personal suffering, but I believed that the same suffering was everywhere. Somehow through all that, *John Wesley Harding* cut like a knife and put everything into perspective.

HANK WILLIAMS

After I left Mick, I didn't listen to records for ages, because I didn't have anywhere. I was living in squats and staying on the wall in Soho. I missed the music
of the end of the sixties and early seventies and when I 'came back' it was different. I didn't like glam rock so I didn't listen to it. I went home and all I listened to for about three years was Hank Williams, Robert Johnson and Billie
Holiday. I found Hank's vision very healing because it was so clear. All country
music is generally so simple. It encompasses all the human moods in a very, very
straight way. 'I love you and if you are unfaithful to me, I will kill you' – that sort
of thing. That I found very reassuring and it was just how I would have liked the
world to be at the time, because I had come off such a strange world – not just
the Rolling Stones, I'm talking about my life on the streets. When I got back I
wanted to be in a place where 'men were men, and women were women and
things were simple'. At the same time I discovered Waylon Jennings, and Willie
Nelson, who is still like that. Yes, it remains an implacable world that Willie
lives in. That's why I like Bob Marley so much, too. He was very dogmatic with
all those stern warnings: 'The small axe and the big tree' and so on.

MINK DE VILLE
WILLIE DE VILLE

Willie was the coolest thing that I'd heard or seen for a long time, and he's very,
very emotional. There's all that cool there but underneath there's this bleeding
heart, and I love people with no defences at all. And when I met him, that is
exactly what he was like. He even married his first sweetheart, his childhood
sweetheart. I remember meeting her. She was a monster.

To be so emotional or so over the top with feeling is one of the reasons
people take drugs, let's face it, because they can't bear their own feelings which
are so intense. Willie de Ville doesn't superficially seem like that, but he is,
because he is a complete sap, as is Chuck Berry and Lou Reed: they all are. Have
you ever heard a more sentimental song than Keith singing 'You Got the Silver?'
on *Let it Bleed*? From Mr Cool himself it's just overwhelming emotion.

ORPHEUS AND EURYDICE
GLÜCK

I went to see this opera about three years ago in Covent Garden with Anita
Pallenberg. It was one of the most emotional, wonderfully moving nights of my
life to sit with her, watching the story of *Orpheus* being acted out and sung to
this beautiful music. I still play it all the time at home late at night. It's not the
sort of thing you can have with other people around. It's the story of Orpheus,
the god of music, who loves Eurydice. She dies and is taken into Hades. He goes
to get her, and his lyre playing is so wonderful that Charon takes him across the
River Styx. He does this trip into the underworld, which no one else has been

able to do alive, and he does it with his music. He endures all these terrible things to get there and once he gets to hell, he finds Eurydice. He plays his lyre for Pluto so beautifully that Pluto weeps and says, 'Yes, you can take her now', which has never happened before.

Eurydice can go back, but there is a condition that she has to stay four steps behind Orpheus, and he must not look back to see if she's behind him. It is wonderful to see that she's there behind him all the way and he can hear her but he can't see her. But just as they're nearly out, and they've crossed the Styx, he can't bear it so he looks back, and as he looks back, of course, she's gone, he loses her. To me that says everything about music.

I feel now there are no delineations. I see Orpheus in the same way as I see James Brown and Buddy Holly and Miles Davis; I see them as all one, I really do. That story is the most wonderful allegory for everything I've experienced in my last thirty years, really being deeply involved in music. It was an amazing experience, and to be there with Anita that night was so wonderful. She has been on that journey with me. We've been there, we went to hell and back, and came out again, and lost a lot of people.

BP FALLON

THE FIRST RECORDS THAT MOULDED and influenced and coloured and changed and warped my life... they're forever young. As I write this, I'm listening to them still. I'm also listening to Underworld and Leftfield and The Chemical Brothers and Tricky and Chuck D. I'm still listening to noise that upsets some people. Thank God. Melodies are made of this.

BP's early top thirteen LPs plus two for luck:

Elvis	Elvis Presley
Here's Little Richard!	Little Richard
Crazy Times!	Gene Vincent
Cliff!	Cliff Richard
The Rocking Chair Album	Howlin' Wolf
Please Please Me	The Beatles
The Rolling Stones	The Rolling Stones
Otis Blue	Otis Redding
In 1966 There Was	Bob Dylan
Astral Weeks	Van Morrison
Sweetheart of the Rodeo	The Byrds
Liege and Lief	Fairport Convention
Gris-Gris	Dr John, The Night Tripper
So Alone	Johnny Thunders
You Can Be Anyone This Time Around	Timothy Leary

Mea culpa, but the very first LP I ever owned ... I stole it from a hardware and all-round whatever-you're-having-yourself shop near that poisoned prison Ampleforth College in Yorkshire. Whoosh! up my sweater it went, this LP, and my karma has paid for it a thousand times. But, Lord knows and the devil does too, I got great value ...

Autumn 1960 and it was a millisecond decision between *The Eddie Cochran Memorial Album* and the ultimate winner, *Crazy Times!* by Gene Vincent. I could hear my heart banging against the hidden acquisition as I stole out of the shop, and I'm sure everyone else could hear it too. Thump thump thump it went over Brenda Lee belting out 'Sweet Nothings' from the record booth. My heart, it sounded like a Sandy Nelson drum solo.

I met Gene Vincent once. York Rialto was twenty-three miles from Ampleforth as the schoolboy hitch-hikes and there he was at the soundcheck, Sweet Gene Vincent, leather-clad and sad and vulnerable and the most magnificent tragedy that ever happened. Standing there on the lip of the stage as his British backing group The Outlaws set up, Gene looked superb, a droopy bunch of greased grapes flopping into his faraway eyes. Around the v-neck of his leather jerkin was sewn a chunky chain, from which rattled a brass medallion. It was the kind of thing you might win in a cracker at a Hell's Angels convention, if crackers were slightly bigger.

Gene, bless his heart, he let me wear it, this leather jerkin thing. I just asked him and he said yeah, okay, pulled it off over his head, messing up his collapsed quiff even more, then went back to holding on to the microphone stand and looking up at the roof of the Rialto.

With coaxing from The Outlaws' lead guitarist Richie Blackmore, Gene and the group bashed into the Bill Monroe song 'Rocky Road Blues'. 'We-e-e-ll, the road is rocky but it won't be rocky long ...' Gene sang, his right knee bent and his dodgy left leg in its leg-iron stretched out behind him. Every time Gene moved he clanked like a prisoner never on parole. Really, the poor bastard was fucked. Pills to kill the pain of the leg the doctors wanted to amputate, booze to blot out the loss of his pal Eddie Cochran when their car had crashed earlier that year. Gene had survived, sorta, but his leg had been mashed up some more. Now, he was like Macbeth or Othello, damned yet singing like an angel as the shadows of hell chased him down the dark end of the street.

The LP *Crazy Times!* was by no means Gene's best work – no Bluecaps, for a start – but it was a fine introduction to the possibilities of the 12-inch long player, with Gene's lilting voice warbling easy on the opening track as he promises 'Crazy times we'll have, for you and me'. There's a blues to one of his unfortunate wives, the self-penned 'Darlene', the woe-is-me rockin' of 'Big Fat Saturday Night' and 'Everybody's Got A Date But Me', a, um, *legitimate* song in 'Accentuate the Positive.' Even a truck-driving song in 'Why Don't You People Learn to Drive' with its indelible couplet: 'There's a big diesel pullin' from the highway ramp/The thing he didn't know was that his brakes were damp.' And on the album, the drummer is Sandy Nelson.

And back at The Rialto... The doors have been opened and into the auditorium swarm these these little blue-haired old dears, here to play bingo. Gene and The Outlaws grind to a halt and Gene haltingly asks me for his jacket back, saying in his sweet Virginia whisper 'Better give it to me before the faces see it.' *The faces!* Rock'n'roll slang. Gosh. The schoolboy, he is so impressed.

Meanwhile, rock'n'roll – *Gene Vincent, f'Chrissakes!* – is stopped for bloody bingo. What the fuck is going on? Hey, what about 'Be Bop A-Lula', mister?

•

I was eleven years old and at Avisford prep school in Sussex when I had my breakfast epiphany. Actually, it was in the afternoon. There's this guitar-like someone, *something*, is kicking at my brain and then this guy is singing 'Well, they say it's gonna die but honey please let's face it, there just ain't nothin' that's a-gonna replace it, ballads an' calypsos ain't got nothin' on, real country music that just drives along, a-honey move it!' Bang! The song is 'Move It', the 'B' side of the first record by this new singer called Cliff Richard. It sure done flip mah lid, or something to that effect. This rallying call to rock'n'roll, it made me want to be *part* of rock'n'roll somehow. I'm still trying to figure that one out.

Cliff was rude then. The *NME* – a musical paper, Godammit – gave out in no uncertain terms about this newcomer, said his gyrations were lewd, that he shouldn't be allowed on TV when children could see him, that he'd better seek medical advice if he thought what he was doing was natural. All he was doing, in retrospect, was aping Elvis but he was England's first real rock'n'roller before Billy Fury, and 'Move It' was the first credible English rock'n'roll record *ever*, before 'Shakin' All Over' by Johnny Kidd And The Pirates and 'Brand New Cadillac' by Vince Taylor And The Playboys. Yeah, Cliff was cool.

And his first LP – titled simply *Cliff!* – was wild mainline rock'n'roll cut live at Abbey Road in front of a screaming shrieking rabid audience. Cliff and The Drifters holler and rave through songs by Jerry Lee Lewis, Buddy Holly And The Crickets, Little Walter via Ricky Nelson (the hepped-up blues of 'My Babe'), Little Richard and Elvis. And then, natch, there's Cliff's own songs like 'Move It' and 'Apron Strings': 'Ah don' wanna be tah tah tied to your apron strings', and everyone goes completely berserk and the audience wail like sea-gulls on amphetamines and The Drifters' bassplayer Jet Harris looks mean and moody and doomed before Brian Jones and the guitarist Hank B. Marvin twangs like a demon and they aren't even Shadows yet.

Primal tinny early rock'n'roll with the brakes off...

•

Luke Kelly made me promise to go and see Dylan when he played at the Adelphi Cinema in Dublin in 1966. Luke, he'd get the New York folk magazine *Sing Out!* and sing Dylan's poems to Irish airs (which was what Dylan, unknown to Luke, had been doing anyway, learning the tunes from his pals The Clancy Brothers. For example, Dylan's song 'With God on Our Side' is the same melody as 'The Patriot Game'). Luke, he loved Dylan's words.

Anyway, I arrive at half time so miss the first half, Dylan as acoustic folknik troubadour. So I wander backstage up these echoey stone stairs and in the dressing-room at the top are these guys who look like a cross between space-men and hillbillies. They're the band, soon The Band, before this incarnation working with crazed Arkansas rock'n'roller Ronnie Hawkins as The Hawks. Actually, the drummer used to play with Kenny Rodgers. Bloody hell.

And then this guy rattles up the concrete stairs. He's almost vibrating, like he got his fingers stuck in an electric socket. Twitch central. He looks like a hobo who struck oil and then plumb forgot where the durn well was. His eyes are like two foxes frantically searching for a hole to hide in. This guy, he'd get bruised by a *shadow*. Bob Dylan.

You go back to your seat. You got your little tape-recorder on your knee. This enormous American roadie like Bob Hite from Canned Heat towers over you breathing sulphur and vicious vibes. 'If you record this I'll smash the tape-recorder over your fuckin' head', he says. 'Is Dylan that bad?', you respond. 'Nah. Worse', he says.

So Bob Dylan and these Hawks amble onto the stage and they piddle about tuning and it's not like when The Beatles or even The Stones played here where they seemed to get straight into it, 1-2-3-4, boom! These cats now, they've got their backs to the audience and they sure are sloppy and actually they look kinda *weird* and suddenly whoosh! 'Well, I see you got your bran' new leopardskin pillbox hat' Dylan is whining with the voice of a goat caught on a barbed-wire fence and the group is exploding in all directions, the lead guitarist burning like Mike Bloomfield on methedrine, the organ wheezing like a dying coal-miner strapped to a rocket. and it's not entirely in tune either but it's a bomb exploding with shards of rock'n'roll, bits of it slicing around your head, never heard anything like this before. My God.

Afterwards you cross O'Connell Street and go to The Club A-Go-Go, where you play your new live tape of Bob Dylan to Max Key-Seymour of the mod group The Next In Line. Max, he agrees that it's incredible. 'Who is it?' he asks, all energized. 'The Isley Brothers', you say. 'Wow' he goes, then 'Wow' again.

And then of course you lose the tape somewhere, a little old reel-to-reel spool, as you move on down the line. What the heck: it's in the ether.

The bootleg *In 1966 There Was*, also known as *The Royal Albert Hall Concert 1966*, is actually The Free Trade Hall in Manchester twelve nights after Dublin. Someone calls Dylan 'Judas!' Dylan is saying 'I don't *believe* you !' To be a rock and not to roll? To be on a roll and not to rock?

Madness.

•

The New York Dolls, particularly their gutter peacock guitarist Johnny Thunders, they were gods to the whole of 1976 punk, and The Sex Pistols, The Clash, they carved themselves from the shadows of Iggy And The Stooges, Lou Reed and The Velvets, Bolan and Bowie and The MC5 and a boy called Johnny.

You meet Johnny in 1972 in the after midnight of a dentist's surgery in Harlem. He's a flash peacock in rags of glitter, platform boots and a jet-black plumage of shoulder-length backcombed hair as if a buzzard has been nesting on his head. On-stage upstairs at Max's his streetwise Italian face pouts as he poses, a cross between Keef Richard and an urban subterranean gutter glam outlaw. A punk. Plus of course Johnny plays the bestest, most exciting, powerful *vicious* guitar in town.

Come '76 The Dolls have collapsed in a storm of too much drink and too many drugs, rejected at large for their Neanderthal rock'n'roll, and Johnny is in England fronting The Heartbreakers, he and The Dolls' second drummer Jerry

Nolan. The first, Billy Murcia, he accidently OD'd on Mandrax. Johnny and Jerry, they're junkies and they celebrate their stupidity with songs like 'Chinese Rocks' and 'Too Much Junkie Bizness'. The Heartbreakers collapse.

At a party for Patti Smith, Johnny Thunders asks you to be his manager. Listen, heroin is the horrors, the darkest of darknesses, a hole into which junkies pour their very life. If you wanted an ad against heroin, Johnny Thunders was it to a T. A rock'n'roll genius turned into shambolic mess.

We managed some gigs at The Speakeasy, Steve Jones and Paul Cook from The Sex Pistols playing with their hero. Sid Vicious got up once. He idolized Johnny and wanted to form a group with him called The Junkies. One gig was billed as 'The Living Dead'.

In interviews, Johnny has kindly said that I was responsible for putting together his best LP, the album *So Alone*. Loyal musicians who lent their support came from The Sex Pistols, The Only Ones, The Heartbreakers, even Traffic. Chrissie Hynde sang backing vocals. On the storming version of Derek Martin's R&B classic 'Daddy Rolling Stone', first Johnny, then Phil Lynott, then Steve Marriott sing a verse. Phil, he was concerned at Johnny's health. 'He's too out of it, knowarramean?' And then there was Johnny's most beautiful, sensitive tragic song. It was titled 'You Can't Put Your Arms Around A Memory' but Johnny, he always sang it 'You can't put your arm around a memory'. Christ, Johnny.

Sunday afternoon at the tail-end of April 1990 and Johnny is over at your house. He's been in Ireland a week or so and the previous night appeared in Dublin at the New Inn. Naturally, it was chaotic. And sad. And brilliant sometimes, like when Johnny's into a rambling blues and he's saying, 'And there's you kids, the reason, the reason why. I tell ya, if it wasn't for the kids!' and the guitar, it cries, a flurry of notes weeping the blues. Johnny is playing his heart out.

Sunday afternoon, sunny, we sit here and play records and talk and Johnny plays a tape of some new stuff he's recorded.

Heroin? Naw, he's just on methadone now he says, gets it on prescription. Doesn't do heroin, no not never. Well ... hardly ever.

He's hoping for a record deal somewhere.

His wife Julie is back in Michigan with the kids, has been for years. He'd been living with his girlfriend Susanne in Sweden but that ... well, that isn't happening either.

And then you put on The Shangri-La's song 'Give Him a Great Big Kiss' from Johnny's *So Alone* album and Patti Palladin, her voice all Noo York sass like all of The Ronettes chewing gum, she teases 'Well I hear she's pretty bad' and Johnny, he responds 'Well she's good bad but she's not evil', and sitting here now Johnny's lived-in face, the mouth grins lopsidedly and there's a twinkle from under the drooping eyelids and for a moment he looks so happy and so vulnerable, the wounded artist touching the sunlight for a moment and you understand again why you love him.

Johnny's leaving now, leaving for the airport. He has no home, no number. Says maybe he'll go to New York after he's played in London, maybe go back to Paris. Says he'd like maybe to live in New Orleans.

Johnny gathers his plastic bag of medications and in the street we hug. Once, he'd had a muscled torso like Iggy. Now underneath his pinstriped suit he seems suddenly frail. This battered artist who sings from the slums of his soul is on the home run.

Six days short of a year later, Johnny Thunders is in New Orleans. He's just done a tour of Japan. Two days ago he's recorded with the group Die Toten Hosen, recorded his Heartbreakers favourite 'Born to Lose'. He's thirty-eight years old. And he's dead. The police find vials of methadone, and in the toilet a syringe. The coroner's report says death may have been drug-related.

Bye bye Johnny.

•

The Rocking Chair Album – Howlin' Wolf.

The Wolf howled, all dark and feral and frightening. You wouldn't want to bump into him under a bad moon rising, this back door man, oh no.

Here he moans through 'Spoonful' and 'Wang Dang Doodle', the third-leg boogie one-eyed trousersnake crowing of 'The Red Rooster' and, too, 'You'll Be Mine' which Marc Bolan transformed into 'Jeepster' just like Zeppelin nicked Muddy's 'You Need Love', just like The Stones stole 'This May Be The Last Time' from The Staple Singers. Steal from the very best, baby.

And then there's the cataclysmic 'Goin' Down Slow': bass-player and producer Willie Dixon, he's doing this dark-voice spoken bit at the beginning, going 'Man, you know I have enjoyed things kings and queens will never have' and now The Wolf's voice, all raw and passionate, it's singing 'I have had my fun, if I never get well no more' and Hubert Sumlin's guitar, it stings and stabs the stratosphere.

A perfect epitaph.

PETER FALLON

WHEN WE ALL DIE AND GO TO HEAVEN, we'll wander forever amid celestial graffiti ('The end of the next world is nigh', 'God is Eric', 'You can take it with you') accompanied by the soundtrack of the sounds that thrilled and soothed us in this life on earth.

As far as I can remember, the backdrop of the early years was singles: the Animals, the Small Faces, the Byrds, the Yardbirds and the Who – most of them English. We'd stack them up and watch them fall. Everything clicked into place. Some of it is a bit embarrassing now. Let's face it. We used to listen to Cat Stevens and Al Stewart. But I'm glad to say I tired early of those three-minute ditties in which women were always, and too often, called 'Baby'.

If I was going to grow, so – I thought – should the music. As Chrissie Hynde (aah!) sings in 'Middle of the Road': 'I'm not the kind I used to be/ I've got a kid, I'm thirty-three.' And a bit. 'Hope I die before I get old' sounds a little silly now.

Most of what I listen to now is American and is the work of the so-called singer-songwriters. Still, there are two English guitar-playing songwriters I've listened to as much as anyone.

It's hard to skip Dire Straits' first LP (remember when they were LPs?) and, in particular, that opening trip and stutter as 'The Sultans of Swing' finds its feet, but *Making Movies* is a more sustained and complete collection. 'Tunnel of Love', 'Romeo and Juliet', 'Skateaway', 'Solid Rock' ... these get quickly up and running and swirl you along with them. And Knopfler's lazy singing and fluid fingerwork work like a dream.

This is scary. It's nearly thirty years since I first heard Richard Thompson. I used to go to see Fairport Convention, with Judy Dyble, then Sandy Denny, in my summers in London. They sang songs by Joni Mitchell, Emmit Rhodes and Leonard Cohen – summer sounds, and we all loved each other – and from there and then, through the aching harmonies of Richard and Linda, to a sterling solo career, Thompson has become one of the few heavyweight contenders from England. (I suppose Costello is another.) *Watching the Dark* contains enough evidence to send you in search of all the sources, if you haven't them already.

Tim Hardin I've loved forever – was he the last Romantic? Imagine attempting, and getting away with, 'You look to me like misty roses/too soft to touch, yet too lovely to leave alone'. *Tim Hardin 3: Live in Concert* included

'Lenny's Tune', which hadn't been recorded previously. This paean of identification with Lenny Bruce's agony and the tribute to Hank Williams – 'I didn't know you, but I've been to places you've been' – were, you might say, instalments of an autobiography. The perfect simplicities of 'Reason to Believe', 'The Lady Came from Baltimore' and 'If I were a Carpenter' (imagine the luxury of being able to omit 'Hang on to a Dream'), those gorgeous jazzy arrangements and the voice that trembled as if it was about to shatter. And of course, it was.

Leonard Cohen's richly textured reports of love and longing have always warmed and comforted me. Again, it could be any one of a handful of records – but for the beauty of this particular song, I'd plump for whatever one 'Famous Blue Raincoat' graces. Was it *Songs of Love and Hate*? As far as I remember, it was.

Joni Mitchell. This could easily be *Court and Spark* or even *Blue* (it's just a touch too high-pitched), but I've always felt that *Hejira* was a special album – complete in its concerns and moods. And the sustained metaphor of 'Coyote' would take some beating. The lush sweep of her voice and insights in her recent *Turbulent Indigo* suggest little has changed. My number hasn't. If you read this, Joni, it's still +353 49 41779.

One pleasure that beats being a fan is being a friend too. Since the early seventies, soon after his first two albums stunned and enthralled me, I've been able to count Loudon Wainwright III in the heart's special place. Maybe he's not yet made a perfect album – he's certainly given perfect concerts – but he continues to compose songs that are as funny and moving and, well, as interesting as anyone's in our age. *Career Moves*, live from the Bottom Line, suggest the crazy camaraderie of his performance, but I'm opting for *History* for a sequence of songs, 'Father and a Son', 'Sometimes I Forget', and 'A Handful of Dust', this last one made of his father's lyrics. Beautiful, mature, wise reflections on complicated family relationships. Which isn't to suggest he can't be a complete clown!

I've always loved women singers. That said, Lucinda Williams' voice does something special to me: it's half-lazy, but it's strong and it's not forced. Usually I give the 'blues' a wide berth – 'twelve-bars' sound more like a night on the town to me – but I listen with pleasure to her laments of love and her *Old Country*, her Merle Haggard and the like. Her own songs get better and better – 'Passionate Kisses' is a pretty nifty pop song – and I'm taking *Same Old World*, especially for that lovely ballad (I know, I know, I'm a sucker) 'Something About What Happens When We Talk'. I'd rush to buy a new Lucinda Williams release as quickly as anyone's. And if you're reading this, Lucinda, see my phone number above.

I'm not wilful enough to leave out Bob Dylan. And this, too, could be one of a handful – two handfuls. *John Wesley Harding*? *Blood on the Tracks*? *Nashville Skyline*? I'll go for *Infidels* and, again, a great ballad ('What's a Sweetheart Like You Doing in a Dump Like This') helps tilt the balance. One way or another, he's just part of a generation, part of our lives.

Paul Simon's sweeter tunes also constitute one of the outstanding bodies of work. There's no doubt about whether they'll endure. *There Goes Rhymin'*

Simon shows all his strengths – that light touch, his way of assembling a verse, that melody, and – exquisite! – 'An American Tune'.

How many's that? Still no Love. No Band. No Lyle Lovett. No Rickie Lee Jones. No Dusty Springfield. No Pretenders. What, no Pretenders!

Still, I want something Irish. Christy's a singing treasure, Arty McGlynn's an unsung treasure and I'm tempted to pick his record with Nollaig Casey for the title 'reel', 'Lead the Knave', but I've got to choose something by Van. *Hardnose the Highway? Tupelo Honey?* No, it's got to be *No Guru, No Method, No Teacher.* Who cares what it's about? The voice, the arrangements, the feel of it ... magic. It's as fresh now as it ever was.

These sounds have been friends and companions on an interesting journey. I'm grateful for them. They'll make heaven even better.

ALEC FINN

BLIND BOY FULLER

I would have been at art school in Sheffield when I first heard him. It was shortly before the Beatles appeared. People were still listening to Max Bygraves and 'Knocking on the Green Door'. I had a little group called the Black Jean Boys who used to wear black jeans, those luminous green socks and winkle-pickers. We had old gramophones which were like little suitcases, or accordion cases, with space for a mike and other things. We discovered that there were a few old shops in town, not really record shops, that had collections of old blues recordings: Leadbelly, Big Bill Broonzy, Blind Boy Fuller playing Blind Lemon Jefferson ... they actually played tunes on the guitars, rather than just the old strumming with a skiffle. I particularly liked Blind Boy Fuller. There was a terrific photograph of him, a bit like that old Robert Johnson photograph. He used to play a National steel guitar.

We formed a small band called the Levee Breaks: a fellow on the harmonica, and a guy called Chuck Ward singing. We used to go around folk clubs which had just started and play copies of all these tunes, which we didn't really understand. Most of them were sexual jelly-rolls. We used to go around thinking we were great at the time. I'm sure we horrified the old-folk types.

SONNY TERRY AND BROWNIE MCGEE

That led on to Sonny Terry and Brownie McGee, who made many albums: amazing harmonica playing, reasonable guitar playing and very good vocal harmonies. We used to play quite a lot of their music in the folk clubs around Yorkshire. I've always remained interested in them. In 1985 the group that I now play with, Dé Dannan, were to do a big film festival in Winnipeg, Canada. Lo and behold when we arrived at the hotel, I saw a poster with Dé Dannan in huge letters and somewhere about five down the billing, Sonny Terry and Brownie McGee, which was embarrassing. I couldn't believe that (a) I was going to meet them, which I intended to do, and that (b) I'd be able to hear them live for the first time. As it happened, I discovered the most peculiar thing while talking to one of the promoters. They said that we couldn't meet them both at the same time because they hadn't spoken to each other for about ten years. One lived on the East Coast and the other, I think it was Sonny Terry, lived in Los Angeles.

They hated each other but because blues wasn't (and still isn't) popular enough in America to make a living from, they had to perform together. They both came on stage together, and slapped each other on the back. Afterwards, they went to separate hotels and never spoke again until they got the money and left. That was quite amusing. But more amusing was when we met Brownie McGee in the lobby of the hotel. He agreed to come and have a drink with us. We ended up going on the piss with him for the night. I remember he drank whiskey and milk, a blues version of Baileys. And he started this amazing *béal bocht* story of how he was born somewhere in the south, and how his father worked in an asbestos factory, and used to come home covered in white dust and would sit in a tin tub in front of the fire while his mother washed him off. Quite the opposite to the coal mine, with a white guy coming home and having the coal dust washed off. Ringo, the bodhrán player from Shantallagh, Galway, not to be outdone, said his mother washed his father off by the light of a single light bulb. I told McGee how amazed I was to meet him, how I'd been listening to them for twenty years, and how embarrassed I was to be ahead of him on the bill.

JULIAN BREAM

At the same time, I got very interested in the stringed instruments, particularly the lute, which I think is one of the most beautiful instruments ever constructed. I went to see an exhibition in London of the beautiful, hand-made Elizabethan lutes, with all the figureheads and the carving. It was very impressive. And then I discovered that there was only one person who played these fourteen-stringed lutes, Julian Bream. He played all this beautiful, soothing Dowlin music and also knew how to play the classical guitar. I wouldn't have been interested in classical in the orchestral sense, but when you heard it played on one guitar it was quite amazing. You could never buy a lute because there were none made at the time. When I moved to Ireland, however, I heard you could buy them in Greece. I asked a friend of mine, Eamon Cannon, to get me one when he went on holidays there. Instead he brought me back a bouzouki thinking it was a lute. This was the only reason why I then began to play the bouzouki. It was a three-paired string bouzouki, not a four-paired one – the older type. It is a complete fluke that I play in that style on that kind of instrument. If he hadn't bought the 'lute', I would still be a commercial artist or something.

OTIS REDDING

Otis Redding singing accompanied by brass was quite remarkable; it is the only music I've ever liked which uses brass sections. Just beautiful, syncopated singing, chopping up and playing around with the notes. Emotional and slow. I like his version of 'Try a Little Tenderness'. I don't like 'Dock of the Bay'; it is a bit too commercial for me. It was during the days of the Dandelion Market and Eamon Cannon and I used to listen to Otis all the time, driving around Dublin, drinking pints of Guinness. After that I moved into a flat with Phil Lynott for a couple of years and the two of us used to listen to him. Then, of course, he had that plane crash. I never saw him live. The last time I saw him on film was at Altamont with the Stones. He was amazing. His music wasn't rock'n'roll or strictly gospel. I suppose you could call it soul, but his own particular brand of soul.

JERRY LEE LEWIS AND LITTLE RICHARD

I'd put Jerry Lee Lewis with Little Richard; they are both fantastic, serious rock 'n'roll pianists and singers; the essence of rock'n'roll. Jerry Lee's music has a bit of country attached to it, which I like, and Little Richard would have sort of black, gay associations. If you wanted anything to dance to at the time, really good rock'n'roll, you couldn't get better. It's just wonderful. Outrageous camp playing and behaviour. 'Good Golly Miss Molly', 'Lucille' – all great songs. My favourite record is one called *The King of rock'n'roll*, and the cover shows Little Richard on this great throne in a bouffant, with a queen's crown, sceptre, ermine robes and a sunset behind. It is a live gig. He slates Elvis Presley and everyone else. He does some preaching before it, complete with alleluias and chorus, and tells everyone how wonderful he is, calling himself the Georgia Peach – wonderful Little Richard from Nathan, Georgia. It is a marvellous album. He is a completely outrageous performer like Jerry Lee, yet amazingly enough neither is highly regarded in the States. I went to hear Jerry Lee play once in Milwaukee with Fats Domino, who was awful. Jerry Lee had a mediocre white trio working with him, but he was great. When he dies, of course, everyone in America will come rushing out to buy his albums.

BOB DYLAN
BOB DYLAN

I heard the first Bob Dylan album at James McLaughlin's house. I'd seen Dylan on TV before hearing the record. He did a small part in a play, set in a tenement in London. He suddenly appears, sitting on a step, playing a guitar. It really affected me – it was real. It was more beatnik than anything. He was able to play the guitar beautifully, and he sang in his old Woody Guthrie voice. It was amazing. And then when I heard his album I thought most of it was a sort of wonderful sung poetry. 'The Lonesome Death of Hattie Caroll', 'Parting Glass', 'Boots of Spanish Leather' – they were all beautiful songs, harking back in a way to Blind Boy Fuller. It was just one person with a guitar: no drums or basses. Unlike many people, I liked the way his music developed: the funny country rock and the queer voices, and now my daughter, who is fifteen, is mad for it. I've often wanted to meet him, but I was told it was not possible. This guy, Johnny Cunnington, a traditional Scottish fiddle player, was part of a group called the Rain Togs in America. They found out they were to support Bob Dylan on a tour about two years ago. He was told by Dylan's manager that he was on no account to speak to him, or look at him, or go anywhere near him during the whole tour. Apparently Dylan arrived in a van which had a dog in it, came onto the stage at the last minute, sang, went straight back into his van and disappeared. Johnny never actually got to meet him, even though they were travelling with him for about three weeks.

ABBEY ROAD
THE BEATLES

John Lennon was the key for me to the Beatles. I wasn't really interested in the George Harrison, Hare Krishna element at all. I liked *Sgt. Pepper* and all that Walrus stuff, and the combination of the orchestra with Liverpool dialect. What was that 'Polythene Pam' line I was listening to the other day – 'She's so good-looking, that she looks like a man' – crazy, but unique poetry from that period of time, from the English working class if you like. I also enjoyed the transition out of the suits and into the dirty old kaftans, and the fact that they degenerated into drugs. I was disappointed when they all shagged off to meet the gurus. But listening to *Abbey Road* the other day in Terry Connaughton's flat, I thought again what an excellent album it was. It was the last one I can remember seeing the movie to, where Yoko comes in and the whole thing starts to crack up. This was, amazingly enough, all in the film. I really like John Lennon. I can remember where I was when he died – in the kitchen at home – and I was horrified that he had been shot.

At the time of *Abbey Road* I was living in a basement flat on Raglan Road, rented from a Doctor so-and-so. My flatmate was a musician called Niall Fennell, a French-horn player with a band called the Press Gang. When he moved out Phil Lynott asked if he could move in, but the doctor didn't like the idea of a black guy moving into his flat. There was nothing he could do about it, however. Once at the Cenor Inn in King's Street the Legion of Mary came up and asked us what we were doing in this pub. Philip pretended he was African and said, 'Well, where I come from, you know, your missionaries went into my villages and took down the totem poles.' We stayed in the flat for about two years, and then he went and did his musical about the orphanage. He had to have his tonsils out to improve his voice. That was a traumatic period. Eventually he moved to London and formed his own group, the Orphanage, and started to do well. At the time we listened to *Abbey Road* and he was very into that as well. Those were the days of the tie-dye silk scarfs, bell-bottom trousers and platform shoes in Dublin. Phil was a natty dresser.

JOE COCKER!
JOE COCKER

I listened to this album in my little gate-lodge in Spiddal, Connemara, where I had moved by that stage. I had opted out after all the Dublin shenanigans and high life, and went to live in Connemara and messed around with hawks and dogs, and did very little. I played Irish traditional music, because that was all there was to play down there. Phil Lynott used to visit quite often which was quite a shock to the Spiddalites. I had my favourite albums with me at the time: the odd old Otis, a double album of Johnny Winter, particularly the track 'Good Morning Little School Girl'. A lot were cover versions of earlier black blues, but they really rocked up with amazing screaming guitars. He was a wonderful guitarist, and still is. I used to play it quite a lot, to the shock of any locals who came in. They all thought I was on drugs down there, because I played this way and had long hair. I can remember the Joe Cocker album – this dreadful photograph of him on the front in red and black with his mouth open and his tongue hanging out. That wonderful version of 'A Little Help from My Friends', with Henry McCullach on the guitar. Cocker was from Sheffield, and I was actually born around there. I was amazed to hear that someone actually sang like that. Johnny Minaghan told me how he apparently sang in that great soul voice, but when he spoke, it was like, 'fish and chips please luv', in a completely Yorkshire accent.

AISLING FOSTER

THE ROLLING STONES
THE ROLLING STONES

In 1964 Kennedy was dead, my big sister could jive and girls dressed like younger versions of their mothers. I stole my sister's clothes and spent Saturday nights at rugby-club hops waiting to be asked 'to shake'. Apart from backcombing and toe-crushing stilettos it all seemed pretty tame. The alternatives did not look too life-enhancing either: I had seen *A Taste of Honey* in a basement theatre and read a slew of kitchen-sink novels; the Leadbelly and John Lee Hooker records favoured by De La Salle boys offered the same hopelessness, only black. I had a horrible feeling the politicians would be proved right: that one day soon every rocker would settle down like the rest of the adult world to a life of quiet despair. Then the Rolling Stones crashed onto our crackly transistors. Here was something different: black American music infused with white man's optimism. Mick Jagger's wheedling tomcat voice and Charlie Watts's drumming wasn't the stuff Radio Luxembourg could sandwich between Bing and the Bachelors. Broadcasting had to change. And when the Stones came to Dublin, convent schoolgirls didn't weep like Beatles fans; we tried to dance in the aisles.

SOLID GOLD SOUL
VARIOUS ARTISTS

[Solomon Burke: 'Got to Get You off My Mind', 'Just out of Reach'; Wilson Pickett: 'Don't Fight It', 'In the Midnight Hour'; Joe Tex: 'I Want To', 'Hold on to What You've Got'; Don Covay: 'See Saw', 'Mercy, Mercy'; Ben E. King: 'Don't Play that Song', 'Stand By Me'; Otis Redding: 'Mr Pitiful', 'I've Been Loving You Too Long']

Today's advertising soundtracks recycle my anthems of escape from hated school and the beginning of real life. A fellow art-student had grown up in East Africa and danced like nobody I knew. This music offered the freedom to try it. Soul hit a nerve in Dublin, expressing a yearning for some kind of freedom beyond our censorious, post-Dev world, away from the number 15 bus-stop on Stephen's Green where an old woman believed in her God-given right to whack mini-skirted legs with a walking stick. Suddenly it was fun to be an object of sin. I hitchhiked in France with an Irish flag on my rucksack. A Breton tried to converse with me as a member of some Celtic revival, using laboriously acquired Irish; I blush at the vehemence with which I told him in bad French that I never wanted to place a fada or learn an 'idiom' again. On television the Atlantic Label singers looked like raddled Bible-thumpers. Yet when they sang about love, even virgins like me knew they meant good sex. This album went to O'Dwyer's and Toner's most weekends. For years it could crash you in the door of the strangest parties and it still bears the scars of a million Saturday nights and Sunday mornings.

SURREALISTIC PILLOW
JEFFERSON AIRPLANE

The sound of pirate radio, Ranelagh bedsits, Smedley's canning factory, doing the ton on a motorbike, crawling down the King's Road in the back of a convertible Austin Healy, thumbing to Greece, sleeping on beaches, on park benches, waking one frozen winter dawn inside a rolled-up carpet in someone's parents' house in Stillorgan. Sergeant Mullins was head of the drugs squad in Dublin then, famed for his one-liners: 'Freeze, lads, this is a burst!' [bust?] Tracks like 'Chauffeur Blues' bring back the horror of the hard drug scene in the late sixties, always looming behind the feel-good haze. I still mourn Jack, a Dublin northsider in Notting Hill who liked hanging out with students from home. I knew he had lost himself when he brought me to visit a heavily pregnant friend: she sat up in bed, injected herself and laughed. Jack died that winter; choked on his own vomit.

ASTRAL WEEKS
VAN MORRISON

This was the first Van Morrison I bought, but I know I'm old when I admit that I first noticed him when Them played a Saturday night hop in Donnybrook. I wore a black-and-red check sack dress over black polo-neck and tights, and Van sang 'Gloria' a lot. Every boy who asked me to dance had a Belfast accent. They opened with the question, 'What school do you go to?' The answer, 'Notre Dame des Missions' was all they needed to know. There was no next dance. Up North, Them were a Prod band, and though Van got away from those mean streets the nostalgia in his songs for the peculiarities of his childhood is always haunting and poetic. He sings, too, about a sixties generation who travelled, crossing borders amongst a youth culture which was happening everywhere and in which everyone seemed welcome. A year or so after this album was released Bernadette Devlin turned up at a Dublin party. She had a lot on her mind I suppose, because when we put on Van she moved to another room where she remained for the night, singing sad rebel songs with her Northern friends and looking disapproving. Yet, it's extraordinary who The Man reached: in 1989 I met an eminent physicist at Princeton who, as a Berkeley undergraduate, had counted how many times Van repeated the phrase 'the love to love' in 'Madame George'. It still seemed important.

VANILLA FUDGE
VANILLA FUDGE

I don't remember ever seeing this band play, which was probably just as well. They had no image, only an amazing sound. The pictures of Timmy, Vinny, Carmine and Mark on the back of the album make it hard to imagine how those four empty-looking, all-American boys in sta-pressed versions of English pop gear made this very disturbing music. They didn't compose much of what's here; most tracks are cover versions. In the same year that the Beatles brought out *Sgt. Pepper* these boys dragged 'Ticket to Ride', 'She's Not There' and 'Eleanor Rigby' underground, slowing them up, tripping them out. This was heavy music, and it got listened to because in those days nobody worth their thong sandals ever talked. Not properly. We were too busy sticking Rizla papers together, while boys said 'Wow! Great stuff!' between tracks and girls sat and smiled and shook their hair. Peace and love. This record cooled for me in a Spanish campsite in October 1970. A month in Morocco with a tent and rucksack had been a month too long. Recuperation by the pool was disturbed by a VW camper from California blasting Vanilla Fudge. After an hour we asked them to turn it down. The owners were horrified. 'But you're Long-Hairs!' It seemed they had a master plan, to build a long-haired town in the mountains. Now we were excluded.

LIVE AT THE APOLLO
JAMES BROWN

This is the best live album ever recorded, the next best thing to being there. Brown and the Famous Flames give it everything they've got, but the audience is wonderful, too, perhaps because the Apollo Theatre is in Harlem and the brethren don't sound phoney when they clap and testify. When Brown sings 'Please Please Please' you know he's on his knees; when he sings 'Night Train' you can see those funny little shuffling steps of his and smell the sweat. Sometimes the sound gets muffled as if he has fallen over the microphone, but the energy comes through, the genius which must have encouraged Brown to pay for this recording himself and strike solid gold. A UCD architecture student who looked like Sam Beckett introduced me to this record. Eventually he dropped out and drifted between Dublin and London where, one summer, we shared a flat with some friends and this LP. Our landlady was West Indian and on the game. She had a huge extended family, notably an elder son who carried a knife on rent day. One weekend we all hitched to the Cambridge Folk Festival and returned on Sunday night to find our belongings tossed into the street, her littlest daughters clumping about in my silk shawls and high heels. It looked like notice to quit, but she took the two of us aside. 'It's all right, you and the boy can stay.' She had not liked a lone female living in her house with more than one male. She didn't know the Irish.

THE ROCK MACHINE TURNS YOU ON
VARIOUS ARTISTS

[Bob Dylan: 'I'll Be Your Baby Tonight'; Moby Grape: 'Can't Be So Bad'; Spirit: 'Fresh Garbage'; The United States of America: 'I Won't Leave My Wooden Wife for You, Sister'; The Zombies: 'Time of the Season'; The Peanut Butter Conspiracy: 'Turn on a Friend'; Leonard Cohen: 'Sisters of Mercy'; Blood, Sweat and Tears: 'My Days are Numbered'; The Byrds: 'Dolphins Smile'; Simon & Garfunkel: 'Scarborough Fair'; Taj Mahal: 'Statesboro Blues'; The Electric Flag: 'Killing Floor'; Roy Harper: 'Nobody's Got any Money in the Summer'; Tim Rose: 'Come Away Melinda'; Elmer Gantry's Velvet Opera: 'Flames']

Everyone had this record. It wasn't a 'best-of' (most of these artists you wouldn't be seen dead with), it was something else – a membership badge, the musical equivalent of the Borges novel or the Che poster, stacked on the floor beside Janis and the Doors. UCD was filling with draft-dodging students. They were heroes, especially after Chris Meehan wrote a song about Tom Casey who had failed his exams and was killed in Vietnam. We hated Johnson and then Nixon, shouted 'Ho, Ho, Ho Chi-Minh!' into the lenses of unmarked TV cameras. This album was also a high-water mark for college-boy rock as the Motown tide came flooding in. Apart from Dylan, most of the tracks were the driving, wind-up sound of hirsute groups; stuff that ripped the inhibitions out of trainee accountants and made straight girls at rock concerts pull off their t-shirts and wave them in the air. My most played track was Leonard Cohen's 'Sisters of Mercy'. The image of nun-like handmaidens 'waiting in line' for Leonard seemed acceptable then, though I could never finish his novels. His philosophy fitted with unequal pay and a summer room in Putney where the landlord liked to brew Turkish coffee when I got home from the factory and discuss female masturbation. One morning I walked into the kitchen and was introduced to his girlfriend, a naked, six-foot Australian who was ironing his shirts. I couldn't help noticing the leather gloves he wore with the palms cut out.

GIANTS OF MODERN JAZZ
CHARLIE PARKER

I bought this in the sixties with another brilliant album, *Kay Starr Sings Gospel*. The sleeve was missing, but the hippie selling his worldly goods off the pavement must have been impressed that I read the disc before handing over the cash. He followed me down the street, telling me who played drums and which session men sat in where. I didn't like to say I had only a vague notion of who Parker was, but when I got the album home and put it on I knew it was great. Here was an artist playing alto sax not because he wanted to change the world or even impress, but because he loved it and it was what he did best. I didn't know then that most of the tracks were recorded in 1947 when Parker had just been released from a sanatorium. To me the creative zip sounded like part of a sixties for-its-own-sake attitude, the mood that supported publications like Hayden Murphy's poetry *Broadsheet* and a snowstorm of student newspapers, and that could fill Dublin's duller pubs nearly every night with performing writers and singers. Someone told me that Charlie Parker had died in 1955 aged thirty-four. It sounded old at the time.

THE BALLAD OF LUCY JORDON
DR HOOK & THE MEDICINE SHOW

Married in London with a stereo whose owner objected to the way I abused his stylus, records had become an occasional buy. Albums like Curtis Mayfield's *Back to the World* and the Eagles' *Hotel California* were played obsessively in brief moments free from work and talk; but they were just more good music, more of the same. We had become introverted, put down roots, even liked our jobs. Friends who didn't had died or become echoes of something that was over. Then, in a hamburger joint where even shouting wasn't possible, I heard 'Sylvia's Mother', 'The Freakers Ball', 'Makin' It Natural'. The music was basic cowboy rock'n'roll, but Shel Silverstein's lyrics could slash through any cliché. Here were Americans giving two fingers to the have-a-nice-day politeness that was washing around the world with Coke and fries; they were still celebrating the briefly opened windows of the sixties, even being ironic, for God's sake, about p.c. issues like gay rights and wholefood. Backing a loser, of course, but they made me laugh. 'Pass that roach, please, and drink the wine, I'll kiss yours, if you'll kiss mine.'

LET'S DANCE
DAVID BOWIE

Every album Bowie produced was different, a real original, though I had never bought one. I suppose I disliked Bowie fans: they seemed the sort of people who bought the cover, not the book. They were also younger than me. Then I got an old *Ziggy Stardust* tape for the car, and from the minute he could speak my son was singing along to 'Star Man' and 'Five Years'. He was nearly three when *Let's Dance* came out, by which time we had done a lot of dancing together to Ella and her Fellas and Motown. Last time I'd tried to dance away from home was when Lynn Geldof took us to the Boomtown Rats. That made me think that dance was dead, unless it meant pogoing and getting gobbed on when you stood near the stage. *Let's Dance* seemed like a return to what good rock music can do, making you 'put on your red shoes and dance the blues'. Yet it had an eighties edginess, a synthesized, digital polish a long way from early Stones. Then I heard Eric Burdon was giving a comeback concert in the Town and Country Club up the road. It sounded like a good way to get back. Like in the old clubbing days, we asked friends round for food and drinks to give the support band time to finish, then rolled up at the door at about eleven. The lights were going out one by one: our old rocking hero had played his gig and gone off home to bed.

JOHN WILSON FOSTER

ON SUNDAY EVENING of 13 January 1963, there was a play on BBC television called *The Madhouse on Castle Street* which I watched through a family quarrel (Sunday evenings were often tense, the work week looming up for my father) and over my mother's ironing board. It was set in an English boarding-house, and one of the boarders was a hunched figure who spent most of the play crouched on the stairs singing mournful songs, accompanying himself on a guitar and a mouth organ somehow strapped around his neck, so freeing his hands for strumming. There was a song about a dying swan, I seem to recall, and as the credits rolled at the end he sang a song about answers to heavy questions blowing in the wind. His name was Bob Dylan and I had never heard music like his: intelligent, poetic images fused to funky blues-type guitar and a voice of premature world-weariness. Hearing Dylan that night became significant in another way, because it was the very next morning that my father died suddenly and totally unexpectedly, and forever Dylan and death have for me a powerful connection, a connection his songs do nothing to dissipate.

To my astonishment, an LP by this human revelation could be ordered from a Belfast gramophone shop – *Bob Dylan* (1962), his first album and easily the most important album in my life, up to then and thereafter. Some years later I had to replace my copy, for it had worn smooth with constant use. 'Man of Constant Sorrow', 'Pretty Peggy-o', 'Gospel Plow', 'Song to Woody' – these took their instant place alongside *On the Road* and *The Dharma Bums*. In their evocation of an endless horizon and of men 'that came with the dust/And are gone with the wind' they rehearsed that bottomless allure of broad America: 'crossing the county line', 'making it to Mexico', 'getting your kicks on Route 66', 'lighting out for the territories'.

It was the mouth-organ that got me most, the low-register locomotive steady shunting and fast rolling-stock intimacies of the instrument, the pocket-sized one-man-band feel to it all: the self-contained poetic *welzschmerz*, take-me-or-leave-me-but-I'm-my-own-goddam-man impression of it all. I had to get me one.

As a start I bought Marine Band harmonicas in Matchett's music shop in downtown Belfast (I already owned a secondhand guitar which I'd bought from a schoolmate for 37/6, hoping to become Buddy Holly) and within a week I could strum three chords with pleasing adequacy and bow my head to play the harmonica balanced precariously on the curving rim of the guitar. Within weeks

I became a man of constant sorrow, going back (just a poor hobo and singing those freight-train blues) to Colorado, 'the place I started from', martyred, sadder and wiser, poor, poetic, dusty, betrayed by pretty Peggy-o, charming, sexy, solitary, yet likely to talk New York and my experiences there like a rambling minstrel ancient mariner, stopping by to see dying Woody on my way west, all the while keeping my hand on the gospel plow, not quite yet fixin' to die (though if I did hoping someone would see that my grave was kept clean) but hoping to meet some baby who would let me follow her down either across the green pastures of Harvard University or Highway 51 to her sad warm pad where I would do anything in the god-almighty world for her before I discovered she was no good and reached into the corner another wearying time for my travelling shoes.

All present and correct, but the real problem was how to free the hands for playing the guitar. Dylan had some kind of metal harness which I'd never seen before. For a packet of twenty cigarettes, a guy in a garage made me one to my guesswork specifications, which worked except there were no hinges and once over the head it resembled a medieval torture instrument. But it passed muster and I set to learning Dylan in earnest and trying my hand at my own Dylanesque songs. Dylan's second album – which I remember hearing for the first time in a record shop booth in London – was a terrific boost to a would-be songwriter. *The Freewheelin' Bob Dylan* (1963) had on its cover a singer both reassuringly and alarmingly youthful (a sly fifteen year-old, perhaps, who should be in school), with his arm-hugging girlfriend showing him the kind of attention no girl had yet shown me. Inside was 'Blowin' in the Wind' and 'Girl of the North Country', but even better was 'Don't Think Twice, It's Alright', painful in its lyrical simplicity and an early hallmark of Dylan's style with its stoic self-pity and blend of vulnerability and on-the-road untouchability.

The best version of 'Don't Think Twice' that I've heard is by Ramblin' Jack Elliott, whom I had the great pleasure of seeing live, and introducing myself to, years later in Vancouver. By then he was a short birdlike man with a cowboy hat and a bemused expression. Like Dylan he had changed his name: he was Elliott Adnapoz (I do believe) to Dylan's Robert Zimmerman: the urban Jew transformed by talent and desire into western goy. *The Essential Ramblin' Jack Elliott* (1976) is one of my own essential albums, though his later record, *Young Brigham*, is even better, with a superb version of 'If I Were a Carpenter' and the wonderful talkin' blues reminiscence, '912 Greens'. I early acquired an Elliott 45 that had on it 'San Francisco Bay Blues', 'Muleskinner Blues' and 'Railroad Bill'. Some years later when I lived in Oregon I gave it away to an even greater Ramblin' Jack fan, the folksinger and playwright Bob Deemer, and I hope he gets pleasure out of it yet.

On that mini-album, Ramblin' Jack drank from the same fountain of inspiration as did Cisco Houston and their mentor, Woody Guthrie. I can't recall if I knew Guthrie's work before I encountered Bob Dylan, with its Guthrie-like homage track, 'Song to Woody'. But later I invested in the crowded three-record album *Woody Guthrie: Library of Congress Recordings* (originally released in 1964), with its interviews of Guthrie by Alan Lomax interspersed with Guthrie's off-the-cuff renditions of his songs.

It's a monumental compilation, as much social as musical history, and when I came to perform I took to singing 'Going Down that Road Feeling Bad' and other Guthrie compositions. I think I'm right in saying that all of Woody's words, and none of his tunes, were original. I suspect his songs were the more haunting because many of them contained the ghosts of folk songs and more specifically of gospel tunes. There was something of the itinerant preacher about Guthrie as well as the wandering minstrel. Dylan picked up on this: Dylan's later 'conversion' to Christianity was much remarked upon (his born-again, Jesus phase), but his entire body of work is full of religious theme and tune. 'Blowing in the Wind' from his second album became the hymn of an epoch, and 'The Times They Are A-Changin'', from the 1964 album of that name (his third), even more so, with its aggressive tidings. *The Times They Are A-Changin'* also contained the apocalyptic 'When the Ship Comes In', though in revelatory force that was to pale beside the later 'A Hard Rain's A-Gonna Fall', Dylan's potent re-working for the nuclear age of the Child ballad 'Lord Randall'.

The old thirties unionism of the Wobblies helped produce Guthrie and Pete Seeger. These singers generalized solidarity and disaffection into a concern for justice and connected folk music up to liberalism (and at times radicalism). This musical tradition was available, via Dylan out of Woody, when the youth of the sixties needed to sing their concern about racism in America, nuclear build-up, and the Vietnam War. By 1965 there was a folk revival under way, mostly white and even middle class, but unignorable, by turns angry and lyrical. *Folksong '65*, an Elektra Records fifteenth-anniversary commemorative album, features most of the names of the revival: Judy Collins, Tom Rush, Hamilton Camp, Tom Paxton, Mark Spoelstra and Phil Ochs. (Missing are Baez and Dylan, not available to Elektra, and a few others, such as Dick and Mimi Farina, Eric Andersen and Buffy Sainte-Marie.) A tacit idealism suffuses the whole, a vague lyrical dissatisfaction which on hindsight stood for these qualities in a whole generation soon to meet (and in part create) its challenge in the selection boards of the U.S. army and the campuses of American universities. One track is by a blues threesome who made at least one fine album together, but seem not to have fulfilled their early promise: Dave Snaker Ray, Tony Little Sun Glover and Spider John Koerner. I have one of Ray's memorable solo albums, on which his guitar work is plangent and brown.

By 1965, I had had the gall to have been singing on stage (a small stage, but a stage nevertheless) for a couple of years. I think I'm right in saying that I was the first to sing the songs of Dylan anywhere in Ireland (this was in 1963), the first Dylan imitator, and one of the first to write songs inspired by Dylan. Most of those who heard me sing back then were hearing the name and work of Dylan for the first time. My most frequent gig was the weekly meeting of the Folk Society of Queen's University (something between concerts and hootenannies), but I also played halls and community centres around the place. My biggest gig in a very modest career was as support act for the Spinners at the Whitla Hall in 1964 or '65, where I was accompanied by George Hayes, who stole the show in a pair of tight white jeans in an era of great conservatism of dress (all was to change within a year or two).

I took to making demos of my own songs, recording them either in John Shannon's house (John was a fine lyrical accompanist) or in a Cromac Square studio owned and run by an Englishman called Peter Lloyd. I spent a few summer weeks hawking these demos around London's Tin Pan Alley (Essex Street, Wardour Street and environs) and managed to sell a song to Tradition Records and, back in Belfast, one to the folksinger David Hammond, then a producer with the BBC, later to become a filmmaker and Field Day Theatre Company director. It was a song inspired by the unemployment at Harland & Wolff shipyard that caused some workers to go to (then faraway) Sweden to ply their trade and who soon came back full of homesickness. David used this song in a documentary on the shipyard but I believe he may have attached my words to an old air. I sent demos also to Elektra, then the most respected American label interested in the folk revival. To my astonishment I received a letter from Judy Collins – then vying with Joan Baez for title of Queen of Folk – who expressed great interest in my songs and persuaded Elektra to take out rights on one of them, an adaptation of a Laurence Binyon poem called 'The Burning of the Leaves'. Whether she ever sang or recorded it I don't know, but she wrote me a second time, though I never sent Elektra any more work.

•

Like a few other privileged Butler Education Act products, I found myself taking the long road to the United States on a Fulbright scholarship in pursuit of a doctorate. You flew BOAC, whose logo had always thrilled me with the promissory music of adventure, escape and money. Until I reached my destination the planes got progressively smaller: from London to New York, New York to Chicago, Chicago to Portland, finally Portland to Eugene, Oregon in a small propeller plane sitting at ten degrees on the runway.

My first night on American soil, in the YMCA on East 47th Street, was like being home: we were all intimate with America, having watched it every Saturday afternoon. As though New York were a film set, I knew how to carry myself, and how to order in the corner drugstore, and to lock my hostel door at night real good. I had applied for admission only to those American universities with names electric with the thrill of boyhood, irrespective of academic reputation: Indiana, Wyoming, Utah, Idaho, California, Nevada, Iowa, New Mexico – and Oregon, for I had read Parkman's *The Oregon Trail*. I won the lottery, for the University of Oregon happened to be a very fine college.

The radical sixties did not get seriously under way until 1966 or 1967, at least not in a small western town like Eugene (pop. 75,000, the welcome-sign told the visitor). It was essentially a college town, but it rubbed shoulders with

Springfield, a tough lumber town of taverns and those ugly but convenient one-storey commercial strips, with their garish signs and cheap eateries, that are somewhere in almost every North American town. Luckily for me, I caught in 1965 the disappearing tail-lights of fifties America, Eisenhower's and Connie Francis's and early Presley's America. The automobiles were still huge, there were still drive-in movie houses, there were still lonesome diners and drive-in burger joints on the edge of town, there were still jukeboxes. McDonalds was already in business but still new enough to post in conceivable numbers the burgers sold to date: I believe it was nineteen million when I hit town.

It's funny how we remember precisely when we first heard certain songs. I was in the Paddock tavern (a vast place, frequented by students, where I first saw frosted mugs in which was served beer so cold it took away your breath) when I first heard 'Hey, Jude' with its tailback refrain, changing it from love-song to anthem. I heard 'Paperback Writer' for the first time appropriately outside the building that housed the English Department; I was opening the door of Dan Tannacito's Corvette Sting Ray, which he had driven clear across the continent from Boston in three days flat to enroll like me as a graduate student at UO.

It was with the *Sgt. Pepper* album that the Beatles began to have an impact on students of culture. Dan studied under the charismatic William Cadbury, a highly respected Victorian literature scholar who had a mesmerized following at UO. (Typically I avoided his regular classes, as I did most classes by gurus. I also gave Timothy Leary the by when he came to campus. Or did I? It's all a bit hazy. Dan meanwhile sold his Sting Ray, abandoned his skateboard, and joined the counter-culture.) It was Cadbury who introduced structuralism to his students, very early on in the Anglo-American enthusiasm for that intellectual fashion. In the one class I sat in on, he covered the blackboard with game theory matrices to explain plots of novels and left his students prostrate with excitement. He then startled us all by publishing a scholarly essay on *Sgt. Pepper* in the respected creative-writing journal that the poet Ralph Salisbury edited out of UO, *Northwest Review*. Cadbury's radical chic credentials were enhanced by his black wife, in a town and state where there were few African Americans. (Though there were sufficient to form a Black Panther unit, some of whom were in my Introduction to Literature course. They occupied the back row, dressed in black leather jackets. One of them gave me Iceberg Slim novels to read, which I did and enjoyed.) I still have Cadbury's essay, a remarkable reading of the *Sgt. Pepper* subtexts and an inventive bridging of the Beatles, the anti-racism movement in the U.S., and a culture tuning in, turning on and dropping out.

Another charismatic teacher at Oregon was Barre Toelken, who taught Chaucer and folklore but was an eminent balladeer and field-collector. At Queen's I had published in a short-lived magazine called *New Ireland* (it was the Lemass-O'Neill New Ireland that was being alluded to) a defence of the folk credentials of Guthrie and Dylan, for they had been dismissed as 'fakelore' by the purists. I submitted this article for publication in Toelken's journal, *Northwest Folklore*, but he rounded upon it in absentia (he was on sabbatical in Utah).

When he returned the following year we nevertheless became fast friends and came to an understanding on Dylan and Guthrie, whose songs (along with my own) I was singing around campus and in the coffee-houses of Eugene.

Toelken was married to a charming Japanese-American but had been married to a Navajo woman, and was an adopted child of her parents, with the anglicized name of Son of Little Wagon. On one memorable trip he and I drove to Salt Lake City, picked up another folklorist called Jan Brunvand (later to become a celebrity through his best-selling books on urban legends), and drove down through the startling Monument Valley, past Goulding's Trading Post and Piute country dotted with hogans, to the Navajo reservation in southern Utah to visit Little Wagon and his family. Toelken would sing ballads for the Navajo children and they would perform the most astonishing cat's cradle string games for us, elaborating constellations and animals.

Another time Toelken and I drove across the desert and through the Strawberry Mountains of eastern Oregon to the Idaho border where we both performed at the National Old Time Fiddlers' Contest at Weiser. After Toelken's solo performance I sang my first Irish song, but started in the wrong key in front of the assembled multitude of five thousand and couldn't get into the right one because Barre would stop playing the squeezebox at the end of my every line just as I frantically tried to pick up his last note. The next day we went into the studio to rectify matters (the Contest organizers released an LP each year) but to this day I wake up in the dead of night to eat a further few hundred stitches of my blanket; so mortified was I on the night that I went to a nearby tavern and sank eight bourbons with absolutely no effect. Nor did I get hold of the Contest's commemorative LP as a souvenir, wishing never to remind myself of the experience, though I heard the album and I passed muster certainly.

Besides doing the coffee-house circuit, I organized outdoor cultural festivals on campus. Festival UO – Culture Alfresco: that kind of thing. It was early in the great era of outdoor and indoor 'fests' – of poetry, jazz, poetry and jazz, folk, folk and poetry, politics and folk, dance and jazz, crafts and politics: a veritable cat's cradle of causes and emotings, songs and declamations. I brought poets to campus – William Stafford, Vern Rutsala and others – and recall Robert Duncan reading memorably against the Vietnam War; one metaphor of his was a startling evocation of the napalm war: 'The Johnson barbecue of Asia'.

I took advantage of my position as festival organizer to invite in person some of my musical heroes, including Bill Monroe and the Bluegrass Boys. Monroe, when I went to greet him in his motel room, seemed an elderly gent in suspenders and I am astonished to find that he is performing to this day. He drew a fine crowd to the Student Union (mostly local Eugene and Springfield folks, loggers and store clerks) considering that he was competing that night with a speech upstairs by a national counter-culture hero, possibly Eldridge Cleaver. I love bluegrass, all the way from the New Lost City Ramblers (whom I had the pleasure of hearing and meeting backstage at Ed Pearl's celebrated coffee-house in Los Angeles, the Ash Grove) through Monroe to the records of the twenties by the Tar Heel Rattlers, Skillet Lickers and others.

The charge was even greater for this Belfast boy when I brought Bukka White and Furry Lewis to town. Booker T. Washington White was the composer of 'Fixin' to Die', which had thrilled me on *Bob Dylan*. Here was a bluesman who had been inspired as a youngster in the twenties by the great Mississippi Delta player Charlie Patton, who met a bad end like many musicians in the violent American South. White speaks homage to Patton on an album that is one of my prized possessions: *Bukka White: Mississippi Blues Vol. 1*. His reminiscence circles around the lines of a song of Patton's that most impressed the young White:

> *Hitch up my buggy*
> *And saddle up my black mare*
> *I want to find my baby*
> *In this great big world somewhere.*

These lines, especially as White speaks them, detach themselves from rhyming blues formula into an existential lament, rather like Blind Willie McTell's 'Reach into the corner, mama/And hand me my travelin' shoes' – death and love, journey and pilgrimage becoming one. Here was a country blues artist to stand alongside Son House, Blind Lemon Jefferson, Robert Johnson, Blind Willie McTell, Leadbelly, Taj Mahal, Rev. Gary Davis, Sonny Boy Williamson (the First) and other legends.

Furry offstage played the part of mischievous elder. Bukka was younger and gave an impression of a man who, though greatly personable, could take care of himself. Indeed, he had shot a man and had done time (both being motifs in the lives of legendary bluesmen) in Parchman Farm, to which he devotes a blues in *Mississippi Blues Vol. 1*. He had been released because of his potent music, and he demonstrated that music in our concert. Like the best bluesmen he had the ability to make every song he sang seem like his own. He would sing the odd classic that wasn't his own, such as 'Baby, Please Don't Go' by Big Joe Williams – he of the nine-string guitar – later sung to great effect by Van Morrison and Them, who were surfacing just as I was leaving Belfast for Oregon.

Fine though the concert was, it was bettered when White and Lewis sat in my house in Eugene later that night, playing, talking and singing. Bukka played that unique careering, slap-strumming style on his National steel guitar, a style that could convey a man on the run or a lover distraught or a train in desperate motion. Furry would play gentler and offer harmonica, a peg-legged legend in his own right.

It was a difficult time for black men like these singers. A new breed of black man, proud, angry, defiant, had grown up. We had some of their representatives in Eugene and they did not come to hear these bluesmen whom they had cruelly translated into Uncle Toms, white men's minstrels. I like to think that African-America has thought twice about this, for when I reflect on these impressive singers, they seem to me to have embodied dignity under duress while carrying the weight of a suffering past which they translated into the weightless power of song. Cadbury's black wife did come to my house and bantered jive talk with White which I'd never heard live before. She was big enough to meet Furry and Bukka on their own terms, though she was a sophisticated and educated woman. During their near rap-talk (rap was a venerable black form of communication: H. Rap Brown, a celebrated black power advocate of the day, got his nickname from his proficiency in this ghetto dialogue art-form), the white boys and girls felt a little shut out, a little 'Other', and why shouldn't we have? Bukka White embodied an experience deeply alien and attractive: the power of his singing and his playing welled up from life as I had only read about it. When he sat in my house, filling it with his personality, I felt immensely privileged and somehow contracted and enlarged at the same time. I only wish George Hayes could have heard this great man, for George could have learned from him whereas I could simply admire and be enthralled and uplifted.

It was around this time that I went north to Portland to hear in the flesh for the first time the great Bobbie Dylan, as he had now become. Dylan was in his electric phase by then, of course, singing stuff from *Bringing It All Back Home*, *Highway 61 Revisited* and *Blonde on Blonde*. He was also in his Afro phase when the famous poster was about, with the light shining behind his head, suiting the guru/LSD/Hare Krishna/Mellow Yellow mood of the time. It was the first time I saw an audience hold up lighted matches in worship-applause (plastic throwaway lighters must not yet have become fashionable). I thought that America was getting altogether too religiose, though I too burned incense and candles (usually homemade, another rage) at all my parties (and I threw dozens of them, at which we danced to Creedence Clearwater Revival, Hearts and Flowers, Moby Grape, Quicksilver Messenger Service, the Grateful Dead, the Doors, Iron Butterfly and the Stones).

I was especially excited to travel north up Highway 99 to Lewis and Clark College to hear Sam Lightnin' Hopkins. I had brought to Oregon from Belfast *Last Night Blues* (1962), an album on which Hopkins is accompanied by Sonny Terry (Saunders Teddell). Hopkins was a Texas bluesman who had once teamed up with Texas Alexander, author of the immortal bawdy line, 'She worked under cover with a boar-hog's eye'. Though not without its humour, *Last Night Blues* is a dark intense session: it is almost as if one hears it through Terry's sightless eyes, the music alone available to the senses. Although both Hopkins and Terry were country bluesmen, one can imagine Chicago electrified blues emerging from this album, and even Chuck Berry, from whom it is a step to early rockabilly and thence Jerry Lee. That night in Oregon, Lightnin' must have been stoned, for several times he sang the same song without realizing he had just sung it. But that was fine with me, since growing up in Belfast six thousand miles away in a different culture I had time to make up when it came to live blues.

One of the two men who wrote the liner notes for Bukka White was John Fahey, the ethno-musicologist and guitar player. Fahey had absorbed the work of the great country bluesmen as well as of the classical composers and the Spanish flamenco tradition. From this he developed a unique sound, fully exhibited in a

1967 album that became one of my favourite records: *John Fahey: Volume 2: Death Chants, Breakdowns, & Military Waltzes*. Fahey was a powerful man for the striking titles and he was inclined to go over the top in search of oddity and effect, toppling often into grandiosity. But they were fun and perhaps self-mocking: 'The Downfall of the Adelphi Rolling Grist Mill', 'Dance of the Inhabitants of the Palace of King Phillip XIV', 'Stomping Tonight on the Pennsylvania/ Alabama Border' were some of his tune titles, *Blind Joe Death* and *The Great San Bernardino Birthday Party* two of his album titles.

His musical promiscuity (from Bach to Broonzy) was perhaps part of the ceilingless mood of the time: everything was available for us in the sixties, especially if you worked out of California as Fahey did. Also, Fahey caught in his preoccupation with death something of the apocalyptic tone of life in sixties America. In 'John Henry Variations' and 'Sunflower River Blues' he translated blues guitar work into a new beauty for the times, while 'Stomping Tonight' is a powerful blues baroque. His music is almost a kind of architecture, spacious enough in its various movements to walk about in, though if so then the gothic cathedral is the inspiring structure of his oeuvre. Maybe Blues Postmodernism is a better way of saying this. Anyway, his was great music to get stoned by, and we did.

The first time I took LSD I did not know it, thinking of a sudden that I was drinking the most potent whiskey I had ever drunk. My girlfriend Maren had spiked it: a stupid thing to do but I forgave her. I was high for twenty-four hours and for part of that time the world and everything I looked at in it had elephantiasis and was green. The next morning – there was no sleep of course – I heard from far away the immensely heavy tread of what in the 'real' world was the paper boy, sounding like the approach of the giant coming down the beanstalk to Jack, and the slow-motion thunderous receipt of the paper by my wooden verandah. It was days before I saw the world aright (or awrong). Beside LSD, pot was a breeze, a relaxation, though when we first got it at a drive-in movie we felt laughably like criminals, which of course we were.

It turned out that Maren was a friend of Ken and Fay Kesey and often babysat for them. Kesey had been a UO student, majoring in writing and wrestling (wrestling Mr Hemingway without a doubt), and had then gone to California where he had fallen in with the legendary Neal Cassady (Kerouac's Dean Moriarty, as I knew from Lawrence Lipton's *The Holy Barbarians*) and had inspired a second wave of the Beats, called the Merry Pranksters, the name befitting the streak of infantilism that animated the sixties, the subversive joker element. After the success of *One Flew Over the Cuckoo's Nest* (which I taught frequently in those days, when students were hungry for anti-authoritarianism in the literature class), Kesey had returned to his beloved Eugene, working on *Sometimes a Great Notion* – the title an adaptation of a Leadbelly line – in a rambling farmhouse outside the city limits, with a macaw and a raven, numerous cats and dogs among the menagerie that was his life, and the Merry Pranksters' bus idling psychedelically in his yard.

MARTIN GALE

MORE CHUCK BERRY
CHUCK BERRY

This album was released in 1960; I bought it three years later, coughing up 12/11 as far as I remember. What an investment! It changed my life: my tennis racket became a guitar, my bedroom was a bandstand, and those tricky years of puberty had a soundtrack. It was easy at the age of fourteen and fifteen to identify with the songs here – the wallflower watching 'Sweet Little Rock and Roller', or waiting to pounce on 'Little Queenie':

> *If it's a slow song, we'll omit it,*
> *If it's a rocker, that'll git it.*

Or more likely sharing the burning embarrassment of 'Anthony Boy' still a million miles from breaking his duck:

> *Hey there Anthony boy,*
> *Why you in such a rush,*
> *The girl she want to talk to you,*
> *Look at him how he blush.*

Everything Chuck did seemed tailor-made for teenagers – the unforgettable melodies, scorching guitar solos and superb lyrics and rhymes, all propelled along by a driving beat that made dancing a must. Even though I was incarcerated in a boarding-school when I first heard this record, and light years away from what Chuck was on about, I still instinctively knew about reelin' and rockin' and Carol and Cadillacs. I suppose it came from American TV sitcoms and teen movies, but somehow it all seemed familiar. Of course the music was so good that it has endured way beyond those early years. Chuck Berry opened so many musical doors for me, from R&B and rock'n'roll to blues, rockabilly and even jazz. This album paved the way for everything that was to follow it into my collection.

LIVE AT THE CRAWDADDY CLUB
SONNY BOY WILLIAMSON AND THE YARDBIRDS

In the autumn of 1963 the American Folk and Blues Festival made its first appearance on a big scale in England. Sonny Boy Williamson was the discovery for European audiences that year, even though the tour included such established stars as Muddy Waters, Memphis Slim, Big Joe Williams, Lonnie Johnson, Victoria Spivey and Willie Dixon. On a night off, Sonny Boy was taken to the back room of a London pub to hear a local band play. They were the Yardbirds and a jam session ensued. It was decided to set up a recording session. Some three years later this album was released. It had been recorded before a live audience at the Crawdaddy Club in Richmond – an early stomping ground of the Stones among others. I don't remember where or when I bought it, but it was sometime in 1966. Either way, it was one of my earliest introductions to the blues harp. Quite apart from being a dramatic and expressive harp player, Sonny Boy was also an excellent singer and a prolific songwriter. He played a huge part in introducing European audiences to blues and R&B at the onset of the sixties blues boom. At that time, the Yardbirds – along with the Stones – were one of the most popular R&B bands on the club circuit. For me, the outstanding cuts on the album were a shuffling, urgent version of 'Bye Bye Bird', the brilliant 'Mr Downchild', the slow, aching 'Twenty-three Hours Too Long' and 'Take It Easy, Baby'. But the real surprise was the beautifully understated playing of the Yardbirds' eighteen-year-old lead guitarist – Eric Clapton.

MOSE ALIVE
MOSE ALLISON

Nineteen sixty-six was some year! I was just seventeen and about to leave school and home. Having made a premature departure from boarding-school in late '65, I was living at home, about twenty miles from Dublin, and going to the Blackrock Academy in Lower Mount Street – Willy Martin's. Being a keen LP fan, there were two problems: no money and a dearth of record shops. 'Pop fans' in our area were served by the local TV, radio and electrical shop, specializing in fridges, washing-machines, cookers and toasters, and they also sold a few records as a sideline, mostly singles (I did find a Fats Domino LP there once, but it was a fluke). But getting into Dublin every day meant access to proper record shops. I spent hours standing around in Tara Records , the record department downstairs in Switzers, Pat Egan's and Murrays' record centres. But for someone developing an interest in music other than 'Hit Parade' stuff, life had its frustrations. Although it was surprising how much you could learn standing around reading sleeve notes, RTV Rentals on the corner of Grafton Street and South Anne Street had listening booths – though they did like you to buy something once in a while. Come June, school was over forever and it was away to London, a flat in Chiswick and a succession of bitty jobs. The city was throbbing with life. We went regularly to the Marquee Club, as well as various folk clubs in and around Soho. And the record shops: there were two Dobell's shops in Charing Cross Road, one dealing exclusively in jazz, the other in folk and blues. It was in the latter that I found *Mose Alive*. I had never heard Mose Allison before, but the track listing looked interesting – stuff like Big Joe Williams's 'Baby Please Don't

Go', Willie Dixon's 'Seventh Son' and 'I Love the Life I Live' (I'd heard Georgie Fame's version) as well as Jesse Fuller's 'Fool's Paradise', plus some numbers written by Mose himself, including 'Parchman Farm', which I'd seen John Mayall do in the Marquee Club. Having listened avidly to Ray Charles *Live at Newport*, I had some idea about jazz-blues fusion. I gambled and bought the album. It was, and still is, brilliant. Allison's blistering piano playing and smooth, laid-back singing combine superbly. Unforgettable. At the time of writing, Mose Allison fans are still waiting for this to be re-issued on CD. I'll be buying it.

BRINGING IT ALL BACK HOME
BOB DYLAN

Having bought Dylan's first album on its release and absorbed every syllable, I was a fan from the word go. However, staying with someone as prolific as Dylan was an expensive business, and my pocket was not up to it, so I ended up buying a lot of his stuff retrospectively. But I bought *Bringing It All Back Home* at the time of its release. I'd missed his first Dublin concert in 1965, due to a combination of poverty, youth and parental guidance. But a friend of mine, Brendan Rush, went, and he stunned me the next day by announcing that Dylan had 'gone electric'. The second half of the gig featured an all-electric backing band, drums and all! I was appalled. How could he do that? He had sold out. Imagine what Woody Guthrie would think.

First chance I had I bought the album. What a surprise: it was brilliant, mindbending, all of those things. He was working with other musicans, experimenting, finding new directions, a new way of expressing himself. The eleven songs on the record were each so strong, so devastatingly good, and, as it turns out, ageless. This was an end to the Dylan *v.* Donovan debate. Things had moved on.

For this selection I could have chosen any one of a number of Dylan albums; *Highway 61 Revisited* came close, as did *Blood on the Tracks* and *Oh Mercy*. But *Bringing It All Back Home* evokes one embarrassing memory which really should be outed. It involves the previously mentioned trip to London in '66, and a short (very) career as a busker. I had a cheap guitar and had painstakingly learnt a song, 'She Belongs to Me', from this album. The career was launched in a corridor between platforms in the Tottenham Court Road underground. The corridor was necessary, because with only one song (and some strumming bits), a rapidly changing audience was essential. Play the song, wait five minutes and so on. Grand as long as no one stopped to listen. Actually there were two of us and a half hour later we took early retirement. An interesting by-product of the album was Solomon Burke's grinding, soulful, rocking cover of 'Maggie's Farm'. That warranted further investigation, and what a find he turned out to be.

STICKY FINGERS
THE ROLLING STONES

Since the release of 'Come On' as their first single in '63, my brother and I were fully committed Stones fans. Between us we bought the singles and the LPs and the EPs also. Brilliant as the Beatles were, it was the Stones for us. They had the attitude. They, and the Pretty Things, made sure that the 'generation gap' stayed good and wide. It may be difficult now to imagine them as a teenage band, but the girls screamed at them and the blokes identified with them. Added to their appearance – image was crucial then – the music was dynamite. R&B, rock-'n'roll, some blues; tough and uncompromising. After the relatively disappointing *Their Satanic Majesties Request*, a rather unfocussed stab at psychedelia, the Stones recorded and released *Let it Bleed*, quickly followed by *Beggar's Banquet*, and then came *Sticky Fingers*. It was recorded between 1968 and 1970, and released in 1971. A visit to Muscle Shoals studios yielded three tracks including the great 'Brown Sugar'. Obviously revitalized and using extra musicans, they produced a record that was their most successful to date, both critically and in terms of popularity. I was studying at the National College of Art in Dublin at the time, and *Sticky Fingers* provided a pretty good soundtrack to the way we were living. A great party album, with tracks like 'Brown Sugar', 'Wild Horses' and 'Sway', not to mention the seedy glamour of 'Sister Morphine' and 'Dead Flowers' – perfect for cruising the kitchen later, looking for dregs and butts. Not forgetting their blues roots, the Stones included a Fred McDowell/Rev. Gary Davis song, 'You Gotta Move' – a real throw-your-head-back-and-bawl-along number. The problem was whether to choose this or *Exile on Main Street*. I went for *Sticky Fingers* because it was so good it made me go out and buy *Exile* the minute it came out. And what a cracker that was.

ST DOMINIC'S PREVIEW
VAN MORRISON

For some reason I had managed to miss out on the *Astral Weeks* phenomenon when it happened. So *St Dominic's Preview* was my first serious brush with Van Morrison since his days with Them. Being an art student at the time of its release, money was extremely short, but I had heard someone else's copy and it was obvious a sacrifice would have to be made. From the opening hand claps and scat singing of 'Jackie Wilson Said' through to the awesome 'Almost Independence Day', Van doesn't put a foot wrong. Great songs, great singing, brilliant arrangements and playing. For me, there are three standout tracks that rank with the very best he has done; the title track, which contains the evocative line 'for every Hank Williams railroad train that cries'; 'Listen to the Lion'; and 'Almost Independence Day', which I once saw described as 'cinema for the blind'. It would be pointless to even try to describe this track, just to say the addition of a Moog brings a whole different dimension to the song; beautifully incorporated into the arrangement, it is never allowed to dominate Van's own twelve-string guitar, but is used for subtle background colouring. Van's singing throughout the whole album is up there with the very best white soul singing.

MEDDLE
PINK FLOYD

I can hardly believe that I am including this in my selection. But it has its place, having once entered the bloodstream, along with God knows what else! I suppose most music fans at that time (1967-70) had some kind of a brush with psychedelia. It may have come late to me, but come it certainly did. Many a nighttime excursion to the stratosphere was orchestrated by these chaps. I am surprised, listening to it now, how short the album is; it seemed to go on for hours in those days. What makes it stand out from similar records of that period and genre is the quality of the playing, and indeed of the songs – especially on side one. Side two is all one track, 'Echoes', and here things could get tricky. A bit of a white-knuckle ride under some circumstances. *Meddle* is perhaps not as well remembered as some of Pink Floyd's other works, but is free of bombast and the usual guitar slaughter at the end.

REFLECTIONS IN BLUE
BOBBY 'BLUE' BLAND

One of the all-time greatest singers to emerge from American popular music, Bobby Bland is peerless in the blues-soul-ballad department. Elvis Presley at his best was in the same league, but few others. I bought this having read a Bill Graham review in *Hot Press*, and for the next two years it hardly left my turntable. By now I was living in County Wicklow with my wife and two children, and life was a lot more orderly than it had been. My painting was beginning to come right, I was attached to a good gallery and my work was starting to sell well. Thus I always associate this album with a positive, upbeat period, even though Bobby Bland was wrestling with demons in nearly every song. He purrs, growls and storms his way through nine titles here, with not a dud among them, a feeling of progressively rising anger and frustration growing from track to track. A real tour de force of blues, soul and gospel influences.

LITTLE CRIMINALS
RANDY NEWMAN

Having always had a leaning towards singer-songwriters cum storytellers, it is very difficult to pick one of particular significance. Country music is full of them of course, with Johnny Cash, George Jones, Lefty Frizzell, Joe Ely, Jimmy Dale Gilmore, Merle Haggard and John Prine all possible choices. Similarly Bruce Springsteen, Tom Waits, Tony Joe White and Dave Alvin (King of California). However, I've gone for Randy Newman and *Little Criminals* because two major events happened during the time I was listening to it regularly. The first was the birth of my daughter Rebecca, and although the record was released a year later, in 1977, I associate it with that time, which was very happy. The second was the death of my father, which was devastating. Each song is like a complete little movie in itself, built on the framework of Newman's understanding of the human condition. He creates songs that are, in some instances, haunting and moving, and at other times quirky and humorous. Among the former would be the touching 'Texas Girl at the Funeral of Her Father' and 'In Germany Before the War'; the latter category includes 'Jolly Coppers on Parade' and 'Riders in the Rain'. Musically it is everything you would expect from Randy Newman – beautiful, surprising, quirky and intelligent.

THIS YEAR'S MODEL
ELVIS COSTELLO AND THE ATTRACTIONS

Well I heard the news ... two bits of news actually, in August 1977. The first was that Elvis Presley was dead at forty-two. The second was the arrival of Elvis Costello. It was while reading about Presley's death in the NME that I came across a small feature concerning the other Elvis. In the interview he sounded like a narky bugger with a lot of attitude – and the review of his first album, My Aim is True, sounded intriguing. So I bought the album. It was raw, raucous, snappy and belligerent as hell. It's worth mentioning that punk had passed me by, probably because I was ten years too old, and most of the bands involved had built their reputations and following on live performances rather than on recordings. Where I was living, I was well outside punk's catchment area. Hippies of varying degrees and vintages were the norm in our neck of the woods. Then Elvis and the Attractions played the Stella Cinema in Rathmines, and we went along. What a gig. Micky Jupp opened proceedings with some excellent no-nonsense Southend rock'n'roll. But Elvis, he was a different animal. He looked like a demented stick-insect and the band never took their foot off the throttle all night. They played most of My Aim is True, but, already well ahead of the posse, they played the whole of This Year's Model, their soon-to-be-released second album. I bought it the minute it came out. It was the first set of recordings that Elvis Costello had made with the Attractions. It sounded as if most of the songs had been put down in one or two takes; immediate, fresh, but still cohesive. A touring band caught in full flight. Actually it sounded like an old beat group LP, open and accessible, quite the opposite of the over-produced, self-indulgent posturings of a lot of major rock bands at the time. I've stuck with Elvis Costello ever since. There have been many highlights, Get Happy, Almost Blue, Trust, King of America, Imperial Bedroom and latterly Brutal Youth and Kojak Variety. But, while My Aim is True lit the fuse, This Year's Model is where Elvis Costello and the Attractions really caught fire.

CARLO GÉBLER

It was 1959; I was five; we were living in the grim suburb of Morden, London, which lies at the end of the Northern Line.

There was a tallboy in my father's study with a drop lid which flapped down to reveal a Ferguson Radiogram system; the gramophone arm was ivory-coloured Bakelite, and the turntable was dull aluminium with a plum-coloured vermiculated rubber cover. My father's records were thick and black and he never played one without first giving it a loving clean. He used a velvet cylinder filled with distilled water; when wet it attracted dirt to itself. My father's musical diet was a strict mix of classical and folk, Gustav Mahler and Woody Guthrie, Sibelius and Pete Seeger. We did not go to church, and perhaps as a replacement for this missing spiritual dimension we often came downstairs on Sunday morning to a heady blast of Beethoven's Ninth or some Delius.

Musically I was asleep; then, one day, I was standing by the stove in the kitchen, watching a wisp of blue-black smoke squeezing from the chimney pipe and curling through the air. At the same time I was rubbing my nose because the anthracite which we burnt was making the nasal passages itch as usual. That was when I heard it: the radio was on in the study and it was blasting out the fifties classic from Bill Haley and his Comets – 'Rock Around the Clock'.

My father was out. He wouldn't have tolerated this. We had a nanny called Sally and perhaps she had turned it on. She sometimes listened to Radio Éireann when she did the housework. Or perhaps it was my mother. But I didn't go through to find out. I couldn't. I was literally rooted to the spot, amazed by the power of what I was hearing. I knew this was a moment I was never going to forget. I didn't, and years later, it still being with me, I bought *Rock Around the Clock*, the LP. It has a brilliant cover of alarm clocks and other horological objects arranged on a garish red background. It's almost punk.

Musically, *Rock Around the Clock* is crude if vigorous, yet it still does sterling service as an ersatz Proustian madeleine, a memory recall device. It's good; it makes me move; and like all the records I remember from boyhood and adolescence, the key to longevity isn't just the memories it evokes; the albums have to be good in their own right, or at the very least they must give pleasure.

AFTERMATH
THE ROLLING STONES

In the middle of the Morden period my parents separated; my mother moved to Putney and I followed some years later. We lived in Deodar Road, named after the Australian tree famed for its fragrance. It was a street of three-storey houses, built for clerks in the 1860s and colonized by artists in the sixties on account of the view; all the gardens on our side of the street gave directly onto Old Father Thames. The Australian painter Sidney Nolan was a neighbour, although in several years of living there I never once saw him.

Walking back from Putney High Street one day, clutching an Airfix model of the *Tirpitz* or the ill-fated HMS *Hood* – it is 1966 and I am twelve – I bumped into David Evans, an older boy of whom I was somewhat in awe. He wore his hair long and shaggy, like Reg Presley of the Troggs (who had a huge hit at the time with 'Wild Thing'). Dave also wore winkle-pickers. He was definitely cool. Dave was carrying a bag – Woolworths, Golden Discs? – I can't remember, so much detail is lost.

We went into his house. He produced an LP from the bag. This had cost many shillings. I was impressed. The front of the record was purple and had a photograph of five men; they had long hair and were staring up into the lens of a camera in the same cheeky way that some of the boys would look up the skirts or down the blouses of the women teachers at school. The Stones looked dodgy to me; appalling but also enthralling.

Silently and reverently, Dave eased out the white inner sleeve that was stamped with important advice, 'Take good care of your microgroove records .... Use "Emitex" cleaning cloth to preserve your microgroove records ...' then freed the record and wiggled it lovingly onto the spindle of his mother's Dansette portable gramophone.

Next he lifted across the arm with the magnet which held the record tight and clicked the mechanism; the record dropped and the guitar cha-cha-cha warbled from the speaker and the hairs on my neck, for the first time in my life, really did stand up as Jagger launched into 'Mother's Little Helper':

> *Things are different today,*
> *I hear every mother say,*
> *The pursuit of happiness is such a drag ...*

A defining moment this, separating childhood from whatever it was that followed, though it was years before I understood this.

It was also years before I really appreciated the neck of Mick and the lads, starting their first entirely original album (until *Aftermath* they'd done a lot of covers) with a song which ridiculed valium and other domestic drugs, when they themselves were not exactly strangers to narcotics.

REVOLVER
THE BEATLES

In 1967 I was sent to a school run on the child-centered principles established by Friedrich Froebel, the liberal educationalist. It was mixed and the girls wore lovely green seersucker frocks and lovely grey straw bonnets. I was becoming interested in sex.

Fanny Sturridge was a willowy Jewish girl with brown eyes and white teeth. She was in the year above but that didn't put me off; dog-like, I followed her about, every breaktime and every afternoon when she was always to be found on the netball pitch. She was school captain. She only spoke to me once and that was to tell me that she was in love with Micky Dolenz from the Monkees. All the girls in the school were in love with someone from that damned group.

One day I noticed Fanny and some other girls gathered in a knot around the lockers. They were peering at a record decorated with four Beardsleyesque line drawings and deciding who in the Monkees were the equivalents of those depicted in the pen-and-ink drawings on the cover of this record; somebody called Ringo I gathered was Tork; McCartney was Jones; Lennon was Micky Dolenz; and George Harrison was Nesmith.

The bell rang and the girls vanished. I sneaked a look in the locker. The record was something called *Revolver* by the Beatles.

I formed a plan. I would buy my own copy and bring it to school; Fanny would see me carrying it around and this would prompt a conversation; thus would begin our courtship.

I bought the record but I don't remember if I took it to school; I certainly know I never talked to Fanny. But what did this matter? *Revolver*, from the first bar of 'Taxman' to the last bar of 'Tomorrow Never Knows', via 'Yellow Submarine' (mad, I thought, but brilliant) and 'Good Day Sunshine' (orgasmic, I thought, a word which I could certainly find in the dictionary then but had yet to understand), was incomparably superior to anything by the Monkees (damn them). How could Fanny and the other girls even compare the Beatles with those fresh-faced preppies who had brought us 'Last Train to Clarksville' and 'Daydream Believer'?

Unsuccessful in love, I had become a budding rock snob. If you can't get the girl, it's the next best thing, or so I thought.

FRESH CREAM
CREAM

A year later I was at a West London comprehensive school. One lunchtime I sneaked down the alleyway at the side where the skinheads lurked and the dope-heads organized their one-pound deals – and made my way to a chipper in one of the streets off Holland Park Avenue.

Here I ran into Archimedes, a Greek-Cypriot and an incredibly stylish dresser. He was wearing a red Victorian soldier's tunic (unlike the rest of us he managed to get away with wearing whatever he wanted at school) and carrying his books in an army surplus cartridge-bag on which he had scrawled in biro the names of his favourite bands. I noticed a new one – Cream.

'What d'ya make of them?' he asked.

Somehow, thirteen years of age and I hadn't heard of them. But I was smart. I kept my mouth shut; peasant reticence was already an established pattern. Without my knowing, I had passed a test. Archimedes invited me to his next party.

Saturday night saw me in a street of crumbling stucco houses at the top end of Portobello Road. I had showered in anticipation of meeting a member of the opposite sex and my hair was still wet. Approaching the Stephenides residence I could smell marijuana; I could see red light leaking from the windows (obviously all the light bulbs inside had been changed to red ones to facilitate snogging); and I could hear 'I'm So Glad'.

Naturally – but how could it have been otherwise? – I now became a Cream fan. And although *Disraeli Gears* was an incomparably better LP – after all, it included 'Strange Brew' and 'Sunshine of Your Love' – *Fresh Cream*, since it was the means by which I discovered them, will always hold a special place in my affections.

SANTANA: ABRAXAS
SANTANA

BOOKENDS
SIMON & GARFUNKEL

THE PROGRESSIVE BLUES EXPERIMENT
JOHNNY WINTER

In 1970 I went to co-ed boarding-school, and one afternoon a Canadian boy in my dormitory said, 'I'm going to London. Do you want to score with me?'

The system in the school was that we boys and girls banked our money with the house masters and mistresses. I went to mine and asked to withdraw a pound, or perhaps two.

'That's rather a lot, Carlo,' he lisped, but he still let me have the money. The school was not just mixed, it was progressive.

Freddie the Canadian took the cash and went up to London. He came back that evening. In the toilets he showed me what he had; a block of brown cannabis resin and a tiny oily pearl of opium.

We agreed to wait until the end-of-term dance. I was to look after our stash. I put it in an empty Cherry Blossom shoe-polish tin which I then hid behind the wainscoting in my dormitory.

The end of term came. The dance started at seven. At nine o'clock Freddie and I slipped out, made our way to the open-air swimming pool and climbed over the fence, the music from the dance booming behind us; it would be the soundtrack for the scene that followed.

In a changing cubicle we chased the dragon with the opium, then smoked an untidy joint made with Golden Virginia and a kingsize Rizla paper. I think the tobacco probably had a far greater effect on us than either of the narcotics. Not that we'd have known.

The sky above was bright with stars, our heads were swimming and in the school dining-room where the dance was continuing, we could hear they were playing (from *Santana: Abraxas* – an album with a painting on the cover of a naked woman and a strategically placed dove – it had made quite an impression on us boys) 'Black Magic Woman/Gypsy Queen'. It was the perfect music for two stoned sixteen-year-olds.

But then we heard footfalls. Somebody was approaching on the other side of the fence. Oh fuck! Now they'd got to the gate. The chain was rattling. It was Philip Harding, had to be, the German master. He was on duty; he was always on duty when there was a school dance and he had a unique talent for ferreting out boys and girls when they were doing naughty things.

Freddie and I got up onto the slatted seat, anxious lest Mr Harding should see our feet below the swing door of the cubicle, and sat in silence, our hearts thumping.

Meanwhile, in the distance the soundtrack changed to 'Mrs Robinson', the Simon and Garfunkel song from *Bookends* but better known because of *The Graduate*. It was a nasty, sinister song, I'd always thought (although I loved the album – particularly track five on side one – a recording by Garfunkel of old people talking and mumbling), and so entirely appropriate. We were fucking dead. In a matter of moments, Mr Harding would be outside the cubicle. He would call us out. We would step forward into the beam of his torch, blinking, and we would hear him say, 'Boys, you've been smoking. Now don't insult me with a lie, tell me the truth.'

Time passed, excruciatingly slowly. All tensed up, we were waiting for Mr Harding's polished brogues to clip along the concrete poolside towards us. But instead we heard – no, it was so inconceivable it was unthinkable – no, it really was, it was girlish laughter. Carefully, quietly, we put our heads over the parapet of the cubicle door and saw that indeed our ears had not deceived us; it was Maeve McHenry, Masie Baring and Emily Ferguson, and they were skinny-dipping, the whole scene lit by moonlight ...

We sat back on the bench, relieved, delighted, and when the girls had dressed and left, we smoked a second joint.

Now the music booming from the dance was 'Rollin' and Tumblin'', the first cut on Johnny Winter's *The Progressive Blues Experiment*, hard, driving, blues-rock.

Head swimming, I looked up at the huge moon hanging in the sky and imagined it was a hole cut in the cloth backdrop of an enormous stage and that if I crawled through I would find myself in another universe ...

Sex (or something on the way to it) and drugs and rock'n'roll had all come together in one glorious moment. I don't think I'd ever been so happy.

THE SONGS OF LEONARD COHEN
LEONARD COHEN

I went to university in 1973, and in the second term I was paired for tutorials with Jane. Jane was blue-eyed, blonde-haired, and spoke with a burr in her voice. Jane was Cornish. Jane wore long vaguely medieval dresses and an ankle bracelet with bells. Tuesdays were our day. Two o'clock sharp we would fetch into Wentworth College for our tutorial on the literature of the Augustan period with Mr Durwood, then every Tuesday evening we would sit in her college room, ostensibly for the purpose of a post mortem on Pope or Dryden or whoever we'd 'done' that afternoon, but in truth to talk, drink and take narcotics.

Jane liked her music melancholy: Joni Mitchell, John Prine and Johnny Cash, but the greatest star in the musical firmament as far as she was concerned was Leonard Cohen, or 'ole lugubrious of Montreal' as we jestingly called him. (Humour was not our strong point.) One image encapsulates the experience: the curtains are closed; Jane is sitting on the bed, turning the bracelet on her ankle and tinkling the bells; I am sitting on the floor, the album sleeve *The Songs of Leonard Cohen* between my knees with its sepia photograph of melancholy Leonard staring up at me; I am cutting the speed on Jane's mirror or crumbling hash into a pipe; and meanwhile, the pained voice croaking from the speaker sings of Suzanne, tea and oranges, her place by the river ...

I was in love with Jane, and I entertained the ridiculous idea that Leonard Cohen (whom I had grown to love because Jane loved him) would help create a mood conducive to sex. It never happened, of course it never happened. We just snorted and smoked, and talked and talked and talked until four o'clock in the morning, at which point I would say my goodbyes and stagger back to my room and fall into an amphetamine haze to the half-remembered words of 'The Sisters of Mercy' or 'Hey, That's No Way to Say Goodbye'.

It's a cliché of course – an unfulfilled student relationship with Leonard Cohen droning in the background – but that didn't make it any less real when it happened. And I really liked the music too. Still do.

TUBULAR BELLS
MIKE OLDFIELD

I met Fiona at a fancy-dress party. (I was in tails; she was in a Biba nightdress, furry slippers and curlers – this was the seventies.) We started living in a flat together above a hairdresser's. Everything tasted of lacquer; it even got into the toothpaste. The landlord belonged to a fringe religion and several of his relatives were buried in the garden.

I was in my first adult relationship and I did what I thought then was the adult thing: hugely embarrassing though this is to admit, I bought a copy of *Tubular Bells*. Yes, it was superficial musically but it was also sweet and engaging and it seemed new; we came to love it; we smoked dope to it; we made love to it. Sex and drugs and rock'n'roll had finally fused.

PRETZEL LOGIC
STEELY DAN

Money was tight at college and I used to frequent the local Book and Record Exchange buying and selling textbooks.

One day when I was in there, a record sleeve caught my eye; it had on it a picture of a monkey-faced street vendor in the middle of some heartless American city. I shouldn't have, but I bought the record on the strength of the picture. I wasn't disappointed. I thought *Pretzel Logic* was magnificent, and it rose even higher in my estimation when someone pointed out that Steely Dan's version of the Duke Ellington standard 'East St Louis Toodle-O' (which ends side one), quotes directly from Mozart's *Requiem*.

Here was rock (or a part of it) doing the same sort of thing as the literature I was reading: quoting others, celebrating a tradition. The downside to this realization was that I now bored more easily; glam and stadium rock, Slade and Cockney Rebel, they just didn't interest me. Too much attitude, not enough content. In that sense *Pretzel Logic* was another demarcation line, for after it I stopped buying records.

THE SUN SESSIONS
ELVIS PRESLEY

In 1980, six recordless years after the above, I happened to be watching a bio-pic of the life of Elvis Presley on television one evening. I'd tuned in because it promised never-seen-before footage of the King pre-'Colonel' Tom Parker; Elvis before his sideburns were shaved and his pelvic movements curtailed; Elvis, in other words, before he became the syrupy balladeer I knew from *Live in Las Vegas*.

To say that I was not disappointed is an understatement; the footage of Elvis singing 'That's all Right (Mama)' on an open-air stage at (I think) a high school prom somewhere in the Deep South inspired something like the same excitement as 'Rock Around the Clock' had inspired thirty years earlier, only this music had buckets more guts and sex than the goodtime rock of Bill Haley.

The next day I went straight out and got hold of the *The Sun Sessions*. It not only had 'It's All Right (Mama)' but also 'Blue Moon', 'Mystery Train' and lots of others. Wow! From this I started listening to the music of the 1950s, the Everly Brothers and Buddy Holly, Chuck Berry and Bo Diddley. This in turn led to punk and suddenly I was buying and listening to records again.

I'M YOUR MAN
LEONARD COHEN

When I drove to Northern Ireland (where I was coming to live) in 1989, Leonard Cohen's *I'm Your Man* was the soundtrack for the journey.

This brilliant work is out of the period and yet at the same time it's not; firstly, Cohen is a sixties figure; secondly, he has not only survived, he has matured; and thirdly, he is supremely eloquent on why it all ended. It wasn't the events in Paris in 1968, or the Grosvenor Square riots, or Altamont, or consumer capitalism, or Richard Nixon, or the Vietnam War, or the 1972 UK Abortion Act; it was selfishness, the old Adam in us all. This is the rock on which every system founders, left and right, anarchist and conservative, ideological, non-ideological, straight and alternative. The sixties are over – but the songs were good!

KATHY GILFILLAN

THERE'S A TOM STOPPARD PLAY called *The Real Thing* with a character, Henry, who's been asked to appear on *Desert Island Discs*. His favourite records are all pop songs but not the kind of pop it's hip to like. Henry likes the Monkees and Wayne Fontana and the Mindbenders doing 'Um Um Um Um Um Um' so he wants to spin a few Beethoven or Bach lies. By the end of the play, however, he's regained his senses and the Righteous Brothers are loving-feeling it up on his desert island. The point is, it's better to be true to yourself than to invent a cool persona, so I'd better say right away that you're dealing here with someone who bought, as her first single ever, the tragically unhip 'Tell Laura I Love Her' by Ritchie Valens. The first single you buy is a crucial matter because it's your own money – albums were given to you as birthday presents. Imagine then my delight, imagine the shiver of excitement, when having carried home 'Tell Laura I Love Her', there was an announcement on *The Six O'Clock News* that 'Tell Laura I Love Her' had been banned in Britain in case it might encourage teenagers to risk their lives stock-car racing to buy their girlfriends diamond rings. WOW. Forget *Natural Born Killers* and its spawn of copycat killers; to me at nine years old, just to hold 'Tell Laura I Love Her' seemed to be flirting with death.

No matter what anyone over forty claims, pop and rock music affect you in a totally different way when you are young. I still listen to contemporary music all the time because I am artificially exposed to it – it is the world my husband works in – but I am detached from it; I no longer have the complete absorption in the music that I had. It is not life and death anymore. Rock music is erratically individual. Everyone agrees that Beethoven, Wagner, Bach have genius; we feel small, flooded by the sound of all that skill, but this kind of admiration always has a barrier. Genius versus ordinary human being. We are not worthy. We are not worthy.

Great rock music is great because you believe that you alone may have discovered it. We take possession of it because it has taken possession of us. The words of the song tell us that someone understands, someone thinks the same, someone shares that feeling. There's no angst like teen angst. Not many forty-year-olds continue to feel this way and if they do, they may have a problem that music cannot solve.

Rock music lyrics don't bear fierce examination. They may sing like poetry, but Bruce Springsteen's songs about the profound anxiety of young freedom in back streets and the back seats of cars don't travel from the musical performance to the bare page. 'Barefoot girl sitting on the hood of a Dodge/Drinking warm beer in the soft summer rain' from his 'Jungleland' means a lot because it time-machines me back to the summer of 1976 when the accidental magic of *Born to Run* bumped into me. Chris Meehan had this album and was carrying it around with him, the way you did, to spread the good news. I grew up on the edge of a wild moor so even the suburbs looked glamorous to me – certainly it was a long way from Tenth Avenue or Jungleland – and here was this cool wraith singing songs about the slamming of screen doors, burnt-out Chevrolets and escape from small-town America. I longed to go to America, any kind of America, small town or big city, but if I couldn't go I could experience it through music.

Essentially the music is about nostalgia and memory. I cannot hear any of these albums without remembering the precise time in my life when they were vital. Sometimes this alchemy loses its potency. I lived in a flat in 1971 where we played the same album every day for two weeks – John Lennon's *Imagine*. As soon as it finished, it was taken off and put right back on the turntable. Consequently I can't stand to listen to it anymore. It's not on my list of ten, proving that memory and repetition don't always work together.

I think it's important that all ten albums – and I have them here in front of me – are big, fat vinyls; the tactile aspect of examining the sleeve, poring over the lyrics, handing them around, was so much part of the appeal. Some people even rolled funny cigarettes on them. And the more you played the album, the more the sound quality was abused, but did that matter? Hell no, it was part of the appeal; those scratches were the initiation rites of the LP. The neat, boxy little CD just doesn't put out like that.

Mick Jagger was the ultimate in cool and still is. At fifteen you had to choose between the Beatles and the Stones. I chose the Stones because they were dangerous and my parents approved of the Beatles, a death knell if there ever was one. *Exile on Main Street* is the Stones album I would save if the house burned down.

There has to be a U2 album, has to be. I picked *Boy* because it was the first and the threshold of everything. It was a thrill to see those eyes on the cover staring from record shops all over the world.

Talking Heads were almost contemporaries of the early U2. In 1981 U2 were recording an EP, *Fire* at Compass Point Studios in the Bahamas. I played *Remain in Light* by the Talking Heads all through that stay. I took the title *Remain in Light* quite literally because we were staying in a white house wide open to the Bahamian sun and bright light bounced around the white walls while David Byrne sang, 'And you may find yourself in a beautiful house, with a beautiful wife/ And you may ask yourself, Well how did I get here?' Quite. I had gone to sleep and woken up in Paradise.

Jimmy Cliff is on my list too because I fell in love with reggae in the eighties. Again it had to do with light, sun and tropical heat. Chris Blackwell is the

Magus of Jamaica and his life was devoted, in the early days, to the promotion of Jamaica's reggae artists. I was an easy convert because I love to dance and it's hard to sit still when you hear reggae. It's all about motion.

In order, then, here are my desert-island discs:

Harvest	Neil Young
The Pretenders	The Pretenders
Born to Run	Bruce Springsteen
Accept No Substitute	Delaney & Bonnie
Cream of Al Green	Al Green
Boy	U2
The Harder They Come	Jimmy Cliff
Exile on Main Street	The Rolling Stones
Remain in Light	The Talking Heads
Sweet Dreams	Eurythmics

ELGY GILLESPIE

TEN MOMENTS MUSICAL, intense enough to be felt keenly. I'm telling you them, children, because now that we've grown old disgracefully, I want you to know how it was to be alive and a teenager in the far-off days they call the Real Sixties. Yes, we made our own amusements then. We listened to these vinyl things called records or albums.

Hearken unto me, my pretties. We put big round 33 r.p.m. records on a red-and-beige plastic thing called a turntable, and, if we really liked an album, we pulled the arm up so it repeated and repeated if we were stoned. And we rolled our own too – joints, I mean, with Job cigarette papers. We didn't need virtual reality because we had our own reality. We didn't need Prozac, kids, because we enjoyed being depressed and crying. We didn't expect to be happy. Pain was life.

THE BEATLES
THE BEATLES

The other day I picked up the phone to find my old friend Harry at the other end in New York. As I heard him say 'Elge?' the vision swung inside my head of Har, wading thigh-deep into an icy river in Provence so that he could bring me a glass of water at midnight on New Year's Eve twelve years ago. I flicked through a few memorable frames, disgraceful and otherwise. We relived the joint fortieth birthday supper with his friend Kev in Montreal, when we played the Beatles all night rather than his McGarrigles or Jean Cabral. Although French-Canadian by choice and upbringing, Har and Kev have Scots and Irish roots; and despite the fact we only shared one year in Paris and live in three cities, we've stayed in touch across continents and time.

So as I talked to Har three thousands miles away, the White Album began to play in my head. Time collapsed, and once again I slid wheeee down the time tunnel all the way back to the late sixties: a musical cue that brought whole tastes, flavours, moods, smells, so near I could touch them. Memory tries to be linear, but not music.

'I'm working on the theory that we are aurally susceptible, all us lank-haired oldies,' I propounded, as I reminded Har of those steaks we took back to the Rue Jeanne Mance and seared in brandy; the four bottles of Merlot, the three joints, their friends Ariane and Françoise – and the five of us singing the entire White Album from start to finish. 'Blackbird singing in the dead of night/ You were only waiting for this moment to arrive,' we sang, word perfect. 'Blackbird fly! Into the arms of the long dark night …'

Abbey Road next: 'And in the end, the love you take, is equal to the love you make … Aa-ah-ah-ah-ahhh!' Not that we would have replied 'the Beatles!' if someone asked us our main musical influence during puberty. That would be like saying our mother was our main influence in utero. My parents, in fact, went to Christmas Beatles concerts and bought their albums for us. Asking if you were a John-girl or a Paul-girl is still a meaningful debate, probably more so than Stones versus Beatles. But back to dear old Har on the line to New York.

'Orally susceptible?' riposted Har with his characteristicaly high insane eunuch's giggle – a Canadian eunuch's giggle. 'I'll say. Orally susceptible, that's us! Heh-heh-heh-heh!' 'Oh Har,' I rebuked.

Har is a respectable father now and a Wall Street journalist for *The Independent*, younger than me and Kev who have the same birthdays and birth year: not yet forty. His woman is an exceptionally talented New York film-maker, while Kev's is a feminist talk-show host in Quebec. Kev, Har and I once made the three points of a triangle that refused to collapse for the longest time. In other words, we were the Three Stooges – would be still if we lived in the same city, maybe.

'No, you dopehead,' I pounded on. 'Not o-r-ally susceptible. A-u-r-ally.' I meant that by contrast with the anal, computer-taught MTV twentyish kids I work with now, we're more musically susceptible than visually imaginative. Those musical buttons that collapse time and linear thought for us and take us home to our precious memories are all on riffs. '… like Clapton and Winwood on "Can't Find My Way Home" or Clapton and Bruce on the John Mayall album we played when we were all on our first three chords.' Though maybe Har had a point with 'orally susceptible'. We were to be, after all, the generation that discovered the mixed blessings of oral sex and all that that entails …

BLUESBREAKERS
JOHN MAYALL WITH ERIC CLAPTON

BLIND FAITH
BLIND FAITH

As I started to hum 'I'm so-o-o tired…' a vision of Ginger Baker leering at my sixteen-year-old self at some gig flashed by (you had only to look at the infamous cover of *Blind Faith* to figure they liked 'em young). Then that Cream bass-riff kicked in, the one all journeymen Fender benders or Les Paul guitar students learn with – you know, da-da da da boom boom ta-dah-dah da – and punched me straight back to nubility, socked me into my red Biba mini-dress with ironed long blonde hair and black eyeliner and Anello and Davide two-tone button shoes. I was a self-punishing, miserable teen, but music was my salvation.

Put in chronological sequence, the coming-of-age anthology does seem to start with the Beatles, though we were listening to Chuck Berry even as we painstakingly saved up six shillings and eleven pence for 'Love Me Do'. 'Long distance information, get in touch with my Marie! She's the only one who calls me here in Memphis, Tennessee,' I sang to our family dog Baskerville while together we lay on our tummies watching the yellow Pye label go around with the arm up. It was 1963 and I was thirteen and had not yet acquired me a miniskirt or smelt the evocative smell of marijuana, later to become so familiar.

CHUCK BERRY
GOLDEN HITS

SMOKEY ROBINSON AND THE MIRACLES
GREATEST HITS

'I don't like you, but I love you/Seems like I'm always thinking of you/Whoa-whoa-whoa you treat me badly; I love you madly/You've really got a hold on me...'

Around puberty too, I found Radio Luxembourg and *Ready, Steady, Go!* and Tamla Motown – at 1.15 a.m. every morning there were three Tamla tracks under the bedclothes: Little Stevie playing 'Fingertips Part Two', the Miracles with Smokey Robinson singing 'Shop Around' or Marvin Gaye with 'Can I Get A Witness' and Martha and the Vandellas singing 'Heatwave'. By fourteen, I was addicted.

What I loved, what I so immediately loved about Tamla Motown, was the way the raw, garage voices just completely sidetracked thought. Sound just poured straight into my veins in the form of undiluted, neat passion and though there were words, they were hardly the important thing. 'Whenever I'm with Bill/ Something inside/Seems to burn me ...' sang Martha Reeves, but Bill wasn't the point. Of course the words were silly and no-count. The point was the sound, and the immediate accessing of this vivid, exotic lifeforce, this rejection of all that was boring, repressed. Remember Joey in *The Commitments*, brothers.

SONGS IN THE KEY OF LIFE
STEVIE WONDER

'You can feel it all over/ You can feel it all over...'

I never lost my passion for Little Stevie and indeed I still play Marvin Gaye and still have to get up and dance whenever I hear the Sir Duke riff banging out: Ta, da da-da dee! Da, da, da, da, tadara dee! But though this led ultimately to Ray Charles, Bessie Smith, Robert Johnson, Billie Holiday, Ella and Louis, Nina Simone and the general conviction that black was what us repressed, pallid honkies should strive for in terms of direct emotional energy and fabulousness, it never stopped deathly pale me from trying to get into a rock band any more than Joey 'the Lips'. It actually came as a shock to discover that white Americans weren't into them and I was unaccountably white too.

WHAT'D I SAY
RAY CHARLES

Like everybody else in the sixties, we lived for the weeklies *Melody Maker* and *New Musical Express*, and starting up bands was our reason for living. My brother Richie and boyfriend George O'Brien actually succeeded, too (Rich sessioned with Joe Cocker and his schoolmate Paul Allen, now dead, with Osibisa. And George, well, George will tell you about George). We haunted the Marquee, Finsbury Astoria, Hammersmith Palais, Hundreds Club, the UFO club, open-air Stones and Cream concerts in Hyde Park, wherever. Open-air fests coated our sleeping-bags with mud and gave us colds. We were never in bed before 6 a.m. In winter I hardly ever saw daylight.

We had a piano on which I'd learned to Grade Eight (I sang in a church choir and played the organ). While my brother sessioned on his Fender and George banged his drums, I dreamt of playing my own Hammond like Georgie Fame, Nina Simone and Alan Price, the consummate and tasty musicians whom I knew to be influenced by Jimmy Smith and Ray Charles (oh, those Raylettes). Ray Charles was better known in France on the French labels than in London, and I took to him while staying with my pen-pal. 'Hey mama don't you treat me wrong ...' I sang for what I fondly imagined was a thumping, thudding little piano left-hand, before switching to descant for the Raylettes' three-part echo. 'Come and love your daddy all night long. Tell me what'd I say!' I would screech. Harmonies, two basses and a Hammond were all I dreamt about.

THE IMMORTAL OTIS REDDING
OTIS REDDING

'She may get weary/Young girls do get weary/Wearing that same shabby dress ...' Later, we encountered that wall of saxes Otis Redding used to bring in on tracks like 'Try A Little Tenderness' that wowed us so, a grand blow-the-roof-off-the-dump slab of saxophones that got picked up by people like James Brown and the Famous Flames. By that stage – late sixties, I suppose – I was finding it hard to listen to anyone white, with the possible exception of Van the Man in 'Chlorine Gardens'. I would no more have gone to Woodstock to get back to the garden than I would go to see Traffic now (Stevie, have you no shame at all?) though I confess to a soft spot for the Incredible String Band – they were much loved in Dublin's Liberty Hall around 1968 and Robin Williamson's 'First Girl I Loved' and 'Waltz Of The New Moon' are lovely songs, reminiscent of George – and later, for Joni Mitchell (*Blue* and 'Free Man In Paris' is her at her best).

When I turned eighteen and moved from Swingin' London to Boozin' Dublin, everyone there got into Dylan, dope and Janis, thanks to our fellow Trinity College student Dan Shine: epitome of New York hip. There was the time Nina Simone came to sing in the Boxing Stadium. She looked a bit stunned when she walked into the ring; but the great warmth of our response for 'I Put a Spell on You' and 'Mississippi Goddam' won her over. I loved Chris

Meehan and his self-penned 'On a Monday Morning'. Dylan was too white for me but I dug his Band and played *Music from Big Pink* unto baldness in Herbert Place. There was the Cuban summer, when I learnt to love Hispanic sounds and fell for Conjunto Rumbavana (oh, mambo!) and a New York summer, courtesy of USIT. Instead of Woodstock, my sister Sonny and I went to the Ann Arbor Blues Festival to hear Howlin' Wolf with 'Smokestack Lighting'. But if you want to know a shameful secret, Crosby, Stills and Nash still sounds like 1969 teen spirit to me; 'Marrakesh Express' brings good old Ann Arbor painfully close.

CROSBY, STILLS AND NASH
CROSBY, STILLS AND NASH

MUSIC FROM BIG PINK
THE BAND

These days I play opera (specially Mussorsgsky), Tito Puente, Celia Cruz, Cesaria Evora, Cole Porter or George and Ira Gershwin, plus a little jazz (Take Six, Dizzy, Bill Evans), Van on *Irish Heartbeat*, Mary Coughlan, that great *Red Hot and Blue* tape, Randy Newman, Paul Simon, Nino Rota, Nina Simone again, Sinéad's 'Love Made a Thief out of Me' and Celine Dion's *Sleepless in Seattle* track with Clive Griffin and occasional weak-minded Sting or Annie Lennox orgies. But it's CDs and Walkman cassettes; and like everyone I know, I'm wondering what became of my albums. Not that I could play them if I had them, but … the trauma of missing records haunts my generation like slow-release memories of abandonment and desolation.

When mine were stolen from Hanbury Lane I took them back from a fence on Kevin Street; then they were stolen from Lombard Street and I found some in a stall off George's Street. I can replace all the Frank Hartes, Freddie Whites, Moving Hearts, Randy Newmans and Ry Cooders. But the very rare ones – Melvin Van Peebles, John Fahey – got lost in some move. The only person I know who's kept all of his (in good nick too) is P.J. Curtis, the Pride of the Burren.

And so these days I work in an office with dozens of Californian kids on electronic guides and CD-ROM books. The poor things had to survive puberty to the strains of Madonna and S.O.S. 'You wouldn't believe the crap my juniors stick on in the office – but they're MTV generation and they have a visual memory of Madonna with her leather bustier so they don't care about sound,' I told Har. 'Sound has almost nothing to do with it now. Very occasionally they actually put on *Diva* or Peter Gabriel and I have to weep with gratitude!'

Har was still hanging onto 'orally susceptible' as I hung up. But, hey, maybe he does have a point. As far as I could tell our generation discovered only the Beatles and the Pill and soft drugs as teens in the sixties. Oral sex was really discovered by Americans under twenty in the late sixties and adopted with great relish as a de rigueur part of sexual liberation – which wasn't really sexual for all or liberating for everyone either, alas.

But you could argue that oral sex changed things forever if not always uniformly for the best – I mean, what else was that Rolling Stones stuff about? 'Love in Vain' and 'Gimme Shelter' are forever hot but 'Sticky Fingers' and 'Brown Sugar'? Gimme a break. No wonder mothers thought Mick was sick. Much though I enjoy Keith (did you see 'Hail, Hail, Rock and Roll'? You must!), the concept of some teenage groupie giving Mick a blowjob in the backseat of the limo is enough to infuriate even me, let alone a suburban mum. On the other hand ... Hmmmmm. It's a Pandora's Box, children.

But we were in Dublin, of course, sweeties, so we missed a lot of that; and anyway, it all seemed like much too much hard work ('Wha'? I have to take all me clothes off and all? Are ye joking me?'). So it probably never really reached us at all, at all. Heh-heh-heh-heh.

TIM GOULDING

THE HIDEOUS SPECTRE OF NOSTALGIA IS UNLEASHED ... 'Time for your Van Morrison darling, and did you take the yellow ones?' Meanwhile here are today's top ten with apologies to k.d. lang, Ry Cooder and the Band.

THE FUTURE
LEONARD COHEN

Having spent the sixties trying to dodge Leonard Cohen freaks and their 'tea and oranges' refrains, what could surprise me more than *The Future*. It knocked me off my prejudicial perch. I'd never heard a voice so low, a chorus so ethereal and words so densely pungent. Leonard Cohen is a masterful poet with a bleak vision of society, not dissimilar to Lou Reed. But 'There is a crack in everything, that's how the light gets in'.

THE MISSING YEARS
JOHN PRINE

Singer-songwriters are ten a penny so it's only rarely that one jumps out of the pack. *The Missing Years* didn't leave my turntable for a solid month, John Prine's Dylanesque voice being so seductive and straight down the line. Couple that with the super-clear production and simple arrangements, and you get a gem.

John Prine, in true country-and-western tradition, sings of the everyday ... but with a sardonic twinge. He also imparts some inside information on Jesus's missing years. It transpires that He saw *Rebel Without a Cause* on His thirteenth birthday, went to Rome where He married His Irish bride, although the marriage failed probably because of those pretty Italian chicks, and then wrote His first song, 'The Dove of Love Fell off His Perch'. So there's one for revealed religion. It reminds me of a friend who was intent on seeing his guru in meditation and after many ascetic hours Mick Jagger appeared. As John Prine says, 'It's a big old goofy world.'

ZOOLOOK
J.M. JARRE AND LAURIE ANDERSON

This was the first album that really excited me about sampling. Always a Laurie Anderson fan, this one fell into my lap with its psychedelic stream of language.

It is something to voyage into, deeper and deeper, as the montage of 'world' languages knit together into a moving organism of sound. If you can travel in that strange land, your pipe is truly burning. For those of a more nervous disposition I would recommend the sublime music of the spheres on Eno's *Apollo*.

SAILOR
STEVE MILLER BAND

1968. Notting Hill Gate. Smoke-filled rooms. Vestal virgins on their way to the coast etc., although some stayed behind. Was it just the bright eyes of youth that made the present so present, that identified the B♭ of the taxi horn and its perfect counterpoint in the D of the bat-winged American matron's call of 'You Betcha'. No wonder the carpet dropped away and it was more like pure cerebral reception that was caught by the first foghorn blast of 'Song for Our Ancestors'. Quite inadvertently you're on the dock of the bay with the drip drip expanding outwards into a new reality and then a new one. Here comes Stevie in his breathy voice thanking Mary, for the day they spent together. 'I'm not sorry, Mary.' Seamlessly it rides through 'Living in the USA' to 'Gangster of Love' and 'Dime-a-Dance Romance'.

Sailor is a stream-of-consciousness album that sounds every bit as fresh today. Two songs by Boz Scaggs's great Hammond organ and the inimitable light bluesy voice of Steve Miller, not to mention the minor fifth in the guitar solo on 'Overdrive' that spawned Strange Lee Strange's immortal question and answer, 'Does she go that Ban Garda ... She Goes.'

GOIN' BACK TO NEW ORLEANS
DR JOHN

Whenever I see the wide grin of an open piano it's time to tootle. So how could I resist *Goin' Back to New Orleans* with Dr John at the helm of the riverboat? He's my keyboard hero for his swampy, bluesy, jazzy informal 'feel'. His music spills across the bars of straight timing and breathes a heady cocktail of derring-do. Spontaneous showers of musical afterthoughts duck in and out of the melodies like so many *rara aves* flashing their wings in the rainforest.

This album is a nostalgic ramble through New Orleans musical history, kicking off with 'Litanie des Saints' inspired by the composer Louis Gottshalk, who was born down there. From there on in it's a bursting package of blues, funk, jazz, trad, rock'n'roll with *gris-gris* inflections. There's a sublime version of 'Careless Love' sung in that unique gravelly, end-of-the-megaphone voice, a moody 'Basin Street Blues' and a toe-tapping 'Goin' Back to New Orleans'. The production is crammed with saxes, clarinets, tubas, trombones and strings, not to mention those incomparable vocalists the Neville Brothers. When it comes to 'Radiatin' the 88', look no further than Mac Rebennack (Dr John).

NEW YORK
LOU REED

> This is no time for saluting flags
> This is no time for inner searchings
> The future is at hand
> This is no time for phony rhetoric
> This is no time for political speech
> This is a time for action
> Because the future is within reach
> This is the time.
>
> Lou Reed

Undermine everything you know, think, believe, are told, have learned, will learn, can conceive, can't conceive, and maybe there'll be a small ring of Truth in the emptiness. Lou Reed exposes and disposes of the Rotten Society we live in with its back-to-front values, and no better place to do it than New York. But out of the eater comes forth sweetness. Know what I mean?

THE HEALER
JOHN LEE HOOKER

This one just peeks over the top on the blues list, partly because it includes other great candidates such as Santana, Robert Cray, Bonnie Raitt, Los Lobos, George Thorogood and Canned Heat. You get the feeling that John Lee need hardly hit a note to make music. In fact he often only just does. The master of one- and two-chord songs with that old brown lived-in voice tells his tale in an unhurried, authentic fashion. They must have invented the phrase 'paying your dues' for him, for that spell he casts from seeming nothings brings me back and back. For further reference listen to the soundtrack from the motion picture *The Hot Spot*, which revolves around John Lee Hooker with guest appearances by Miles Davis and Taj Mahal amongst others. And while we're on the subject of the blues I can't let Eric Clapton's *Unplugged* go without mention.

BLONDE ON BLONDE
BOB DYLAN

A Whistling Hammond and a voice that is so laden with intent stopped some of the best minds of my contemporaries in their tracks. A man, like Dylan Thomas, drunk on words who seemed to articulate meaningfulness and life 'like it is'. Often that meaningfulness was far from meaning but we seemed to intuit it. Anyway, even today 'Sad-Eyed Lady of the Lowlands' raises gooseflesh with its mantric layers of bitterness and love. That selfsame indictment of relationships and society can be heard on John Trudell's excellent album *Graffiti Man*. It could be said, why rail against others when 'the other' is ourself, but for some curious reason it makes great music.

INARTICULATE SPEECH OF THE HEART
VAN MORRISON

It was a toss-up between this and *No Guru, No Method, No Teacher*. For me Van is a teacher. His lessons include how to play the human voice like a sax, how to release music from its overcoat of form and let rip. When he bursts from speech to song on 'Rave on John Donne' the tie ropes of normality are slashed. The albums he made around this time reclaim his Irish roots and when I hear the music I see hills and valleys, passion and meditation.

GODDESS OF FORTUNE
THE HARE KRISHNA TEMPLE

I actually bought this in a shop and not at the airport from a hairless one. Whether you swallow your leader or worship a little bronze creature on a velvet cushion you have to admit that when the human voice aims for 'The Measureless', magic can ensue. Could it be the longing to eschew the washing-up that produces the molten quality of 'Desire Without Sex'? Listen to 'Govinda' and see if those encrustations down the back of the oven don't appear to be very significant marks of excitement. So what if it's another illusion, it's also music for the soul.

BILL GRAHAM

PERSPECTIVES INEVITABLY CHANGE as you traipse down the winding road of equally changing taste. Records that once provoked fanatical listening can now seem of fantastical folly, while the ones that initially lingered at the bottom of the collection eventually became the subjects of a more durable loyalty. And of course there are always some that symbolize personal watershed moments that only oneself can fully appreciate.

I think I may have lingered in a peculiar cutting off the main sixties railroad. Sequestered in boarding-school, I could get envious of my day-school Blackrock colleagues. I hardly saw *Top of the Pops* and couldn't scoot off into the Dublin club scene. Instead radio was my unsteady and irregular guide, listening to Luxembourg between the sheets in the dorm. But then maybe I wasn't that exceptional, living on the cusp of the sixties and trying to make sense of it in its aftermath. Politically and socially, it's arguable that the seventies were the Irish sixties – the watershed decade. In pop culture we also had to fillet out the superfluous, irrelevant and distracting.

Of course, some records were bound to ambush you. The Beach Boys' 'God Only Knows' was my first experience that Pop might be graduating to a new language. Jim Webb's production of Richard Harris's 'MacArthur Park' can now seem hilariously overblown but someone had definitely put out a strange new cake in the rain and I wanted to eat it.

And then there were those soul records that passed you by, since boarding-school just didn't encourage appreciation of rhythm sections. What was that instrumental they kept playing on Radio Caroline? No, I didn't appreciate King Curtis's 'Memphis Soul Stew' till a decade later.

Then psychedelia began to drown out Stax and Motown. I first heard Radio London at midnight while on holiday in – of all places – Inishbofin. The disc-jockey, who sounded like another Liverpudlian version of Kenny Everett at 33 r.p.m., was grumbling about how the station bosses were compelling him to play this predictable soul track. He was John Peel; the record was Wilson Pickett's 'In the Midnight Hour', and no, I wasn't then convinced by it either.

Then there was my first album purchase, a CBS compilation of folk-rock acts featuring three tracks each by Bob Dylan, Simon and Garfunkel and the Byrds. With the latter's 'Eight Miles High' began my taste for transcendent guitars. Nobody since has consistently created the majestic rush of McGuinn's mob at their most majestic.

But I know the artist who really started me – Mississippi John Hurt. In my final year at Blackrock, you were allowed a double room and your own record-player. My cohabitee hung out with a gang – which included Bob Geldof – who were fixated on the blues; but most of their records were too harsh and dense for my immature ears.

But not Mississippi John. Born at the start of the century, he'd been re-corded briefly in the twenties and then was rediscovered in the sixties, a benign pensioner wowing the Newport Folk Festival.

His music had an exceptional benevolence with a lucid, fluent guitar style that leads to J.J. Cale rather than the hard-rock demagogues who later mis-translated the Chicago blues. But there was far more. Languishing in a Catholic boarding-school with Mass five days a week before breakfast, I was smitten by a singer who could be gently eloquent about sex and religious belief and not see the two impulses as enemies for eternity. Unawares I'd stumbled onto the crucial dual strengths of the Afro-American tradition. Aretha Franklin and Bob Marley would make far more sense later.

Escaping to Trinity in autumn '69, I began to explore jazz for hipper-than-thou reasons. Hippiedom was tempting but somehow its Irish political passivity didn't make complete social sense. Or at least not when the North was erupting. The Doors and Jefferson Airplane might link to Americans protesting against the Vietnam War but Pink Floyd hardly connected with Burntollet. And some-where along the way I got some half-baked notion that black militants might teach me more enduring lessons.

In the summer of '70 I got my first part-time job and with my pay I went on a jazz binge. But I did it backwards, starting with the avant-garde not New Orleans. Like I said, I was hipper than thou. But also very lucky. The majors did-n't abandon jazz till the seventies so the bargain-bins were littered with all these John Coltrane, Ornette Coleman, Cecil Taylor, Archie Shepp and Sun Ra albums for a pound or less. With so little competition I feasted, but it took me months to digest their impossibly intricate musical language with their alien rhythms and harmonies so far beyond the established Western canon.

Then, one evening, I broke through. *John Coltrane at Newport* was the record, 'My Favourite Things' the track, and suddenly I was redeemed by the elo-quence of his soprano saxophone – not even knowing until years later that Coltrane had been the most significant influence on 'Eight Miles High'. Then I cottoned onto Charles Mingus but the quality of his vast output is such that I can't isolate one record.

Exit the apprentice hippie. At the Isle of Wight festival, I'd dashed down to the front to hear Miles Davis and then overdosed on *Bitches Brew* but now I just couldn't stomach the inept pretensions of fusion and most progressive rock. And though I didn't know it, I'd also found the funk. But we were all lousy dancers then, head- but never hip-shakers.

Increasingly, I've realized that that early jazz experience gave me three benefits – I wanted instrumental music to be anarchic, transcendent and usually drenched in blues dischords; I escaped the traps of those who favoured only one particular black music style and who couldn't perceive the linkages; and, because I was so suspicious of most seventies white art-rock, I came back to the artists, producers and songwriters who were inspired by the principles of the two-minute thirty-seven-second single.

The experience also led me on to my own peculiar connection with Irish traditional music, with which I had no prior connection. As ever, bargain-bin excavation gave me the boost. In Murray's on Ormond Quay I found my first B.B. King single, his cover of Willie Nelson's 'Nightlife' with its outrageously brief and strangled guitar solo. Within a fortnight I heard Tony MacMahon playing accordion in Slattery's and ran to buy his Gael Linn album, 'Lament for the Wounded Hussar'. Twenty years later both Van Morrison and Sinéad O'Connor prove that it's no outlandish heresy, but then I was both devastated and exalted to realize that the blues and Irish music were expressing parallel experience in parallel musical lines.

Of course, like most of my generation, I was still antagonistic to rock-'n'roll. Elvis Presley was distastefully alien, the saint of the showbands, a man who made lousy gimcrack B-movies and sucked up to Richard Nixon. Merle Haggard's Okies from Muskogee were just Presley and Nixon's loyal damnfool infantry – rednecks forever self-condemned to the backwaters of their boon-docks. And if I liked Gram Parsons and the Byrds in their country phase, well they were Californian exceptions with a future vision.

HUGO HAMILTON

WHEN BOB DYLAN TURNED TO RELIGION in the early eighties, it felt like a Stanley knife between the ribs. It was the big betrayal. Up to then, I had spent most of my semi-waking hours listening and muttering along with *Highway 61*, *Blonde on Blonde* and *Blood on the Tracks*.

I knew every word that ever made its way out of his goddamn throat. Everywhere, in pubs and flats from Dublin to Berlin, London to Halifax, I met people who spoke or whined the words at random like a ubiquitous text that could be uttered or understood anywhere and in any situation.

There was no need to talk. At parties, all you had to do was to gaze into somebody's eyes and say: 'The past is close behind ...' They would nod and whisper: 'Something is happening ...' You concurred wholeheartedly with a blink, and while not wishing to accuse anyone, you would add: 'But you don't know what it is ...' They would be taken aback a little and you would both pause for a moment, look at each other and together, in perfect timing, say: 'Do you Mr. Jones?'

It was like the People's Front Judea. Everybody knew everybody through this arcane code of Dylan-speak. I heard people conduct in-depth discussions on any subject from politics to war using Dylan's caustic words. I remember couples arguing in lyrics. 'Give me some milk or else go home ...' there was a phrase for every occasion in the Dylan repertoire. The worst thing you could say to an ex-lover was to tell them you couldn't touch the books they had read. And in general you lived your life according to certain prescribed norms. You drove that car as far as you could and abandoned it out West, somewhere near Oranmore.

What could you do to defend yourself against the invective of a Berlin or Munich ticket inspector only to argue back in whole chunks from 'Desolation Row'. That was the only way of dealing with them. Leave them puzzled, but unyielding. As a last resort, you could even translate it into German for them, like 'Bitte, schicken Sie mir keine Briefe mehr ...'

Fair enough, it didn't always work out right. And as they hauled you off the U-Bhan and you gave the V-sign to the stunned and righteous onlookers, you went on babbling those prophetic words like a possessed moron, because they were all you had. It was your language.

No matter where you were in the world, there was an underground cabal of Dylan disciples which you could latch onto and communicate with. OK, once in a while, somebody rolled a joint and announced with great solemnity: 'Take this, all of you, and smoke it.' But that was as close as we ever got to religion. Unless you count the few people who kept saying: 'Amen' or 'Oh man'. Even if you include Dylan's own line, 'God said to Abraham, kill me a son', our faith was only expressed in a collective use of his self-mocking vernacular. We were without faith. Anarchists. Infidels. Guided through the labyrinth of everyday practicalities by Dylan's unstable, nonsensical parables.

It was a case of 'Do this in memory of me.' It was a case of a few of us gathering in Dylan's name. It was *Mollaigaí an Tiarna*, baby. He was the shepherd, so to speak, and we were the flock of wasters issuing his gospel until the moment of the big fracture. Until Dylan decided to revert to religion himself. Jesus, we all felt like a flock of shagged sheep.

It was a big blow, right enough. Like your greatest hero being struck down by multiple sclerosis or cancer. Alright, we stood behind him through his darkest hour – 'right before the dawn' – but it was no longer the same. We could have accepted anything but that. Dylan down on his knees, going to Mass, receiving Holy Communion; that was unbearable. This was a vision of the scorched earth after World War Three with nothing left on the landscape but a few charred tree stumps. We were waiting for the joke. Waiting for Dylan to announce that he had been up to see the Pope in the Vatican and that he found him wearing the leopardskin pill-box hat.

At the time I was in a relationship with a woman who had long brown hair and long brown boots of Spanish leather, who proclaimed that her only ambition in life was to sleep with Bob Dylan. I could live with that somehow. It was shelter-from-the-storm stuff. I was willing to accept my role as a Dylan substitute, even on a semi-permanent basis. But when I found out that Dylan was flirting with God, I was forced to confront the situation. I could no longer live with this pretence and deceit. It was Big Jim versus Jack of Hearts, I told her. It was either me or Dylan. And there was no way I was going to put up with the three of us in the big brass bed together. Him sitting up late at night on the far side of her with the light on, reading the Bible. I drew the line. She had to make a choice.

Some of us had made the all-important discovery. The sun was not yellow, it was chicken. Dylan had been faking it like a woman all along. After he turned to Gawd, there was a big schism. Some thought it was alright to continue buying Dylan albums and following him through thick and thin. But they were stuck inside of Mobile, basically, whereas I was determined to get out. I could not bear the disillusionment. I lost heart. Memphis blues, big time. Went off food and began wasting away in a dingy flat in Dun Laoghaire. One of my best friends emigrated to Australia, which was the right thing to do.

Another of my friends went to live near Thomastown where he devoted a room in a big country house to the memory of Dylan. There is nothing in the room except a Stratocaster and some Dylan lyrics lying around. A simple shrine in the middle of Ireland somewhere. Every now and again he locks himself into this museum for hours, days. I worry about him from time to time.

Most of us went our own way after that. Some people began experimenting with Van Morrison, Thin Lizzy, the Chieftains and God knows what. Some people began mainlining on country music and inevitably ended up on Randy Travis and Garth Brooks. There was a level of feckless promiscuity that was previously unknown to man or woman in history. I saw people succumbing to all kinds of unlikely musical ordure like Heaven 17, Simple Minds, Bon bleeding Jovi. Some went back to the Eagles, for Gawd's sake. But who could blame them? I heard of casualties on detox programmes with Verdi and Joan Sutherland. Some extreme cases even descended down to bottomless pits and ended up knocking their heads against the wall and growling pitifully along to Leonard Cohen. All about Eskimos and frozen bodies.

I came out of my own deep catharsis by leaping on to Roxy Music and the 'bogus man' or father of punk, Bryan Ferry, until he too went soft as dogshite in my own hands. I went through a metamorphosis. I began eating out of bins. At one stage I was deluded into thinking that I could live with Bono as an acceptable substitute. Perhaps only because of the sound of his name and the fact that he sang 'Maggie's Farm' in all his 'raging glory' at a point when I was extremely low and defenceless. But then he started singing all about salvation, stagnation, indignation and constipation, so I was homeless again.

I was lucky to be alive though. I ran into some tragic, forlorn cases dabbling with Oasis and Blur recently, looking back in anger like they were dazed and doomed. My heart goes out to them. I knew another man who got stuck on Mary Black, or any other Mary he could find. What can you do for them? I mean, I went in for a lot of home-grown stuff, like Joe Heaney, Joe Cooley, even Dé (techno) Danann, but I never descended as low as Ireland's Nana Mouskouri. And somebody should take the bleeding Woman's Heart out of its misery.

In the end, if it wasn't for Talking Heads and David Byrne, I don't know where I might have ended up. I picked myself up. 'Found myself another city to live in.' I began to perk up and sing 'Psycho Killer'. I was also helped out by Elvis Costello and Morrissey. 'I've been stabbed in the back.' 'I'm sick down to my heart' I sang in my box-room, suburban-blued until I found Nick Cave and the Bad Seeds. Took some comfort in his 'Murder Ballads'. There's some hope left for me now.

Nowadays I meet occasional heads who have come through a similar ordeal. But I can tell the genuine bad seed from a not-so-bad seed a mile away. There are only certain levels on which you can communicate with them. I don't talk to people in just any language. I say to them: 'Mister Motherfucker, you know who I am?' And if they're up to it, they'll come back with the right response. 'Yeah, and I don't give a good God Damn.'

MICK HANLY

I RANG DES KELLY'S OFFICE in the afternoon to find out what time the van was leaving. I was told to be at the Terenure Inn for four o'clock on Friday. I was slow to put the phone down. The answer was too cryptic. I wanted to talk more, even talking to the office was exciting.

The year was 1972. The day was like any other biggest day in your life. I'd had a call from the office a few weeks earlier.

'From someone in PLANXTY,' my mother said.

'Jesus Christ, what did they say?'

'They said you were to ring them back as soon as you can.'

'Who was it though?'

'I don't know, someone from PLANXTY.'

Oh, fuck. It's Friday evening, seven o'clock, no answer. Saturday, no answer. Sunday, just in case, no answer.

Monday, ten past ten. 'The lads were wondering would you be available to do an Irish tour with them, in February.' I was playing in Slattery's of Capel Street, one night a week for a ten-bob note.

'I'll check, I think so.'

PLANXTY, PLANXTY, PLANXTY, even my mother knew the name. This strange new word had become a household one in the space of a couple of months. Every time you turned on the radio, you heard 'The Cliffs of Dooneen' uilleann pipes, mandolins, Christy's strange velvety voice, all arrestingly new. The word PLANXTY was on everyone's lips. Everyone's lips that mattered that is. Back then, I thought that everyone with lips knew about music. Loved music. Thought music was more important than sport, or books, or trainspotting. I had a lot to learn.

On the sixth of February 1972 I made my way to Terenure. I found a pub as near as possible to The Terenure and I stayed there till as long after four as I could bear.

At five past four I sauntered in the door. I was being as casual as I could be. Cool would be today's word but then it still applied to tea and the weather. There was nobody there. No one real. No musicians. No PLANXTY.

A barman was giving the tables a cat's lick with a cloth. An old man was giving his terrier some crisps and nursing a pint. I got a coke for myself and sat down to wait.

After about twenty minutes I began to suspect that I got the time wrong. They'd hardly be this late going to Sligo. I sat and waited. I watched people come and go, study the racing page, have quick ones. I wanted to be going. This was my first big gig. I was anxious. They couldn't be this late. Sure Sligo is the other side of the country, for God's sake.

A couple who had come in, settled down, had a drink, were now leaving. Jesus Christ they've forgotten to collect me.

Quarter past five.

'Hello, is that Des Kelly's office?'

'Yes.'

'This is Mick Hanly.'

There was a covering of the mouthpiece at the other end and a far off conversation.

'What's it in connection with Mick?'

'I'm playing with PLANXTY tonight in Sligo.' More hesitation. More consultation.

'I'm sorry, Mick. I didn't know who you were there for a minute. Des isn't here at the moment and the lads have left. They must be on their way over to you.' I wanted to burst into tears, but I was too old for that now. The next twenty minutes was like waiting for Santa, despite having been told it was all a cod. At quarter to six Liam O'Flynn arrived. I waved. His first words were,

'Are you ready?'

'Yea, just about.' I'd been ready for four and a half weeks.

I climbed into the converted Ford Transit. There were two rows of airline seats in the midsection, a wall of plywood which sectioned off three to four feet of equipment space, a few straggly bits of carpet on the walls, no less, and a three-seater seat up front. A palace on wheels. For the record, this wonderful machine housed Christy Moore, Andy Irvine, Liam O'Flynn, Dónal Lunny, Nicky Ryan (soundman), Johnny Diffley (driver), and Mick Hanly (support act). All the sound and lighting gear, plus the instruments. I don't think one ever truly appreciates the stretch limo without having sampled the Ford Transit first.

So this was it. The big league at last. The Supergroup. Dónal was trying to reassemble the crotch of a very worn pair of jeans with a needle and thread. Andy was stuck in an adventure book on Antarctica and demolishing his nails. Christy, the biggest of the big-leaguers, was looking out the window. I said hello and sat beside him. He said hello, but not much else. He seemed preoccupied. I noticed he was smoking something unusually large. I was familiar with roll-ups but this was a strange variation, more like a badly constructed ice-cream cone. I knew nothing about dope at that time so I presumed that Christy was just an oddball as well as being a big-leaguer. A minute or so passed while Christy pulled on the cone like a man who had just gone under for the third time. He then took a turn at doing Dizzy Gillespie before a blow out that would have done Orca the Whale proud.

'Would you like a draw 'a this, Mick?'

'No thanks, Christy, I have my own.'

I knew the moment I said it that I'd put my foot in something, because the joint was then passed to Dónal, who took it, despite having twenty Rothmans and a lighter among his sewing gear.

Ten minutes later I took out my twenty Players and turned to Christy.

'Will you have one of these, Christy?'

'Bejasus, I will. Fierce strong, these yokes.'

I wasn't allowed to forget my faux pas. Anytime there was a yell of, 'Has anyone any draw?' from the front of the van. Christy usually piped up with, 'Jaysus, Mick has great cigarettes there. Break 'em out there Mick and we'll all get high as Croagh Patrick.'

The van broke down in Chapelizod. Fortunately, some showband on their way to a gig in Dublin spotted their fellow 'Transiteers' in trouble and stopped. The driver told Johnny that a simple timing mechanism was jamming and that all he had to do was give it a gentle tap of a spanner and away we'd go. Away she did go but only thirty miles down the road. When she cut out again Johnny leaped from the cab with the flourish of a man who doesn't know an oilcan from a beancan but has the vital piece of knowledge.

'I'll fix that,' said Johnny. He did and away she went again. This time she did ten miles before another gentle tap was required. After a series of diminishing distances and 'I'll fix thats' the stoned occupants were now getting ever more fretful. A call was made to Ben Dolan of the Drifters. Sorry, the bus is gone to Mallow.

When the 'I'll fix thats' didn't work anymore, Johnny left for Mullingar to get the simple timing mechanism, while frantic calls were made to the office in an effort to find a van. Nobody wanted a cancelled gig. The punters don't believe the 'broken van' or the 'sick singer' story, they prefer to see the corpse.

Even Harry Secombe says that once, when having to tell the audience that one of the lead players in the Panto had a heart attack and 'is on the way to hospital', he was greeted with 'Oh no, he isn't.'

We sat in the van, ten miles from Mullingar, helpless and despairing. It was agreed that if Johnny didn't return by nine-thirty the gig would have to be cancelled. At twenty-five to ten, and still no sign of Johnny, several joints were lit and the atmosphere lightened considerably.

When Johnny finally got back, at around quarter past ten, he found the van of gloom was now rocking with high hilarity.

PLANXTY didn't play Sligo that night. My first big gig was no gig at all. I smoked my first joint. Maybe playing a gig on top of all that might have been too much for a Christian Brothers' boy.

Rumour had it that Christy was at a funeral with Barney McKenna in Clare and was the worse for wear. Andy had missed a plane from Bulgaria. Dónal had a burst appendix. Liam and Séamus Ennis were on the batter. The truth is that everyone stayed in a hotel in Mullingar and got the worse for wear into the small hours.

DERMOT HEALY

I GREW UP AMONG SINGLES. We had a small blue portable record-player that saw out Presley, Billy Fury, Tommy Steele, Del Shannon, Frankie Avalon, Fabian, Helen Shapiro and a few others. When it went defunct I never bought another.

So all the music I've heard since has been in pubs, on the radio or TV, at concerts, supermarkets, banks and, most especially, in other people's homes. I can't remember ever buying an LP. I've bought the odd disc of traditional music, true, and even worked for a couple of years as a questionable roadie with Planxty, and though I ended up at the wake for Brian Jones in Hyde Park, it never meant I had a Stones tape back home to remember him by.

The first real long-playing rock album I heard was after Mrs Galligan died. She was wife to Dr Galligan who co-founded Comhaltas, and was friend to Séamus Ennis, Brendan Behan and Gareth Browne. Séamus Ennis used to arrive in Cavan off the Dublin bus to dry out in Dr Galligan's surgery. He'd arrive a wreck, gaunt-featured and sickly, with his pipes in a box. A week later he'd emerge from the doctor's house a new man, trim, dapper and nimble-fingered to open up the sounds in the Farnham Arms.

It was the doctor, after Séamus was gone, that went round Cavan like a lost soul ... holding on to the railings in Farnham Street. When Mrs Galligan died the Galligan lads came to stay with us and they brought their record-player with them. We sat in my mother's room and listened to an LP their father had brought over from his last trip to America. It was, he said, the first recording by a young traditional singer who he thought would do well.

And that's how I discovered Bob Dylan. We played it over and over – 'Hey! Hey! Woody Guthrie', 'A Hard Rain's A-Gonna Fall', 'Corrina, Corrina', 'Talking World War III Blues', 'Girl of the North Country' – and these would have been the tunes we heard in our heads as we stood in the graveyard.

In Denbight Street in Pimlico in the late sixties, John McCaffry, a Cavan man also, kept a fine display of records. A hairdresser by day, he was a playboy by night. He'd cut our hair and we'd head up to tour Soho. The first acid we took was made of aspro. We sat round for hours waiting for it to happen. A few nights later we found the right stuff and the wall began moving. I remember sitting up late into the night listening to Crosby, Stills, and Nash – the LP that contained 'Marrakesh Express' – and anything from that album makes the hair on my head stand.

Dermot Burke, my next-door neighbour, communicated with me through a cord tied to two tin cans, one in his room and one in mine. We'd listen to the top twenty from Luxembourg, then beat out a signal as to what number we thought was best. 'Love Me Do' had just entered at number sixteen. We gave it a great clatter. We thought the Beatles were from another world. A few summers later I heard 'Please Please Me' on the Isle of Man as I walked the promenade between jobs as a waiter and night porter. The song was blasting ashore from Radio Caroline into the transistors of the South England boppers. The Kinks were playing up the road, there was live wrestling in the casino and single Belfast ladies were walking the streets for love.

A couple of years after came *Sgt. Pepper*. I saw many mornings in with 'Here Comes the Sun'. Got up and dragged a comb across my head, found my way over St James Park, round the circus and up the stairs bleary-eyed into the Westminster Insurance office overlooking Eros. I was a clerk there for over a year. The manager and I used to look down with dismay on the hippies scattered across Piccadilly. Someone sold me strychnine instead of acid about a year later, and I left London, joined the hippies for a while, wandered Soho buffeted by flashbacks, then took off to Wicklow sleeping with dogs and dreading direct eye-contact.

In a pub in the village of Malin on the Inishowen peninsula there's someone loves that old fundamentalist, Cat Stevens. His songs were like a breath of fresh air to the guilty psyche. That one album, *Tea for the Tillerman*, they played over and over, and looking back it was his spiritual quality that beckoned you in, with songs like 'Morning Has Broken', and it still does, despite everything.

On Ravenhill Road in Belfast I discovered *Love and Affection* by Joan Armatrading. In Ryan's Hotel at Rosses Point, Sligo, the manager was a fan of the Pogues. At first they sounded loud, brash and hickory-dickory. Then I got to know 'A Fairytale of New York'. This was a drinking song with a difference, far removed from the gentility of the marijuana numbers of a few decades before. The punch was calypso, raunchy, and lyrical. I love 'You scumbag, you maggot, you cheap lovely faggot, Happy Christmas you arsehole'. I heard a crowd of Irish girls singing those lines with relish around a pool in Crete in 1994, as years before I heard the cashier girls from the Bank of Ireland in Cavan singing along with the love songs from *Tapestry* by Carole King.

Always in those days James Taylor was knocking about, as was Neil Young, and earlier, Gene Pitney. An old pro came back to top them all later with *Imagine*. John Lennon dealt with jealousy well. Then suddenly Roy Orbison surfaced again. Crossing the Irish Sea and taking the Holyhead train to London an Australian girl handed me her headphones. It was my first time to have a personal stereo round my skull. She was playing Moving Hearts, Robson and Michael Coleman.

I once lay late in a bed in an old parsonage by Lough Oyster on the Erne. I spent a beautiful hour listening to an album on BBC Radio 2 when the station played mainly classical music. It was a recording of bells ringing in Tibet. I don't think I've ever bettered that experience, once-off, magical and lost.

To finish with I have to return to Cullen's Amusements, which came year-ly to the egg market yard in Cavan town. Over the speakers for three nights they played Buddy Holly's album with the track 'I Guess It Doesn't Matter Anymore!' Maybe it was only a single, but the album it was on will do as a final choice, but one, for I've sneaked in another LP in the title *Redemption Songs* which comes from Bob Marley who used sing out of a jukebox in Drogheda during the last World Cup in America. Somehow it all makes sense.

DESMOND HOGAN

FOR ALMOST A YEAR NOW I've been living in a town in west Limerick which in many ways is like Ballinasloe where I grew up. Sometimes on the street by the bridge there's the chimera: the bird-of-paradise red of a teddyboy's shirt, the roach of black hair, the plush locks, the phantom moustache, very pale, almost white rose-petal skin as if he'd been a weakling child, grease in the black hair making it look like wet tar. Only the children talk to you – a little boy virtually swimming in a big bicycle he manoeuvres with determined effort, a little girl pushing a go-car with a Saint Bernadette's scarf on her head. In a place called Gort I swim where the river is tidal, a mixture of river and sea. Gort means field, field of corn, in Irish. It is very like Gorta, which means hunger, famine, and that's very much like my life, the vicissitudes, and being here, being back almost where I began – the custard-coloured, the jonquil-coloured shop- fronts – I fre-quently hear songs, the voices of singers, like the voices who wrote the stories I read, or the voices of the children. They are the voices that have survived over a few decades.

You walk in the late summer fields of yellow agrimony, used for the diges-tive system or to heal skin rashes and external wounds, and yarrow, said to cure the innards it looks like, and burnet-saxifrage, and, like a banshee you hear Sandy Denny's aqua-clear voice. Sandy Denny died young and tragically two decades ago.

'Farewell' – a farewell to one who must always walk 'in the cold north wind'. And I think of all the walks I've done and the pilgrimages and peregri-nations and something stays me to the homeless. In my last months in England I talked a lot. I lingered with the homeless.

'They took my invalid's allowance. They asked for a second birth certificate.'

'What do you expect me to do?' I said to them.

'Swim back to Ireland,' a lady in signal-red socks and a flop hat informed me.

'I stay with me mates and lie on the floor with them,' a boy from the Rhonda Valley in Roman sandals told me. 'I don't speak Welsh. Rhonda Valley and all that. I've been here too long. I went to Southend with me mates today. Jumped a train.'

'Stay close to me. Just to be warm,' a woman, hunched up, said to a friend. 'I don't like what I'm going through.'

'Do a bit of shoplifting to make ends meet,' said a man in black Marks and

Spencers trainers. 'Shower every day in Squire Lane Baths in Finchley. Sleep in a football field in Stepney Green. Saw my wife the other day. She bent her head when she saw me.'

Two boys hugged one another. 'Don't want to live.' 'Take it easy. There are a lot of people behind you.'

'Where are you going to sleep tonight, Yvonne?' came a boy's voice.

Tramps around fires late at night. Sandy Denny's voice had survived two decades and spoke for them. It linked the London of then – Edwardian squats, girls with lips like war-paint, in black hobble coats, with torboushes like jet spaghetti hurrying along these streets, tramps from Mayo coming into view on them like boats on an Irish river and standing against a piece of graffiti by a famous Irishman ('Life to those who understand and fuck the begrudgers') – and now – the dunes in the face of a boy in a Prussian crewcut or a turf cut, fake roses in a station café in a Panda orangeade tin, yellow prayer-beads on a viridian string with tassels going through the hands of an Arab boy on the tube, underwear hanging up to dry in underpasses.

One song gives way to another like photographs in an accordion frame – 'Farewell' was written to the tune of 'Willie of the Winsbury' sung by Pentangle.

> The king has been a poor prisoner
> A prisoner long in Spain.
> And Willie of the Winsbury
> Has lain long with his daughter at home.
> Take off, take off your berry brown gown
> Stand naked on a stone
> That I might see by your shape
> Whether you be a maiden or none.

The king returns from captivity to discover his daughter has slept with someone. When he discovers it's not a knight or a nobleman he ordains the death of the culprit until he comes face to face with him and finds that his beauty is such that he too would have slept with him had he been a woman.

'You're as sweet,' says a young bilberry-blackcurled tramp with bow lips, in thin black spectacles, sitting in an arcade: 'I want to go home to Liverpool. Worked as a rent-boy there. But I don't want to do it anymore. What's the second city after Dublin? Liverpool.'

In Hampstead, having moved there, I looked at an elderberry tree, its pink and yellow leaves. I too wanted to go to a home.

Again in the woods of west Limerick, with the great stalks of Himalayan balsam with their delicate white flowers and cirrus pink underneath, I hear Sandy Denny's voice – 'The Men in the Forest'.

> The men in yon forest
> They ask it of me,
> How many strawberries grow in the salt sea?

And I answer them back with a tear in my eye,
How many ships sail in the forest?

I used those words to preface my novel *The Ikon Maker* – a tribute to Sandy Denny and the England she represented – an Irishwoman meanders through squats in London seeking her lost son.

And in west Limerick I thought of words of Spenser's which described that England:

Hither came Joseph of Arimathy
Who brought with him the holy grayle (they say)
And preacht the truth, but since it greatly did decay.

I began that novel after reading a quotation from Willa Cather: 'Where there is great love there are always miracles,' and after hearing a song, 'Seasons in the Sun', which derived from a Jacques Brel song. 'We had joy. We had fun. We had seasons in the sun.' I walked into Easons on O'Connell Street one day, just after hearing that, to read that a young friend had been killed hitch-hiking in France. I went hitch-hiking in Europe then myself, including France, and wrote half that novel on the sides of motorways or in motorway cafes or in a house in Haute Savoie, near where my friend was killed, where I dined at a table in a garden overlooking a field of potato stalks.

By the sea in Saintes Maries there had been bumpers and litle dark kiosks and jukeboxes with effects on them like costume jewellry. Lone young gypsy men wandered on the sands.

In west Limerick a traveller boy shampoos in a stream after a swim. His underpants are blue and white.

Three summers after I'd been to Saintes Maries I wrote a story, 'Afternoon', in which an old traveller woman is brought to a crossroads at Aughrim to die and then gets up, well again. Saintes Maries, where *The Ikon Maker* was partly written, came into it.

'Our secrets are the secrets of the universe,' said Joseph, 'a child, a woman with child, a casual donkey. We are the sort that Joseph was when he fled with Mary.'

I wrote that story on the B&I Liverpool boat to Ireland, bronzed with the sun of Crete and Greece. I'd had an absolute loss. But I'd never felt more absolutely alive. I came from the antique world with a zeal to live.

In a different part of France in the summer of 1970, with fungus sidelocks, I'd walked into Chartres Cathedral on an evening of young men in blue denim outfits on motorinos in the streets below the cathedral and heard a black American girl sing, 'There is a balm in Gilead'. Nina Simone's version was the one I was familiar with. I used the song in my play 'A Short Walk to the Sea', which was staged at the Peacock in 1975.

'All this talk about churches. I've never been to any,' says one girl and then another girl who's been to many wonderful churches comforts her, taking her in her arms. And we hear the echo from a cathedral:

There is a balm in Gilead
To make the wounded whole.
There is a balm in Gilead
To heal the gin-sick soul.

When I walked into Chartres Cathedral that summer I still possessed a Bob Dylan album with Dylan's face on it with an expression like a gunshot. In west Limerick, swimming in the river, I heard his scrannel voice again.

How many roads must a man walk down
Before they call him a man?

And the rasping indignation of Buffy Sainte-Marie's voice. 'Needle of Death.' She sang of 'a troubled young life'.

And the mountain-waterfall clarity of Joan Baez's voice. 'Diamonds and Rust.' A song about a glamorous and ambitious love, and the loss of it.

Songs that accompanied me to the river in Ballinasloe when a rope was held on either side of it, pulled up and down, swimmers holding on to it, shivers of sun on them. I had a mandarin shirt then, with rose and intent-blue speckles on it.

Another song that went with me was the Byrds' 'Turn, Turn, Turn'.

To every thing – turn, turn turn,
There is a season – turn, turn, turn,
And a time to every purpose under heaven.
... a time to kill, a time to heal.

Later I was to read in the memoirs of Nadezhda Mandelstam, and in the *De Profundis* of Oscar Wilde, that only through pain do we come into existence. By that river in west Limerick, on a darkening afternoon, streamers with the Limerick green and white blow, just as I remember the American flag in fields by the Pacific in the late fall on an evening, I was to make love by accident when my body had been robbed by a few years of loneliness.

In the late sixties I left the river and went to Dublin. My first years were unhappy but then I met a girl with crock-of-gold hair and we ceaselessly played the *Ó Riada sa Gaiety* album which had a damson cover. '*Do bhí bean uasal ...*' 'There was a lady with me for a while.'

Leonard Cohen came to Dublin in the years of the early seventies and sang 'Kevin Barry'. 'Just a lad of eighteen summers ...' (There'd been marigolds on the station platform of the town I'd left behind, marigolds I'd find again in a café in Belgrade in fall, a bunch of them on a shelf beside a carafe of white wine, oxen in the fields of Serbia, followed by women in scarves of Slavonic scarlet.) I never heard that on record. But Tim Hardin with his crescendo head came and sang Leonard Cohen's 'Bird on a Wire', and the misfit-boy-voiced anguish, testimony, confession of his version I did have on record. 'And if I, if I have ever been unkind I hope, I hope that you can just let it go by.'

One of the stories I re-read in Limerick was Ernest Hemingway's *The Snows of Kilimanjaro*: 'He has seen the world change; not just the events, although he had seen many of them and had watched the people, but he had seen the subtler change and he could remember how the people were at different times.'

I revisited Chartres with the gold-haired girl one fall. There was a pardon on – a procession filing through the alleyways leading to the hill-top cathedral. A week or so before we'd gone to another pardon – the horse-fair at Ballinasloe. The following fall we went into a church in Italy together. Outside, the crepuscular gold of Italy in the fall. There was a gold crucifix and we felt the tremor, felt our lives would be governed by this cross. Italy that fall, the landscape, was the elixir.

Later that fall, travelling alone, I was on the beach in Ostia outside Rome with an ox-horn moustached boy from Dublin I'd met in Rome. The ancient Romans hadn't just come here to swim, to picnic, but to debate, to have conversations.

'Do you have a lady?' he asked in the light that was shattering.

Hannah Arendt wrote a beautiful book called *Men in Dark Times* and I feel we are living in very dark times now.

When Caesar Augustus couldn't sleep he called the storytellers in and sometimes at night I remember a story Pasternak's cousin Olga Freidenberg tells of a pianist, Maria Yudina, who used to come to Leningrad during the siege and give piano recitals, and who walked back in the black-out to her room on the seventh floor of the Astoria.

Finally in west Limerick it is not the voices of the singers I hear but this nameless piano music.

JOHN HUTCHINSON

I FIRST HEARD 'LAYLA' and other assorted love songs, by Derek and the Dominos, at a friend's house in Notting Hill Gate. It was late in 1971, about a year after the record was released. I had been an enthusiastic fan of Eric Clapton's music since his days with the Yardbirds – we listened to bootleg tapes of early Cream, before the first album came out, in the Common Room at school in England – but after I left Oxford I lost touch. *Layla* seemed unmercifully powerful, and I could scarcely listen to it all the way through.

I love the record's unadulterated passion, and the way the title track evokes a vision of supreme earthly beauty that is about to pass away for ever. There is something in *Layla* that is simultaneously physical and otherworldly, and it made me aware of feelings that I did not know, until then, that I possessed. They were about women.

The album still moves me.

•

It is difficult for young people, today, to realize just what the Beatles meant to many of us in the late sixties. They were the manifestation of a generation's hope and optimism. I first listened to their records at school in 1963 and became a devoted follower, even joining their fan club. *Revolver* was probably the Beatles' finest album, but *Sgt. Pepper's Lonely Hearts Club Band* is my favourite, because it defined a moment, a Utopian moment, that appeared to justify all the energy and commitment that I had lavished on pop music. I was sixteen at the time, and it pleased me that even adults admired the Beatles' accomplishments.

I used to buy all the Beatles' records the day before they were officially released, usually at the local shop in Godalming. I was playing cricket for 'Second Tics' the day *Sgt. Pepper* went on sale, and when I returned to my study that afternoon, it was waiting for me on my desk. A friend, at my request, had bought it. I had already heard most of the album on the radio, and I'd read the previews in the music papers, so it felt very familiar, even in its newness, and I was aware, in a vague way, that it was going to prove to be a masterpiece – and a kind of blueprint for my late adolescence.

I cannot decide whether 'Strawberry Fields Forever' or 'A Day in the Life', the final track on *Sgt. Pepper* was the best song of the Beatles' maturity. Both of them are steeped in John Lennon's melancholy world-weariness, but at the core of 'A Day in the Life' is a passage of Paul McCartney's chipper hopefulness, which gives the song a wonderful poignancy. And when the staggering orchestral glissandi finally fade into chords of nothingness, an infinite and unintelligible message remains. I thought that it said: 'Although I never could be happy ...'

•

The only thing that marred the seamless *Pet Sounds* by the Beach Boys was the absence of one of the greatest pop singles of all time, 'Good Vibrations', which they released some months later. Even I, a staunch Beatles supporter, had to admit that *Pet Sounds* was a gift from the gods. Like *Sgt. Pepper*, it was both a peak and an end, because within a year the Californian sound had become defiantly countercultural: the Beach Boys were eclipsed by the Doors and Jefferson Airplane. *Pet Sounds*, however, was the *ne plus ultra* of white U.S. pop music – banal, maudlin, and singularly transcendent. Brian Wilson, as we now know, was in another space when the Beach Boys made this brilliant record. And, like John Lennon, he knew that this moment of epiphany couldn't last. At the time, though, many of us thought that it would.

•

When the Beatles broke up, my allegiance was transferred to George Harrison. This was because it was his interest in matters Indian that had led, more or less directly, to my decision to read Sanskrit at Oxford. I had already developed an enthusiasm for Buddhism and Indian music at school, and when it became clear that my philosophy and psychology degree was going to focus more on behaviourism and logical positivism than on Freud, Jung and Heidegger, I decided to try my hand at Oriental Studies.

George Harrison's boxed set of records called *All Things Must Pass* was the result of his deep immersion in Indian culture and several years of frustration with the internecine bickering of John Lennon and Paul McCartney. Listening to it today, I find the record over-produced and a little sanctimonious, but at the age of twenty it seemed wise and magnificent. The monochrome cover photograph, showing a long-haired and bearded Harrison in wellingtons, surrounded by garden gnomes in the estate of his mansion, Friar Park, made him look like an eccentric hermit. The devotional lyrics to Harrison's songs, which were applicable either to a woman or to God, reminded me of the poems of the Bengali poet, Rabindranath Tagore, that I loved deeply at the time. Other than the big house, to which I did not aspire, it seemed to me that I would like to live like Harrison – gardening, listening to Indian music and jamming with Eric Clapton. I even bought a pair of black wellingtons.

•

Shortly after I arrived in Ireland, just before Christmas 1967, I noticed that the Incredible String Band were going to play in Dublin. I didn't get to see them, but it was a good omen with regard to my future in this country, because their second record, *The 5000 Spirits, or The Layers of the Onion*, was already a firm favourite in my collection. Some months later, I worked as an extra on a film called *Where's Jack*, which was being shot in the Reformatory in Glencree, starring Tommy Steele. One of the few qualifications for selection as an extra was the possession of long hair, which meant that the cast featured a large proportion of the local hippie or neo-hippie community, most of whom normally gathered, during working hours, at the Bailey in Dublin. Many of these people had been at, or claimed to have been at, the Incredible String Band gig.

I was particularly partial to *The Hangman's Beautiful Daughter*. (My vinyl copy is almost worn out and has a burn mark I left by a falling joss-stick. I recently bought a CD version, for sentimental reasons.) Fey, folksy and utterly charming, its stoned tales about witches' hats and the Emperor of China were hugely engaging, and my friends and I all decided to tramp the hills and return at nightfall to country cottages, where we would live in quiet oneness with nature. I even made myself leather jerkins, moccasins and waistcoats fashioned from multicoloured 'Crock of Gold' rugs to further that aspiration.

Some years afterward the Incredible String Band took on extra members and their records became insufferably twee. But their second, third and parts of the fourth LPs are fantastic.

•

I can still recall the sound of Garth Hudson's intro to 'Chest Fever' echoing around Tom Quad on a warm summer's afternoon in 1969. My chest, like the music, swelled with waves of warmth and pride. This, I thought, was a sound of which a generation could be proud. *Music from Big Pink* came with a myth built into it – not alone was it made by Bob Dylan's backing musicians, in the very house to which he was reputed to have retired after the infamous motorcycle accident, but they were so self-assured that they chose to refer to themselves, quite simply, as the Band. The cover was an ugly, humorous daub by the master himself. *Music from Big Pink* is not quite such a fine album as their second record, *The Band*, which is one of the greatest rock'n'roll discs ever made, but it certainly had a profound effect on me.

Why? Because it was a curiously adult record. The Band, in 1968, were experienced veterans of the road, less concerned with individual bravado and musical self-indulgence than with crafting tough, frontiersman tales of sheer beauty and exhilaration. The Band knew about fear and loneliness, and their musicianship was gritty, instinctive, economic. They were able to describe lived experience, to draw on resources that were unavailable to other groups. In short, the Band had grown up.

•

The Band's earthy realism and terror-filled humour, like Eric Clapton's anguished passion, are – in part – direct descendants of Robert Johnson's blues. I have owned the two volumes of *King of the Delta Blues Singers* for a quarter of a century, more or less, but only recently have I begun to come to terms with them. So simple and unassuming on the surface, they are in fact immensely difficult and uncompromising records, quite overwhelming in their intensity. My initial experience of the blues came through the first Rolling Stones album, and then via John Mayall, Paul Butterfield and Cream. But Robert Johnson is where it begins and ends: 'Rambling on My Mind' says it all.

•

Another rock'n'roll record that deals in parables of love and terror is Bob Dylan's *Blonde on Blonde* – one of the very few double albums that couldn't advantageously be reduced to a single LP, just as 'Sad-Eyed Lady of the Lowlands' is one of the handful of long rock songs that justifies its ten-minute length. *Blonde on Blonde* is a harsh, bitter record, full of ambivalent emotions. Curiously, although I would have expected myself to opt for one of his earlier classics, this is the one Dylan record I wouldn't want to be without. It tells me something about my shadow.

•

Nor would I wish to be without Brazilian music. I was brought up in Rio, and I believe that part of me was left behind when the family left in 1966. (Sadly, I've never been back to find out whether this belief has any substance.) I remember listening to a record my parents owned, called *Dois na Bossa*, by two Brazilian popular singers, Elis Regina and Jair Rodrigues, on the evening I left Brazil for the last time. My father, who seldom listened to anything other than classical music, was immensely fond of this duo, and, in later years, used to play *Dois na Bossa* to remind himself of the days gone by. Now I do the same, having rescued the disc from a village sale in Wicklow where my mother – inadvertently, I think – had deposited it with other items of bric-a-brac that were cleared out after her house was sold. It is a wonderful record, full of tenderness, joy, sadness. Brazilians, on form, are able to combine extraordinary physical grace with *joie de vivre* and a touch of melancholy. When I hear good Brazilian music or watch their footballers in top fettle, I wish that I had been able to spend the rest of my days there.

•

I was at school with Peter Gabriel, and I took photographs of him for the school magazine when he was the lead singer of the band that was shortly to become Genesis. Years later I interviewed him for an American magazine just before the release of *So*; I hadn't seen him since we were at Charterhouse. When my father died, one of the pieces of music that meant most to me during the emotional turmoil of that period was 'Passion', a track on Gabriel's album of the same name. This record brings together Brazilian, African, Indian, American and British musicians, drawing unselfconsciously from all their traditions. It is 'world' music that shouldn't succeed, but does. The album manages to juxtapose moments of celestial beauty with others of devastating pain; it is about dying and being reborn.

Passion throws me back to where Peter and I began, listening to Eric Clapton sing Robert Johnson songs with the Bluesbreakers; it also propels me forward, ineffably, to places where I do not especially want to go.

MARY KENNY

I WAS TOO LEFT-WING to be interested in rock music when I was young during the sixties. Before 1968 the Left, particularly the French and Italian Left to which I was drawn, deplored rock or pop as a lowering manifestation of American capitalism and decadence. Gramsci believed the role of the intellectual was to develop political and cultural consciousness in the masses, not to sink to commercialized sentimentality. The French Communist Party boasted of the fact that a quarter of their members preferred colombophilie (pigeon-fancying) to television and its collateral Americanized culture, but all that changed after 1968, when the French Left imported American ideas – from Marcuse as well as from Simon & Garfunkel – and after rock music was declared subversive to bourgeois society, and thus OK. This was too late for my tastes, however, which had been formed on such gems as *Canti Rivoluzionari Italiani*, the unforgettable album featuring 'Bandiera Rossa' and 'L'Internazionale'. (I had always liked older men, so I was most impressed when Dick West, who I came to marry, told me he was old enough to have sung 'Bandiera Rossa' when the choral refrain had included: 'Viva Stalino!' He had sung that as a teenager back in 1949.)

The sixties for me began in Dublin, where I was a strange, weird loner of a teenager, went on to Paris, where I was poor and gave English conversation lessons to rich families, and ended in journalism in London, a city which was then officially dubbed 'swinging', though in truth it was still awfully stuffy in many respects. Privately, I always had a taste for smoky nightclub music: I loved an album I had of Charles Aznavour, singing 'Tu te Laisses Aller', a theme which occasionally returns to haunt me as I slop around in a dressing-gown until lunchtime. I particularly adored the earlier Dietrich; Marlene became more mannered as time went by. She was at her zenith in the 1939 recording of 'Falling in Love Again' – all the power and the helplessness of sexuality commingled in a great tune. Lotte Lenya singing the low-life ballads of Kurt Weill – 'Mack the Knife' and 'Surabaya Johnny' – pleased me with a harsher kind of night glamours, though Dietrich's half-regretted enchantment proved more lasting. I actually think 'You've Got that Look' the most erotic song ever written.

In youth I often felt filled with a kind of nostalgia for a past I did not yet have. At sixteen I loved to imagine tragic loves and burned-out desire, which was why I liked Ella Fitzgerald singing 'Begin the Beguine', with the allusion to 'a desire I can only remember'. Ella Fitzgerald was a truly great musician – you might call it rock, you might call it jazz – and her voice was her instrument.

My yearning feelings were often satisfyingly evoked by thirties and forties music: Charles Trenet singing 'Que Reste-t-il de Nos Amours' (englished as the banal, though possibly more altruistic, 'I Wish You Love'). His 'Douce France' and 'Revoir Paris' were of course magnificent French Resistant music, sung during the Occupation to resonate of Free France.

The album *Over the Rainbow* with Judy Garland was much played because of its unsurpassingly maudlin 'But Not For Me' ('They're playing songs of Love/But not for me'). It has the most wonderful line about love bringing more skies of grey than any Russian play. I also adored Richard Harris's album *A Tramp Shining*, because of its glorious mixture of defiance and self-pity, though that came out in 1968, which is just the end of my coming-of-age.

I was fond of Sinatra (still am), and particularly liked listening to him at third-bottle-of-wine stage of the dark watches of the night. I had a Sinatra album that contained the irreplaceable 'One for my Baby (And One More For the Road)', which is every boozer's most self-indulgently maudlin idea of bitter-sweet pleasure.

When drunk and nostalgic, I played, endlessly, Seán Ó Riada's music from the albums of *Mise Éire* and *Ó Riada sa Gaiety*, a compilation of traditional airs, folk songs and reels given the special Ó Riada harpsichord treatment. Every emigrant should have something to cry to.

MICHAEL LINDSAY-HOGG

IT'S HARD FOR ME to choose albums that affected me because I'm more of a singles guy, having grown up with the radio in America, then Radio Luxembourg when I was at Oxford, and then the pirates. Albums, early on anyway, seemed to fall apart every so often and it was hard for the one or two or however many voices to hold my interest on the tracks that really shouldn't have been there. This started to change with the rise of the singer-songwriters, although not entirely. So I suppose what I liked was the one perfect track, any early Phil Spector, say.

However, there are a few albums that do mean a lot to me because at a certain stage I was there, in the sense of being physically present. I used to direct a TV music show called *Ready, Steady, Go!* and as a result got to know a lot of musicians from that extraordinary time in the mid- to-late sixties when English bands were exploding and sending their shards of brilliance all over the world and into the history of our century.

After a time some of the bands didn't like appearing on the TV shows (*RSG!* off the air by now) and also wanted more influence over the way they were presented, so we did a few of what are now called videos and were then called promos, some of the early ones being 'Jumping Jack Flash', 'Hey Jude', 'Revolution', 'Happy Jack'. And then the prime bands, the Rolling Stones and the Beatles, became interested in longer-form presentations.

Beggars Banquet: Not necessarily to promote this album but around the time of its release, the Rolling Stones, the original ones, with Brian Jones, decided they wanted to do their own TV special which we called *The Rolling Stones Rock'n'Roll Circus*. (This film is going to have its first public screening at the 1996 New York Film Festival. After almost thirty years of not being seen, it is now going to appear, like one of those soldiers who didn't know the war was over and emerges from a jungle hiding place, blinking, into a new world.) To celebrate the release of *Beggars Banquet*, the Rolling Stones gave a lunch in a large dark restaurant in Kensington. 'Don't wear good clothes,' they said to me. Cream cakes was the why. At the end of lunch, large cakes with whipped cream topping were put in front of the band members who picked up gobs of aerated froth and, laughing and snickering like the naughty children of tabloid dreams, pressed it into the face of whoever they were next to: girlfriends, Lord Harlech, anxious press agents, drunken journalists, whoever. The photos in the paper the next day made it look like a very festive occasion, with Brian enjoying it the most.

We shot the *Circus* in a converted warehouse near Wembley the week before Christmas. After the Who, Jethro Tull, Marianne Faithfull, and a Lennon-Clapton-Richard-Ono band, the Rolling Stones went on stage to do their part in their own show.

It was 2 a.m., and they had been hanging around since noon, when we'd shot their entrance into the Big Top. They were tired and irritable and, in one or two cases, a little unsteady. But think of it this way – if a group of nuns had been sitting around for fourteen hours, with only their guitars for company, and drinking nothing stronger than tea, they too might be in a fractious mood.

'You Can't Always Get What You Want' went okay after many takes, then lots more of the album, take after ragged take, and then it was 5 a.m. and time for 'Sympathy for the Devil', the one we'd all looked forward to, when we were fresher and clearer earlier in the day/night. We did a take which was a shambles, for Mick, for them, for me, for the cameras. Pissed off and tired, Mick went to talk to his troops, a little touch of 'Harry in the night', and then when the music started again, he forced himself into a performance, teasing, innocent, jaded, electric, the like of which I'd never seen before. Then, the song over, the twenty-five-year-old boy, half-naked, stood up, his sharpshooter's mind relaxed, the marathoner's body drooped. He looked at the others, smiled and yawned. Brian smiled back. It was the last time he played with the Rolling Stones.

Less than a month after shooting *The Rolling Stones Rock 'n' Roll Circus*, I started working on *Let it Be*.

I'd worked with the Beatles before, first 'Paperback Writer', then 'Revolution' and 'Hey Jude'. When we were doing 'Revolution', I remember two things. One is when going into the studio before we started shooting, I fell into step with John Lennon. He didn't look his best, a late night or something. I asked him if he wanted make-up so he'd look a little 'healthier'. He said no. 'Why?' I asked. 'Because I'm John Lennon.' What's important to make clear is that he didn't mean he was too grand to be made up, but, instead, he was going to perform as himself, not as an actor pretending to be someone. If he looked a little ropey, that was the way he looked that day. The next thing I remember was that John wanted a big close-up on the lyric 'If you go talking about Chairman Mao, you ain't gonna make it with anyone anyhow', because he thought that was the key lyric of the song.

For 'Hey Jude', we had a crowd as part of the production, for the chorus, meant to represent all different sorts. So for the last four minutes of the song, take after take, the Beatles were surrounded by a mix of male and female, young and old, students, businessmen, housewives, kids, the postman, and the Beatles found they were more or less enjoying playing again with live bodies around them. Remember they hadn't worked in front of any kind of audience since they'd stopped touring in 1966 and so, because of the 'Hey Jude' experience (perhaps not unconnected with the massive record sales and the acknowledged aid the video had given), they thought that they wanted to do some sort of show which would be recorded as a TV special, and that there would also be a documentary of the making of the show.

So, early in January 1969, the Beatles, myself, a couple of cameramen and other technicians met at Twickenham Studios, where we'd shot 'Hey Jude'. The first thing I realized was, and this may seem dopily obvious, that they were musicians first, not actors. And what they wanted to get right were their songs, their music. And that at this early stage of their work, the cameras were intruders, more so now probably than they would have been before. There had been a major shift in the way they worked since they had stopped touring. Touring and then going into the studio and then touring again and then recording again kept the songwriters writing together (look at the Rolling Stones now, thirty years later). But because the Beatles, principally Lennon/McCartney, weren't constantly with each other, they had started to write separately, and so there'd be a song written by one of them and the others were more more like sidemen, instructed and rehearsed but not particularly collaborative. Also, during this time, John had met Yoko Ono and, because of their closeness, there were now five people in the mix, not four.

Rehearsals in theatre, dance, music, whatever, take on their own life and personality. Here the personality was curdled. Different, usually unspoken, aims were pulling the participants in conflicting directions. An inspired day would be followed by lackadaisical ones, no-shows, rows about what the TV special should be (shoot it in the Cavern or an amphitheatre in Tunisia), George leaving, John wanting immediately to get in Eric Clapton, George returning with the proviso that there be no TV show, only an album. By this time, our small film crew was an accepted nuisance, like wasps on a summer's day. We left Twickenham and all moved to the un-wired basement studio at Apple in London. Things seemed to improve here: back in a hermetic studio again the tensions simmered, didn't bubble. These four men, in their mid- to-late twenties, tested together by unique experiences, were entering a different stage of their lives, and not a very tidy one. Jealousies about credit and acknowledgment, inequalities to do with songwriting percentages, vastly different personal lives and desires, money worries (uncollectable royalties and a cash-haemorrhaging Apple Co.), were forces ulcerating what had seemed eternal friendships – or maybe that's just what we'd hoped they'd be.

We in the film crew felt we were actors in an updated version of Sartre's *No Exit*, where people meet in hell and can't get out. What was going to become of all this stuff we were grinding out, two cameras for eight hours every day?

One Saturday, the Beatles and I and a few others were having lunch in the boardroom – which was also the dining-room – discussing what we were going to do, whether it would just be another unrealized and junked rock'n'roll project. My version of what happened is that I said we needed some sort of resolution to the film, a sense we were going somewhere, a sort of conclusion. 'You wouldn't do it at the Cavern, or in the amphitheatre in Tunisia. Why don't we just do it on the roof?' The reason I say 'my version' is, in light of events, there are several claimants for this suggestion including, I think, the cook who'd made the apple crumble.

So, after lunch, while the others went off to different pursuits, Paul, the late Mal Evans (later shot, like John, in America) and I went up on the roof and had a look, and the idea started to take on a life. The rest is part of rock'n'roll history.

We had decided to start playing around 12.30, to get the lunchtime crowds. The Beatles were, typically, still arguing at 12.20 if they'd really do it and then, enthusiastically or reluctantly, according to character, they finally went up the narrow staircase onto the roof. It was the last time they, as a performing group, as the Fab Four, as the repository of a generation's dreams and happiness, ever played together. The final words of the film were John's: 'I hope we passed the audition.'

SHANE MacGOWAN

SEVEN DRUNKEN NIGHTS
THE DUBLINERS

One of my favourite groups and one of my biggest influences in Irish music. I had all these cousins who were in Dubliners-type ballad groups; Frank and Tony Gleeson and Gerry Lunch never really got anywhere but they played sessions all around Tipperary. They were friends of the Wolfe Tones. The Dubliners were the first of the sixties folk revival groups who weren't clean-cut like the Clancy Brothers in their Aran jumpers. This is not to knock the Clancys, because I like them in their own way – but they were like the Beatles while the Dubliners were like the Rolling Stones. I remember all the old people being shocked by the long beards. The Dubliners had brilliant musicianship as well as two great voices – Ronnie Drew and Luke Kelly. Luke Kelly was a travellin' man, a rolling stone. As a young man he travelled across Europe with his banjo, and he had a brilliant voice and a very broad-minded attitude to music.

CAROLAN

Carolan was a harp player who was one of the last Irish wandering minstrel bards. He played in the big houses and in the bars and shebeens, for varying amounts of money. He drank whiskey in the ditch and was blind.

He learned music by ear and gave a baroque phrasing to the Irish music of the day, which is still there. He wrote a lot of classic Irish tunes, a lot of them anonymously; knowing the author of a lot of these old tunes was an unusual thing. Derek Bell, the harpist from the Chieftains, made two great tapes of his music.

MISE ÉIRE
SEAN Ó RIADA

He broke all the rules – the Comhaltas rules of the time. There is still a stultifying force in Irish music that doesn't like anything new but Ó Riada and Carolan kept the tradition alive by doing new things with very old music, at times when interest was flagging among the people.

He encouraged the use of the bodhrán as the traditional Irish drum. Even though it had been used by peasant musicians for hundreds of years, the bodhrán was not regarded as a true Irish instrument by Comhaltas until Ó Riada encouraged its use.

The Chieftains were Ó Riada's band when he did *Mise Éire*. I like the Chieftains on their own but they don't have the magic they had when they were with Ó Riada.

ELECTRIC LADYLAND
JIMI HENDRIX

Along with Jerry Lee Lewis and Elvis Presley, one of the ultimate men of rock-'n'roll. Everything about Jimi has already been said. I'm really into him and have him on my wall; it's one of my favourite pictures. I don't know why he looks at me, he looks at everybody. And when you look back into his eyes it's like looking into the eyes of God. He said he was from Mars and I believe it; if he said it was so, why not? He could have been joking of course, he was a jokey kind of guy.

JERRY LEE LEWIS
JERRY LEE LEWIS

Jerry Lee is enlightened as well. When I met him I went in there quaking. He offered me some whiskey. He said 'You either drink with me or I shoot you', so I drank with him and we got on great. He wanted me to write a song for him and I've been trying to get it done.

THE SUN SESSIONS
ELVIS PRESLEY

Pop, rock, white soul, country, whatever; a giant of a man both musically and physically.

SAM COOKE

Beautiful. Great rock'n'roll with loads of gospel and melody.

Now I've only got three left and there are far more than three that I want to do. These are all people that I feel an affinity with, because they're telling it like it is. They are all unique in their own way, yet they are all coming from a tradition. Carolan did it in his own way. He wrote the most popular tunes of his day and they are still popular, so he's the longest-lasting of these, but I think they will all last equally in the long run.

RAIN DOGS
TOM WAITS

Tom Waits comes from the American blues, gospel, country, jazz tradition but he's still unmistakably Tom Waits.

Like Jerry Lee Lewis, Tom Waits is a really nice guy. I never met Elvis but I'm sure he was a very nice guy too. Just guys who get down and do it.

My favourite Tom Waits record is 'Downtown Train'. I like the tune, I like the words, I like the fucking music on it. You could shag to it, but I find it too diverting to shag to it. It's the sort of record for after you shag. It's a great story that demands all your attention, so I suppose it isn't really a good shagging record at all. Good shagging records are the ones with a good beat and a smoochy melody.

JOHN COLTRANE

Then there's Coltrane. We're talking about weirdos here; all people who didn't have many hit records and should have had a lot more.

Coltrane is a guy who went through a musical trip. He started off as a jazz, R&B sax player and by the end of his life he was scaling transcendental peaks, making music for meditation.

LEE PERRY

Comes from the black music tradition. He's ahead of his time, every step of the way. He's cheeky, the way he does stuff. He has been known to bury his records in the ground to make them sound 'earthy' – he's the original insane genius. He is incredibly creative and is still going today. He has taken things to the limits like Carolan or Ó Riada during *Mise Éire*.

PATRICK McCABE

BLONDE ON BLONDE
BOB DYLAN

The high metallic sound of this album, along with its high-voltage imagery, reveals for the first time where exactly it is that one might locate the ghost of electricity – howling in the bones of some woman's face to be precise – not to mention practically blowing everything that rock and folk and any mixture of the two had given us before it right out of the water, with a menagerie of surrealist images and truly mental rhymes and metaphors which make no sense at all and yet make just about as much as it is humanly possible to make. Hearing 'Sad-Eyed Lady of the Lowlands' – a whole side of the most glorious music in all of rock's history – at what was essentially the beginning of my creative life, had me heading off in the direction of the river, there to end it all, until I realized of course that if I did dip my head therein, I would never again be able to savour the delights of 'Absolutely Sweet Marie' or '4th Time Around', not to mention 'I Want You'. I mean – where did you ever hear electric piano like that? So back I came and on she went and it's been spinning since.

THIN LIZZY
THIN LIZZY

I realize of course that there will be any number of people lining up to say, 'What? Thin Lizzy? Their first album? In second place! Are you mad?', but I don't care because from the very first day I heard this album I've loved it and I've every intention of going on loving it and putting it in whatever place I want. I think it is because it contains one of the best songs about any city anywhere that I've ever heard – 'Dublin' – which shows just how good Phil Lynott was before he started wearing spray-on jailbreaks and choppers and all that old codology. It seems to be a really Irish record but none the less powerful for that, and is it any wonder that after I heard it I started wearing bolero shirts and saying to women, 'Howya!', letting on I was from Crumlin and knew Diddy Levine, who in the later forties lived with Judas King – I mean what more do you want than that beauty?

GUNFIGHTER BALLADS AND TRAIL SONGS
MARTY ROBBINS

I suppose there will be plenty who will ask what Marty is doing here but that is only because they have never sat down and listened to the heartbreak in his voice when he is singing about his woman, his wife, or the anxiety he faces when he's out El Paso way and all hell breaks loose with mustangs rearing and guitars playing and wild Mexican women doing dances that would blow the togs off lesser men. Let there be no equivocation, this man is truly the opera star of the mesa and if anyone can honestly sit down and listen to 'Cool Water', 'Big Iron', or 'Little Green Valley' without saying, 'This man more than any other knows what the sound of a swinging sign or a skittering tumbleweed can do to a man's heart,' then they deserve to be taken out and dry-gulched.

LIVE IN EUROPE
RORY GALLAGHER

The question was: where was Rory from? Was he from Donegal as the men from Rannafasht loudly insisted or was he from Cork city born and bred and liable to take your head off if you suggested otherwise? To tell you the truth, I didn't know and didn't care – all I knew was that once he got on that stage and shouted, 'Thaggew!', before going into the opening bars of 'Messing with the Kid', if he had asked me to hump his gear from Youghal to Yokohama for the rest of his axe-wielding days, I would have been more than glad to do it. To show that I was serious about this, for many years I committed myself to the wearing of lumberjack shirts and baseball boots, and without the slightest provocation at all would grab brushes, sticks, lumps of plywood and anything else that was going and go down on my knees saying that it was good to be here in Hammersmith Odeon and, without stopping once, go right through the entire set of the above album until the sweat roared off me like Niagara and off I went to sit in my hotel room, listening to Big Bill Broonzy and Leadbelly, two of the best who would never have been bettered – if the long-haired Cork-Donegal poet of the Strat had not happened along and stole their blues away.

HAPPY TO MEET, SORRY TO PART
HORSLIPS

This had all the impact of an atomic explosion, not just as far as my consciousness was concerned, but that of anyone who had ever heard a jig or a reel and hadn't given tuppence either way, for whatever reason, famine or church or oppression or a mad mixture of the whole lot, none of it making a blind bit of difference now, for the second you walked into the ballroom where bomber-jacketed, self-styled heads were clapping their hands with such a ferocity that they soon had the consistency of raw steak, crying, 'Horslips! Horslips!' until at last on they came, the glam-rock jig merchants, launching into every shining nugget from this seminal, concertina-shaped album, 'Furniture' being the highlight, then on to 'Scalloway Ripoff' and ending with the show-stopping medley of rock'n'roll, proving at last for a salivating, redeemed generation, that Johnny B. had been, all along, one of the Goodes of West Clare.

FILL YOUR HEAD WITH ROCK
VARIOUS ARTISTS

I got this for 29/11 in Enniskillen with the money I earned from delivering messages on a bike around the town. It was a compilation of the kind that were very popular in the early seventies, a sort of showcase of the very best that, in this case, CBS had to offer. And boy, had they plenty to offer! Was it any wonder I crashed the bike on the way home? For there they were in all their gatefold glory, your man with the electric fiddle out of Flock, Leonard (Ha! Where are the cynics now!) 'Genius' Cohen, Argent, Tom Rush, Black Widow (who, incidentally were a black-magic band but managed to get the blame put on Black Sabbath), Santana, and the late-lamented, quintessentially ethereal hippie band of all time, Trees. Don't ask me where they went – all I know is, if I had known where to get illicit substances in them days, I would have smoked my way to Cavan town. I include this because its mind-blowing eclecticism indicates just what a vibrant time the much-maligned seventies was – and how good we dinosaurs had it before those spiky-haired counter-jumpers came along calling us names. Oh, and also included on this black circle of joy (!) is Al Stewart, with a song about an orange. Literary types in long coats will remember that he used to write for Eamonn Carr's *Capella* magazine. (See Horslips above).

SHAG TOBACCO
GAVIN FRIDAY

If you look at Laurence Harvey, you think to yourself 'now there's a nice, well-mannered man who would never cause trouble at a dinner party', but that of course is just because you don't know that he has a microchip planted in his head which if it goes off will blow both you and this whole book to kingdom come. Gavin Friday on the cover of this album looks a bit like Laurence and I am glad to say that the similarity doesn't end there. For, like the *Manchurian Candidate* man, young Friday can be velvet-voicing away there with nothing to bother him only the cigarette smoke and the sighs of lonely lovers as they shuffle by on the blue-lit streets of early morning. Except that next thing you know, you're away off up the river on your way to a night-time Cambodia of the soul, locked in mortal combat with the ones you love, the ones you hate, the future, the past, all about you tracers and dum-dum bullets fragmenting in the sky. This is very much an end-of-the-millennium record, and makes it very clear to all but those who have turnips for heads what Friday is and always has been, a very funny man who has no problem taking himself intensely seriously and then laughing at himself all the way to the early-opening houses. Which I mention because, although this record floats out into the middle of the world, it also puts its arms around Dublin and makes that city its own, as much as Joyce and Behan did in their day. Because the album smells and feels and crashes all about you like the strangest black silk, you're never sure from one moment to the next whether it's going to strangle or sweet-talk you – just like your average Dublin night.

COSMO'S FACTORY
CREEDENCE CLEARWATER REVIVAL

It's hard to make up your mind which album by this band to include in your top ten. In their heyday they were so good and produced so many, any of their records from *Green River* to *Willie and the Poorboys* right up indeed to John Fogerty's solo efforts could happily have filled this spot. I chose this one because there is a picture of that very man on the cover, doing his best to look like me, or at least me in the early seventies, when I was doing my best to look like him, sporting a Davy Jones haircut and a Rory Gallagher lumberjack shirt, the outfit which was *de rigueur* if you were off to the Sports Centre in Cavan or Mullinavatt Marquee to say to girls, 'Creedence! Aren't they something?' as she said, 'Wha?' and the relief band went blue in the face trying to get the top notes of 'Travellin' Band', having sandpapered their throats in the dressing-room, all to no avail. For nobody, but nobody – not even the great Rob Strong – could come close to anything this band did at their best. And *Cosmo's*, with its spectacular 'purgessive rawk' extended version of the Marvin Gaye classic 'I Heard It Through the Grapevine', must surely rank as one of their best, seriously electric cowpunching that has never been bettered.

FIRE AND WATER
FREE

I know it's a sad state of affairs that most of my albums come from the early seventies and feature people who spent a lot of their time wearing three button t-shirts of the tie-dye variety but if you think I'm going to get embarrassed for one second by that then I suggest you go out and buy any number of gatefolds and stick them where the monkey stuck his nuts. For, what with the astonishing dialogue that's going on here between Paul Kossoff's lead and Andy Fraser's bass, you simply have to say that if these men were writers, one of them would be Joyce and the other Beckett. And that's not to run down the rest of the band either for if any rock vocalist has ever come near Paul Rodger's melodic growling then I'm afraid I have been living in a Buddhist monastery for nigh on twenty years. What do you think of 'Mr Big'? I mean have you ever in your life heard heavy gutsy rock so tight and so controlled? I put it to you that you are a liar sir. Like Creedence, there are any number of Free albums I would gladly put in this spot, such as *Tons of Sobs*, but I think, having given it a lot of thought, this emotion-charged offering, which showed the rest of the orgiastic heavies just what rock was really all about, just gets in there by a nifty whisker. Just a pity thousands of other bands of the period didn't pay more attention and learned from Free's subtle, weaving melody lines that gutsy and ballsy doesn't mean you have to play Popeye.

IRELAND'S REQUESTS
EILEEN DONAGHY

I'm not saying that this is the best album ever made or anything like that but because it was never off our record-player when I was knee-high to a dockleaf, I couldn't, morally, bring myself to leave it out. It might well be used as the soundtrack of *Kitty the Hare Goes to Hollywood* or *The Stile My Father Built* for it has all the charm and gaiety of those heart-warming water-colour worlds that I used to inhabit not when I was eating dried banana skins but when I was young – stone walls, cowslips, warm buttermilk and little cottages with women in headscarves shouting at you, 'Good man, young McCabe!' as you happily ramble horizonward with a jamjar full of bees, all these songs in your head and at your back – 'The Old Water Mill', 'Who Put the Overalls in Mrs Murphy's Chowder?', 'A Wee Cup of Tay' (incorporating the famous Ulster soda farl) and many other gems that no one who claims to be an admirer of *The Quiet Man*'s magic can afford to leave out of their dreams. This golden-studded world of wonderful waxen mini-symphonies first appeared in the early sixties and belongs to the noble tradition of Percy French, Johnny Patterson, Bridie Gallagher, Maisie McDaniel and many others, and if anyone out there has a problem with that, take care would they get chased across a golden field of long ago by a ten-best-album-list compiler with a hayfork in his hand, yelping, 'Will you g'wan to hell and buy these rekkirds before I ventilate ya!'

NELL McCAFFERTY

SURE WE NEVER HAD ALBUMS. We had a factory in Derry producing record-players we couldn't afford to buy and when the Birmingham Sound Reproducers closed down in the late fifties, thousands of families were thrown out of work, reducing our prospects even more. The civil rights movement and the twenty-five-year war with Britain followed soon after. We managed to grow up as rock-'n'roll kids anyway, because we did have the jukebox. The jukebox was better than any hi-fi collection in any home in the world today. Standing in the corner of every ice-cream café, it was the centre of the universe. Every week the records were changed, bringing the Gods into Derry. For threepence a play, five for a shilling: Jerry Lee Lewis, Fats Domino, Buddy Holly. Elvis, of course, was never changed. His listings on the jukebox, for the three short years he was among us before being drafted, just grew longer and longer. By the time he got out of the army, the jukebox had virtually disappeared. People had stopped eating ice-cream and moved into the sixties, into the pubs. There was no music in pubs in the sixties. The sixties are overrated. People who grew up in that era never knew what it was like to worship before the jukebox in a neon-lit, ice-cream cool public sanctuary that was devoted solely and exclusively to rock 'n'roll. There are jukeboxes in Irish pubs now but they are ridiculous. You either drink and talk, or you don't.

Macari's café was the best place, because the sailors who came into port for the day came into Macari's to eat ice-cream, buy sweets, drink lemonade and spend their money like ... sailors ... on the jukebox. (There was no mortal sin, no sex and no booze in Derry in the fifties.) Derry was an international port then. The sailors came from France and Portugal and Holland and America. AMERICA. You could sneak a look at their tans, listen to their accents and simultaneously think of Elvis. If you've never moaned along with a Yankee sailor to the words of 'Heartbreak Hotel', you've never lived. You can't truly sing the chorus of 'All Shook Up' unless you've learned the sound – it's all sound, no words – from an American sailor. 'Unh huh huh, huh huh hunh ...' Something like that.

What's more, rock'n'roll, buried in concept albums, doesn't cause riots any more. Derry had its first (and only) rock'n'roll riot when *Rock Around the Clock* came to the city picture-house. The police couldn't cope with the dancing in the streets as they poured out of the cinema, led by my neighbour Gerard Sharkey, from number 3 Beechwood Street, five doors away from our house. Let his name and address be carved with pride; he was eighteen and he was fined for jiving. Rebellion spread and soon everybody was dancing outdoors. (The Royal Ulster Constabulary have never managed to get things right.) We didn't need the record-player, or the record – never mind the album – because we learned the words off by heart, and percussion was provided by hand-clapping, 'One, two, three o'clock, four o'clock, rock, five, six, seven o' clock, eight o'clock, rock ...'. My sister Muireanna and her boyfriend Maurice taught us the dance-steps, moving from street corner to street corner. It was lovely in the summer evenings when she came down to the foot of the street where the crowd was waiting, ready and eager to sing along and learn how to dance rock'n'roll. Why my father worried about her sometimes hanging out with the sailors around the jukebox, I'll never know. She and Maurice emigrated to England, made a fortune in the building trade and voted for Margaret Thatcher.

The change came when a Belfast boy erupted. Van Morrison and Them sang 'Here Comes the Night'. Suddenly everything was personal. He was mean and moody, and marvellously in your face. We couldn't hide behind Elvis anymore, couldn't claim sanctuary in the ice-cream parlour, couldn't dance innocently at the crossroads, couldn't shyly content ourselves with the fictional fights that stars put up against the establishment in rock'n'roll movies. Van was one of our own, an ordinary Northern Ireland person, just like us. He called on us to be, not to follow. It was frightening. He created the impression that you had to have sexual intercourse in the swinging, sinful sixties. It sounded alright in 'Madame George', but in your own flat it amounted practically to running a brothel. Who, us? Doing it? That?

I'm not the only one who reached for the safety of the record-player and the album and the non-sexual collective piety of folk-song protest. The answer, my friend, was blowing in the wind, the choir kept singing of freedom, and Dylan and Baez saved our virginal bacon. This culminated in my arrival in Israel to work for ideals and no pay in a kibbutz, coinciding with the outbreak of the Six Day War. Hundreds of young, heaving bodies were crammed into air-raid shelters. To save on fuel, the lights went out. Never have so many minds been concentrated so heavily on one single album in an effort to avoid the obligations of sexual intercourse. The Beatles' *Abbey Road* had arrived in the kibbutz the night before war broke out. Over the next six days we put together all the words, calling out remembered snatches, singing in the dark to save our virginities. That was just the men: the women imitated the orchestral bits. Lucky man who made the grade: ... in the sky with diamonds ... after being alone for so many years ... something about the Albert Hall. How we sang, emerging word perfect.

In the seventies I turned to opera and feminism.

CIARAN McGINLEY

But of course the sky does not wake
There is no open grave, no resurrection
Only silence. We live and die in the cage.
Music, at least, gives the living grace.
          — Chet Raymo, *The Dork of Cork*

TEN HUGELY INFLUENTIAL RECORDS from 1969 to 1994. Twenty-five years since I pawned my soul to rock'n'roll.

The most I can claim from the sixties is that just as it came to a close I got my first LP. Before that I was a typical Irish teenager. Then I saw the film *Easy Rider*, bought the soundtrack, and nothing has been typical ever since.

EASY RIDER
VARIOUS ARTISTS

The *Easy Rider* album was filled with rock anthems, but my favourite track was and is 'Born to be Wild' by Steppenwolf; riding a low-powered bike around Connemara roads, I fantasized I was Dennis Hopper on his super-bike 'doing my own thing, man' in the movie. Seeing the film on holiday in Dublin, it epitomized and crystallized my thoughts of the time, and for years afterwards the record turned merrily on whatever record-player I had. Other powerful tracks were 'The Pusher' and that piss-take of a ballad 'Don't Bogart that Joint'.

For millions of people *Easy Rider* opened the way for mass-appeal rock music, with drugs a fairly integral part of the attraction. Unlike Mr Clinton, I inhaled, and often. And although I would counsel caution with hard drugs, the album's extolling of freedom and non-attachment are central pivots of my present life.

DARK SIDE OF THE MOON
PINK FLOYD

In the early seventies this bunch of musicians, having lost their inspired leader Syd Barrett to drug-induced psychosis (today finds him communicating in dog-like barks), wrote a series of songs that played the most formative part in my development. Apart from occasional gimmicks, like the cash-register sound in 'Money', the music's quality and the haunting, wailing singers make the album a piece of audio theatre. The sleeve must have been tacked to walls from Dublin to Madras: a rainbow prism-reflecting designed by the studio Hipgnosis.

TRANSFORMER
LOU REED

This is an enchanting collection of songs produced and arranged by Reed's friends David Bowie and Mick Ronson. This was the next major record to encourage my progress into the degenerate I am today. Funnily enough, I bought the record for a friend whose parents had just committed him to St Patrick's psychiatric hospital in Dublin. The night after he asked me to get it, he was given ECT and lost his memory, so I held on to it for twenty years, airing it at least once a week. The classic track 'Walk on the Wild Side' was produced by Bowie and Ronson at the height of their careers, as well as the more gentle 'Perfect Days', and the adrenalin rush of 'Vicious'.

PIN-UPS
DAVID BOWIE

His finest work was from the early- to mid-seventies, and I played records like *Hunky Dory*, *Ziggy Stardust* and *Aladdin Sane* until the groove literally wore away. *Pin-Ups* was Bowie's tribute to the hits of his youth; songs like 'See Emily Play' by Pink Floyd and 'Here Comes the Night' by Belfast-based Them (featuring Van Morrison) were polished further by Bowie in a stunning production.

I played 'Friday on My Mind' every morning before the soul-destroying job I once had in London.

Bowie influenced style in London at the time, and both he and Elton John did a lot to combat bigotry towards gays and transsexuals. His music, unlike others with psychedelic influences, had a sharp, urbane amphetamine buzz.

NEW BOOTS AND PANTIES!!
IAN DURY AND THE BLOCKHEADS

As Johnny Rotten and the whole explosion that was collectively called 'Punk' had turned the music industry upside down, for me the star of the whole lot was the witty Londoner Ian Dury. I certainly identified with 'Wake Up and Make Love to Me' and the lovely dreamy tribute to his hero 'Sweet Gene Vincent'. And then the four 'genuine as Tower Bridge' London ballads with 'Plaistow Patricia' as my favourite. I've always loved 'lawless brats from council flats' and this song captures the defiance later demonstrated by the many 'Patricias' at the poll-tax riots near Plaistow less than a decade later. 'Billericay Dickie' tells the ribald story of a genuine London Romeo and would have Dury in front of a jury today for political incorrectness.

I saw this maestro perform in the tragic Stardust Club in Dublin, just as Thatcherism marked the beginning of a severe era, and his music directed me to choose my own course and life. This is the album I'd take if stranded on some desert isle.

REMAIN IN LIGHT
TALKING HEADS

Just when I despaired of anything worthwhile emerging from North America, the late seventies delivered a group called Talking Heads. The band was fronted by the gaunt figure of David Byrne, a musical genius, and the music somehow made me face the realities of becoming, as I was then, part of a village community in western Ireland.

'Psycho Killer' followed my passion for 'Born to be Wild'. Byrne managed to penetrate each line individually, counterpointed by his bassist, Tina Weymouth, and her husband Chris Frantz on drums. Once, when I gave an interview on radio over a fishery rights issue I was involved in, part of the deal was that I could select the tune of my choice. Without hesitation: 'Psycho Killer'. The band sadly broke up, and although Byrne has released several records since in a solo capacity, little has been heard from the others. As the Tom Tom Club they performed in the tiny McGonigal's nightclub on South Anne Street in Dublin, a terrific performance without their mentor. Byrne is still making some of the finest music I've heard, with the same power, the same alertness to possibility.

SUNSHINE ON LEITH
THE PROCLAIMERS

'Brilliant', I remember thinking when a friend gave me a copy of this album. 'Here are Scottish twin brothers articulating with beautiful melodies the pent-up feelings of those marginalized by Thatcher.' Craig and Charlie Reid looked like a cross between Kenneth Williams of the Carry On films and Benny Hill. They delivered incisive lyrics and strong social commentary with manic guitar-bashing crescendoes, leaving the casual listener mesmerized.

'Cap-in-Hand', my favourite track, has the same international relevance as Jim Larkin, and could be the cultural anthem for Scotland's Mrs Ewing and her SNP members. I played it once to young guys in Sri Lanka and they loved it.

'It's Saturday Night' must someday become the anthem of degenerates of all shades, from football fans to lager louts. 'The drink that I had three hours ago has been joined by fourteen others in a steady flow.' There's anger towards exhibitionist wealth when the lyrics menacingly forecast that the singer is 'going to scratch cars with my key again'.

WRONG WAY UP
BRIAN ENO AND JOHN CALE

The coming together of these two legends got the nineties off to a fine start for me. John Cale had spent the sixties in the Velvet Underground, and by the eighties he was back living in Wales making an odd guest appearance here and there. Brian Eno had been in several supergroups in the seventies but had become best known as a visual artist and producer of other groups' records in the eighties, including his work with U2 on *The Unforgettable Fire*.

According to media reports, tension between the two remained charged throughout the recording of this record, and Cale blew up at one stage and headed to America from Eno's recording studio in blissful Suffolk. There are ten songs on the record and without doubt my favourite is 'In the Backroom'. I have been lucky in life to work often in the proverbial 'backroom', and this song captures the mood and rhythm of life on the edges. Captured by Francis Ford Coppola in the filming of Brando in *Apocalypse Now*, the disjointed approach adopted by Eno on 'In the Backroom', 'Cordoba' and 'The River' lets the listener do his own visualization, and the images are rich.

I can honestly say this record saved my sanity. I once had a ten-hour stopover in Bombay airport and the youth of the soldiers walking around with machine-guns sort of got to me. It must have been the heat. Noticing my restlessness, a lovely woman came over to me and loaned me her Walkman, as she planned to go to sleep. *Wrong Way Up* was the tape on the machine. On seeing this I almost kissed my benefactor. Within an hour, I was smiling relaxedly at the young soldiers as they strutted around.

AM I NOT YOUR GIRL?
SINÉAD O'CONNOR

Hardly any Irish musician has given me a real lift. The classical guitarist John Feeley and the virtuoso accordion player Máirtín O'Connor would be the only two men. Thankfully the brilliant voice of Sinéad O'Connor has touched every sinew of every nerve in my body.

There had been the early promise at the end of the eighties with *The Lion and the Cobra*, but with this simple collection of other people's songs, Sinéad gives all the emotions a thorough wringing-out. Her version of 'Scarlet Ribbons' is the best song I have ever heard her sing and the final lament with uilleann pipes closes the song wonderfully. Opening with 'Bewitched, Bothered, and Bewildered', the album brings together diverse songs from four decades, mostly with lavish orchestra backing to O'Connor's voice. She dedicates the album to the people of New York, and that indeed is the cityscape most of the songs draw on.

AMERICAN CAESAR
IGGY POP

I play a record of Iggy's every day and last year's *American Caesar* perfectly hit many nails on the head. There are sixteen songs, and all carry a rage and a bite that sadly has all but vapourized for most of the performers of Iggy's vintage. The album sleeve carries a pointed warning to parents that the record 'is an Iggy Pop record'.

PATRICK McGRATH

I RAN AWAY FROM STONYHURST COLLEGE in October 1967, a rebel, a poet, an artist: Padraic McGrath del Mundo. In those days Stonyhurst was a hardline institution where a boy's physical and spiritual sinew was toughened with early morning runs, daily Mass, Latin, CCF, and the ferula, this last a slipper-shaped tongue of supple black whalebone applied with vigour to palm or arse by a bluff beefy Jesuit called Pounder Magill. What place was this for a poet and artist with every lyric, every chord of *Sgt. Pepper* etched in his soul? I sold my guitar to Johnny Butt for five quid and with that five quid caught the bus into Preston and the next train to London. Christ, this was the real stuff at last, this was life. It was dark and raining when the train pulled into Euston and the song that's burned into the memory of that charged journey oddly enough is 'Massachusetts'. Didn't the lights always shine in Massachusetts? It spoke to me of travel, experience, large movements of the heart. It gathered up every adolescent yearning I'd known since the day childhood ended (the day I heard 'Love Me Do') and wove them into the grand foolish gesture of flight that shifted the course of my life and found me four years later in a maximum-security lunatic asylum in northern Ontario.

Rock music was central to everything in those desperate years. This is because identity, at seventeen, is a structure of such fragility it must be buttressed by myths that elevate and romanticize its paltry experience. Mine was certainly paltry; at seventeen I hadn't done anything except run away from school and screw up my education and forfeit a place at Oxford, so I thought. I needed to give meaning to all the clumsy groping, all the inchoate emotions, and this is what rock did. It stood for the personal history that had yet to happen. Through identification it allowed me to believe I was something when I was still nothing. I was the Walrus, goo goo g'joob.

In due course I savagely fucked up my A-levels and 'won' the last place in the last English department still hawking for the dregs of the 1968 school-leavers. This was the City of Birmingham College of Commerce, which offered external degree courses. I was less than rigorous in my attendance. Moseley was the place to live in Birmingham, and the place to be in Moseley was the King's Head, and that's where I misspent my youth: drugs and music and very long hair, and a sort of tough, Brummy, working-class hero sort of ethos. My mate was Pete Butler, and we'd sit in the kitchen of our cold shabby flat in Chantry Road warming our hands in the oven till the King's Head opened. *The Who Live at Leeds* was important (I was there), and Led Zeppelin, the 'Whole Lotta Love' album, and Traffic – some of the King's Head regulars knew the band, and every so often we'd get thrilling bulletins: 'Stevie's cancelled the gig. Broke his thumb tripping' – and Cream, 'Sunshine of Your Love', and of course Pink Floyd, *Ummagumma*. *Ummagumma*, more than once, did me in totally, as I sat on the floor of some threadbare flat in Moseley hugging my knees at four in the morning while the acid lifted me by stages to a plane of experience beyond language where matter turned into energy and pulsed atomically for hour after hour after hour. Then the creeping out into the dawn, shattered and battered and helpless and depressed, because it was always laced with speed, and there was no chance of sleep, you just had to suffer the bleak grinding circuits of your own sad mind till it worked itself out of your system. Never again, you said, but when that American guy in the pub told you he had tabs of white lightning or blue streak or whatever, there was no refusing.

With the acid it all got dark and complicated and gothic. There were other albums that harrowed my soul in the long strange reaches of the night: Dr John the Night Tripper, one track in particular called 'Mama Roux'. There was an Eric Burdon album, with a track of Eric talking, telling a grim, ghastly story whose details are lost to me now but whose menace and violence and madness remain, similar in feeling to the Doors number with the line, 'The killer awoke before dawn'. There were others, but I've bricked them up in some deep vault and can't get at them anymore. I hung out with the art students, cool, laconic guys I never felt I really knew. Most of 1969 and 1970 seems now a vacillating nightmare, days of lethargy and depression spent in cinemas and pubs, and long nights in an acid-fuelled ecstasy of terror and wonder, my own private dark side of the moon. Time and again the teetering, flimsy structure of the self fissured like the House of Usher and threatened to collapse and go under, though somehow it never quite did.

Though many of the albums that counted were benign. The first grand passion was conducted with Donovan very much in the vicinity: *A Gift from a Flower to a Garden*. Donovan had always been there, right from the moment 'Catch the Wind' gave me a glimpse of a life so utterly enchanting that my silly, overactive imagination recoiled from economic history and French irregular verbs and began to edge toward that wet October day I caught the bus to Preston. He sang of a life of constant travel, fleeting emotional contacts, poetry, poverty, and faded denim jackets. Wire things you wore round your neck to hold your mouth organ. It was romantic, pacifist, irresponsible and anti-materialist. Donovan had always been there, and now, in my summer of love, roughly March to August 1969, here he was with a double album. He was the flower, we were the garden.

Her name was Eve, she was boisterous, Birmingham-Irish and wild. She had glorious thick yellow hair. My parents hated her. Her father had been a legendary Brummy drinker, and when more than once we fetched up by chance in some dour workingman's pub, a vivid pair of hippies in our scuffed suede and patched jeans and our long, long hair, Evie would recognize one of her dad's old cronies and then we were welcome. We hitch-hiked to the Isle of Wight festival and saw Dylan. Back in Brum we smoked hash joints and listened to Jethro Tull, *Aqualung*. I lost her after five months to a small-time thief and dope-dealer I liked enormously called Coker. He was a cheeky irrepressible little guy even when he was being busted, which was often. He'd come into the King's Head and buy me a drink and tell me about knocking over the Curry's in Balsall Heath, five tellies and a stereo. But it broke my heart when Evie started going to bed with him. I waited outside her house all night once, watching her window. It was a Leonard Cohen sort of a night.

I went to Canada in September '71 and worked in the lunatic asylum. Mellowing occurred. Neil Young, the 'Heart of Gold' album. And the Eagles. *Desperado* I still adore. I always wanted someone to tell me, 'You're a wild one, but I know you've got your reasons,' or perhaps, gazing deep into my eyes, 'Your prison is walking through this world all alone.' Music was still important, but not vital, as it had been; it was no longer the scaffolding of the self. I didn't really believe anymore that my prison was walking through this world all alone. I began to listen to the blues. One night, years later, living in a small cabin on the north shore of the Queen Charlotte Islands, I jammed with Sonny Terry. At the time I was earning my living in the local bar, playing guitar and singing blues and country and western.

At the end of the seventies I started to write fiction and music fell away completely. By the time I got to New York in late '81 my albums had all been lost along the way. Now there's only one tape I absolutely must have in the car, the Stones, *Hot Rocks 1964-71*. 'Honky Tonk Woman' still fills me with joy every time I hear it, though the greatest rocker ever in my opinion is 'Brown Sugar'. I still feel undefeatable when I hear that song.

FRANK Mc GUINNESS

THE BEATLES
THE BEATLES

They have to be number one. The White Album is wonderful, an unwieldy, crazed mix of styles, funny, gloriously indulgent – the best, the only kind of rock madness. 'Helter Skelter' is the best answer to the cretins who dismiss Paul McCartney, 'Blackbird' always puts me in good form and Lennon was at his wicked best singing 'Revolution'. Great stuff.

BROKEN ENGLISH
MARIANNE FAITHFULL

I dislike heroism, but I love courage. This record is Marianne Faithfull as Mother Courage. Is it any wonder that she is the world's best interpreter of Brecht's lyrics and Weill's music? *Broken English* was her training ground.

THE JULIET LETTERS
ELVIS COSTELLO AND THE BRODSKY QUARTET

Costello has matured into a really good poet. His early writing was as sharp as it was deep, but these songs together have a marvellous diversity. Their savagery, despair, tenderness and joy are all beautifully served by the accuracy of the playing. The singing, as always, is superlative. A great meeting.

BLUE
JONI MITCHELL

I collect all of Joni Mitchell's music, but *Blue* is special. It comforts me. All things that comfort you should also frighten you. All I'll say is that I should not be let listen to 'The Last Time I Saw Richard' in the company of men. It frightens them.

MIDNIGHT
HERB ALPERT

Does Herb Alpert qualify as a rock musician? Do I care about this when I'm smooching to his gorgeous version of 'In the Wee Small Hours of the Morning?' Do I hell.

BLOOD ON THE TRACKS
BOB DYLAN

Every bloody track a winner. I have a dream. I'd love to let a real supper-club singer like my loved, late Mabel Mercer loose on 'Lily, Rosemary and the Jack of Hearts'. Dylan gets the violence of the song – and by Christ, this is a violent record – but Mercer would get the suspense. Dylan's lyrics can be extraordinary whenever he remembers that he is a really good storyteller. When he is in supreme form, there is so much happening in his music. His only rival is Van Morrison, which leads me to –

ASTRAL WEEKS
VAN MORRISON

Yes, oh yes, the one and only, yes.

LIONHEART
KATE BUSH

This woman deserves all the praise she gets. She has a unique imagination. *Lionheart* is a lovely recognition of England, a true national anthem. 'Wow' is a pantomime, and both 'Symphony in Blue' and 'Kashka from Baghdad' are erotic, so very, very erotic. What more do you want? Perfection? Then listen to her entire body of work.

THE MISSING YEARS
JOHN PRINE

The wisdom in this man's voice breaks my heart, it is so full of sorrow. 'All the Best' is a song that could melt ice, and 'Jesus: The Missing Years' is the fairest and funniest piece of biography I've heard for years.

DUSTY IN MEMPHIS
DUSTY SPRINGFIELD

The woman herself. I include this as a warning to the world that when I meet anyone who doesn't have this record, I know it in its entirety and SING it to them. Spare yourself, buy a copy now. Make Dusty really rich. A glorious, generous voice.

PAUL McGUINNESS

I think this record, the first record I ever bought, had something to do with a movie that was out at that time. I remember the chorus. 'Sink the Bismarck' was the battle-cry, 'over all the seven seas.' That was when I was about six or seven years old. I wasn't a serious record-buyer until later. It was one of several novelty records that appealed to me because it wasn't about girls, something you're not interested in when you're seven or eight. I was living in a military environment in Malta at the time and all my friends were service kids, so our lives were very disciplined. We were like little soldiers and had to wear khaki uniforms to school. Johnny Horton was a mad rockabilly singer and it seems unbelievable that he was part of the movie campaign of *Sink the Bismarck*.

PLEASE PLEASE ME
THE BEATLES

The first song that really turned me on was 'Please Please Me' by the Beatles, which I heard on a homemade record-player in 1962 when I was ten. Somebody at school had made the machine and this was the only record he had. He didn't have a speaker, so to hear you had to put your ear very close to the needle. You could just about make it out. Even under these inauspicious circumstances, it was quite clearly wonderful.

I saw the Beatles in Bournemouth in 1963 at the Gaumont Cinema. I had three tickets, each costing seven and six – one for me, one for my brother and an extra one for a schoolfriend of mine who then couldn't come. I scalped it to a middle-aged woman outside the cinema for ten shillings, something I would disapprove of nowadays were it a U2 ticket. As penance I had to sit beside this woman throughout the show while she complained about not hearing anything because of the screaming. It was a big mistake to have sold it to her.

EXILE ON MAIN STREET
THE ROLLING STONES

In the sixties there were lots of great records and they were, of course, dominated by the Rolling Stones, the Beatles and Bob Dylan. Probably it was through watching these groups and seeing them develop that I made up my mind to get into this business. I knew I wasn't musical, but I was always aware of the manager's role. I thought that managers like Brian Epstein, Andrew Oldham and Albert Grossman must have great jobs. I knew these people's names when I was thirteen, fourteen, which I'm sure nobody else did at that age. I was very keen to get into the business. I was lucky growing up in Bournemouth because it was a mod town; all the major ballroom tours would come through, and I was able to see these bands. There was a lot of black music. The mods, amongst whom I counted myself, were into Tamla and Philadelphia music.

By the time *Exile on Main Street* was made in 1970 or 1971 I was reading *Rolling Stone*. I think Mick Jagger was a partner in the magazine so there was a lot of coverage of the making of this album. It confirmed my wildest imaginings: there they were in the south of France living in a mansion, with a recording truck at the back door, doing all sorts of illegal but enjoyable things. The result was an astonishing double album. I think it's fair to say there are hardly any double albums that wouldn't be better as single ones, but *Exile on Main Street* is absolutely the exception to this rule. For me, anyway, it was a defining record – it defined rock'n'roll and the Rolling Stones. I was very surprised recently to read an interview with Mick Jagger in which he seemed to be saying that he really didn't rate it that highly nowadays. Maybe it was because it was more Keith's record. It was, of course, largely a work of fiction. These were guys from the London suburbs writing as if they were dispossessed Southern white trash. They have this extraordinary ability to imagine a place and write from it with conviction. At the same time this insolent 'fuck you, I don't care' stance was delivered on every single lyric in that album. It's quite an achievement.

NEW MORNING
BOB DYLAN

I associate this record very much with Dublin. I've bought it many times when I'm in a new place and I've got no tapes or records with me. I was a philosophy student at Trinity when I first heard it in around 1972, smoking a certain amount of pot and taking acid a few times. It was very relaxed in the early seventies. I didn't have very much work to do and indeed didn't do the full amount I was supposed to. I eventually got thrown out of TCD by Brendan Kennelly who didn't like the way I edited the college magazine. But my main interests while there were directing plays, listening to music, getting to know the world after six years of boarding-school. It was like a big blast of freedom and my affection for Dublin developed from that time. Apart from frequent absences I've been here more or less ever since.

I never skip tracks on this album – 'Time Passes Slowly', 'Winterlude' are great and 'New Morning' has the sense of waking up and feeling happy. It's not generally regarded as one of Dylan's classics, but it is by me. For a long time it wasn't even available on CD after the rest of his catalogue had appeared. It's got bounce: it's almost a pop album. Dylan's intent was always creative and although he's made some terrible records along the way, I think his inconsistencies are probably a part of his integrity.

STEELY DAN

I have to confess I usually buy the greatest hits of Steely Dan's when I'm buying records for a hire car. There are quite a few compilations. Barry Devlin of Horslips turned me on to the band when he came back from the U.S. They had these deeply enigmatic lyrics about taking smack and getting into dangerous situations in Harlem. They were these white middle-class guys who had been to this interesting college called Bard in upstate New York. They were obviously very sophisticated musically. I liked the jazz feel and deftness and elegance of what they did.

THIN LIZZY

In 1971 I was starting to promote a few concerts with Michael Deeny. I was a student and he was the accountant at Kennedy's bakery. We put on a few shows and through that got to know Horslips, who were happening at that time, and Michael became their manager. I wasn't at all fanatical about buying records or going to concerts then but I did go to Thin Lizzy shows. They took off to England and got record deals, and even though they weren't really happening there, they seemed to understand that coming back to Dublin was something they should do strategically but rarely. Even though Phil Lynott would be living in a broom closet in Notting Hill, he was still able to come back to Dublin and sell out the National Stadium. I'm all for smoke and mirrors. We don't necessarily want to know the precise truth. The illusion is more exciting; Phil was a big star at home. He later became a big star elsewhere but early on he was a master of concealing how small they were in England. Their live album *Live and Dangerous* (1978/9), recorded when they were at their peak, was wonderful. It catches the excitement of a great rock'n'roll band on the crest of the wave and I used to urge U2 to listen to it because it seemed to me to embody the dynamics of a great stage show.

ZOOROPA
U2

Towards the end of the seventies I started managing U2. It was the time of Boz Scaggs, Fleetwood Mac, and the kind of smooth adult music that was alright in the background but was very hard to get excited about. I think there was an expectancy that music was going to change and perhaps become exciting again. Of course, what happened was the arrival of the Sex Pistols and the Clash in Britain and Talking Heads, the Ramones, Blondie and Television in America. That explosion really led to the formation of U2. I had only dabbled in management before that. I used to have these late-night conversations with Bill Graham in Leeson Street basement clubs about finding a band in Dublin and conquering the world using Dublin as a base. After these discussions had been taking place for quite a while, Bill called me and said he'd seen a group that I should manage. They were called U2 and they were still at school. They had tricked him into going to see a rehearsal of theirs and he'd gone. Even though they'd been playing Ramones songs, he was sufficiently impressed by them to recommend them very strongly to me. I went to see them in the Project, which was being run by Jim and Peter Sheridan at the time, and I became their manager that night. It was quite a slow start. We were all trying to figure out how committed we were. Edge was at college, Bono was waiting to go, and I was working as a freelance film technician. The levels of commitment varied somewhat. We circled each other for a few months before we all plunged in. Edge left Kevin Street, where he was doing engineering, because his course was taking too much time from the band. We got a record deal eventually and made a record in 1980.

I listen to *Zooropa* quite a lot nowadays. It was difficult for the band to make because they recorded it while they were on tour in 1993. In our business lots of people have tried to do a one-two punch but rarely pulled it off. This means releasing two albums in the same cycle – big album, big tour, big silence is the norm, and then start again. We had thought how wonderful it would be if you could produce a record and then, during the course of the tour for that record, put out a second one while people were still paying attention. Creatively it gives an enormous opportunity to the artist. U2 had very much reinvented themselves in the album before *Zooropa*, *Achtung Baby*. They'd come from the low point of the *Rattle and Hum* movie, which was, in the end, overblown, self-reverential and over-marketed. As a record alone it would have been perfectly good, but associated as it was with this enormous movie campaign, it got up everybody's noses. It was too big. People who buy records are used to the sensation of discovering a record for themselves. Movie marketing doesn't work in that way. It smashes you over the head so you pay attention. Coming back from that low point with *Achtung Baby* was brilliant. It was an ultra-modern record and it established them once and for all as the sort of rock'n'roll band that can reinvent itself creatively, and in a kind of cyclical way, like the Stones or the Beatles or David Bowie. It was quite a stretch for the U2 audience to take that in but they did and then while they were still fresh, we were able to release *Zooropa*, which if anything was more demanding of the audience. I don't think it could have been released in isolation. So *Zooropa* is the album that I like most because of what it achieved for the band and also because the music is most demanding and intricate. It's very modern: melodic with strong dance rhythms going through it.

THE PRETENDERS

I came across the Pretenders while trying to find out how bands got their records played on the radio. I remember hearing 'Brass in Pocket' for the first time and thinking, despite a lot of assertions that they were finished, that it was going to be a worldwide hit. It was a very exciting, puzzling, enigmatic record. The Pretenders were a great live group in the early days when they were all still alive. Years later I became Chrissie's manager for a few years, but it was a bad time because she was very involved with her children and wasn't really that interested in making records. I became her manager because I was a friend and after a couple of uneventful years with no touring or recording we parted by mutual consent. We have remained friends. She's a great singer, songwriter and guitar player and is smart and funny. She has the glow. I did something terrible to her once. She phoned me to tell me that the guitar player in the band, Robbie McIntosh, was leaving. I said that was too bad. There was a bit of a silence on the phone and then I said cheerfully, 'Look, at least he's not dead,' which was a singularly tasteless remark because, both Jimmy Honeyman Scott, the guitarist, and Pete Farndon, the bass player, had died. There was a long silence and then she started laughing.

RID OF ME
P.J. HARVEY

She is the only other person I represent besides U2. She opened for them during the last part of the *Zoo TV* tour in Europe. She was an extraordinary sight on stage: a tiny girl in daylight without any kind of production. She was unknown, so the audience weren't very interested in her, yet she had great presence as a performer. She has that absolutely indefinable quality which makes you want to watch her on stage even if she is standing still. A few months went by and then Island, U2's record company, asked me would I manage her. Her music suggests a great deal and reveals very little; I always imagine I hear references to Captain Beefheart, Leadbelly, Robert Johnson – swamp music. Her parents were hippie promoters in Yeovil so she grew up with that kind of music playing in her home. She is bewitching and beautiful, with a voice that seems to come from somewhere very deep within her. Though very small, she doesn't look it because like a lot of artists she has a big head.

STABAT MATER
PERGOLESI

The last record is a piece of church music. The recording I like best is on Deutsche Gramaphone. Clare Enders, who works at EMI, gave it to me five years ago to pass on to Bono. I played it and liked it so much that I actually bought another one for him. I've given it to many people since then, and have bought other versions of it. Some months before Denny Cordell died I laid it on him.

He looked at it and said he didn't like that kind of music. A couple of weeks later, however, he phoned me up and said how much he had been playing it and what an extraordinary record it was. Stabat Mater is a standard prayer. Lots of composers in the seventeenth, eighteenth and nineteenth century composed their own versions of it, and this one is quite amazing. If you close your eyes and listen to that music you really do imagine you're in a different place. And now Denny is … there was little that could surprise him about music, so I was delighted to be able to do that with this record.

PADDY MOLONEY

THE LONG BLACK VEIL
THE CHIEFTAINS

This album sticks out because every track on it has a story attached – a party, disasters. It was all made inside of eight months, with a day here and a day there. But every track only took a day with each artist – there was no sitting down and reading the dots and dashes – it was a jam session for each one.

Each track was a live performance. There were no separations anywhere, just a couple of over-dubs here and there to enhance the whole thing. But the music could have been taken out of that room, or that studio, or that person's house and brought right on stage, as it was with Sinéad O'Connor. We played Carnegie Hall and did 'The Foggy Dew' and 'He Moved Through the Fair'.

Probably the most enjoyable session was one with the Rolling Stones. The day before we had Mick doing 'The Long Black Veil'. Incidentally, I had tried to get him to do a rebel song. I wasn't trying to be clever or anything; I had in mind the fact that he had done 'Ned Kelly' so well, and I thought an Irish rebel song would come in handy, but we didn't do it. We agreed on 'The Long Black Veil'. He was familiar with the song, came in the first day, and did it in two or three takes – that was it.

When I went down to Ronnie's house to talk to the lads about the Stones session, we went straight to his bar. We got stuck into a bottle of 'Middleton Special', which was one of my favourite drinks from the past. I couldn't believe he had a bottle of it, so that was the end of that. When they got to the studio I had put a little piece of 'Satisfaction' into the middle of 'The Rocky Road to Dublin'. There was a party going on, and it was about twelve o'clock before we decided to put anything on tape. I thought I was going to lose the track and that the opportunity had gone. But the music went down, and there was dancing and shouting in the studio with about thirty or forty people: it was incredible. Mick came back that day for more punishment. He knew there was going to be fun, and we all ended up guzzling pints of Guinness until all hours of the morning – it was a great, great night.

The same happened with Sting. We went into his ancient house and had a great session in the large front parlour. We had lunch out on the lawn first and then went in and recorded 'Mo Ghile Mear'.

ANOTHER COUNTRY
THE CHIEFTAINS

Years ago I got a book from a returned emigrant, Rory Butler, of music that went from Ireland to North America – most of it Irish, some of it Scottish. There was a whole history there which enlightened me on the relationship between Irish, American, and particularly Canadian music. I did a series of programmes for RTÉ at the time and thought that I must do an album exploring these musical links. I put it off and put it off, and eventually I brought it out about six years ago.

We spent a week in Nashville making this album : it was like going on holidays and having a session every minute of the day and night. We even did two shows at the Grand Ole Opry one week. They treated us like the returned sons. Wonderful musicians kept coming out of the woodwork and we did this grand session at the end where everybody sang 'Did You Ever Go a-Courtin' Uncle Joe, Uncle Joe?' which we gave to the Scots years ago (like the bagpipes, and they haven't seen the joke yet). This is the extraordinary circle music makes as it travels throughout the world. I'm sure that we have got some of our tunes from China and North Africa, and India in particular. The Nashville musicians can pick up a tune immediately, without ever having heard it before. They are magic.

The sessions reminded me of my younger days, going to the mountains of Laois, up in the Slieve Blooms. We used to have these parties – they were called dances, house dances. The dancing would go on all night, sometime during the evening someone would start to sing songs, and you'd have the likes of 'Coast of Malabar' (which Ry Cooder sings on *The Long Black Veil*). I can still see my grandmother singing that song – sitting up on an old wooden milk-churn in the kitchen. The dancing was wild: wild Irish men and women, mountain people. No televisions, no radios: dancing, telling stories, playing music was our entertainment. And they had these same parties over in America when they emigrated from Ireland. This is where some of the American country music comes from. I can recognize their tunes immediately and get the same feeling, the same buzz as I do from our own traditional music.

THE HORN CONCERTO IN E
MOZART

I love Mozart because I feel a great kinship with him, albeit in a different world of music. *The Horn Concerto* is very close to a jig called 'The Piper's Chair' and I'm fascinated by the relationship between this piece of music and Ireland. Mozart's favourite tenor was Michael Kelly, a Dubliner, who sang at the first performance of *The Marriage of Figaro*. They were very close friends and used to socialize together. I'm sure that this is where Mozart got the inspiration for this concerto.

MISE ÉIRE
SEÁN Ó RIADA

The music for *Mise Éire* was what turned me on to the genius of Seán Ó Riada. People said that it wasn't his music, that he was just an arranger. But to me his genius was in his arrangements; they were as good as composition. People had listened to a lot of these tunes before but nobody had paid much attention, and it was Ó Riada's orchestration that actually touched the audience.

I used to go and see Seán and talk about music and songs in the Trinity Bar in Pearse Street every Monday. He asked me if I would help to put together Ceoltóirí Chualann. That group took off in 1961, so I was part of all that scene. During the fifties I put together various groups – quartets, duos etc. – and with the assistance of my good friend Garech de Brún, formed the Chieftains in 1963. I was a bit of a rebel in traditional Irish music, because I did things that didn't please the purists very much. If you listen to Seán Potts and myself playing tin whistles, we had this tremendous bond in style and in understanding of music. Our approach to it, jazzwise, soulwise and most importantly traditional-wise, was as one, like two minds playing off one another. We'd often get into a session and play a tune for twenty minutes – the same tune – and just improvise on it, maybe with a little bodhrán in the background. That's why I do love the tin whistle, it has something very deep in it. When you play with somebody it's not so much the instrument, it's the mind and the music within the man that's coming out.

Nowadays I think the oyster has opened: people all over the world have become more aware of the relationship between different sorts of music. Galician music from the north-west of Spain is so close to our own music. After Scottish music, it is probably the closest there is to Irish music. That in turn has travelled to South America and to Mexico and to places farther away. The Chieftains have explored this connection on our new album *Santiago*.

LONNIE DONEGAN

Although I loved traditional music in my teens, Lonnie Donegan was an artist who really impressed me. I had this band called the Three Squares, a skiffle group with a washboard and a couple of guys playing guitar. I used to love to sing quite a few of the old songs in that wild kind of style, but I used to throw a few reels and jigs into the middle of the songs just for good measure.

CLYDE VALLEY STOMPERS

The Clyde Valley Stompers were a jazz group and I thought they were the bee's knees. Their LP was the first present that my wife Rita gave to me, although we weren't married then. I was just leaving school and starting work as a clerk in an old builders' providers. An LP was a big present in those days, huge in fact, and I still have this one at home. It's got a bunch of hats on the cover: trombones, saxophones and straw-boaters with a band around the top.

COLUMBIA LIBRARY OF FOLK AND PRIMITIVE MUSIC

This was a brilliant record, produced by Alan Lomax, with a great selection of music from all over Ireland, including some tracks from Séamus Ennis. Séamus was a most colourful character. I loved listening to his piping and to the stories that he would tell. Séamus was just a whole bundle of folklore, a great Irish-speaker, the sort of person that would make you want to speak Irish: it came out of him like music. His music was a whole story. He didn't just sit down and say nothing and play a few tunes. There were stories attached to the songs, and a whole ritual of getting together and putting on the pipes.

Something that is little known is that the Clancy Brothers brought Séamus to the Newport Jazz Festival in the early sixties. The Clancys were big heroes at the time. I can just see Séamus walking out onto the stage in his big long raincoat and those long limbs he had – a hugely tall man in a massive hat. A chair was put down for him and he opened up the case and started to talk to the people. They were enthralled before he played a note. They were just sold on him – he got to them before he even had his pipes put together.

KING OF THE PIPERS
LEO ROWSOME

Leo Rowsome was my tutor from the time I was eight years of age. And this album, which was brought out by Garech de Brún, was the first LP of uilleann piping. I can still hear Leo playing the double chanter, something you never hear tell of nowadays. It is like two chanters stuck together, you just spread your fingers across the double holes. It has a magical sound, like two voices in unison.

THE CHIEFTAINS
THE CHIEFTAINS

By 1963 Garech had put out a couple of albums, including a poetry record by Paddy Kavanagh and a trad album by Dolly McMahon. He approached me about forming a group and I picked my old favourites who I'd been associated with. But we needed a bodhrán player and Garech says, 'I know the very one – Davy Fallon who lives down in Castletown Geoghegan in County Westmeath'. We ended up out in the country someplace in the middle of the night, at a small farmhouse. We weren't allowed to go in to ask if he would come out, because Davy's wife didn't approve of him playing the bodhrán. Somebody had to go in and tell him, so he came out and we went off out to a barn where he had hidden the bodhrán. We went off out into the night into this small little cottage somewhere, and Davy started to play. I thought I knew what a bodhrán should sound like, but I was totally amazed by his style. It started into a session, of course. And the next thing someone put this glass of brandy into my mouth. I had never taken alcohol before, and God I nearly died. I don't have to tell you who it was – that was just my first introduction to many things through the years from the colourful Mr Garech de Brún.

The album was recorded in a mono studio and took about five evenings, from seven o'clock in the evening until ten. It is still one of our greatest. It has a simplicity and a quality you could never recreate.

It was a great record to do and it got us into some strange places. People like Mick Jagger, Marianne Faithfull, got to like us. They came to an open-air concert that we gave in the fields at the back of Castletown in 1966. Brian Jones also liked us. I went to his flat in Eaton Square and was amazed to hear the Chieftains being played. Then there was the occasion when Marina Guinness brought me to visit Peter Sellers, who was staying in Carton at the time. There was the bold Peter with his social-welfare glasses and a glass in hand. Spike Milligan was there and they were listening to the Chieftains too. Peter introduced me to the music of Ravi Shankar that night which was something I subsequently really got into.

IRISH HEARTBEAT
VAN MORRISON AND THE CHIEFTAINS

To be honest with you I never listened to Van's records until I went to see him in the Gaiety Theatre. I was so taken by his relaxed improvising style that I went around to see him after the performance. There was something that drew me to him, to the music, the way it was played, the way it just flowed without being at all harsh. I just don't like noise and can't understand why everything has to be played so loud, because you miss all the subtleties. I love his improvisation. You know that he'll never do a song the same way twice, it's always a first for every piece of music. As it was when we came to do *Irish Heartbeat*. I've done other collaborations, with Jimmy Galway, Paul McCartney, Mick Jagger and so on. But to work with Van was a great experience. There's a whole book to be written about it.

DANNY MORRISON

Psychologists say our conscious selves inhabit only a brief moment of the present – a little moving slot of individual time six to twelve seconds long that we carry along with us all our lives. The present cannot be instantaneous, or we would not be able to make the connections between words or music or other stimuli that transform them into coherent experiences.

– John Boslough, *The Enigma of Time*

I HAVE THIS CRAZY THEORY that the real meaning of life is the sensation of epiphany we experience when we touch the quintessential past, those promontories of innocence, melancholy, suffering and love. No other stimulus is greater than music to bring back those exquisitely painful times.

I am sixteen, the nights have become dark and cold. Angela, the girl I think about constantly since I kissed her in August, loves Pat, my boring but good-looking friend .... It is Sunday evening and I am listening to Alan Freeman's *Pick of the Pops*. He introduces a new LP. Within seconds I know it is incredible! Quickly, I switch off my lamp, stand up and – my bedroom softly illuminated only by the beads of light from the back of my old valve radio – I become a member of Led Zeppelin. 'Way down inside. Honey. You neeeeed lovvve! Wanna whole lotta love ...' I buy the album, *Led Zeppelin II*, and inflict it on my family who just don't understand my Robert Plant persona. The LP steers me through the winter of 1969. Later, Pat's mother sends him to America to avoid the Troubles and there he joins the air force. Angela marries another mutual friend and is happy. (I bumped into her a few weeks ago and for an hour we had a laugh at my seriousness and what we thought of things back then. 'What is and What Should Be.')

Our old music teacher, Tommy Cooney, carried a strap which he never used and so his pupils tortured him. Asked to play a note on the recorder that a monkey could grasp, the class would produce a cacophony of veritable Schoenberg. Asked to produce a simple uniform hum, forty hysterical bees would be abuzzing around the room. When he became angry it was impossible to keep a straight face. He taught music because he loved it: it was his life. He had begun his musical career at the age of sixteen with the BBC Northern Ireland Symphony Orchestra where he played under such famous conductors as Elgar, Henry Wood, John Barbirolli and Hamilton Harty. One day he came into class with ... oh no! Not another record which he's going to ask us to listen to and analyze! Half the class reckon this is their cue for a nap. I'm considering writing a love letter to Angela or reading *Anna Karenina*. He places the disc on the player. I don't know where he got *Abbey Road* – it has just been issued! The class becomes alert, electrified, as he explains the Beatles' music, takes us through 'Something' and 'Here Comes the Sun', and compares 'Because' to the second movement of Vivaldi's 'Autumn'. He is so taken by our response, by the questions, by our interest, that he is grinning at the end of the class and we are impressed by how he changed our point of view and talk about him for a long time afterwards.

It is a Saturday morning, February 1970. My brother Ciarán is a fifteen-month-old baby and I take him into bed and force him – 'hothousing' is the modern expression – to listen to music as part of his cultural education. Dave Lee Travis announces a radio exclusive, the first broadcast of *Bridge Over Troubled Water*, and he plays every track! I can hardly move. 'I'm the only livin' boy in New York.' 'I do declare, there were times when I was so lonesome I took some comforts there.' 'So long, Frank Lloyd Wright.' To illustrate the eponymous lead track, *Top of the Pops* uses a film of a ballerina dancing alone – so vulnerable. 'If you need a friend, I'm sailing right behind. Like a bridge over troubled water I will ease your mind.' On St Patrick's Day my girlfriend (another Angela) and I queue with hundreds for entry to the *Radio 1 Road Club* in the Romano's Ballroom where that song and 'Cecilia' are played. We arrange to meet again at eight o'clock outside the Bee-Hive pub. At twenty past eight I realize I have been stood up ....

It is 1994 and Ciarán, having been sentenced to twenty-six years, is with me here in the H-Blocks. He hands me a letter from my friend Chrissie. She has met Angela in Switzerland and taken her to task for ditching me. She writes that Angela says that that night back in 1970 she couldn't get out of the house until half-eight and that she showed up! Very interesting. Angela became an opera singer, is married to a German musician and lives in Munich .... I am out of jail. After twenty-five years we meet again. She has just performed 'Song to the Moon' from Dvorjak's *Rusalka*, and Glück's 'What is Life to Me Without Thee' and I'm absolutely moved. And guess to whom she dedicated them? Yip, her husband Nico! Ciarán tells me not to worry, the sea is full of opera singers.

Pat's cousin, Tony, introduces me to Fleetwood Mac's *Then Play On* but it is months before the hormones are ready, though I've been practising suffering and self-pity for some time. Then I'm struck down with the blues and until the end of time Peter Green is a god. I repeat, Peter Green is a god. 'Without You.' 'Although the Sun is Shining.' 'Coming Your Way.' I shall feel forever the deep loss of a woman I've yet to meet.

Thérèse is demure and intelligent and middle class. I walk her up and down the Falls Road like a greyhound .... Right now, I can't even remember if we held hands, but I doubt it .... I want to explain the Troubles to her, the recent curfew, why there'll be a war, but all she is interested in is my friend Noel. What does he eat for his breakfast, is he the lonely type, has he ever mentioned her?

Agggh. 'Have you ever heard of Leonard Cohen?' she asks casually. Leonard who? I borrow her LP. *Songs from a Room* as a clue to her soul. Goodbye Thérèse, Hello fuckin' Leonard Cohen! 'And why are you so quiet/Standing there in the doorway/You chose your journey long before you came upon this highway.'

I am driving fast through England at night with my girlfriend. We can see the stars in the sky. She is reassuring. The car heater is on and Radio Luxembourg is coming in on the radio, then fading for a few seconds. The last time I heard Stevie Wonder was in early 1970 when he sang, 'Yester-me, Yester-you, Yesterday'. It's his voice again but the song is long and in two parts. One: 'Mary wants to to be a superwoman/But is that really in her head/But I just want to live each day to love her for what she is.' Two: 'Spring will fill the air and you will come around/But is it summer love that will let me down/Where were you when I needed you, last winter, my love?' ... I am in Long Kesh Internment Camp, alone out in the transline hut with the radio, cold early Sunday morning, January 1973, thinking about everything, dead friends, the long future, and 'Superwoman' comes on the radio and I'm back in England with her by my side though we're no longer together but have created a future. And the moment is caught in amber because even now I am looking into that moment and I am there ... I am in Nottingham, 1974, sleeping on the floor of my future sister-in-law and listening to *Music of My Mind*. 'I'm happier than the morning sun, because that's the way you said that it would be if I were to bring you inside my life.' My wife and I honeymoon on the Norfolk Broads and Stevie is still going through my head: 'Little girl it seems, in all my dreams/Your happiness is due/ But still they last/They're in your past/Events that make you blue.'

Seven years elapse. Marriage, fatherhood, separations, reconciliations – later, divorce, but before that, the longest seven months in history, the heroic H-Block hunger strike of 1981. It is beyond discussion or dispute, it is so huge. That autumn Gerry Adams asks me have I heard of Moving Hearts. No. I hear the album in a flat in Dublin where we have retired after producing *An Phoblacht*. A fusion of jazz, rock, protest, traditional. It says things I want to sing and lose my head to .... I am in the Baggot Inn with my girlfriend, it is 1982, and Moving Hearts are playing. I have never heard a live performance like it. So we go back two nights in a row to be intoxicated, to be moved. 'So let the music keep your spirits high/Let the buildings keep your children dry/Let creation reveal its secrets by and by/By and by/When the light that's lost within us reaches the sky.'

My girlfriend and I are sleeping. I wake up and switch on the radio. That's a good song, I say. She murmurs. We can't catch the name of the group. It's the same the next morning but this time a different song. There's a unique alchemy at work. Here. There. 'You're the best thing that I've ever found/Handle me with care.' George Harrison? 'I'm so tired of being lonely ...' Roy Orbison's plaintive voice? We fall in love with the Traveling Wilburys. On Friday nights when the dance is over, we go home and continue the dance to 'Not Alone Anymore' and 'Tweeter and the Monkey Man'. Drinking in a club with my Da, all eyes on the

TV, complete silence, watching Israeli soldiers break the arms of a Palestinian youth. The Intifada. Then Roy Orbison's death is announced. The meaning of life is the past living into the present, our little moving slots of individual time … Watching the video for the song 'End of the Line', the rocking-chair, Roy's, is empty, but it still rocks. It still rocks. 'Well it's alright … remember to live and let live … the best you can do is forgive.'

1994, I buy from the prison tuck shop *Debut* by my Icelandic beauty, Björk, and promise that as soon as we meet I'll bowl her over with an offer of marriage and she can lullaby me throughout our nights with 'Big Time Sensuality' and she can growl and yelp and nip. I walk the exercise yard singing 'Venus as a Boy' and 'Come to Me' and it is generally believed that I've flown over.

Freedom. I have wangled four VIP tickets for REM at Slane. At Kennedy Roundabout, Belfast, the driver of our bus falls off his seat and out the door. There is still some blood in his alcoholstream and he is answering to the wrong name but so does everyone in this life. To revive him he is given more drink. He comes around, addresses me and says, 'You better drive.' I drive. 'What if you rocked around the clock/Ticked, tocked.' *Automatic for the People* is blasting out the speakers. I look down the aisle, which is full of Martians singing in strange tongues, and it is great to be alive. They drink Dundalk dry then we speed off to 'The Sidewinder Sleeps Tonite'. Slane village becomes global. It is an asylum but there is no aggression. We find our position on the embankment, part of a natural amphitheatre, and the numbers of people innocently enjoying themselves is breathtaking. Night falls. Michael Stipe is illuminated on stage and enlarged on a video screen. As he begins, thousands in the valley below us light candles and there is one anthem. It is of solidarity with the lost and lonely. I look at my sons and my niece and we smile and all stand and join in, one huge swell of humanity. 'When the day is long, and the night, the night is yours alone/And you're sure you've had enough of this life/Hang on/Don't let yourself go, 'cos everybody cries/Everybody hurts/Sometimes.'

There is only one generation – this one. And the meaning of life is our individual little moving slots of time, often converging in or forged in joint experiences, which we look back upon with a sigh, ten minutes or ten years or ten thousand years later.

My sons and I are at a special reunion and my eldest and I discover our affinity with Peter Green, with Fleetwood Mac, 'Before the Beginning', and we dance with each other and look into each others' eyes saying, 'Welcome Home'.

TERRY MOYLAN

PEARL
JANIS JOPLIN

Released after Janis's death, this is the tightest collection of tracks she ever recorded. The album could have been called 'Pearls' for it contains a string of superb performances. 'Me and Bobby McGee', written for her by Kris Kristofferson, is probably the best-known song. It has been done by hundreds of others, but not like this. Janis sets it alight. On a lot of other recordings her voice sounds as if it was not up to the demands she was making of it, but here she proves that her skill was equal to her ambition, filling this, and every song on the record, with passion and energy. Nothing is fumbled. One never feels that she has reached her limit, emotionally or technically. And what emotion there is here! Janis's first recordings were covers of Bessie Smith numbers, done in Smith's style. She held the 'Empress' in such regard that she organized and paid for a headstone for her grave. I think she always wanted to be a blues singer. The songs here are not strictly in the blues style, structurally or melodically speaking, but in terms of feeling they are probably closer to Bessie Smith than anything that has been recorded since that great lady's death.

Other tracks include 'A Woman Left Lonely', 'Half Moon', 'Get It While You Can' and the humorous, slightly out-of-place 'Mercedes-Benz'. For good measure there is an instrumental version of 'Buried Alive in the Blues', a song Bessie Smith was due to record the day that she was found dead. The name is as apt an epitaph as could be devised. The track itself is a superb piece of rock music and displays the skill of Joplin's band to the full.

I bought this record in London around 1973 and I have so far got twenty-three years of pleasure out of it. Poor Janis! If there is any justice she and Bessie are grooving together now. In Heaven, of course. The blues ain't really the devil's music.

LIEGE & LIEF
FAIRPORT CONVENTION

When a friend first played me his copy of *Liege & Lief*, being a pain-in-the-neck folk purist at the time I was not impressed. But it weaselled its way into my psyche and shortly afterwards I had my own copy and was telling friends, and strangers, that I had heard an LP which had changed my life. And so it did. In this record Fairport Convention demonstrate how the rock'n'roll style can be applied successfully to ancient songs. I had never believed that it could be, and I was, and remain, utterly unimpressed by Irish attempts at the time to do the same thing. Fairport's secret was the respect they had for the material they worked with.

In Sandy Denny they had a singer who was able to carry any kind of material. Based in folk song, she subsequently extended her range of material to everything from the Ink Spots and Chuck Berry to traditional British and Irish song. She wrote a lot of fine songs herself. Here the songs are mainly traditional. The outstanding pieces include the gentle and brooding 'Crazy Man Michael' and 'Reynardine' and the ballads 'Matty Groves' and 'Tam Lin'.

ISOMETRIC BOOGIE
THE GUTTER BROTHERS

One of the delights of life is the Saturday morning stroll around town, a pleasure to which I am trying to addict my son. On one such outing four years ago we came across a trio playing at Switzers' corner. They were the Gutter Brothers: a young black percussionist extracting amazing rhythms from a single drum and a variety of unlikely objects, a tough gent who looked like a serving marine and played the tea-chest bass, and the front man a singer/guitarist with an American accent. With this skiffle-group instrumentation they were belting out raw, powerful rock'n'roll. What impressed was the combination of skill and energy. Each of them was brilliant at what he did and they meshed together so well it was the tightest combination I had heard for years. They were flogging their tape, and I bought it. It's good, driving music, and it reminds me of a pleasant Saturday morning in the summer of 1990. I came across them again just once, in a notice of a gig in the *NME* or *Melody Maker*. They will probably never be massively popular; they were too good.

BOP TILL YOU DROP
RY COODER

I understand that this was the first popular music LP to be mastered digitally, and it was criticized by some at the time for having a 'cold' sound on that account. I could never see what the critics were getting worked up about. Perhaps you need far more sophisticated equipment than mine to be able to discern such niceties. Whatever about the sound, the music itself is hot enough. Cooder is something of a musical curator. He has devoted each of his LPs to a different aspect of America's popular music: the blues of Blind Blake, Blind Willie Johnson or Sleepy John Estes; cowboy and badman ballads; Woody Guthrie and Leadbelly songs; the civil war; Tex-Mex; jazz; and fifties rock'n'roll, all with equal ease and ability. This LP he devotes to a funky city-based rhythm and blues style. He has a four-piece band and three male backing singers with the most amazing vocal ranges. I didn't realize they were all male until I saw them in the Stadium at what turned out to be the best rock concert I've ever attended.

The tracks include 'Down In Hollywood', 'Little Sister' and 'Trouble'. My one gripe is that 'Crazy 'bout an Automobile' ought to be on this LP instead of on *Borderline*.

LIVE IN EUROPE
RORY GALLAGHER

While buying a pair of jeans in a shop in Talbot Street in around 1974 I heard a great piece of guitar playing and singing over the shop's audio system. I asked what it was and ended up buying Rory Gallagher's *Live* album. The track was 'Pistol Slappin' Blues', originally recorded by Blind Boy Fuller in 1935, and just one of the old blues songs in Gallagher's repertoire in which he displays his astounding skills as a guitarist. The rest of the songs are performed with his standard blues-band line-up. I subsequently got all his records and started going to his concerts. There was a period of a few years when he stopped touring, in Ireland at least. During the break punk happened, and when Gallagher next played Dublin gigs his old blues-loving audience were out-numbered and overwhelmed by hordes of youths who found in Gallagher's energetic playing some of the buzz they enjoyed in punk. They behaved like louts and effectively destroyed Gallagher's concerts as a source of pleasure.

However, that phase passed and Gallagher did return to playing to a blues audience, and the LPs are there to be enjoyed. This was my first taste of his music and remains the one I prefer.

THE HISSING OF SUMMER LAWNS
JONI MITCHELL

My record shop of choice was, for many years, Murray's of Grafton Street, underneath Captain America's. I remember reading of the release of *The Hissing of Summer Lawns* in America and visiting Murray's every day until it arrived. It was a Saturday when I eventually got it, my brother having given me a lift into town.

Everything about this record is brilliant, from the sleeve image (derived from a *National Geographic* photograph) of South American Indians carrying off a slain anaconda, to the lyrics, arrangements and singing. This LP was Mitchell's definitive break with the folk style and sounds as powerful now as it did then.

The title track deals with the boredom of the suburban housewife, caught between her desires and ties, between 'the Latin drum, and the hissing of summer lawns'. 'Harry's House' has a similar theme. 'In France They Kiss On Main Street' depicts that wonderful mixture, young love and rock'n'roll. 'Anima Rising' tells of youthful and/or feminist rebellion. The highlight track for me is 'The Jungle Line' which explores the parallels between actual and urban jungles. The instrumentation consists solely of Moog synthesizer and Burundi drummers, and it was the first time that I had heard of either. It is an extraordinary piece of music. It has a pulse rather than a beat, and it abounds in memorable lines.

As she developed and tried jazz and experimental music Mitchell's records became more difficult and less accessible. This LP is at the junction between the simplicity and openness of her early music and the dense sophistication of the later.

IN MY LIFE
JUDY COLLINS

The track list on this LP is like a name-check of some of the best songwriters of the late twentieth century. Bob Dylan, Jacques Brel, Lennon & McCartney, Bertolt Brecht, Donovan and Leonard Cohen are represented, along with fine songs from lesser-known writers. In fact every single piece on this record is wonderful. From Dylan's bleak 'Just Like Tom Thumb Blues' to the heart-warming reading of the Beatles' 'In My Life' it never hits a low patch. In between come Richard Fariña's 'Hard Loving Loser', Cohen's 'Suzanne' and 'Dress Rehearsal Rag', Brecht's 'Pirate Jenny', Brel's 'La Colombe', Donovan's 'Sunny Goodge Street', 'Liverpool Lullaby' by Stan Kelly and 'I Think It's Going to Rain Today' by Randy Newman. For good measure there is the 'Marat/Sade', a suite of songs from Peter Weiss's play. I like to listen to this album at a sitting, for it seems to hang together so well, conducting the listener through a range of emotions, truculent and tranquil.

TO LOVE SOMEBODY
NINA SIMONE

When Nina Simone sings, you believe her, no matter what she is singing about. This was my first taste of her, heard on a copy belonging to my ex-girlfriend's brother. When she dumped me, not being able to hear this record was not the least of my regrets. I eventually got my own copy, in a shop on Ormond Quay as I remember, and was I the happy boy. There are several wonderful things on it, including the other definitive version of Leonard Cohen's 'Suzanne', covers of the Gibbs Brothers' 'I Can't See Nobody' and 'To Love Somebody', Pete Seeger's 'Turn! Turn! Turn!' and the Beatles' 'Revolution'. The cream is provided by the three Bob Dylan songs – 'I Shall Be Released', 'The Times They Are A-Changin'' and 'Just Like Tom Thumb's Blues'. The first is transformed into classic soul in her hands, and the second becomes positively apocalyptic. The third is probably my favourite track of all time. Its depiction of a mood of weary hopelessness is unmatched. This is done, not in story form, but in a series of unconnected word-pictures that are almost anecdotal in tone.

> *Sweet Melinda, the peasants call her the Goddess of Gloom.*
> *She speaks good English and she invites you up into her room,*
> *And you're so kind and careful not to go to her too soon,*
> *And then she takes your voice, and leaves you howling at the moon.*

By the time Simone reaches the end and sings 'I'm going back to New York City, I do believe I've had enough', you know exactly how she feels.

INFIDELS
BOB DYLAN

This is his most recent great rock album, from 1983. He is the greatest word-junkie in popular music. I understand why people give out about Dylan's singing, but I also pity them because once you get accustomed to his voice there are enough musical riches in his recordings to keep you going all your life. I suppose I was blessed that I came up in the traditional music scene where conventional beauty of tone is not the most highly valued feature of a singer's voice. That said, the unconverted have in this album Dylan's voice at it's most mellifluous in years. He uses it to deliver a splendid set of songs. He is surely the most literary songwriter around. He employs references from biblical and political sources, popular song, the worlds of art and the cinema – just about everything, in fact, that might be of interest to an educated person in the last part of the twentieth century. He can take a well-known phrase, give it a little spin and turn it into something striking, as in the song 'I and I':

> Took an untrodden path once, where the swift don't win the race.
> It goes to the worthy who can divide the word of truth.
> It took a stranger to teach me, to look into justice's beautiful face,
> And to see an eye for an eye, and a tooth for a tooth.

To use the expression 'an eye for an eye . . . ' in the sense of 'call a spade a spade' has the simplicity of genius.

There's the most outspoken politics here since his 'protest' days in 'Neighbourhood Bully', 'License to Kill' and 'Union Sundown'. There's the vicious 'Man of Peace', and no one can do vicious like Dylan. There's the apho-ristic, mystical 'Jokerman', which had one of the best videos I've ever seen. Finally there are the three songs of love; messy, complicated love: 'Sweetheart Like You', 'I And I' and 'Don't Fall Apart On Me Tonight'. He says what's on his mind in so many utterly different ways in each song that you end up knowing exactly how he feels. He switches from reflection to direct speech to recollection to whatever will serve to convey the mood he wishes to create. These songs are achingly beautiful. And they are uncommonly well served by the musicians. Dylan is not known for the care he takes in the studio. Here, however, Mark Knopfler leads a great band in providing the finest of backings for a fine set of songs.

HIGH TIDE AND GREEN GRASS
THE ROLLING STONES

When this record came out I was a holier-than-thou folkie who thought that if you liked one kind of music you couldn't like another. My brother used to play this and I could never see what he liked about it. Eventually I got into it from the bottom up, as it were. The Clancy Brothers led to Joan Baez; Joan Baez led to Woody Guthrie, who led to Leadbelly who led to Robert Johnson and Muddy Waters, who were two of the Stones' most important sources. So I got into the Rolling Stones through folk music. Tommy Makem would be appalled. Considered in this light the early Stones records have as much interest for folk music enthusiasts as for the rock-heads.

With this record the Rolling Stones defined the shape of rhythm and blues, on this side of the Atlantic at least, as a separate genre from the blues. It reminds me of an impressionist painting, acceptable and unremarkable today, but revolutionary and outrageous in its day. It is just bursting with energy and originality. I can never hear 'Satisfaction' anymore, however, without thinking of the riverboat scene in *Apocalypse Now*.

PAUL MULDOON

SLEEVE NOTES

ARE YOU EXPERIENCED?
THE JIMI HENDRIX EXPERIENCE

'Like being driven over by a truck'
was how Pete Townshend described the effect
of the wah-wah on 'I Don't Live Today'.

This predated some months the pedal
Clapton used on 'Tales of Brave Ulysses'
and I'm taken aback (jolt upon jolt)
to think that Hendrix did it all 'by hand'.

To think, moreover, that he used four-track
one-inch tape has (jolt upon jolt) evoked
the long, long view from the Senior Study
through the smoke, yes sir, the smoke of battle
on the fields of Laois, yes sir, and Laos.

Then there was the wah-wah on 'Voodoo Chile
(Slight Return)' from *Electric Ladyland*.

THE BEATLES
THE BEATLES

Though that was the winter when late each night
I'd put away Cicero or Caesar
and pour new milk into an old saucer
for the hedgehog which, when it showed up right

on cue, would set its nose down like that flight
back from the US ... back from the, yes sir ...
back from the ... back from the USSR ...
I'd never noticed the play on album and 'white'.

210

ASTRAL WEEKS
VAN MORRISON

Not only had I lived on Fitzroy Avenue
I'd lived there with Madame Georgie Hyde Lees,
to whom I would rather shortly be wed.

Georgie would lose out to 'The George' and 'El Vino's'
when I 'ran away to the BBC'
as poets did, so Dylan Thomas said.

461 OCEAN BOULEVARD
ERIC CLAPTON

It's the house in all its whited sepulchritude
(not the palm-tree against which dogs piddle
as they make their way back from wherever
it was they were all night) that's really a list.

Through the open shutters his music, scatty, skewed,
skids and skites from the neck of a bottle
that might turn on him, might turn and sever
an artery, the big one that runs through his wrist.

EXCITABLE BOY
WARREN ZEVON

Somewhere between *Ocean Boulevard* and *Slowhand*
I seemed to have misplaced my wedding-band
and taken up with waitresses and usherettes
who drank straight gins and smoked crooked cheroots.

Since those were still the days when more meant less
Georgie was herself playing fast and loose
with the werewolf who, not so very long before,
had come how-howling round our kitchen door

and introduced me to Warren Zevon, whose hymns
to booty, to beasts, to bimbos, boom boom,
are inextricably part of the warp and woof
of the wild and wicked poems in 'Quoof'.

THE JOSHUA TREE
U2

When I went to hear them in Giants' Stadium
a year or two ago, the whiff
of kief
brought back the night we drove all night from Palm

Springs to Blythe. No Irish lad and his lass
were so happy as we who roared
and soared
through yucca-scented air. Dawn brought a sense of loss,

faint at first, that would deepen and expand
as our own golden chariot
was showered
with Zippo-spears from the upper tiers of the stands.

GRACELAND
PAUL SIMON

Little did I think as I knelt by a pot-hole
to water my camel with the other Kaffirs,
little did I think as I chewed on some betel

that I might one day be following the river
down the West Side Highway in his smoke-glassed
limo complete with bodyguard-cum-chauffeur

and telling him that his lyrics must surely last:
little did I think as I chewed and chewed
that my own teeth and tongue would be eaten by rust.

I'M YOUR MAN
LEONARD COHEN

When I turn up the rickety old gramophone
the wow and flutter from a scratched LP
summons up white walls, the table, the single bed

where Lydia Languish will meet her Le Fanu:
his songs have meant far more to me
than most of the so-called 'poems' I've read.

212

OH MERCY
BOB DYLAN

All great artists are their own greatest threat,
as when they aim an industrial laser
at themselves and cut themselves back to the root

so that, with spring, we can never be sure
if they shake from head to foot
from an orgasm, you see, sir, or a seizure.

VOODOO LOUNGE
THE ROLLING STONES

Giants' Stadium again ... Again the scent of drugs
struggling through rain so heavy some young Turks
would feel obliged to butt-hole
surf across those vast puddles

on the field. Some might have burned damp faggots
on a night like this, others faked
the ho-ho-hosannas and the hallelujahs
with their 'Tout passe, tout casse, tout lasse.'

The Stones, of course, have always found the way
of setting a burning brand
to a petrol-soaked stack of hay

and making a 'Thou Shalt'
of a 'Thou Shalt Not'. The sky over the Meadowlands
was still aglow as I drove home to my wife and child.

KEVIN MYERS

IT WAS A CHILDHOOD of the family in exile, the fantasy-images of Ireland weaving into the ordinary experiences of life in England which shaped and formed me. The English singer Michael Holliday on the radio singing 'Hot Diggity. Hot Diggity, Boom What Do You Do to Me?' or my father lying upstairs in bed in the morning while we breakfasted below, singing 'The Kerry Dances' or 'The Rose of Tralee'. Maybe he would arrive at the breakfast table before we all left for school. Little pieces of newspaper on cuts on his cheeks, the smell of shaving soap.

In the playground at Christ the King Catholic primary school in Leicester, talk of rock'n'roll. Johnny Ray was a sissy; he wept. Around Elvis Presley, Bill Haley, real men, factions formed in rival loyalties. And all so mysterious, because I knew, without knowing what I was knowing or why, that it was to do with sex. I didn't know about sex, but something inside me sensed its existence. I knew that there was some unexplained mystery which referred to unexplained commandments and unexplained rules and unexplained faintly stirring yearnings within me.

I fell in love first of all with my sister Ann's friends, ten years or more older than me, Freda and Brenda and others, before beginning to fall in love hopelessly, endlessly but most of all secretly with a series of nine- and ten-year-olds; Celia Lynch, Catherine Carey, Patricia Freeman, you never knew, did you? I dreamed of rescuing them, of finding them naked, of covering their nakedness. That was it; covering their nakedness.

These were not overtly sexual thoughts. The key was nobility, the gallantry, the decency of my deeds. I told my friend Marcus about them. He regularly rescued a girl, her name was Patricia Greenwood, and she too was always naked.

What? Naked as well? As well as Freda and Catherine and Celia and all the others? How odd. All this nudity. We sang a song: 'I'm Popeye the sailorman, I live in a caravan, I like to go swimmin' with lots of bare wimmin, I'm Popeye the sailorman.'

Marc's brother had a Mitch Miller LP, the first LP I ever heard. Marc and I played 'The Yellow Rose of Texas' on the Pateman radiogram endlessly one summer's lunchtime, and then I crossed Medina Road singing 'The Yellow Rose of Texas' and looked up outside my home and saw right above me an American troop-plane, a Fairchild Flying Boxcar.

I was nine. There was not a plane in the sky – de Havilland Vampire, Douglas Attacker or Handley Page Victor – I could not identify by engine noise alone (the Boxcar, as you know, had two Wright Cyclones). That moment I was transported to America, to Texas and its yellow roses, in that Flying Boxcar.

America. What was the mystery of America? Music, girls dancing, showing their knickers. America.

Like Ireland, it haunted my English childhood, as did reverberations from the war. In garden sheds there were gas-masks and steel helmets. There were war-widows and odd boys, older than me, troubled boys who were not quite right, boys whose fathers had been killed.

My family got a Dansette record-player, and someone gave us a Delia Murphy LP. This was strange music indeed. I played 'The Spinning Wheel' endlessly, convinced that this was authentic Irish music, as I was convinced that my father's strong, melancholic baritone voice from his early morning bed carried authentically traditional songs rather than the music-hall nostalgia that in reality they were.

Delia sang:

Mellow the moonlight to shine is beginning,
Close by the window young Eileen is spinning;
Bent o'er the fire her blind grandmother, sitting,
Is crooning and moaning and drowsily knitting.

My mother came into the dining-room. Why are you playing that, on and on? 'Because it's Ireland,' I said. But there was something else about it. I didn't know what, but I knew that mysteriously it belonged to me.

My mother said nothing, just a look on her face.

In fact it was the very song which back in Dublin was playing on the radio when my mother's younger brother set off to cross the Irish Sea to join in the war against Hitler's Germany. Many months later, she and her mother were sitting in Dublin listening to the radio. The same song was playing ...

Slower and slower and slower the wheel swings,
Lower and lower and lower the reel rings ...

when the doorbell went.

My mother took the telegram from the War Office announcing the death on active service of Captain Kevin Teevan, RAMC, West African Field Force. The next two males born to members of his family were called Kevin. I was one of them.

Ireland for that Kevin in the following few years was Haffner's sausages on holiday in Greystones in the 1950s; fly-fishing with my father in Wicklow; red lemonade and cream cakes in the Metropole café; my father telling me about the Black and Tans; visits to Aunt Ellie and Pat and Uncle Martin in Rathmines.

On television *The Six Five Special* speeding down the line brought us Tommy Steele and Dickie Valentine, check shirts and brylcreemed hair. What were the thrilling dangers of Elvis's 'Hound Dog'? Why was the menace of that beat, that rhythm, those mysterious, meaningless lyrics, so thrilling? Why did my breath catch whenever I heard those words?

Gallantly I sang 'The Minstrel Boy' at the St Patrick's Day concert in Leicester, the smell of crushed shamrock sent from Dublin by my Auntie Ellie yielding from my lapel the mysteries of the bog to my exile's nostrils. That year the Catholic lads of Christ the King soccer team, with me at right half, cut a swathe through our schoolboy division. Played eleven, won eleven. Ten Irish outfield and a Polish goalkeeper.

A fat Polish goalkeeper.

Coming home from football practice we were singing Frankie Vaughan's 'The Garden of Eden', which was dead rude, because you knew you were bare and the woman was bare, in that garden of Eden.

On the Glenfield Road, just down from Danehill's convent, one boy said, 'Have you heard? John Skelly fucked Elizabeth Gowan.'

'What does that mean?' I said, my muddy boots swinging by their laces from my hand and bouncing off my shins. I merely knew fuck was a rude word.

'He put his cock inside her cunt,' said my friend.

We all made vomiting noises.

That was what my fellow footballer said. Cock inside her cunt. It meant nothing to me. Absolutely nothing. Cocks were what boys weed out of, girls weed out of their cunts. I knew I liked looking at girls' cunts, but I didn't know why. Fuck had no meaning. It was a word. A rude one. If that was what fuck meant, it wasn't rude, it was disgusting.

I continued singing, Paul Anka's latest hit. We all joined in, together, 'Oh please, stay by me, Diana.'

I used to stand outside the Frears Biscuit factory in Woodgate, close by Frog Island, a couple of hundred yards from the Myers household, so that I could hear the pop music being played to the workforce on the assembly line. I listened to Michael Holliday's 'The Story of my Life' one darkening February evening on the way home from school, a book about aeroplanes from Woodgate library under my arm.

Night fell on a cold, smoggy city. Back at home we warmed ourselves before coal-fires. My father heard the news on the television and told me there was a plane crash in Munich, the lads from Manchester United were dead.

They were in an Airspeed Ambassador (two Rolls Royce Centaurus piston engines).

Next day Christ the King football team gathered in the playground, disbelievingly. Our centre half Denis Moran – we even pronounced his name the Irish way – sang, 'Manchester, Manchester, they're a bunch of Busby Babes,' and then fell silent.

And Bobby Charlton? How was Bobby Charlton? Alive. Duncan Edwards? Alive, but only just. And Harry Gregg, the Irish goalkeeper?

Harry Gregg was a hero. He went back into the crashed plane to rescue people. Harry Gregg was going to get the Victoria Cross, said one boy.

I knew why Harry Gregg was brave. It was because he was Irish. Irish meant brave. Everybody knew that.

Munich, Kennedy. The two imperishable disasters for my generation.

Then secondary school. On my first spectacular day, a boy called Saunders grabbed from my new blazer – my black blazer – the biro which my big sister Ann had brought back from Heidelberg (it had a picture of Heidelberg on the side) and he picked a lump of snot from his nostril with the ballpoint tip. Then he told me the facts of life. All of the facts of life, from homosexuality – they do what? – to conventional intercourse, to masturbation, to lesbianism, WHAT?

Well good God almighty.

Even now I wonder: so John Skelly and Elizabeth Gowan really were ...? At the age of eleven?

'Your parents do it too,' said Saunders, and he sang: 'My Bonny lies over the ocean, My Bonny lies over the sea, My Daddy lies over my Mummy, And that's how they got little Me.'

I got my pen back and cleaned it in the washroom, reflecting that this adult business seemed all very bizarre and disgusting. Leicester City Football Club – five of the first team were Catholics, tremendous! – and rock'n'roll were much more interesting.

After mass at St Peter's Church – where, little did we know, Canon Gilleran, a remote gruff Irishman, was with the assistance of his housekeeper discreetly producing a few remote, gruff little Gillerans – I would gaze avidly at the Top Ten listed in the record shop doorway opposite. Those names – Adam Faith, Russ Conway, Conway Twitty, Craig Douglas – pure fifties naff.

Elvis was in exile doing his military service. We waited and waited while the loathsome poseur, Cliff Richard, pretended so futilely, so pathetically to be Elvis. Words do not exist to describe our contempt for the creature Cliff Richard. The Shadows were different. 'Apache' would cause bubbles to form in my blood. We'd vocally imitate the chords, plucking imaginary guitars, making anguished faces at one another. Even now 'Apache' does things to my corpuscles.

And the summer of 1960, the Everly Brothers produced one of the greatest songs of all, 'Cathy's Clown'. That hot summer we used to go to Leicester's outdoor swimming-pool, the Kenwood. My friend Marc Pateman saw, but I did not, a young woman's bikini top fall off.

He saw her breasts.

He saw her naked breasts.

When he told me I was ill with envy, that summer of 'Cathy's Clown'. Throughout the days that followed, Marc used to sing 'Itsy Bitsy Teeny Weeny Yellow Polka Dot Bikini', week after week, to remind himself and me of his vast sexual experience.

'Go on. Tell me, what were they like?' I would beseech him.

'Oh they were so ...'

Boarding-school followed that summer. The damp and the cold of the following winter haunt my memory with the sounds of Elvis Presley, by 'It's Now or Never', the ensuing spring by 'Wooden Heart', the fine summer which followed by 'Surrender'. I hear those songs on my cassette-player in my car and am instantly catapulted back to Ratcliffe College, to the last days of my childhood, to floundering in the mud on the rugby pitches on the old converted wartime aerodrome, and to the solemn clonk of leather on willow. There is a perfection to that sound upon a summer's day, while sandwiches wait on trestle tables and tea steams in big steel pots, which is known only to those who spent their childhood in the English countryside.

One winter's night in the dorm Paul Chatfield said, 'Have you heard this new group, the Beatles?' 'No, not yet.' 'You must,' he said, 'you must.'

Next evening I sat in the common room, listening for them on Radio Luxembourg and heard, for the first time, 'Love Me Do'.

It was incredible, new, inexplicably strange. Everybody who heard that record knew something was happening; we were young and could like chickens uniquely sense the earthquake coming.

That night in the dormitory we talked about the Beatles. What was special about this group we hadn't even seen? We didn't know. They had a sound we liked, and we loved the name, because the Prefect of Studies was a Father Moss, whom we had nicknamed Beetle.

That night I was woken by a hand on my shoulder, and a voice, saying, 'Kevin'. It was Beetle Moss. Not a dream. Beetle Moss. 'Get dressed', he said, 'your father's unwell.'

He wasn't. By then he was dead.

That was the winter of 1963. A sheet of white iron covered the English countryside for months on end. Fields vanished beneath packed and frozen snow and Liverpool began to unleash its Mersey secrets as the Myers family plummeted into poverty.

Day after day I wandered the icefields around Ratcliffe in leaking shoes, baffled by grief and guilt while my poor mother had to make sense of a moneyless world with children galore and not a penny left, right or centre.

I remember the tunes of that long, long winter in 1963: 'The Wayward Wind', 'From a Jack to a King' and, most of all, 'Please Please Me', by the Beatles.

The Beatles filled my youth. They seemed to fill the world. Everything was Beatles. Nobody who was not alive then can understand the power they had over our lives. There is barely an event over the following half-decade that was not flavoured by some memory of the Beatles and their music. There are no pre-Beatles sixties, merely fifties by another name.

We played the first Beatles album endlessly at school dances; and the second album and the third. My growth hormones stayed inert; I had not developed, and I remained a pathetic, beardless little boy at sixteen, with absurd, ambitious longings. I fell hopelessly in love with Katie O'Hara, still one of the most beautiful girls I have ever seen. It was a futile, doomed devotion which lingered with me for years.

Shortly afterwards my voice broke and at one of the school dances, a girl – not, alas, Katie O'Hara – took me behind the stage and put my hand on her breast. I nearly had a coronary.

'She was just seventeen, you know what I mean.'

Oh by God I did indeed.

I played the Clancy Brothers and Tommy Makem records in the prefects' common room, at full blast, joining in 'The West's Awake' with tearful passion.

I marvelled at the speed and cleverness of 'The Rocky Road to Dublin' and 'Follow Me Up to Carlow'. Most other boys thought the music bizarre. Only the Murphys, whose family came from South Armagh, shared my taste.

I fell for jazz and big band music. Though I had virtually no money, I managed to buy a Buddy Rich-Gene Krupa album which brought me out in goosebumps. I listened to all the jazz I could – Gerry Mulligan, Stan Getz and especially Coleman Hawkins, one of whose albums I had found on a stall in Leicester market. My nervous system would cease at some of his solos. One tune, 'El Salon de Gutbucket', remains the most perfectly thrilling single piece of jazz I have ever heard.

Obsessed with music, but of course with no money, I borrowed a transistor from one of the boys at school to hear a jazz programme on BBC. The radio was promptly stolen from me. Transistors were incredibly expensive in those days. My entire earnings working in Lewis's department store in Leicester that summer went to pay for the stolen radio. I was so poor that that was a lunchless summer. My mother, God help her, was poorer still that terrible year.

I came to Dublin, full of anxiety, but with an English public-school manner and accent which was taken for self-confidence – actually the one quality that was lacking. Thinking sarcasm was witty, I was sarcastic. Thinking sarcasm was not, girls avoided me. Soon I personally knew, with an absolutely unshakeable certainty, that I would die a virgin.

The Dublin of the mid-sixties was still very much the city Joyce had walked. Funny corner huckster-shops with flitches of salty, fly-walked bacon dangled like shrivelled trophies outside a headhunter's house. The city died a complete death at Saturday lunchtime. Weekends were nightmares of loneliness stretching like full archaeological epochs between college days. Saturday nights were so acutely terrible that they cannot be written about, a great aching emptiness in a bedsitter from which I could hear the sounds of a city in apparent revelry.

A girl who lived in the same tenement in Harcourt Street got pregnant. Her parents came to collect her one May afternoon and the mother threw a fit of hysterics on the stone steps where I was sitting. 'I will not enter this house of sin, I will not enter this house of sin,' she shrieked.

What fucking sin, I wondered, an evening and then a night of vast emptiness before me.

My isolation was not made easier by Bijan Emmanuel, an Iranian Jew in the bedsitter above me. A small, ugly, hairy man, he was my best friend. Processions of women arrived at his flat for one purpose. I could hear his bedsprings through the night, the women's cries. Once three women arrived simultaneously. Bijan came down to me and apologized – was it possible for me to entertain the surplus while he attended to the first?

I gave the two women tea and made feverishly anguished conversation, plucking at my hair while my ceiling vibrated. The turn of the second came, leaving me alone with the third, a generously built African nurse. I was in a state of dementia. What does a gentleman do in such circumstances? Should I propose myself as an alternative?

Upstairs, thud thud thud.

Barely able to think, I gibbered and scattered hot tea about the place. Bijan was still doing his manly duty feet above my scalp, his companion wailing and grunting. My companion meanwhile, apparently not noticing the din overhead, flashed white beguiling teeth at me and sipped tea. I looked out the window. Months passed.

Finally, Bijan came to collect the third girl, escorting her upstairs while the second tottered downstairs. Two down, one to go. Then mutely I sat in my room while the floor above me thudded and my African nurse ululated in Ashanti, ending in shrieks, howls, a violent hammering, and sounds like murder. I ran upstairs and there was the African girl, completely naked, hammering on Bijan's door, her vast breasts lolloping up and down. 'Sorry,' I murmured, and retreated.

'What in the name of Jesus was all that about?' I asked him later.

'She a very selfish fuck. You notice that, how women selfish fucks? So I make her nearly come, and then throw her out, till she promise not to be selfish fuck again. She promise okay. She come back tomorrow.'

She came back all right, my lightbulb dancing on the ceiling.

Bijan's elemental sexual magic defied belief and enraged virginal me. I was with him in some godawful place in Parnell Square when he picked up a quite ravishing sixteen-year-old blonde girl. The three of us walked back to Harcourt Street.

Again, grimly, I had to endure her happy Teutonic yodels of joy through the plaster above my head. A couple of months later her father, a German Nazi living in exile, arrived with a gun to shoot Bijan, my swart, hairy Jewish friend. But joy. My swart hairy Jewish friend survived, and the German, white with rage, was led away.

Two girls in the bedsitter next to mine played the Tremeloes' 'Silence Is Golden' for hours on end, weekend after weekend. One Sunday evening I nearly kicked in their door and told them to shut the fuck up with their fucking record. Silence is fucking golden, ohfuckingkay?

One of the girls was at that time sedulously collecting the virginities of the male population of the house. After this, she crossed me off her list and so, uniquely, did not collect mine; and uniquely in that house – apart of course from Bijan – I was not obliged within a few weeks to present myself before the VD clinic at St Vincent's Hospital.

The sixties finally arrived for me in 1967 when I hitchhiked around Europe, alone. Great earthquakes were circling the world, from Britain, from America. There was Vietnam and there was music and there was that unstoppable tide of sex.

One morning on a campsite in Switzerland, after I turned off my shower, I noticed that the pool of water on the floor had turned into a sort of mirror. The cubicle walls ended about a foot from the floor. In that pool I could see an upward reflection inside the cubicle next to me. In that cubicle, I saw a young woman masturbating. I couldn't see her face or even her feet, just her thighs, her hand, and her legs apart.

Technically I knew that women masturbated, but it was an uncertain knowledge. This made it a physically assured truth that women were as I was. Did she know I could see her? And knowing it, did she continue anyway? It was a moment of extraordinarily powerful sexuality and of reassurance; we are prey to so many needs and lonelinesses which can so easily hunt us down and destroy us. The power of the message and the joy of discovering the commonality of the sexual need was a liberation in itself.

I watched her pleasure herself and then she turned on the shower and the mirror beneath my feet disappeared. I left my cubicle and did not wait to see my liberator leave hers. The mystery woman of my life.

That same day I was sitting with two Americans at a pavement café beside Lake Geneva. The sun was hot, the sky blue, the water shimmered, and I was eating diced green beans, laced with garlic and fried in butter. French cuisine had not crossed the English Channel – never mind the Irish Sea – at that point, and the dish seemed incredibly sophisticated.

A brand new shining white Ford Mustang stopped outside the café. The driver and his blonde companion got out and stood with the doors open, the radio on, playing at full volume 'A Whiter Shade of Pale'.

Suddenly I felt giddy with happiness, with freedom, and most of all, with possibilities. This was me beside Lake Geneva. Me. The world was mine and I was the world's. Something within me changed that day, and changed for all time.

That summer the Beatles' 'All You Need Is Love' and Scott McKenzie's 'San Francisco' accompanied me on car radios to Matala, in southern Crete. We smoked dope and drank ouzo and ate fried fish and had sex there on the beach; and afterwards swam nocturnally naked in the moonlit sea.

Are there middle-aged women in Ohio, in Bristol, in Brighton, who pause in the middle of the day and think upon such things?

In the caves we listened solemnly to Gregorian chant on a portable record-player – there were no tape cassettes in those days – and we endlessly played the album that defined the sixties, the album of albums: Sgt. Pepper.

Why did Sgt. Pepper have this effect? Perhaps because we were all waiting for a cue, a cue first promised that night in Ratcliffe four years before, and now this was it, a secret sign between a community of young people, a free but unmasoned freemasonry, that all was changing; nothing was the same. The old order was over.

This was the cusp between generations, between chronological cultures. We went over the edge of the waterfall, and nothing was the same. Some people I knew, the same age as me, were in the old culture and lost their virginity on their wedding nights. Some tinkered a little bit and then married. But for a certain few of us, the old world was gone – socialism and sex were our future, our present, our everything.

Many women students in UCD remained aloof. The ghastly eligible-husband-hunting species was commonplace; more commonplace in UCD were the furtively secret ones, whose sexuality and passion and individuality and ambition and self remained cloaked behind austere and mimicked indifference to the world. The nuns had done a good job. These students were projectiles fired from de Valera's fifties into an entirely different time. They had been robbed of joy.

The next year I earned money in Philadelphia and hitch-hiked America's great wide width. Sleeping rough in fields, I fell in love with America, the land of the Fairchild Flying Boxcar, as that day on Medina Road gaping upwards I knew I would. And it was money that I earned which paid for this. Money I earned. Me. I was free. Adult.

Simon and Garfunkel kept me company as I crossed the continent, my heart spinning with joy, singing – for me, it seemed – 'Looking for America' as I travelled through small-town Pennsylvania, my heart aching with discovery and happiness. The Beatles' 'Hey Jude' was alongside me then – I cannot hear that tune without thinking of heading west towards a westering sun plummeting vertically before my eyes on that road, the light incandescing blindingly on its deadstraight two-lane blacktop heading straight towards the Pacific rim.

Cheyenne, Laramie, Medicine Bow in silence watched me and my long hair pass through. At night I curled up in ditches and listened to my radio – Tom Jones's 'Love Is Like Candy on a Shelf', Mary Hopkins's 'Those were the Days my Friends' – and slept. In the Rockies I woke covered in snow. Another time I woke up with a snake in my sleeping-bag and I lay there till the heat of the steadily rising sun drove it slithering out through the pall of my muck-sweat.

I knew freedom. It is my fond belief that nobody in the world sensed freedom as we did in the late sixties. No doubt it was illusory. But freedom is spiritual. We felt free, and the music of that summer told me I was free. Sleeping beneath the tall clear sky, walking the long highways of America, I knew I was free.

As I drove into San José, the radio played Dionne Warwick's 'Do You Know the Way to San José?'

I did now.

In California I smoked dope that late summer and early autumn of 1968 and then travelled on. At midnight, somewhere, I swam in the Pacific, alone, naked, and then slept on that Pacific shore. I have not seen it since.

Back in Dublin we gathered to foment the revolution. Bach and Handel had won me. I listened to the *Double-Concerto in D* performed by the Oistrakhs, to the *Water Music* performed by Yehudi Menuhin and the Bath Festival Orchestra, and had sex with as many women as I could.

Which was not many, and certainly not as many as I wanted, but the world was good and easy and there was an insurgent happiness which filled our hearts. That happiness, I believe, was unique to that time. All around me were happy people determined on revolution and change. It was bliss. It was. It was.

We played Handel. The White Album. Bach. Dvörjak, Brahms, the White Album, some dope. The White Album.

January, 1969. Snow in Dublin, sitting round the gas-fire in the roof-flat in Upper Pembroke Street, snow encrusted on the windowsills, ice on the inside of windowpanes and listening to Bach or lying in bed in the morning, thinking of the nameless woman in the shower in Switzerland.

On the radio, Patricia Cahill singing in that icy, frost-decked morning 'Slieve na mBan', tribal follicles quivering.

And later, when that winter had departed, listening to the unbelievable pretentiousness of the Incredible String Band in the middle of the day and having hurried lunchtime sex with a woman before my flatmates returned.

Student occupations, Vietnam marches, sit-ins, teach-ins; all very silly, very sixties. Yet it did not seem so, and we were dizzy with possibilities and happiness.

A party that warm summer of 1969, Leonard Cohen's preposterous and mournfully sententious songs which somehow captured something of the very last year in that decade year with sixty in its name. Then walking home with a girl, and in a front garden near Baggot Street, in a strange front garden, making love to her and hissing to her, shush, shush, while lights came on. A man at the door muttering, 'Oh for Jesus sake,' and closing the door behind him, underwear across his lawn and the melancholy notes of Leonard Cohen ringing through my brain. We lay that warm summer night on the stranger's front lawn, sweet with grassy sap, and laughed and laughed and laughed.

Ó *Riada sa Gaiety* appeared and revealed a treasury of music and fun and self-mockery that had been hidden in the over-reverenced world of traditional music. Irish music kicked open the cupboard and came dancing across the kitchen floor and into the world, never to return to the dreary pieties that had imprisoned it before. We played Irish music and had sex with one another and visiting Americans.

Oh yes, God be good to the visiting Americans.

Then the North erupted and the world began. The ceremony of innocence was over.

I left UCD in 1969 and listened to little rock music afterwards. But I had built up a wonderful collection of records – jazz, rock, traditional, classical, plainchant – which were musical registrations of my life from childhood onwards. In a way they defined my life, from Michael Holliday to Bizet to the Clancys to the Beatles to Coleman Hawkins and the Incredible String Band and

Ó Riada sa Gaiety. Barely a note existed on those albums that hadn't got some resonance for me and my life.

In January 1972 my flat in Belfast was broken into and my entire record collection stolen. The theft would have netted mere pennies for the burglar. Worse things have happened in my life and I have forgotten them; but the loss of the music of my youth follows me down through all my days and will do so, I think, always.

CHARLES NAPER

NOSTALGIA ISN'T WHAT IT USED TO BE. People from our generation seem certain of one thing: music will never hold the same place for any other generation. We arrogantly assume that our music (the music that appeared from nowhere, identified itself with a few signposts like Buddy and Elvis, and snowballed into a full-time, all-embracing ingredient of life) was better than anything on offer now. This assumption is not founded solely on evidence and common sense (listened to the radio recently?) but on the fact that we identified with it. Didn't we all feel personally possessive about our favourite records? It wasn't always due to the possessiveness that comes from 'discovering' something (I still feel I own a part of Steve Miller because I take credit for being the first European to listen to *Sailor* and *Brave New World*). It was, above all, that we identified with it – it enveloped us on multiple levels, it spoke for us, we spoke for it (I used words like 'crash out', 'heavy', 'vibes', and of course 'man', without self-consciousness in the naive belief that this was our language, born of our music). Such arrogance! And such indulgence! Lecturers, parents, employers, everyone capitulated and let us dress, speak, intoxicate ourselves in the style we knew to be true and right; I suppose they thought it was an adolescent phase that would go away. So it did, but not the music; the good records didn't get discarded, just borrowed or stolen.

My father must have been particularly indulgent. During my brief career at Trinity College, Dublin, a consortium of delightful people whom he could only have described as Hippies used to spend weekends with us at Loughcrew bringing the entire 'Trackless Transit' sound system, crates of appropriate records (Beefheart, Yes, Pentangle) and a comprehensive range of drugs, chillums etc. Naturally we were meticulous in keeping evidence of our various entertainments from my father. After their first departure I nervously asked him what he thought of my new friends. He considered, 'They were very nice people, especially Orla. But tell me, were they all so ill because they smoked so much dope, or did they smoke so much because they were ill?' A valid question.

There was no doubt, in my mind anyway, that our music was a major development in world culture. I once made my father listen to the Emperor Concerto followed by *Deep Purple in Rock*, then lectured him on the similarities in mood, classical integrity, blah blah between the two. I also made him sit through the whole of *The Hangman's Beautiful Daughter*, libretto on his knee. (He got his revenge later – he developed a taste for operatic arias.)

My parents weren't musical. Our first record-player arrived soon after the black-and-white TV – the chosen records were *The Black and White Minstrel Show*, *Songs of Percy French*, and Pat Boone's single 'Johnny Will'. Heady stuff. But they did buy me a clarinet and a Hohner accordion, perhaps hoping for signs of natural talent.

The clarinet reappeared at Trinity, when I rather nervously approached Jolyon Jackson to ask if he wanted to replace Jazz Therapy's wind section, whom they had carelessly lost in Canada or somewhere. 'What music do you like?' 'Charles Lloyd'. (I had him there, didn't I – who the hell was Charles Lloyd?) 'Wow! Charles Lloyd! We're doing the College of Surgeons Ball next week. Come and jam!' I am in no doubt that anyone who attended that ball will remember my distinctive public début. My microphone was hooked up to the in-house speakers, which were inaudible to me. The clarinet, when played with excess enthusiasm, is prone to 'overblow' – a piercing, ghastly wail like an impaled pig. Totally unable to hear myself, but confident that I was doing a pretty impressive solo to Therapy's favourite show blues, I stood there, posing and blowing like a veteran, while the hall filled with terrifying howlings and wailings and hundreds of budding surgeons made for the exits, as in a fire alert. Brian Masterson, courteously in the circumstances, thanked me. But I'm afraid it was a case of 'don't call us, we'll call you'.

My next excursion into the world of music found me as assistant roadie to the Woods Band, then reduced to Terry and Gay Woods, an enormous Mercedes van, two unfeasibly large speaker-bins and a variety of delicate stringed instruments. Oh yes, and Liam, the farting groupie/soundman. (Terry seems to have been unfortunate in his roadies. One of his records features an instrumental entitled 'Noisy Johnny' – a tribute to an earlier flatulent roadie.) Terry was, and is, a grand-master of guitar, mandolin etc. However, it was Gay's voice that grabbed me; in an era of remarkable female voices, hers was the greatest. Her songs were the highlight of my brief roadie period.

My role as assistant roadie was rather undefined; sometime driver, sometime sound-mixer (don't ring us, we'll ring you), sometime banker, full-time opener of windows when Liam was around. Irish tours consisted of tearing round the country on a schedule organized by a plausible but incompetent agent called Des. These terrifying drives led, typically, to a gig that didn't exist, or at best a gig in a pub up the back-end of Clare, run by a priest who wouldn't pay us but suggested we might make a contribution as 'the gate wasn't very great'.

One non-event was scheduled at University College Galway. Having arrived after a particularly harrowing drive by Liam (Des had skilfully organized a lunchtime gig in Dublin the same day), we found that no one at the venue had been informed of the gig (except a journalist from the *Sligo Champion*. Des was a divil for the Advance Publicity). However, Thin Lizzy were playing the Talk of the Town so we joined them, Terry playing a few sets with them while the rest of us composed curses for the discomfiture of Des. Afterwards Phil Lynott invited us to his hotel room for some challenging refreshments, a plan thwarted by an hysterical night-porter who denied us entry. Phil, clearly used to these situations, exhorted us to jump up and down. So the musical cream of Ireland jumped up and down in the lobby while the hysterical night-porter phoned for the guards (in vain – they knew his form).

As we left town in the morning, we observed Lizzy's three-tonner, parked in Eyre Square, coming to life. The gear was topped by several mattresses, from which emerged four dishevelled girls followed by two exhausted roadies. Some were getting famous, some were getting rich, some were getting laid. Not me, Bob.

Next was a tour in Holland, where Terry and Gay had a sizeable following. Des had omitted to book any tickets, so I was able to establish my usefulness with my credit card. After a few nights sleeping on wooden floors in crappy youth clubs, I decided the Woods Band and I were superfluous to each other's needs and got out of the wagon in the middle of nowhere to seek my fortune. Terry must have taken this rather to heart – I think he had had a bad run of absconding roadies, Farting Liam being the only one with stamina. Anyway he wrote a charming ditty in my honour called 'Sorry Friend', which appeared on a subsequent album – the nearest I ever came to getting on record.

My fortune took me to London, where, in the naive belief that the Music Business was about Music, I became a recording engineer in the Marquee Studio. A plus was nightly free entry to the Marquee Club. (The best act I heard there was, yes, Thin Lizzy.) The minuses included permanent loss of much of my hearing and the confirmation of my suspected incompetence with a sound-mixer. As I left, I was informed that the only reason I had got the job in the first place was the numerous rings I had been innocently wearing on my fingers when first interviewed. That kind of place.

While all this was going on I was listening to records. I didn't buy many; very selective I was, and tight with it. But what I bought I loved excessively, taking more care of the records and sleeves than of domestic hygiene. I never had this respect for books; I'm perfectly happy with paperbacks; I even lend books to people. The only singles I ever purchased were by Elvis Presley – the greatest being 'Such a Night' (which I have never, ever, heard on the radio) and 'Viva Las Vegas'. I was introduced to Elvis by one Antony Farrell, who used to bring me to a smelly cinema in Mullingar to see Elvis beach movies. I think we were both impressed by the amount of female skin on display; skin, sand, surf, silly hairdos, above all, sun. Stepping out into the rain of Mullingar was a bit of a comedown. What I don't remember is the music. God knows where 'Such a Night' and 'Viva Las Vegas' intruded from.

At prep school, Antony and I unimaginatively developed the same tastes, and the most important feature of days out from school was the chance to listen to the Top Ten. 'Little Children', 'Glad All Over', 'Searching'. Blood was shed over the respective merits of the Stones and the Beatles. Their pictures had a huge currency – far greater than, say, boob magazines or even war comics. I didn't go mad for the music, but I subscribed to the hype, cunningly sitting on the fence by cultivating a haircut that I thought resembled both Brian Jones and John Lennon.

My choice of acceptable music has, in some cases sadly, always been conditioned by anti-fashion. Thus as my contemporaries immersed themselves in the Beatles and Stones, I turned my back on the music out of, I suppose, bloody-mindedness – why should I lower myself to enthusing about what everyone else was enthusing about? Incidentally, this attitude later stood me in good stead in my pose as a jazz-fancier. Essential to this pose is an encyclopaedic knowledge of names to drop, the more obscure the better. This was, of course, easier in the days before CDs. Jazz LP covers always included detailed biographies, with cross-references to other obscure musicians. Occasionally the jazz-bluffer comes against his match (e.g. J. Jackson/Charles Lloyd) but as we bluffers tend to talk at the same time one usually gets away with a good deal of rubbish.

Anyway, the attitude didn't matter much. In time I moved on and got quite excited by the Stones – even some of the Beatles. Did I ever buy their LPs? Yes – *Between the Buttons* (probably because nobody else had it.)

Much more serious was my avoidance of, in turn, Bob Dylan, Jimi Hendrix, the Grateful Dead, Cream. Everyone was listening to them. My school went in for enormous halls divided into cubicles – one each – the walls of which, stall-like, stopped short of the ceiling. Senior boys were allowed to play music. Outside class or study or sleeping hours one's environment was filled with up to a dozen small music devices each at full blast, like a flock of gannets proclaiming their territory. Thus: 11.15.00 am. Bob Dylan's *Route 66* from James Naper; 11.15.09 a.m.: Bob Dylan's *Route 66* from Nick Dent; maybe ten recordings of the same Bob Dylan track, all out of sync, all full blast. Where to hide? At meals, during games, between classes, there was at least one bastard humming or singing *Route 66*. Refuge was the Music School, with its listening room complete with crappy stereo and comprehensive classical library. Or my mentor, Sam Brigstocke, who patiently introduced me to a new world – Miles Davis, Charles Mingus, Lightnin' Hopkins, Champion Jack Dupree. I was pretty clueless, but desperate to be trendy (or anti-trendy). Thus: 'Hey, Sam, is this BLUES or JAZZ?' 'Jazz.' 'Fine, Thanks.' Pause. 'Hey, Sam, how can you tell?' 'Oh, shut up and listen to "Green Onions".' Sam was a philosophical chap, also a genuine lover of blues and jazz; in the end I got the idea; I even gave a potted jazz lecture (my excuse to introduce Paul Barbarin's 'Tiger Rag' to the world). And Sam even consented to form a band with me – he was a rock-solid and inventive drummer, I was a talentless, tuneless, fumbling sax-player. ('The ill woodwind that nobody blows any good' – J. Dankworth.) Garth Cruikshank played string bass – he looked great, like a grinning, short-sighted Donald Duck wrestling with an upended boat.

I had a really flashy bit of kit – the original Phillips stereo cassette-recorder. We started recording ourselves, then stopped. The shed allotted to this fountain of talent was a ten-by-ten-foot shack with one power-point, on the extremity of the school's service buildings; rotting lawn mowings, burning leaves, rusting iron, illicit cigarettes provided the atmosphere. Sometimes, still, when a certain whiff of decomposing garden matter hits me, I recall Garth thudding and buzzing away, his bleeding fingers, Sam's toneless crashing and whacking noises and the honking-in-an-oil-drum sound of my borrowed saxophone. I fortunately couldn't really hear myself playing; others could and kept away. We retained sufficient dignity not to give ourselves a name, but we did resort to trying unorthodox Dave Brubeck-type rhythms (5/4, 9/8 etc) – always a sure sign of true incompetence or creative poverty in an aspiring jazz group. Why in God's name didn't we just play blues? Probably in those days we thought the blues had to be sung; I had my mouth full and the idea of Sam or Garth singing was too horrible for consideration.

My first LP purchases were jazz – Dave Brubeck, Charlie Parker, Lester Young, the usual trendy incomprehensibles – and classical. My clarinet appeared (unobtrusively) in the school orchestra, which was seldom allowed out in public; my borrowed saxophone (Tenor! Big and shiny!) appeared in the Cadet Corps Band and the Brass Orchestra – both very accomplished, huge fun and a wonderful opportunity to show off. We even got on television, at the Earls Court Royal Tournament – annoying the Combined Marines Band by playing all their new tunes before they came on. My music teacher was a dear man; he got cross only once, when I ungraciously suggested we spend time learning some music rather than smoking and gossiping.

Having survived by taping other people's records on my prototype cassette-recorder, I eventually progressed to my trusty PL12 D deck with Sansui 101 amp and Wharfedale Linton speakers. An unpretentious but perfectly formed system. I've always found that, no matter how crappy one's stereo is, it's perfect until one experiences something better. (Rather like cars and wine.)

And thus to Trinity – and encountering the records of Our Generation in context: *Stephen Stills* (Terry says 'Black Queen' has to be dubbed, afficionados insist it's a live take); Leon Russell – the first, with 'Delta Lady' – and all the gang there (Delaney and Bonnie, Bobby Whiplash, Jim Horn, and, I notice now for the first time, produced by the late lamented Mr Cordell); Al Kooper's *Super Session*; Deep Purple; Led Zeppelin; the Who (not *Who's Next* – like piles and the Golf GTI, sooner or later every arsehole gets it), but *Tommy* (perfect from beginning to end – on record anyway). And then the expensive habits – collecting Van Morrison and Elton John's LPs (they both had more stamina than I did – I gave up at about a hundred or so – and they're both still at it!). What do you say about these men? Both satisfy my yen for over-engineered, studio-perfect production; yet both have made superb live LPs. All these early albums had fantastic tunes, fantastic arrangements, good or great lyrics, superbly sung. Oh yes, and nice sleeves. One of my school heroes had his room papered with his obscure record sleeves. Hell, I could do it now with Van and Elton sleeves alone. Talking of sleeves, let's not forget John Mayall's greatest work, *Laurel Canyon* – only slightly marred by the excruciatingly pompous lyrics and the smug credits on the cover (ending 'cover design – John Mayall'). A whole weekend symposium for psychologists on the subject of the Ego could be devoted to that cover. Has this man really no sense of humour, no shame? But what music! What musicians did he (not modestly) hatch!

Then to America, in 1972; the discovery of Jeff Beck's *Truth* (Rod Stewart on vocals); King Curtis and the Kingpins, including drummer Bernard Purdie and Billie Preston, all backing Aretha Franklin with Ray Charles at Fillmore East; the other gang, the Clapton/Leon Russell/Delaney and Bonnie crowd; Bobbie Whitlock; Jim Keltner; Duane Allman, etc etc. I returned with a back-pack full of rather bent LPs. In return I left in America a trail of *Hangman's Beautiful Daughter* copies which I bought on sight and left with people who gave me a bed and were, well, nice to me. My contribution to transatlantic culture exchange.

Bob Dylan caught up with me at last, in the form of the Band's *Before the Flood* – the ultimate live album. Terry Woods introduced me to Ry Cooder's first (the one with 'One Meat Ball') – the first of many from the 'musician's musician' who declined to gather no moss.

Well, that's got most of them in, plus a few more. Being asked to choose ten albums made me feel like the captain in a life raft with only ten places, and fifty or so drowning souls in the water. So I cheated a bit. Anyway, where would rock'n'roll be without a bit of name-dropping. God, we're so old. But don't we feel superior?

His Band and the Street Choir	Van Morrison
Captain Fantastic and	
the Brown Dirt Cowboy	Elton John
Sailor/Brave New World	Steve Miller
Delaney and Bonnie and Friends,	
Live at the Fairfield Hall, Croydon	
The Yes Album	Yes
Ry Cooder	Ry Cooder
King Curtis Live at Fillmore East	Curtis Ousley
Leon Russell	Leon Russell
After the Flood	The Band
Eat the Peach	The Allman Brothers Band

GEORGE O'BRIEN

REVOLVER
THE BEATLES

I always said I didn't like the Beatles. That was my fashion statement. Then they broke up and I had quite a John Lennon phase ('I'm Only Sleeping'). But he went and made *Two Virgins*, and I thought maybe they weren't so bad, hairdos, suits, and all. It was just that at the time I thought they were mannequins. Their successes made everything around them look too good. Life was fab, and society classless. Any day now, the Beatles would officially become jolly old pillars of the jolly old establishment, four corners of a pantomime horse playing at the Empire and the Queen's Award for Industry, booked for eternity on the never-ending Sunday Night at the London Palladium. Being 'the greatest songwriters since Schubert' (Tony Palmer on Lennon and McCartney) was fine if you knew anything about Schubert. Give me a working-class hero like Eric Burdon.

So, how come I remember vividly being on the Tube with a crowd of people I can't remember ('all the lonely people'), singing to the air of a well-known *Revolver* track, 'We all live in a house in Golders Green'? The Beatles might not have been irresistible, but they were unavoidable. I did admit I liked the cover, the flow and flower of it (a lost art, now, album covers). The disarming pun of the title appealed too. Eventually I sat on somebody's dhuri and even listened to the thing. It was upsetting. Behind the Top Ten stuff, the sweetness and light, there was metallic 'Taxman', hypnotic 'Tomorrow Never Knows'. Those two alone were material enough for a Pseuds' Corner into which I could have painted my very own Beatles. And what was 'Dr Robert' about?

PET SOUNDS
THE BEACH BOYS

Liz and I hadn't a red rex between us, which was serious because we were both dying to be with it, London was swinging and we would gladly swing for it, and this meant money. So we had to do the next best thing: if we couldn't afford it, we could secure possession by knowing. We started living together in a booth at the HMV shop in Oxford Street, where they'd play you records before you bought them. Later we found what we wanted ... Cathy Berberian, Coltrane's *Ascension*, Love. But to begin with we had only what we'd heard about to go on.

And *Pet Sounds* was supposed to be right up there, a step forward from the rather infantile 'fun' of the Beach Boys' earlier stuff. American pop was fighting back. Brian Wilson was an auteur. It just had to be interesting. And Liz was delighted because she found how years of poking around preludes and fugues could at last pay off: 'God Only Knows'.

But that cut was the only novelty *Pet Sounds* had. Bach, but no bite. We listened again, and still didn't get it. All the Boys could think of it (that is, It) was that it would be nice. That was as puerile as the Beatles wanting just to hold your hand. The album cover showed them in the Kiddies' Korner of a zoo. Their idea of escape was 'The Sloop John B' (a choirboys' outing compared to Lonnie Donegan's earlier version). Where was the rude noise, the danger, the Blackness? The urgent drive to the impersonality of harmony was the sound of whites aching to be innocent. The way it echoed our own callow pining was so perfect it was intolerable. 'I Just Wasn't Made for This World'.

DA CAPO
LOVE

There was Moby Grape, Steppenwolf, Quicksilver Messenger Service, Spirit, Big Brother and the Holding Company, It's a Beautiful Day. Guitar bands, the sound of San Francisco, but with the wattage to wilt flowers and vocals by people who didn't sound especially beautiful. Love was a relief, mellow, spacy; a flute that was all woodsmoke, like an offspring of Charles Lloyd; a simmering organ, not that piping-hot thing that surged to light our fires. 'Orange Skies' and Arthur Lee's fragile vocals ... those were Love's limit.

I didn't even understand the title of *Da Capo*. The thing you strapped to an acoustic guitar, something to do with the Mafia? The title of the next Love album, *Forever Changes*, made a lot more sense, and had their best music on it too. But not understanding didn't matter, or rather it mattered in the same way as the fact that the album was on the Elektra label, like Country Joe and the Fish. Novelty lived in these words without nuance or context or relevance, and freedom was its countersign. Taking up one whole side of the album with just one instrumental cut, that was freedom. And if that didn't say it all, the proto-punk drive and loopy 'Oowawa-Oowawa' figure of '7 and 7 Is' did. Who could ask for anything more? Not I, and I was as demented as any bourgeois in my quest for rarity and richness.

This music was fog in the bay, visionary mist in a sunlit bedsit. 'She Comes in Colours.' I met a girl from California who said she'd been on a plane with Arthur Lee. 'He's a really sweet guy.' I smiled. I knew. I'd had that dream as well.

FRESH CREAM
CREAM

The Bonzo Dog Doo-Dah Band asked, 'Can Blue Men Sing the Whites?' But nobody stayed for an answer. Everyone was waking up this morning and dusting brooms ... dingedy, dingedy, dingedy, dingedy, ding-ding (with heartfelt apologies to Elmore James). The blues were tradition and discipline, a kind of scouts' honour, high church of the low church of charismatic, extrovert pop. The blues were for shy people, technicians, craftsmen. The blues bred snobby sniping ... urban against country, acoustic against electric. Fans were sanctimonious, obsessive, collected records with trainspotters' ardour.

Cream took the mumbling and jangling of Tooting and Tottenham and turned it into something else. That was the plan, anyhow. And there definitely seemed to be a plan. I knew because I was deep into the scene, the biz as much a fetish with me as the show. Take the hype that heralded them, a coming together of the princes of the House of Mayall (Clapton) and the House of Bond (Bruce). A supergroup. Take the hubris of the name, of a group with three leads. Why call a song 'NSU' (non-specific urethritis)? Was 'Spoonful' really about drugs? Drive and voltage came for answers, thunder and lightning and lashing out. 'Rollin' and Tumblin'.' Ginger the dervish with two bass drums. Clapton's keening. The menace of the big fat bass. The high-wire tension of those strained vocals. The unheard-of loudness. They were redefining 'high'. *Fresh Cream* ... soppy, pop-y title and all ... remains a spark from that fire. But really, you had to be there.

HISTORY OF OTIS REDDING
OTIS REDDING

I was busy collecting the credentials to be progressive. I read Wilhem Reich and the *International Times*, dug Soft Machine and 'Arnold Layne', wondered about Situationism and Dutch Provos ... And whatever happened, I made sure to turn on to John Peel, the Perfumed Garden, Radio London, twelve until two every night. Soul was not in my vocabulary.

But from Dollis Hill to Penge there were blokes practising how best to croon and cry it out. 'Call me Mr Pitiful.' They were the counter-revolution, short hair and mod-ish, clerks, draughtsmen. If they were busted or arrested on a demo, they'd lose a lot more than a night's sleep ... the job, probably; house-room, possibly; 'Security', never mind 'Respect'. The Emperor Rosko was their main man, Caroline their station, Tiles their club, the Stax label their salvation. Hippies had ideas, but Otis had heart, and every worker knew that that was what it took.

Powerful as the pulse of his up-tempo stuff was ('I Can't Turn You Loose'), it was more of a band thing: Jimmy James and the Vagabonds could do that. Otis slow, though, was when pain's raw rasp came through ('These Arms of Mine'), came true. Steve Cropper's guitar melted into metal tears. Booker T's electric Hammond was a case of nerves. A music of singles, not albums. Unprogressive in that too. Pub jukeboxes were full of them. Couples listened moonily, turned on by the losing, the doing without, obviously at home with each all-or-nothing drama. Abashed by passion, I listened and looked on, nursing my light and bitter, as if I'd been cast adrift by my pretensions.

BOOKENDS
SIMON & GARFUNKEL

I was scrounging off Ed, Ron and Mick in an old pile on Herne Hill, convenient to the Southern Region and the Brockwell Tavern, where there wasn't any talent and the jukeboxes played 'Hey Jude' all the time. The lads were art students at Camberwell, and the flat said so loud and clear. Mick's floor looked like an accident in a nail-varnish factory. A giant stain of scarlet polyurethane cut every crack and knothole to the quick, sped under skirting boards and up the blocked-off chimney. Definitely ahead of its time, a heavy-metal landscape.

We were all devastated when Mick found love and moved out. She was an older woman from down Norwood way. Mick had to be serious. She had a child. Mick had to be kidding. This we had to see. After a few Saturday lunchtime pints we went round. But all I remember is 'Save the Life of My Child' booming out to greet us from spanking new speakers. Cohabitation was a jejune form of duality compared to this stereo system of theirs. The crump and clash of *Bookends'* opening track switched channels with abandon. Mick had us where he wanted us: speechless. Before long, we were hymning 'Mrs Robinson' and looking Pauline boldly in the eye. We slapped in unison to 'Hazy Shade of Winter', and never missed a beat except when it effortlessly swung into 'At the Zoo'. Clever, that. Pauline made tea. There was a feeling that maybe Mick had done the right thing in going to look for his America after all.

Twenty-five years later, Ben and Nick O'Brien do their loon dance and are absolutely citizens for boysenberry jam fans.

THE BAND
THE BAND

Pam and I had been married almost a year before we got our first consumer durable, a record-player, at Boots in the Cornmarket, Oxford. Now the problem was records. Should we get everything we wanted – *Electric Music for the Mind and Body*, *A Quick One*, *Surrealistic Pillow* – or should we concentrate on current musts? We were entering the marketplace, growing up. But we were still flashing cultural tail-feathers at each other too. Pam came from banjo country, spoke of Bill Monroe and the Bluegrass Boys. Not to be outdone, I bought *Hot Rats* by Frank Zappa, which was the sound of God knows what.

What we found in the Band was a sweet meeting-place. And then, too, it etched some of what was seriously different about America on my mind's eye. But I didn't quite appreciate that until I visited Brown Country, Indiana, saw places called Bean Blossom and Nawbone, heard the industrial-strength, incessant susurrus of insects in the black woods at the fall of velvet night. Cripple Creek did not seem far away, old rocking chairs creaked on ruined porches, gold harvest was king in the baked fields, and pines whispered with the hickory, live oak, dogwood. Mandolin, jewsharp, and scrawny backwoods vocals provided just the right accents for such extraordinary ordinariness. The Band did not take

America for granted and their offbeat rhythms remain a true picture of a strange climate. This is not where the old friends chatting on *Bookends* live. 'When you awake you will remember everything.' The whole album might be a soundtrack for early Cormac McCarthy.

MOONDANCE
VAN MORRISON

I knew the North had music, what with Ruby Murray and Ronnie Carroll, Eileen Donaghy, Bridie Gallagher smooching 'The County of Armagh', not forgetting Tommy Makem, and on the Walton programme on old Athlone, 'Charlie Magee and his gay guitar'. All on record, mind: very modern – though the North was considered backward. The Clipper Carlton. Besides, I'd been taught how seriously they took their music up there, all that marching and the rattle of the drums like the horrid knocking of your four bones. But when I heard Them I never thought of the North, because Them was rock'n'roll: hormone pinball, gurrier fury, trouble in mind. It wasn't until *Moondance* that I listened to Van Morrison and heard where he was coming from.

'And It Stoned Me.' Beery brass and reed, remnants of New Orleans funeral bands. Flutes such as were never heard at Finaghy, and a gospel choir and a piano fluent in all sorts of sweet inflections. Apart from anything else, there was that mastery of idiom to admire and to identify with. 'Glad Tidings.' This was being international by being yourself, and vice-versa. That came through to me loud and clear. Especially when that was not just a style. It was the theme, the subject, the quest, the visceral vehemence of it all. 'Into the Mystic.'

The voice records the cost. There's something in it that badly wants to hang on. It would like the gospel truth and the safe haven. But at the same time it must break out. Freedom must sing. 'Brand New Day.' (Blood on the streets of Belfast. Froth at the mouths of the politicos.) 'Stoned me just like going home.'

KATE AND ANNA MCGARRIGLE
KATE AND ANNA MCGARRIGLE

The album cover is in black and white and grainy. The two girls looking out from it are not beautiful. I don't think they're wearing make-up, their hair isn't styled, and their clothes look much like anyone's. No sequins, no frills, no jewellery. Instead of image there's expression. One of the girls looks back, knowing that somebody's looking at her. She's holding her own. Her eyes are frank, bold. She isn't smiling. Her sister looks away, taken up by her own thoughts, soulful. She's not smiling either. It's the awful seventies, age of glitz. There isn't much to smile about. For this appearance of sincerity, much thanks. (The album is dedicated to Gaby and Frank, the parents.)

And the voices are as unadorned as the looks, stronger than Joni Mitchell, richer than Judy Collins. Haunting, gaunt, undaunted. The voices of experience, not interpretation, as it must be in the ballad, the lay, the hymn, the plaint ('Go

Leave'). The sad songs struck me most the first time round at Linda's snug little house in the Liberties. Reports from an empty country. 'Heart Like a Wheel' and 'Tell My Sister'. Later I heard the fairground in 'Complainte Pour Ste-Catherine', and noticed that their 'Swimming Song' lacked the original's zany grin, and thought the sound was like the Band's, just lighter.

It was the summer my father died. I was back in Dublin. 'My Town.' Linda was my oldest friend, the only one in Dublin then, and badly needed. I wanted to talk about this suitcase of my father's old shirts I was taking back to England. But 'Mendecino' kept calling me. Another country. 'Jigsaw Puzzle of Life.'

THE SPECIALS
THE SPECIALS

Coventry: a place to be sent to, not to go. 'Cuvventry' they said in Lismore, revealing oven and coven, shades of dark, satanic mills. Pam and I moved there from Oxford. Big lorries, grey faces, clouds of steam, ring roads, not enough trees ('Concrete Jungle'). We didn't go out much, watched *Top of the Pops* on our 13" rented telly. Slade, Bowie, disco, Elton John. Jimmy Hill singing the Sky Blues seemed a slightly more genuine article. Soon soccer edged out sounds. All over the men's bogs in the University of Warwick library, huge graffiti read, 'Radford is God'. Hendrix and Redding were dead.

Soccer was where the police came in. These were the specials, with the black-and-white check band around their caps, vans of them under the overpasses, squads of them frisking, herding, pouncing, collaring. 'Doesn't Make It Alright.' It was terrible: six or seven years since 1968, and how hard being young was … Talk about Boomtown Rats.

The Specials took those check markings and reinterpreted them in a seven-piece (!) band with – for – blacks and whites. 'A Message to You, Rudy', without the sarcasm. The markings trimmed the album. Even Jerry Dammer's gap-toothed grin looked chequered. Right there in Cov. there was verve, brashness, a rude shout of refusal, the music of two fingers flipping. Black and white mixed wasn't grey. 'It's Up to You.' A far cry from the sixties – balls where petals had been thought sufficient. My job at Warwick was cut. Pam and I went to America: eight-track, oldies, rhinestone cowboys. 'Do the Dog.' Come on you Specials!

JOE O'CONNOR

MADE IN JAPAN
DEEP PURPLE

My school pal Nicky O'Sullivan had a big brother called Mal who was heavily into Deep Purple. (This was back in the seventies when people were often 'heavily into' things.) When you are an impoverished teenager you can't often afford to buy albums of your own, and thus Nicky and myself and another pal called Andrew Deignan spent a good deal of our pubescent years listening to this monstrously over-the-top double live album (perhaps triple? I can't remember now), a work so utterly bombastic that it makes the more excessive moments of Spinal Tap seem like Little Jimmy Osmonde. *Made in Japan* has all the great Deep Purple songs – 'Smoke on the Water', 'Child in Time', 'Lazy', 'Space Truckin'' – in extended versions which feature tortuously baroque five-minute-long, eyes-closed, tongue-protruding guitar solos by Ritchie Blackmore, a man whose amplifier definitely went all the way up to eleven, in blissful counterpoint with the screeching vocals of lead singer Ian Gillan, which are disconcertingly reminiscent of an asthmatic cat having frenzied sexual intercourse with a lawnmower. One track, 'The Mule', lasted twenty minutes, a whole side of one of the discs. This, at the time, seemed very impressive indeed. I guess length means quite a lot to adolescent boys.

DESIRE
BOB DYLAN

Another teenage friend, Ciaran Farrell, had a big brother who was a Dylan fan, and one afternoon in his house I found a tape of this album. I had never heard songs quite as strange and beautiful as these before. 'Isis' is still the weirdest song I've heard in my life, though it's shot through with a glum and murky humour. 'The wind it was howlin', the snow was outrageous/We chopped through the night and we chopped through the dawn/When he died, I was hopin' that it wazzen contagious/But I made up my mind that I hadda go awn.' Brilliant stuff. I know there are better Dylan records than this, but it's still my absolute favourite. It's got some fine tracks: 'One More Cup of Coffee', 'Oh Sister' and the tremendous song 'Joey', about the New York hood Crazy Joey Gallo. And it's got 'Hurricane', the best protest song ever penned. But I should add that I was in love with a girl called Sarah at the time, and the fact that His Supreme Bobness had been in love with a girl called Sara, that he had married her, and that he had written a song on *Desire* for her appealed to me greatly. Even though 'Sara' features perhaps the very worst rhyme in the history of popular music – 'now the beach is deserted, except for some kelp ... you always responded when I needed your help ...' – I still can't listen to it without my upper lip trembling just a tad. Actually, now that I think about it, 'Joey' has a pretty dreadful rhyme too – 'one night they shot him down in a clam bar in New Yawk/He could see 'em comin' through the door, soon as he lifted up his fawk' – but I don't care. It's brilliant.

THE TAIN
HORSLIPS

Horslips were the first band I ever saw play live, and they really were fun. They emerged in a frazzled and vaguely absurd musical era when setting an ancient Irish mythological text to a heavy-metal beat seemed like a good thing to do, and, hey, who's to say they were wrong? Yes, they were sometimes pretentious, and the in-clothes were bloody awful; you could have housed an entire chamber orchestra in Barry Devlin's flares. Yet they were tremendous fun, like I say, and they really could play their instruments. Witness how even today a sad thing happens to people of my generation when, at a wedding say, somebody digs out a scratched old copy of 'Dearg Doom' and sticks it on the turntable. It's like someone has blasted the dancers with happy gas. But Horslips had a serious side too. I bought my first Seán Ó Riada and Planxty and Carolan records because of the Horslips. I really do think they were important. People of my parents' generation tended to be suspicious of traditional Irish culture, whatever that is. But Horslips proved that Irish music was as full of raw visceral energy as anything else in the world. And that you could dance to it without having to keep your hands straight down by your sides. Along with other brilliant artists like Christy Moore, De Dannan, Paul Brady, Andy Irvine and Moving Hearts, Horslips saved Irish music from the museum, and are in some important way to be thanked for the music's popularity today.

NEVER MIND THE BOLLOCKS, HERE'S THE SEX PISTOLS
THE SEX PISTOLS

I can clearly remember the first time I heard the Sex Pistols. It was on the John Peel show on BBC Radio One in the summer of 1976, when I was thirteen. I was nailed to the floor by this music. It was mesmerizing, irreverent, passionate, funny, everything that great pop music should be. I bought the album in Freebird Records, which was then in a dingy and evil-smelling basement on Bachelor's Walk in Dublin. I don't know how many times I must have played it but I can assure you that there is not one grungy chord, sneered vocal or clumsy drumbeat that I do not know as intimately as I know my own grandmother, which is to say, very intimately indeed. This is still the classic punk album, although, oddly enough, I never thought it was in any way serious. When Johnny Rotten sang about achieving 'Anarchy in the UK', I never really thought he meant it. I always saw the Sex Pistols as the most English band you could imagine. I thought they had more to do with music hall or pantomine than with changing society, man. They just loved dressing up and swearing on television and pretending to be naughty and they didn't seem to believe in guitar solos, and y'know, when you've been brought up listening to Deep Purple, believe me, that's quite refreshing.

THE CLASH
THE CLASH

The Clash were kind of an enigma, really, for despite being musically talented and genuinely politically committed, they managed to make it in punk rock. The Clash were to the late seventies and early eighties what the Stones must have been to the sixties. It sounds a bit This-Is-Your-Life to say they both defined and reflected the bewildered *zeitgeist* of a generation, but I think it's true. And despite the fact that the Clash generation – which pogoed and spat and sang along loudly to 'White riot, I wanna riot/White riot, a riot of my own' – all grew up to vote conservative and want Filofaxes, you still have to love the Clash for at least giving it the full welly before ultimately selling out and allowing their music to be used in jeans adverts on the television.

A TONIC FOR THE TROOPS
THE BOOMTOWN RATS

I loved the Boomtown Rats more than I've ever loved any pop group. I can still quote huge chunks of their lyrics by heart. Several members of the group went to my old school, Blackrock College, and the week 'Rat Trap' got to number one in the British charts, myself and my friends cut a photograph of Bob Geldof out of the *RTE Guide* and stuck it up over a picture of Archbishop Croke (of Croke Park fame) in the school's gallery of famous past pupils. This revolutionary gesture had the kind of cheap symbolism which appeals very greatly to fourteen-year-olds. It felt like a victory at the time. If I am honest, it still does.

LIVE AND DANGEROUS
THIN LIZZY

Philip Lynott was raised in Drimnagh, like both of my parents, and so, like most Dubliners, I always felt an odd kind of connection with him. I remember feeling genuinely upset when he died, even though I never met him or even saw him play. But I don't think I was alone in that sadness and sense of loss. For me, he personified all that is best about Dublin. I loved his eloquence, his playfulness, his mischief, his rebellious spirit, which is captured so brilliantly on this live album. It's hard to explain my affection for Lynott, because I'm not actually that crazy about the music. Apart from a few of the songs – 'Dancing in the Moonlight', 'The Boys are Back in Town', 'Don't Believe a Word' – the music is sort of naff and clichéd, and the toe-curling between-song patter – 'anyone here got any Irish in them? Any of the girls want a bit more Irish in them?' – is, shall we say, not exactly influenced by the collected writings of Andrea Dworkin. Still, you kind of miss having Philo around. And when they played the *Live and Dangerous* version of 'Rosalie' every Saturday night at the Presentation College Disco in Glasthule, even the shyest of the shy would get up and go mad on the air guitar. I can still see it now. A frenzied head-banging scrum of cheesecloth shirts and dandruff. And I can hear it too. A chorus of appallingly unbroken male voices yelping, 'Rosa-Lee Bam Bamma, Ba Bamma Bamma Bamma!!!'

ASTRAL WEEKS
VAN MORRISON

I bought this album second-hand in Dublin's Dandelion Market the year I did my Leaving Cert. To be honest, I didn't think I'd like it much. The music I was listening to at the time was punk, new wave and ska, and Van Morrison had the reputation of being something of a boring old fart. But I bought it because it was cheap, and I was glad, because these songs are simply magnificent. The menace of 'Slim Slow Slider', the tenderness of 'Sweet Thing', the swirling kaleidoscopic majesty of 'Madame George' where Van sings 'And you know you've gotta go/ On the train to Dublin up to Sandy Row'. This line astounded me. It was the first time I had ever heard the word 'Dublin' in a song that wasn't a folk song. Here was Van Morrison, from Ireland, singing in the black American soul/jazz tradition, about the city I lived in. I couldn't get over that. It was amazing. The sheer confidence of it. *Astral Weeks* is a work of unparalleled genius, and even though, strictly speaking, it predates my generation by a few years, it's one of the few pop music records that is genuinely timeless. It was recorded in three days, when Van was twenty-three years old. Scary.

BURNIN'
JOHN LEE HOOKER

My best friend John McDermott's late father was a Dublin policeman who was also an avid collector of all sorts of records and books. One day when I was a student in UCD John arrived up to my flat with two records his Dad had given him. One was *Muddy Waters Live at the Newport Jazz Festival*, a terrific record. But the other was *Burnin'* by John Lee Hooker, and this was the one that really had a lasting effect on me. Nowadays blues music is more popular than ever before; we're used to hearing it in everything from TV advertisements to movie soundtracks. Back then in the early eighties, after its resurgence of popularity in the sixties, blues was kind of in the doldrums. But the first time I heard *Burnin'*, I fell utterly in love with it. This was the blues at its darkest, its most elemental and disturbing. John Lee played in a guitar style of his own, stripped down to the basics, raw, pared back, full of space. He almost used the guitar as a percussion instrument. Unlike the white English blues revivalists of the late sixties – Clapton, John Mayall, the early Fleetwood Mac – he really knew how to let the music breathe. And there was such pain in his beautiful voice. A harrowing, memorable and extraordinary record. I am also grateful to John Lee Hooker for leading me to the work of the late Rory Gallagher, Ballyshannon's own king of the blues. Many Gallagher fans went on to explore the various forms of the American blues that he loved so much. I came to Rory the wrong way around, in that sense, but I'm glad I did, because, for me, no Irish rock musician ever has had his breathtaking skill, modesty and sheer love of the craft.

THE SMITHS
THE SMITHS

In the early eighties, as New Wave music became more and more mannered, the names of bands – Duran Duran, Spandau Ballet, Cabaret Voltaire – became increasingly pretentious and the dread use of the synthesizer spread like a virulent cancer. Punk and New Wave finally melted into the vulgar chaos of the New Romantic bands, whose members wore pirate shirts and satin trousers and looked for all the world like the smacked-out hippies they had once detested so much. Then the Smiths burst on the scene. And even the very name of the band seemed to spit in the face of prevailing orthodoxies. No cod-French appelation and no synthesizer. They had one guitarist, one bass player, one drummer and one singer, a scrawny genius-cum-loon called Stephen Morrissey who capered about the stage wearing NHS spectacles and a hearing aid, with a bunch of bedraggled daffodils hanging out of his trouser pocket. The songs they wrote were about everyday life and were full of satire. One went, 'Hand in glove, the sun shines out of our behinds/Oh, it's not like any other love, this one is different because it's ours'. Another went, 'I need advice/I need advice/'Cos no-one ever looks at me twice'. A song from a later album contained the truly unforgettable lines, 'Sweetness, sweetness, I was only joking when I said/By rights you should be bludgeoned in your bed'. In 1985 I went to see the Smiths play the SFX centre on the north side of Dublin and my friend John Bourke spent the evening helping bouncers pull people off the stage. It was mad. It was the greatest pop concert I had ever been to. Thinking back now, it still is. It was absolutely unforgettable.

TIMOTHY O'GRADY

MY MOTHER HAS RECORDED in a blue book containing notes about my infancy that my first favourite pieces of music were 'The Yellow Rose of Texas', de Souza marches and an advertising jingle. Later, I read a garish war novel called *Thirty Seconds Over Tokyo*, Hardy Boys mysteries and *The Stan Musial Story*, the biography of a baseball player. I did not read Dickens, Victor Hugo or even Mark Twain until I was nearly an adult and the only classical music I can remember hearing was the opening bars of Beethoven's *Fifth Symphony*, because it was in a cartoon. Nearly all of what came to be among the most important aspects of my life endured extremely long periods of gestation. The advertising jingle I was so fond of was for the toothpaste Pepsodent. I remember it still. Was it because my father was a dentist?

The first record I bought was Duane Eddy's 'The Guitar Man', with the accent on the first syllable of Guitar. I listened to the main Chicago pop station on my transistor radio sometimes, but a little less often and perhaps a little later in life than my hipper contemporaries. I was too young and preoccupied to take in the emergence of Elvis, but eventually I came across him. I liked 'Hound Dog' a lot. I bought 'Return to Sender'. Soon it became apparent that you could no more be unaware of Elvis than you could of your schoolteacher or the President. My first memory of him was connected with two very good-looking teenage girls, one with black hair and the other with blonde, who lived in the flat across from ours and who occasionally babysat for me. I remember seeing on the landing where the rubbish was left a booklet full of colour photographs of Elvis with his face covered with lipstick where one of the sisters had been kissing him. I imagined it was the black-haired one, who was the eldest. She seemed the more alluringly licentious of the two and confirmed this as far as I was concerned when she eloped at seventeen with the boyfriend she snuck into our flat when she was looking after me.

I was better prepared for the arrival of the Beatles. I liked them right from the beginning, when they came along with 'I Want to Hold Your Hand' and 'She Loves You'. I began to increase my expenditure on singles.

The way that I related to music changed when I arrived in the parking lot of my high school in a friend's car and first heard Bob Dylan singing 'Like a Rolling Stone' on the radio. I didn't know very much about myself then, and I certainly didn't know how to find out about who I was through listening to music, but I felt this song getting through to me in a way that no other piece of music ever had. I would have had no direct way of relating to a diplomat on a chrome horse. But there was the intensity, the scorn, the shockingly vivid images, that 'wild, high mercury sound' he later talked about. It lifted me, and it made me curious.

The gaining of self-knowledge, it would seem, is a collaboration, and when in my late teens and early twenties I began to find out about who I was and how that person I was discovering might become free, I collaborated with Albert Camus, William Faulkner, Thomas Merton, my first girlfriend, Ken Kesey, Eugene O'Neill, William Blake, red wine, mountains, LSD, Orson Welles, Malcolm X and Dostoevsky, Gogol, Jack Kerouac, forests, pool halls, surrealism, islands and dancing, Picasso, Garcia Marquez and John Berger, Manhattan, Muhammad Ali, W.B. Yeats, San Francisco, Donegal, Marlon Brando and Zen, among many others.

Like everyone else I knew, I listened to a lot of music. Literature altered and shaped me, it gave me hunger and aspiration, and the territory it occupied seemed vast and endlessly absorbing. I could not imagine ceasing to be interested in it. But its effect tended to be cumulative, to be tied to consecutiveness, duration. Music was instantaneous. It could stop the world, bring you right into the moment that was happening. I sat in rooms and listened to albums. I went through lyrics like a cryptographer. I went to see Wilson Pickett, Joan Baez, Sly and the Family Stone, Duke Ellington, Junior Wells, the Grateful Dead, James Brown, Crosby, Stills, Nash and Young, Laura Nyro, B.B. King, Linda Ronstadt and John McLaughlin. Much of how I would think, act, feel, eat, drink, look, relate and learn took definition at this time.

Music was at the centre of this, as it was for most people, and at the centre of the music was Bob Dylan. I listened to him persistently, hungrily. He seemed connected to some place wondrous and electrifying and only dimly perceivable by me, and he had the power with language to bring it back into the world.

I finally saw him live around the time *Street Legal* was released, at both Earl's Court and Blackbushe, after sleeping on a pavement in Soho to get tickets. He was in a rich vein at that time, with his band of violinists, horn players and back-up singers, his surprising and inventive arrangements and his generous theatrical performance. You could never know with him. His greatness seemed connected somehow to his fallibility, his capacity to become completely lost from whatever it was that fuelled his brilliance. He took big leaps, and sometimes he landed in a ditch.

Years later I wrote an essay comparing him to Hamlet. What I felt they had in common, among other things, was their myriadness, their wearing of masks to unmask others, their capacities to hurt and be hurt, their venom, wit and tenderness expressed in a poetry so pure as to make all around it seem prosaic, their seductive mysteriousness, their almost incandescent intensity. As with Hamlet, I get the sense in Dylan, at his best, of the world being looked upon in a way that it has never been looked upon before, and of the language arriving whole from the unconscious. They both say the unsayable.

I read an account once by a woman who knew Dylan of a walk they took together from an apartment in New York to a shop, when Dylan was in his early twenties. It was only a few blocks, but, she said, it felt like it lasted a month. He was amazed by everything – dogs, cars, faces, bricks. He wrote it all down in a little book. Great artists seem capable of opening themselves like that, of facing the world without defences and attempting to deliver it whole. Whether by design or by some freak operation of the genes they will uproot and demolish themselves, enter exile or wilderness, and struggle blindly to remake themselves, perhaps partly in a spiritual quest, perhaps, as Freud contends, through psychological instability, but I think finally to create art. I learned more about the connection between an artist and his work from Bob Dylan than from anyone else I read about or met.

Choosing an album by him to place among the ten was difficult. I had become acquainted with his work through listening repeatedly to *Bringing It All Back Home* and *Highway 61 Revisited* and believe there are three or four songs on each, such as 'Just Like Tom Thumb's Blues' and 'It's All Right, Ma (I'm Only Bleeding)', which are among the finest he ever wrote. *Blonde on Blonde* has such varied brilliance as 'Leopard-skin Pillbox Hat' and 'Visions of Johanna'. I would listen to *John Wesley Harding, New Morning* and his soundtrack, *Pat Garrett and Billy the Kid*, any time and I am apparently one of the few with a high regard for *Street Legal*, primarily because of 'New Pony', 'Señor (Tales of Yankee Power)' and the agonized 'Where Are You Tonight? (Journey Through Dark Heat)'. My choice, though, is *Blood on the Tracks*. I heard it first late one night in the darkness and sensed from the opening bars of 'Tangled Up in Blue' – from the unaffected authority of his voice, the wholeness of the music, his belief in his story – that after years of stabs in the dark he was united again with the great depth of his talent. It hasn't the social rage, the wit, the boisterous frivolity, the surreal flights, the visionary intensity evident elsewhere, often on the same album. It is more modest in its range. It is composed of varying reactions – sadness, scorn, tenderness, resignation, yearning – to lost love. But these reactions are wonders of eloquence, authority and authenticity. I love this work for its audacious rhymes ('Verlaine and Rimbaud' with 'make me lonesome when you go'; 'I like the cool way you look at me' with 'Everything about you is bringing me misery'), its surprising stings ('Shelter from the Storm'), its brief, elliptical tales ('Simple Twist of Fate') and its driving narratives ('Tangled Up in Blue' and 'Lily, Rosemary and the Jack of Hearts'). This is fine, emotive, mature, true work written by an artist who seems completely to possess and inhabit – like a man who has dreamed, built and lived in his own house – the language with which he works.

I first heard my next choice in the same dark room where I heard *Blood on the Tracks*. It is probably on almost everyone's list. It is that kind of defining work. With its soaring, impassioned searches and evocations it can make walking along the road an act of wonder. Like Beckett with his beyond-the-grave voice or Edward Hopper with his figures trapped in light, Van Morrison found a sound with this album that was entirely his and that he could work with throughout his life. I used to pass afternoons with him sometimes in a café in Notting Hill Gate. 'I did something once,' he said. 'It happened, it was right. I thought it would always be like that. But it wasn't.'

'What was it?' I asked.

'*Astral Weeks*.'

This record is an illumination.

I can no longer relate to the Beatles as I once did. Even with John Lennon's caustic digs, driving rock'n'roll, anguish and undermining astuteness, they evoke for me a lightness and sunniness, an innocence I do not feel, though I believe I once did. I liked *Revolver*, *Rubber Soul* and *Abbey Road* very much, but probably the White Album most of all. It is in part the unity of my two previous choices which makes them great. With this it is the disparateness. The whole band and their varying styles get a shout.

The Rolling Stones, like the Beatles, passed through stages as they grew in sophistication, the Beatles fairly consistently Apollonian and the Stones Dionysiac. The Beatles would not preen and snarl and pout. They would never release a song like 'Under My Thumb'. I remember trying to analyze the sexual content of 'Satisfaction' in the schoolyard and I stayed with the Stones, if at a slight distance, for years. I can still get a charge when I hear the opening of one of their songs. I owned *Let It Bleed* and loved playing it, but because 'Sympathy for the Devil' could send me past myself – it certainly did once in a room full of dancers, throbbing and wild-eyed – I choose *Beggars Banquet*.

One night I was sitting up late with my father watching a talk show and Jimi Hendrix came on. He looked like he had arrived by rickshaw from an opium den. He slouched languorously. His satin clothes emitted a debauched, purplish sheen. His hair looked like it had sprung free from a jack-in-the-box. My father, I noticed, was watching with steely concentration. What was he making of him? Hendrix talked about his days in the service, the blues bands he played in, what the music meant to him. When it was over my father looked at me with an expression of rather startling alertness and said, 'That is a very interesting man.' I think he's interesting too. I remember hearing someone who stayed with him for a while talking about how as he sat around the house through the day his guitar never left him. He even took it into the loo with him. He picked constantly at its strings. It was the means through which he related to the world. He was a great live performer and I think his 'Star Spangled Banner' at Woodstock was an act of brilliance, perhaps genius, but most of all I like the slow mysterious blues songs, like 'Red House' and 'The Wind Cries Mary'.

The era of which I am writing, with its large-scale enthusiasms, hypocrisies, indulgences and astonishing discoveries, was, I think, lived more collectively, for better or for worse, than those which followed. It has many anthems. The one which for me most eloquently celebrates the tenderness and dignity among those at or outside the margins of power is 'No Woman, No Cry' by Bob Marley. I think I love listening to it more than any single song I have ever heard. My choice from his work is *Legend*.

The development of music, particularly in this century, has been propelled by adaptation and synthesis. Some of the most buoyant, truly enlivening music I have heard has been produced by the adaptation of Irish music to rock, jazz, classical, blues, punk, country, reggae and rap. I like the Saw Doctors, Waterboys, Fleadh Cowboys, Marksmen. The Chieftains' live show with Van Morrison was among the best I've ever seen and I like their collaborations with, among others, Ry Cooder, Tom Jones and Sinéad O'Connor, particularly her 'Foggy Dew'. There's a reggae version of a song from Cork I heard years ago on a jukebox that I would love to hear again. The Pogues are one of the great bands I have known. I first heard them in a basement in Islington and thought they were both stunning and hilarious. I could listen to 'Fairytale in New York' once a day from now on and not feel aggrieved. Moving Hearts were not the first to enter this territory, but they played as though they were. I loved their sense of discovery, their need to communicate it, their unapologetic republicanism. I choose their first album.

I first saw Martin Hayes playing with a band called Midnight Court in a bar in Chicago. To one side of him was a lead guitar player from the south side of the city and to the other was a bass player who I think is Japanese. Martin was in the middle playing an electric white violin, his long hair flying. At some point he played a reel called 'The Pope's Toe' while the two guitarists banged out the 'Ode to Joy' from Beethoven's *Ninth Symphony*. It was both witty and dazzling. I have passed many hours with him since then, talking with him through the night, listening to him play. He is an exceptionally interesting, courteous and talented man. He comes from a family of musicians in East Clare, but to find the heart of his music and his sense of Irishness he travelled far from there, in both mind and body. For most of the time that I knew him in Chicago he was after something – a style of playing, a sound that was his own, but also something larger and deeper. He didn't want to go on playing notes that together would make something conveniently shaped, pleasing, fun, merely entertaining. Playing the music was about getting to the heart of the emotion that had produced it. At its purest, it could produce a profound experience. He seemed to be able to taste it but not yet possess it. Then I think he broke through. His playing is lyrical, delicate, empathetic and emotionally rich. I choose his first album, *Martin Hayes*.

There is not another single work within the specified time frame that immediately declares itself, though there is a great deal of music that has got and continues to get to me in an immediate way. This music can alter the way you look at things and feel; it makes things move inside you. There's Joan Armatrading's first album, Ray Charles, UB40, some of the Velvet Underground and Bruce Springsteen, Otis Redding, Tom Waits, a lot of bluegrass and Motown, particularly Aretha Franklin and the song 'Dancing in the Street', Janis Joplin, John Lennon's solo work, Chrissie Hynde singing that song with the refrain 'I'm special' and Cyndi Lauper's 'Time After Time', Bette Midler, Marianne Faithfull and Gregory Isaacs, B.B. King, Prince singing 'Purple Rain' and 'Walking on the Moon' and 'Every Move You Make' by the Police, some of the Band and Neil Young, Howlin' Wolf. I've liked most of the African music I've heard, such as the Bhundu Boys. There's an album by a guitarist named Leo Kottke which I haven't heard in over twenty years and which I would love to hear again. My choice is in acknowledgment of that powerful, passionate music associated with the city where I was born, the blues. It is *Electric Mud* by Muddy Waters.

My final choice is not an album. It consists of parts or perhaps all of two albums placed on a tape by someone that I know. She gave it to me as I was falling in love with her. Part of it consists of a jazz group unknown to me playing compositions by Bach and the other is *Watermark* by Enya. We played this music in rooms in Chicago, Wisconsin, New Orleans, Louisiana, Mississippi and London while we were finding out about each other. I associate it with one delirious moment when I had the sensation of being composed entirely of light. I have played it often in times when we have been apart. The sounds are ethereal, delicate, beguiling and mysterious. I would think: This is her, she loves this music. This is the woman that I love.

FINTAN O'TOOLE

THE SUBJECT OF RECORDS was always a touchy one in our house. When I was six or seven, we got our first record-player, one of those square plastic boxes with a creamy lid and a blue base, gilt clips on the side, grooved knobs on the front. At first we had two records, one by the Everly Brothers, the other by the Clancy Brothers, and for a while I imagined that making records must be a strictly fraternal affair, that the Beatles and the Kinks – the only pop bands I had heard of – must be brothers as well. But after a while my father started to accumulate LPs that clearly confounded this rule: Rossini's overtures, Beethoven's symphonies, Mozart's cello concertos, Bach's *Brandenburg Concertos*. No family could be large enough to spawn all the people you could hear on them.

My father's records were a problem. There was only one room in the house where you could sit and listen to music, just as there was only one room where you could sit and watch the television, or where you could sit and read a book, or sit and do your homework. The problem was that all of these rooms were one and the same. And because my father worked shifts, he sometimes wanted – I would now say needed – to listen to Beethoven at odd times of the day, while someone else wanted to watch television. When he got his way, there would be tension as well as music in the air. My mother and grandfather didn't seem to approve of Beethoven.

I think it was because of this that the idea of bringing records into the house didn't occur to me. And if you didn't buy records, everything that went with rock music looked dangerous and disturbing. The image of absolute degeneracy in my childhood was that of a young fella in the Green Olive café on Leonard's Corner, bawling out his own version of the Kinks' 'Lola': 'La, la, la la, Lola'.

I disapproved of this kind of thing, so I missed out on the sixties, remaining a child of Mother Church rather than a child of the universe. My father, my brother and I were actually in London when Brian Jones died and the Rolling Stones played their free concert in Hyde Park. My father asked us if we wanted to go. But we didn't: we knew the place would be full of drug-crazed hippies. Our English cousins had a copy of *Magical Mystery Tour*, and played it over and over, but the line about letting your knickers down in 'I am the Walrus' was just too uncomfortably embarrassing, knowing that adults might walk in at any moment, and I couldn't enjoy it.

I became a capo in the Sodality and joined the Red Cross. When I won a record token on *Ken's Klub* on the radio, I exchanged it for Gilbert O'Sullivan's first album.

It was, oddly enough, the Red Cross that brought me to perdition. In the summer of 1972, when charity walks were all the rage, there was one from Dublin to Baldoyle to raise money for the Central Remedial Clinic, led by Jimmy Saville, and I was sent out with my first aid kit. At the end of it, on the racecourse, there was a concert. A few bands played, but I remember only one – Horslips.

I'm not sure if it was the first time they played, but for me it will always be a first time. They took all the stuff that formed a continual, immeasurably dull background to childhood – stuff that you were forced to sing at school, stuff that might be on the radio when you were eating bacon and cabbage – and injected it with angel dust. They turned 'Óró Sé do Bheath Abhaile' into a rock anthem, 'Furniture', which seemed to go on forever with its byzantine guitar solos and dreamy flutes. They played 'Dance to Your Daddy' as if it had been washed up from the Caribbean on the gulf stream. They were loud and lurid, completely kitsch (did Barry Devlin really have a shamrock-shaped bass guitar, or had I mixed too many aspirins in the cider?) and utterly exhilarating. They made it impossible to believe that there was Ireland and there was rock music and the two things belonged to different categories of existence. I went to see them in the Stadium and bought *Happy to Meet, Sorry to Part* when it came out. I also bought, with money from a summer job in Dunnes Stores, an orange shirt with huge white flowers on it and a pair of purple seersucker thirty-six inch flares.

Around the same time, there was Thin Lizzy. 'Whiskey in the Jar' came out, and it seemed to be the same kind of thing that Horslips was doing, but when I bought *Shades of a Blue Orphanage*, I realized that they were something altogether different. Phil Lynott and Brian Downey were locals from Crumlin, and the places mentioned in the songs were mostly familiar, but Lynott was also wildly, wonderfully exotic. We knew he had been at Clogher Road Tech, and everyone claimed to be his best friend, but he seemed much more like a reincarnation of Jimi Hendrix than a local boy made good, more like someone who had descended from on high than someone who had risen from our very own obscurity. His voice was as lithe as his body, and his Dublin accent on 'Sarah' or 'Buffalo Gal' seemed to reshape our own voices, to make our flat vowels all of a sudden sound cool and confident.

At Dunnes, one of my friends had all the Beatles albums, and although they had been there all through my childhood, it was only in his house that I started to really listen to them. I taped his copy of *Abbey Road* and brought it home. There was – is – a special kind of bittersweet allure in listening to it with a sense of retrospect, knowing that it was the end of something you had missed. What I have always loved is not so much the individual songs, but the long, elegiac, fragmentary sequence of half-songs that runs from 'You Never Give Me Your Money' to 'Her Majesty'. It makes no attempt to hide the sense of breakdown, of things falling apart. You can hear a band dissolving into its component parts right before your ears. But it turns that dissolution into a celebration, a glorious reminder of what you're missing. Melodies and images are tossed out with apparent abandon, as if there's no tomorrow. Which, of course, there wasn't.

Coming to the Beatles in the aftermath of the sixties, I was, I suppose, enthralled and sceptical at the same time. The scepticism was sour grapes, but it gave me the best of both worlds – *Sgt. Pepper's* and the Mothers of Invention's great, hard pissing on hippie mysticism, *We're Only In It For the Money*. That, in turn, led me on to the greatest of all satires on rock folly, *Mothers Live at the Fillmore East – June 1971*. I had started to go to the theatre around this time, and I love the way this album was like a play, not a pompous 'rock opera', but a real drama with characters and a plot and a brilliant dénouement. In it, Mark Volman and Howard Kaylan, formerly of the Turtles, play a rock star and a groupie, their dialogue weaving in and out of Frank Zappa's music, building, as the price of Volman's virtue, towards a wonderful rendition of the Turtles' hit, 'Happy Together'. It is funny, cruel, and indescribably filthy. So filthy that you could safely play it in the house, knowing that even if your mother heard it she couldn't begin to imagine what they were singing about.

Once you'd discovered Zappa, ordinary guitar heroes could never be quite enough. At the Stadium every Christmas there was Rory Gallagher. After school, in somebody's house, there was always Eric Clapton – old Cream numbers, then 'Layla'. We went to most things in the Stadium: Thin Lizzy, Status Quo, Tir na nÓg, and even, because someone had read in *NME* that their female dancer sometimes took her clothes off, Hawkwind. She didn't, but the ringing in our ears for days afterwards proved that thinking about sex could make you deaf.

The albums I listened to most, *Next* by the Sensational Alex Harvey Band, and *The Doors*, were both dominated by edgy, dangerous male singers, and both seemed to come out of a darkness and violence that seemed more honest in the cruel early 1970s of Bloody Sunday and the Shankill Butchers than the optimism of the sixties. Some of the songs from them – Harvey's brilliant, demented version of Jacques Brel's 'Next', Jim Morrison's mean and melancholy 'The End' – showed that rock could delve into hidden corners. But I still hankered after something with a bit more uplift.

Then one night on *The Old Grey Whistle Test* there was the Mahavishnu Orchestra – John McLaughlin with his double-necked electric guitar, one six-stringed, one twelve-stringed, fingers flying up and down the frets, face contorted in concentration, the ultimate guitar hero. Their music – guitar, violin, drums, bass, synthesizers – seemed to be everything at once: rock and jazz, Indian and classical. It took all the pomposity of rock stars wanting to be artists, all the vague dabblings with eastern music – George Harrison messing about with a sitar – and made it serious, clear and hard as nails. With speed and virtuosity, with aggression and energy, with a sound at once mystical and industrial, they took electric music as far as it could go. Their second album, *Birds of Fire*, is possibly the best use of electricity since the invention of the light bulb, and even in middle age, when you want your music unplugged, I still find its combination of subtlety and attack worth every volt. Electric rock couldn't really go any further. McLaughlin returned to his roots in jazz, and I've followed him most of the way. But for the first half of the seventies he was just what I needed – a kind of rock star who seemed to owe nothing to the sixties, and on whom older, hipper heads had no claim. He even helped me to lose my religion. He was a devotee of some fat guru, and since I had stopped going to Mass I imagined for about a week that I might be, too. The guru's followers had a meeting in Trinity and I sneaked in, half-hoping that John McLaughlin might be there with his double-necked guitar. His wife was, but he wasn't, and I sat through a cringe-making film about the guru's goodness before sloping off. But I still wonder whether, if he had turned up, I might not have ended up as a by-election candidate for the Natural Law Party.

Instead I spent my spare time, and a lot of time that wasn't supposed to be spare, in vaguely political activities. At the time politics was dominated by the conflict in the North, and there was still a deep layer of ignorant nationalism in the Republic. Catholics were our side, Protestants were blind bigots, dupes without a culture. I think one of the things that made me think again about all of this was hearing Van Morrison's *Astral Weeks* in about 1973.

It affected me, of course, because it is a wonderful album – literate and lyrical, immediate but infinitely lingering. It has the melodic appeal, the lightness of touch to be accessible on first hearing, but it is also full of the dense textures that make an album last, and stop it from ever wearing thin. And Morrison's voice on it is extraordinary. It still has a light, youthful layer on top of the deep, bluesy Belfast growl that remains now. That extra stratum of sound makes possible the most heart-stopping swoops ands swirls – listen, for instance, to the rainbow ribbon flutter and shine in 'Cypress Avenue' or to the intoxicating sight of the forgotten glove in 'Madame George'.

It helped, too, that the album's dominant mood is that of remembered adolescence, all moody despair and dreamy lust, insides shaking, tongue tied in your own mouth when it should be twisted in someone else's. Obscure objects of desire – hair-ribbons, gloves, high-heeled shoes – move across the streets of Belfast, London, and even, for one fleeting moment, Dublin, the first time I ever heard the city's name in a great rock song:

> And you know you've gotta go
> On the train from Dublin up to Sandy Row

The soundscape is that of familiar city streets – barking dogs, church bells, heels clicking on concrete – all sufficiently ordinary for a spotty youth to identify with, but sufficiently transformed to make even the condition of spotty youthfulness seem somehow marvellous.

But there was something else about the album, too. It was the first real encounter with a Northern Protestant sensibility, with a voice that was unmistakably that of urban Ulster, lyrics that reeked of kingdom halls and evangelical rapture, but music that seemed to have seeped out of some steamy delta. It seemed, effortlessly, to be better at being American than Elvis, better at being Irish than the Clancy Brothers. And it made it impossible to think of 'Irish culture' in narrow terms ever again. At the time, it was both humbling and liberating. Ever since, it has been just pure pleasure.

After it, no album ever quite carried the same sense of revelation. But there were others that have lingered. With Bob Dylan I was even slower on the uptake than I had been with the Beatles. When I was eighteen and in my first year at UCD, there was a girl whose house we used as a headquarters for election campaigns, and her sister was one of the first people in Dublin with a copy of *Desire*. It seemed to be always in the background, behind the dull beat of the Gestetner machine that was churning out hastily written leaflets – the wailing violin and spitting words of 'Hurricane', the warm fantasy of 'Mozambique'. Whether I still play it because it's so good, or because the girl and I got married a few years later, I'm not sure, but either way it earns its keep.

After that, rock became more of a background noise, and I started to listen much more to other kinds of music. Last Christmas, though, my nine-year-old son got a CD of Oasis's *(What's the Story) Morning Glory?*, and listening to it with him has helped me to place my own youth: too late for the sixties, too early for the sixties revival. It reminded me, very pleasantly, of *Abbey Road*, and of the way rock songs, as well as bringing back the past, can give you footholds in the sheer and slippery surface of the future.

RHONDA PAISLEY

IT IS NOT EASY, this writing about music! It is like asking me why I used blue in a certain painting.

My earliest memories of music come from religious services. Both of my favourite hymns commence with the word 'all' and both refer to creatures!

ALL THINGS BRIGHT AND BEAUTIFUL,
ALL CREATURES GREAT AND SMALL

We fairly belted this out in school assembly but our enthusiasm made it lovely! From the 'tiny wings' to the 'purple-headed mountains' it was all recognizable, very like our own environment and landscape.

ALL CREATURES OF OUR GOD AND KING

Along the same lines only more sophisticated, while adults can't do justice to 'All Things Bright and Beautiful', they most certainly can do so to this hymn. To my great pleasure, this hymn was sung at my graduation, which took place on a Sunday.

THE BLUE DANUBE

Many years ago the BBC created a series entitled *The Strauss Family*. I was about twelve or thirteen at the time. Being exposed only to classical music as a young-ster I found it fascinating to learn about the people who wrote the music which I knew by sound but not by title. In bizarre fashion 'The Blue Danube' is associ-ated in my mind with raiding orchards – one in particular. We were forever being chased by an old brute of a man whose sprawling orchard ran along the back of a row of houses where my best friend lived. We shook trees and dropped apples to 'Da, da, da, da, da ... da, da ... da, da'.

I CANNOT TELL WHY HE WHOM ANGELS WORSHIPPED

I wasn't much older than those orchard-raiding days when we had a visit from an American Negro singer – Bertha Norman. This large and lovely lady was touring churches in Ulster and she was amazing. I'd never heard a voice like this, nor seen emotion so openly displayed.

She sang this hymn to the tune of the 'Londonderry Air'. Now I mean you can't go wrong with this tune in Ulster! Add to it the pathos of Calvary – you just don't forget the power of the message with a Negro singer. The words that conclude the verse are 'he looked beyond my sin and saw my need'. To this day I still think that is the best summary of the gospel which I believe in.

MUD, SLADE AND DAVID ESSEX

Moving from the sublime! Mudd, Slade and David Essex were all adored in turn. The dance that Mudd performed was carried out by a long row of us down the hockey pitch. Slade's 'Merry Christmas' continues to complete the season for me as it blares out of the car radio en route for home with rolls of wrapping paper, a sprig of mistletoe dangling from the central mirror and the smell of a box of oranges wrapped in their fine purple tissue paper.

As for Mr Essex: yes, I still think the husky, flat voice and the messy hair perfectly acceptable – for him! And although one of my brothers-in-law swears it's not singing, his wife (whom I confess to introducing to the one he so despises) agrees with me!

PAUL SIMON

Paul Simon has endured from these young days and survived as a long-time favourite. *Rhythm of the Saints*, in particular 'Obvious Child'. Why that piece? The drums, no doubt!

MARY BLACK

Mary Black also has this enduring quality, although I was in my twenties before I first listened to her. *Holy Ground*, in particular 'Flesh and Blood'. (And I don't subscribe to the criticism of her recent *Circus* album.)

ENYA

Finally, Enya. Wonderful, peaceful Enya. *Shepherd Moon* in particular. 'How Can I Keep from Singing?' – a Celtic hymn. Methinks I've come full circle! Well you know about Miss T, don't you?

> *It's a very odd thing*
> *As odd as can be*
> *That whatever Miss T eats*
> *Turns into Miss T.*
> > – Walter de la Mare

NOEL REDDING

BOOKER T AND THE MGS

I first heard this band while playing with the Burnetts, near Maidstone, Kent – I think it was 1962 – at an American airforce base. They had 'Green Onions' on the jukebox. Pete Kircher and I 'freaked' and I think the guys stopped the juke-box and got the single out. Pete and I then ordered a Booker T album, but could only get an EP. I found this music so different from stuff in England at that time. A lot of people don't know what the MGs stand for. Some say a car; actually, it is the Memphis Group!

OGDEN'S NUT GONE FLAKE
THE SMALL FACES

When I first heard this the phasing effects really impressed me. It was a different sound – the band had produced it themselves, but with a lot of help from either George Kyantsitz or Andy John, the engineers. I did some demo tracks with Steve Marriot in 1995 (my Clonakilty Cowboy Band!) at his cottage in Essex. He hadn't forgotten the phasing sound, God bless him.

KINK-SIZE
THE KINKS

When I first heard 'You Really Got Me' in 1964. I was an instant Kinks fan. Some of their earlier stuff written by Ray Davies (a brilliant songwriter) was wonderful. The Kinks were a truly big influence on my listening to music. Mick Avory and I have recently toured New Zealand and Europe with the band Shut Up Frank. Yet another story.

THE NOTORIOUS BYRD BROTHERS
THE BYRDS

I think this came out in around 1968. It was a brilliant album, the songs, the sounds etc. Could it be called psychedelic? Wonderful, altogether. It also had a lot of phasing. I had the pleasure of meeting all these guys at Monterey in 1967.

BEST OF THE MOVE
THE MOVE

I managed to find a complete selection of the Move's output in the U.S. a couple of years ago. Roy Wood is a brilliant songwriter – we toured with them in 1967, and got to be good buddies. This is still one of my favourite CDs.

AXIS: BOLD AS LOVE
THE JIMI HENDRIX EXPERIENCE

Recorded in 1967, produced by Chas (Brian) Chandler. Although I played on this album myself, I feel it still stands up compared with recent music. I still play tracks off this. God bless, Jimi.

THE JOHNNY KID MEMORIAL ALBUM
JOHNNY KIDD AND THE PIRATES

Johnny Kidd and the Pirates were, and still are, a favourite band of mine. Consisting of Mick Green, guitar, Johnny Spencer, bass, Frank Farley, drums with Johnny Kidd (real name Frederick Heath) on vocals. I saw this band in Folkestone, Kent in around 1963. Johnny Kidd died in a car crash in October 1966. I still play this album.

MARTIN ROWSON

IN RETROSPECT, I NOW REALIZE that my adolescence coincided with the High Summer of The Album. That this was also the deep, hard, barren mid-winter of Music was, perhaps, more than coincidental. Still, all too soon it was gone; ultimately fucked by the bright, airy spring of the New Technology and the advent of the CD; more immediately stuffed by Punk. It was Punk, after all, which awoke us all to the truth that music was only actually valid when it came in singles, preferably in a two-minute, twenty-second thrash. In earlier, more innocent times we had, of course, abjured singles as terminally unhip. They were the crassly commercial province of bubble gum, teenyboppers and other vile-nesses no cool middle-class kid worth his (and this was gender specific) salt would ever deign to contemplate. As a result, for most of the mid-seventies my friends and I wasted our lives transcribing pages and pages of lyrics from inner sleeves onto our Economics 'A' level folders, later in the day slouching around in each other's bedrooms in glum concentration listening (without ever saying a word, mind) to *Led Zep IV*.

And, of course, it wasn't just about the music. As an artefact, The Album defined (and was defined by) its age as exactly as any muddy old pot shard encapsulated the Etruscans. For a start, you could do so many things with it. During *longueurs* in yet another bloody John Bonham drum solo, you could scru-tinize the Hipgnosis sleeve artwork; then you could read, try to understand and then memorize the lyrics. Then you could fold it out so that it became enormous. Moreover, you could roll joints on it, which was perhaps the greatest contribu-tion of The Album to the ur-culture it defined. After all, you wouldn't eat your dinner off it, fill in your pools coupon or write a short shopping-list on it (although you could write a poem on it, cribbing from the inner sleeve, or do your English homework on it, maybe simultaneously). But it was quite clear there was nothing else at all worth skinning up on. (The supplementary strange role of the cassette case for storage deserves deeper examination elsewhere.) It even supplied a vast reservoir of cardboard after you'd torn all those handy little bits out of the insides of the fag packet. A significant imaginary scene springs to mind here: thin hairy git shuffles into general retail outlet, *circa* 1975. Coughs nervously, then mumbles, 'Er, yeah, could I have, right, twenty Benson and Hedges, um, a packet of green Rizlas and, ah ... (gabbled rapidly in nascent beard) that "Fleetwood Mac" album, yeah!' before fleeing as assembled shopkeepers and customers chorus, 'We know what you're Dooo-ing!' What, on the other hand, can you do with a CD box? Snort cocaine off it, I suppose, but that's about it. And cocaine is not, of course, a drug conducive to musical appreciation of the lilting cadences of *Focus 3* or, for that matter, a higher appreciation of the guiding aesthetic of Roger Dean, which, shrunk down to four square inches, tends to look just plain daft anyway.

And there was more. The cardboard sleeves used to scuff, particularly on Dylan albums, in a particularly satisfying pre-Grunge, grungy sort of way. On older albums, the pretensions of the cover artwork would give way, on the inner or 'dust' sleeve (and what role, in the brave new CD Age, does dust fill in the aural dialectic of sound reproduction, synthesizing clarity into reassuring scrunge?), to an echo of Recorded Music's Tin Pan Alley origins, with adverts for the record label's backlist. Thus Matt Munroe, Roger Whittaker, Harry Secombe and Mrs Mills would all grin cheesily at you while you, simply by listening to Donovan, were complicit in sweeping away that old, unmourned world. Later, with *Wish You Were Here*, there was the delightful dilemma of how you removed the black, shiny, shrink-wrapped plastic outer cover with the nice sticker on it: did you rip it off in a frenzy, or carefully razor open one side, slip it off like a condom and then stick it on your bedroom wall? (I did the former, and immediately regretted it.) Then there were the accessories. In a one-stereo household, if you wanted to listen to Bee-Bop Deluxe's *Drastic Plastic* while your parents were watching *The Onedin Line*, you had to listen to it on headphones. These weren't the discreet little Sony deaf-aids (stereos weren't 'personal' then), but chunky old monsters that wouldn't have looked out of place on a Lancaster Bomber's radio operator somewhere over Dresden. Then, of course, you had to worry about the care of your record. You could, to this end, buy a nice maroon spongy thing from Boots, or a kind of bright yellow duster – although an old hanky usually worked just as well. Later, my flashier friends with richer and more indulgent parents and a developing anal obsession with the impedimenta of sound reproduction would have little brushes or statically charged rollers that were dragged over the record as it went round, strobing nicely with the little orange light from the turntable which told you it was rotating at the right speed. Then there was your stylus, but by the time any of us got to caring about that it was usually too late. But the scratches were merely another part of the pleasure. To this day there are two tracks on *Space Oddity* that I have never heard properly all the way through. And then there was the smell ...

But I'm in danger here of overlooking the actual music. Which I suppose was what it was meant to be about. As I suggested above, the light of experience has taught us that the majority of the music brought into our homes and our lives through the agency of The Album was crap. Our excuse, of course, was that we knew no better. Perhaps, even now, eager little post-modernists are planning the rehabilitation of Emerson, Lake and Palmer; kids in the suburbs are ingesting substances unknown to previous generations and grooving to *Tales from Topographical Oceans*, while an encyclopaedic knowledge of the Supertramp discography is *de rigueur* in gaining access to the smarter dives in Berlin and Barcelona.

However, while we breathlessly await the Bread revival it's worth remembering how liberating Punk was for us munchkins back then. I remember, for instance, slouching round my friend Tony Walker's bedroom and being forced to listen to the soundtrack of that monumental turkey of a concert movie, Led Zeppelin's *The Song Remains the Same*. I gritted my teeth in rage and frustration as Jimmy Page played on and on and on for what seemed like (and probably was) hours. Tony, inevitably, had the orange turntable light and the little brush, but by this time I was beginning to fall out of love with the whole thing. Shortly thereafter I cut my hair, threw out my flares and went to a Jam gig. Then Elvis died, we all guffawed callously, and by the time I went to university about a year later, when a new chum sheepishly admitted that he thought the greatest song ever written was 'Stairway to Heaven', we all laughed him to scorn. By then I was far more in sympathy with my college's resident Organ Scholar, who earnestly insisted that the highest achievements in the History of Music were 'God Save the Queen' by the Sex Pistols and Beethoven's *Emperor Concerto*.

Still, that pile of old albums stacked horizontally under the hi-fi (the what?) must once have held some significance for me, before I stopped listening to them about twelve years ago. Whether or not they were a soundtrack to my adolescence is now questionable. I remember being driven mad during my Maths 'O' level by Pilot's 'January' going through my mind over and over again, and that was a record neither I nor any of my friends would ever admit even to exist. So what were the criteria that informed our aesthetic? Mostly, I suppose, it was your standard laddish game of one-upmanship, intensified by the struggle, fey and gloomy though it was, to attain the required status of neurotic boy outsider. So, how did this ghastly cocktail of hormones and snobbery manifest itself? To start from first principles, it was universally acknowledged that concepts were where it was at, but thereafter you had to choose your concepts carefully. (It goes without saying that our contemporaries who expressed a fondness for Motown and Slade were roundly despised, even though they later turned out to be right.) That said, to take just one example of the rich pickings from the period, Pink Floyd provides a useful template for our mindsets at the time.

Pink Floyd, it hardly needs saying, were the apotheosis of the art-school, hippie-wank band, and in aspiration I really liked *Dark Side of the Moon*. But I was also slightly suspicious of it. It was, after all, so common. By which I meant that far too many other people liked it too. On the whole, *Wish You Were Here* was preferable, but even then I had nagging doubts about it: there was just a chance that all this heady concept stuff might become pretty uncool pretty soon. I was already vaguely aware that scruffy oiks were rucking it up in King's Road, Chelsea, wearing t-shirts bearing the legend 'I hate Pink Floyd'. Not certain which way the wind might blow, I comforted myself by constructing an escape route to what then passed for credibility by going for the Exegesis School of Rock Appreciation. This entailed, by and large, ignoring the music as such, and instead disturbing your mates as they slouched around their bedrooms listening to The Album with lengthy discourses on what it all meant. Thus did Syd Barrett prove my salvation.

The *cognoscenti* already understood that Roger Waters, Pink Floyd's main man, was a fucked-up shit; a minimal amount of research allowed you to conclude that he had probably betrayed something once, something artistic, something beautiful. So, once I realized *Wish You Were Here* was about this person called Syd Barrett (which it was), then it followed that further research was required. Finding out more about the Madcap Martyr of British Psychedelia, I soon appreciated that the only point of listening to *Wish You Were Here* was because it was about Syd, and that it existed purely in order to be filed with all other Syd references I could find in order, like a dogged and dutiful biographer, to build a complete picture of The Artist. Thus, a couple of months after getting *Wish You Were Here* for my sixteenth birthday, I'd bought the double reissue of the Floyd's first two albums (were they Albums yet? Hard to say) as well as Syd's two solo albums.

For the pretentious, arty adolescent Syd Barrett had everything going for him. First, he was a Rock Martyr, but a different kind of Rock Martyr. After all, he wasn't actually dead, so one could immediately distance oneself from the necrolatry of one's mates with their sniffy reverence for Hendrix and all those other martyred stiffs up in Rock'n'Roll Valhalla. (By the same token, I entertained a passing enthusiasm for the late Paul Kossoff, who died of drug-related almost everything five miles above the mid-Atlantic, thus becoming the only Rock'n'Roll Martyr to die in an aeroplane not in violent collision with the ground at the moment of his death.) Instead, Syd's fate was far, far worse – and consequently far more romantic and Romantic. Having sunk into irreversible drug-induced schizophrenia (R.D. Laing said he was incurable, for what that was worth) he'd become a kind of hippy Sleeping Beauty, doomed never to awaken. This was all pretty cool: madness coming equal tops with death in the Romantic league of *Sturm und Drang* angsty dreadfulness; it also made him a kind of internal cultural exile, a lost leader within reach, but always out of reach.

Second, Syd was weird in a specifically English way, a way I found increasingly alluring. In the great global community of hippiedom, while one could acknowledge the validity of hairy post-Beats chewing peyote in the Desert, and appreciate the indisputable grooviness of slightly confused twerps heading Eastward in broken buses, there was another English strand. It smelled strongly of patchouli oil and compost, had lurid streaks of paganism and pantheism woven into it and owed as much to Edward Lear and the Levellers as it did to Captain Beefheart and Timothy Leary. And in my mind's eye it was summed up by Camden Lock in about 1971, on a rainy summer's day, its denizens dressed in tie-dye and stinking knee-length sheepskin coats, exuding all the while a mesmerizing miasma of compost and patchouli. I don't even think this is a personal memory; it was more than that, it was a dream, a glimpse of paradise. And all this, for me, was exemplified by Syd.

(Later, much later, when my monopoly on fandom no longer mattered so much, I discovered other devotees who, like me, had been led by their devotion into deeper, uncharted regions; into listening to Gong's *Camembert Electrique*; into a post-Syd enthusiasm for the Syd-inspired Soft Boys lead by Syd manqué, Robyn Hitchcock. Together we would sing Syd's terrible, pitiful song of catharsis, 'Dark Globe' and then cheer ourselves up with 'Gigolo Aunt'. Some of us even admitted to liking the Floyd's early post-Syd albums like *Obscured by Clouds* and *Ummagumma*, although these fans were the real basket cases, and generally suspect.) I still, twenty years on, nurse a fondness for Syd, still presumably living with his mum somewhere in Cambridge. But best of all, as I discovered when I listened to *Syd Barrett* and *The Madcap Laughs* again recently, these two solo albums, recorded just before he sank forever into silence, were still almost unlistenable to, and guaranteed to drive anyone except a true fan screaming from the room. Just perfect.

My passion for Syd Barrett demonstrated the abiding tenets of my developing tastes. Best of all, if I was going to like an Album, it had to be produced by someone both difficult and unpopular; more significantly, my tastes were retrospective. Someone, or something, originally obscure, but further obscured by age, was best of all. Failing that, one could always reappraise something firmly in the popular domain according to the strict rules of The Exegesis School of Rock Appreciation, just so long as it was old.

Take David Bowie as a case in point. Aged about twelve, I sneered at my sister's adoration of Bowie. Four years later I would bore people for hours discussing the significance of *Space Oddity*, *Hunky Dory* and *Aladdin Sane* (*Ziggy Stardust* was excluded for reasons of popularity – see above – and *Diamond Dogs* was crap, as was everything that followed it). Actually, to be honest, the only one of these albums really worth talking about was *Hunky Dory*, and this was because it was all about Nietzsche, you bet it was. At university, indeed, some of us nearly reached the point of creating shadow seminars, late at night, convened merely to explicate further upon this precise point. Had I thought about it more at the time, I could have proposed complementary auto-didactic classes on those influenced by Bowie (and vice versa) with courses on, respectively, Iggy Pop and Lou Reed, under the general title 'D. Bowie's Influence on the Revived Careers of Various American Clapped-out Junkies as Producer and Patron'. Of these two, my preferred option was Lou Reed, on *Transformer*, which I listened to almost continuously throughout my final year, by which point I was less interested in analysis than in the noise. Still, at least The Album was over ten years old, and even older was the Velvet Underground and Nico. This once more fulfilled my needs for something old, cliquish and impenetrable. Then (we thought) the Velvets were a secret known only to a very few, very wise, very cool nineteen and twenty-year-olds, and you could sort the cool from the uncool in seconds by slapping 'Sister Ray' on the turntable and whacking it up to maximum volume. (You could do the same, only more so, with the endless track 'Interstellar Overdrive' from the Floyd's first album *The Piper at the Gates of*

Dawn, leaving, if you were lucky, about three people at any party where the trick was pulled, the rest having fled the appalling discordant row and, more often than not, abandoning their booze and their stashes in their haste to escape.)

At roughly the same time I discovered the importance of earlier investment. Records bought on a whim when I was about sixteen or seventeen, and for the most part unplayed since became, three years later, potent talismans of deep cool. *Apocalypse Now* turned my copy of *The Doors* into a highly coveted possession. (For reasons I can no longer remember, my copy of *The Doors* was kept in the outer sleeve of someone else's copy of King Crimson's *In the Hall of the Crimson King*, leading to considerable perplexity and confusion of cool judgment among passers-by scouring my record collection.)

But despite the undoubted pleasures of getting stoned out of your box and reciting great passages of Marlon Brando's monologue in the role of Colonel Kurtz while listening to 'The End' at full volume, my relationship with The Album was drawing ever so slowly to its end. I certainly never bought records as a student, mostly through meanness. I remember borrowing Patti Smith's *Horses* and Springsteen's *Born to Run* and *Darkness on the Edge of Town* (both of which I thought hilariously funny) on a pretty permanent basis, and would listen to them, secretively, late at night through the monstrous old headphones. The one exception, the last Album I ever bought, was ABC's *Lexicon of Love*, a wonderfully schmaltzy concoction of post-Punk torch songs; though, coming in 1980, and despite its vinyl mien, I doubt it was really, truly an album at all. Coming when it did, it was almost certainly an LP, a completely different thing altogether. Soon, other things intruded, like love. My wife-to-be was gloriously and liberatingly out of touch with contemporary notions of Rock cool, so we settled down to listening to Mozart, Ella Fitzgerald and early Motown, while the first song we ever danced to was a wonderful piece of camp trash called 'It's Raining Men' by the Weather Girls. You might double-take here, and insist that the whole point of Rock'n'Roll was sex, that I should here be listing all those rockin' tracks I fucked my youth away to. Well, for me it was about credibility, peer-group pressure and the constant need to stay a couple of yards ahead of the pack. So now all my old Albums gather dust, rendering them, no doubt, even more distorted than I remember them being all those years ago when I last listened to them.

Nor do I necessarily mourn these neglected trappings of late childhood. Indeed, when I learn that contemporaries of mine have just bought the new Portishead CD, or evince a keenness for Nirvana or Blur or Suede, to the extent of actually bothering to buy their products, I feel slightly embarrassed on their behalf. People in their mid-thirties and beyond have no business dabbling their horny toes in this kids' stuff, I convince myself, conveniently forgetting that now it's no longer about 'Yoof' or rebellion or generational ghettoizing: now it's about product placement. What were previously the provinces of subcultures are now part of a great big post-modern supermarket, where the trade is in nostalgia and endless youthfulness in equal measure, and rather than dying before we get old, we bop, literally, till we drop.

Which leaves us with one last record, which fits some of my criteria, but not all. I 'discovered' *Abbey Road* when I was about seventeen (I was eleven when it was released) and in many ways it was a revelation. I'd grown up, almost literally, with the Beatles. *Please Please Me* came out when I was four. I remember, when my older sister and her friends mimed to all those early singles, how somehow or other I always ended up playing Ringo, for Christ's sake. I remember – just – going to see *A Hard Day's Night*, remember it being black and white, which was weird, because the cinema was in colour, and the telly was in black and white. I remember all the Fab Four being on the Juke Box Jury. These are standard memories of my generation, I'm sure. They do not constitute my golden memories of childhood, which are quite different. I was, in childhood, aware of but indifferent to the Beatles. In adolescence I was, for a long time, reactively dismissive. And yet, as I said, my musical tastes were retrospective. The times, to a large extent, demanded it, as one stared into the vacuous heart of the midseventies for want of the Rock'n'Roll inspiration which, even then, was considered to be 'Youth's' birthright.

What else did we have? Someone said, or at least should have said, that the sixties ended in 1976, and as my generation was pre-pubescent when they actually did end, we had to make do with what was on offer, or the long, lingering hangover of what had been: pompous post-hippie longhairs like Led Zeppelin, art-school acid-clowns like Pink Floyd or, differently but also horribly similar, Bowie. The Song, indeed, Remained the Same. We had to look back even when we wanted to look forward, waiting unknowingly for Punk to rip off our blinkers. Which is why *Abbey Road* was so important for me, because it was about the Beatles having the decency to finish when the sixties finished. To call it a day with an acrimony which belied the legend of the Golden Age everything else around us implied we'd miss, and we had, it seemed forever, to suck the dregs of. That whole second side, rolling haphazardly towards a crescendo and that final, dying chord could be heard as sniffily elegiac. For me, it was the sound of a concrete curtain crashing down on the end of a decade of which, over half a decade later, we'd had enough. And, best of all, it was followed by a bad joke.

JIM & PETER SHERIDAN

SGT. PEPPER'S LONELY HEARTS CLUB BAND
THE BEATLES

JIM: *Sgt. Pepper* was the first record that felt like art as opposed to rock-'n'roll. It's the dividing line. My Da had a second-hand record-player, a big stereo deck thing. It had huge speakers, the lid opened up and it wasn't very good. It was in the front room and he had a lead down to a tiny speaker and you'd have to go and hear *Sgt. Pepper* on that tiny speaker in the kitchen.

PETER: Then you had to run up to the front room to put it on again. He'd always say, 'They don't play their own instruments, of course.' That started no end of rows.

JIM: I remember *Pepper* as the final put-down of my father's generation – this was better than anything they had ever done. *Pepper* was like a ...

PETER: ... a breakthrough. 'A Day in the Life' is on that – about the kid dying in the car accident. The record just resonated in a different way from any other music at that time.

JIM: There wasn't much hash around then. There was more acid. I never actually took acid, but I was one of the few who didn't.

SIN AND SOUL
OSCAR BROWN

PETER: I think that was a weird record to like, because he was a black cabaret performer, more cabaret than anything.

JIM: But he rapped a lot, he spoke a lot, and I used to do a crazy song of his that I heard sung by a fella at the Five Club. We had a band, Peter and myself, Peter played lead and I played bass, and I found it easier to rap, to talk songs. Oscar Brown was really brilliant – his album had that identification which the Irish have with the blacks.

PETER: Forty acres and a mule.

JIM: That displaced sort of thing. Oscar Brown was way ahead of his time. He was also slightly misogynist.

PETER: Very much so. The songs were very anti-women.

JIM: Misogyny something the Irish will never admit but it's there.

PETER: Well, Phil Lynott has it. Women are all chicks. Chick culture. That's a very definite thing about that Thin Lizzy vibe. It comes from Oscar Brown – 'black bitch' and so on. One song, 'Brother Where Are You?', that we always associate with our brother Frankie, is on that album. He died in 1967, and I'm moved every time I hear it. The passion in Oscar Brown's voice is very powerful.

JIM: Frankie had a tumour on his brain and it took him a long time to die. There are a lot of people who in their teenage years experience the death of a parent or somebody close. You could say this about a lot of people like Bono, Larry Mullen, Sinéad O'Connor and Daniel Day-Lewis. It makes you erect an alternative reality to the one we live in, and you protect that alternative reality with a savagery much deeper than that with which you protect reality, because it's a safer place to be. Nobody dies there; you feel like a protector, you actually prevent anyone from dying. People say Bono's really tough. I don't think he is at all. I think he's a pushover, but when it comes to protecting his work, I think he's a man. And that's a different thing. It's a kind of fear of death.

JACKIE MCGOWRAN SPEAKS BECKETT

JIM: This is what we listened to at university in the late sixties. Everything Irish was mother love and in Beckett's work you have this completely anti-mother feeling, with a total love for the father. I was always fighting with my father, so I don't quite know why I was so attracted to Beckett. It was the Protestant version of things, which seemed to be the flipside of the Catholic version. Beckett represented that kind of Protestant world where you didn't give that much away, yet there was huge pain, nevertheless.

PETER: And not much guilt, which is extraordinary. Here were characters who were very much on the edge of experiences, but they carried very little guilt. They seemed free in a peculiar kind of way which was really attractive if you were brought up a Catholic. I remember one passage where McGowran reads this litany about 'My mother's mother's mother's mother, and my father's father's father. My mother's mother's father, and my father's father's mother'. And he goes through this list of people which he makes really funny. All it is is just a list of the people you can't marry. So it's like making the telephone directory funny, a little bit of insanity. Jackie McGowran's extraordinary voice doing that list of people in an unstoppable flow is intensely funny.

JIM: There's something about Jackie McGowran's voice which summons up the Anglo-Irish world, a world that the ordinary Irish don't penetrate. Beckett's world is not normal Dublin, but it's very interesting, and it has a kind of moral integrity. This world has nothing to do with Catholicism and yet Beckett is much more profoundly confessional than any other writer. The confession is personal whereas in Joyce even the confession is part of the structure of *Ulysses*. Beckett is just me, one person, making his own decisions, personally Protestant. It's protesting in that way.

GHOST TOWN
PHIL CHEVRON/THE RADIATORS

JIM: After UCD where we put on some shows, we went into the theatre and started trying to incorporate the Project with the music of the time.

PETER: Phil Chevron came into the Project and said he was a musical arranger and asked if we had any gigs going or were we doing any theatre. This guy looked pretty young and when I got talking to him, it turned out he knew Kurt Weill, and he sang some on the spot. Jim and I were practically kids, but Phil was actually even younger than we were and it turned out he was, in fact, mitching from school. He'd decided to come into the Project and sell himself as a music arranger, which I thought was quite extraordinary.

JIM: The Radiators album *Ghosttown* is seminal: it's punk with brains. It's a kind of aural world of pictures. It's the great album of the Irish music scene. It didn't get enough attention.

PETER: The problem with the album was it was too good to succeed, too deep and complex. There were songs about Kitty Ricketts, who was a character in *Ulysses*, a prostitute who Phil made into a symbol of contemporary Ireland. What Phil Chevron was dealing with in this album was corruption and the Church and everything that was seething underneath.

BOY
U2

JIM: When we first went to the Project, it seemed as if U2 were playing there almost every second week. They caused a stir from the word go and I remember one night in particular, a group called the Black Catholics, who were against U2 for some mad reason, tried to get into the theatre and caused mayhem.

PETER: I thought that U2 were guys just like us, that used to play in the Oriel Hall, and they weren't that good musically. In fact, in the initial stages, they were probably one of the worst bands that we had, but they had something, especially through Bono, that you couldn't define – just brains. It's a kind of combination of instinct and brains.

JIM: Because we had been in a band ourselves, we could judge how good a band were. What U2 had was an unadulterated lack of fear of trying. I would have been much more closed off or conservative than Bono. He acted completely like a star from day one, he even had the walk. Niall Stokes of *Hot Press* gave them a big award that year, and I thought what the hell, are they that good? I went into see them and there were only three notes, 'If you walk away, walk away ...'. I couldn't believe this song. It was the first time I'd ever watched anyone transform, it was like the Frog Prince. They were unbelievable and maybe that confirmed my belief about the death thing. I asked Bono later, 'What's that song about?' It turned out, I think, to be about his mother. It was the first time that they cracked it. Somebody was speaking about their own life as opposed to trying to speak about America. Songs like 'Bloody Sunday' were firmly rooted in

Ireland and dealing with Irish things.

PETER: The Radiators felt like they were carrying a tradition on their shoulders. They were carrying the weight of something even if they were brilliant. And U2 felt free, they felt like they were lights. Obviously, in their early days when they weren't musically very good, you thought they'd come and go, but as they progressed, it was like a series of transformations.

NEVER MIND THE BOLLOCKS, HERE'S THE SEX PISTOLS
THE SEX PISTOLS

JIM: *Never Mind the Bollocks* reminds me of the time when I was nearest to a nervous breakdown; the Project board had decided to knock down the building and rebuild it when I was fucking on holidays. When I came back, the place was destroyed, and it took us nearly a year to reopen, which we did with a twenty-four hour event called the Dark Space. The band that was to headline it was Johnny Rotten's Public Image Ltd. We hadn't sold any tickets so I said to a kid with a mohawk, just a bit of hair in the middle of his head, why haven't any tickets been sold? 'They won't show up,' he told me, 'that's their gig. Their whole thing is to undermine.' I rang Johnny Rotten who said, 'Fuck off' or something on the phone. So I got pissed off and went over to London. Rotten's brother answered the door, I kicked it in, then they came downstairs and kicked the shite out of me in Gunter Grove. I'll never forget it, there we were, just off the Fulham Road, and here I was fighting with these guys who I totally loved and adored.

This made a change for me; now I was being the responsible one, the producer and the gig owner. I'd been in a band, and I loved these guys' madness, and deep down, I must admit, Johnny Rotten had charisma. But after all, the true artist is more responsible than anybody in the world. He can't be in constant infantile rebellion. That only carries you the first six months, and that's how long it carried Johnny Rotten. He was a bit of a fucking idiot after that. He needed McLaren and he needed the others and now he's like some cynical, dried-up prune. When you listen to the album, you're better off not knowing him.

NEVERMIND
NIRVANA

JIM: Kurt Cobain, who didn't know Johnny Rotten, took the *Nevermind* album title from *Never Mind the Bollocks*. But he made the superior album. Although *Never Mind the Bollocks* is a historical album with great power, *Nevermind* is an album forever, it comes from the same source as Beckett. Kurt wasn't wanted, he knew he wasn't fucking wanted. He had this maniacal responsibility; you can look at him as an alco head, taking heroin, a fucking lunatic, but I think the songs he wrote were trying to find a spiritual centre in a world without any, and that's where rock'n'roll is purest, going back to gospel and blues.

IF I SHOULD FALL FROM GRACE WITH GOD
THE POGUES

JIM: The Pogues were on the same wavelength as something I was trying to do in the Irish Arts Centre. Suddenly they went mega and I thought Shane MacGowan was the best lyricist since Bob Dylan. He's up there with the greats, and again, there's a great spiritual quality in what he does. What I remember most of that album is playing the songs with Tess, my kid, because I had to mind her every morning and she used to dance dementedly to them.

PETER: All the work we'd been doing with our band, through the Project, and doing stuff with me Da was all some kind of interpretation. Our concern was, What's going on in this country, what's happening here? Are we relevant? And suddenly here was this voice doing Irish music but it wasn't an Irish voice, he was a cockney. Suddenly, there was something happening over in England about Ireland and the Irish that was really radical. It was impossible that Shane and the Pogues could ever have come out of Dublin. This music didn't feel like it had the weight of the world on its shoulders, it was fresh and alive and kicking at everything and wonderfully fucking anarchic, beautifully lyrical when it wanted to be. It was just extraordinary.

SNOOP DOGGY DOGG

JIM: Some of this music I actually hate and then I hate myself for liking it. It produces that kind of effect; I think 'Murder was the Case' was an extraordinary song. Snoop, Doggy, Dog reminds me of a more masculine and violent Keith Richards, he's the really dark side of rock. The production on that album is infernally brilliant. It's just complete gangster in music. It's kind of like Sicily or Ireland. It's just on the edge of being everything you hate, and it's wild and weird. Just like Snoop!

SYMPHONIE PATHETIQUE
TCHAIKOVSKY

JIM: This is just dear because it's something Fran and I would play in the front room when we were going out. We still play that one. I remember we went to see the Tchaikovsky Sunday Night series at the Gaiety. We used to have a few gin and tonics in the bar and get locked. I love that music. Tchaikovsky was an amazing character.

THE CHORALE, THE NINTH, THE EROICA, THE PASTORALE
BEETHOVEN

PETER: Beethoven would always be my choice: put these pieces on full volume and it's the only music I could honestly say is composed by a genius. It feels like genius to me. The breadth of vision in it, the power of it, the sense of fun. It does something for me. It lifts me off my fucking feet.

PETE SHORT

WHY DO I HAVE TO MUSE?

Would it be worth it after all,
to force the moment into its crisis.
— T.S. Eliot

After Fifty Years of Hearing THE MUSE,
and Forty Years of Listening,
It's Kamikazidical to Choose
Ten Units of Packaged Art.

After all the Songs, the Movements and
Improvisations,
the Shellac, the Cardboard, the Vinyl,
All curious shapes, Bizarre Coloured,
Hybrid-summated,
Collected and Collated,
LIVE, Studio and Open-Aired,
Why Do I Choose?

Still More
Why Should I Do It
and Bow Allegiance to Hedonism
Wrought from Sound-Encrusted Bellows
which Churn, Desperate to Graph the Personal,
Torrential History of Sound,
Borne of Inter-Relatedness
and Convoluted Revolution
that Only MUSIC defines,
and Memory Encrusted words
fall well short of defining,
and Recalling, *Précisèment.*

JAMES SIMMONS

His songs came to us as part of the folk revival in Great Britain and Ireland. 'Blowin' in the Wind' seemed to me a blurred and unsatisfying protest song; but 'The Times They Are A-Changin'' was almost perfect, lucid, original and given special weight by that young/old voice that weeds out the self-admiring charm of the crooners and anchors the lyric in character. There were also long complicated love songs, never totally clear, in which he seemed to be saying things about relationships that had not been coped with before. I was thrilled by the way he could make simple harmonies sustain complicated thoughts, and irritated by a lack of coherence. There was obviously something odd about a young Jewish boy pretending he was Woody Guthrie; but also something exhilarating about what he achieved.

I guess I felt really happy about him when he became more country and western and produced those simple, deft, original songs in *Nashville Skyline* like 'Lay Lady Lay', 'Country Pie', 'Peggy Day'. There was real sex and a real bed, without being too heavy.

Paul Simon is all charm and style (like the crooners), and the content of most of the songs might blow away in a light breeze. I really hate the lyrics of 'The Sounds of Silence', though it is a pretty tune; but 'America' has lovely detail and a good tune and suits his modest musical voice and great musicality. The ambition fits the talent exactly and catches the ambience of these half-free young people exploring their world, the mixture of impotence and excitement.

He is an ordinary sort of singer, but there is a lovely wit and warmth and detail in the great songs, like 'Me and Bobby McGee' and 'The Best of all Possible Worlds', 'Blame it on the Stones' and 'The Law is for the Protection of the People'. That is the way another songwriter hears songs. It isn't the night you slept with somebody, but the night you sat back and listened to a new LP, and heard really good new songs.

DANCE BAND ON THE TITANIC
HARRY CHAPIN

I had seen posters advertising his concerts in Belfast, but would never think of going to a rock concert. Then, poking about in Dougie Knight's record shop when it used to be a cycle shop in Great Victoria Street, I took a chance on *Dance Band on the Titanic*. I didn't much like his big sound or the title track; but there were four brilliant songs: 'My Old Lady', 'Bluesman', 'Country Dreams' and 'I Wonder What Happened to Him?' Here was someone who knew about life and could make moving songs about it. In the first a roué husband is shattered by his wife sleeping with a young man, and generously inviting him back to her bed. All details perfect ... she is 'splashing around upstairs'. In 'Country Dreams' an ex-hippie works for a real estate company to sell country dreams to ordinary punters. The last song examines a common form of jealousy that most of us try to suppress: 'OK you love me now, but what happened to the love you felt for the last one?'

The words say real things. In the late sixties I had a small try at free love and found it just as difficult as Chapin portrays it.

BLUE
JONI MITCHELL

I was attracted to the lyricism and good singing on the early albums, especially 'Yellow Taxi':

> Late last night I heard the screen door slam,
> and a big yellow taxi took away my old man,
> Don't it always go to show,
> you don't know what you've got till it's gone,
> They paved Paradise and put up a parking lot.

Her songs, here, but not everywhere, seem to come out of her life in a good way that clearly illuminate other lives, and her way with stanzas is original, and she sings and plays guitar and piano so well.

SONGS OF LOVE AND HATE
LEONARD COHEN

He doesn't play or even sing well, but at good moments the voice fits exactly what he has to say: '... he seemed so much older/The famous blue raincoat was worn at his shoulder'.

So it is with *I'm Your Man*. I play again and again 'The Tower of Song'. Nothing else. It has a glorious moment of self-mockery where he tells us he was 'born with the gift of a golden voice'. The dire accompaniment somehow becomes a plus in this ambiguous world he creates. I'll bet he isn't a humble man, but he knows about humility.

SAIL AWAY
RANDY NEWMAN

I was bowled over by 'Political Science', a really funny and imaginative presentation of the ugly American. He played the piano with a command of the half-jazz, half-cabaret style that was pleasurable in itself, and was musically literate in a way that tied in to an imagined mainstream, even to the American musical, without preventing him from expressing an iconoclastic vision.

CHEAP THRILLS
BIG BROTHER AND THE HOLDING COMPANY

Again there are just two tracks, 'Summertime' and 'Bobby McGee'. I remember listening to those in our house in Portrush and feeling my connection with a younger generation healed by the passion and musicality of the singing. Janis Joplin was something comparable to Bessie Smith. But, poor child, an awful lot of it is shrieking rubbish.

HOTTER THAN JULY
STEVIE WONDER

Every time his LPs are put on I just want to smile and dance. He is such a beautiful singer and musician, nearly as good as Ray Charles; but he writes his own stuff. I feel ambiguous about his songs. It is part of this ego-ridden scene. Because he has the musical talent to write endlessly inventive tunes and riffs, one is willing to take on his ebullient adolescent lyrics. It is hard to imagine a grown-up person actually learning any of it to sing. Now we talk of 'cover versions'. Earlier, singers picked good songs out of the existing canon. Now anyone can write ... and you wouldn't want Stevie Wonder's songs not to exist. You only wish they could be stiffened by a little more discipline. And yet there is a lot of style and originality there ... a naive boldness in 'Happy Birthday'.

SGT. PEPPER'S LONELY HEARTS CLUB BAND
THE BEATLES

Quite early on their catchiness recommended itself. 'Yesterday' is a lush melody, but it is even more meaningless than your average lush Jerome Kern number. This becomes strikingly apparent when a serious interpreter of songs, like Frank Sinatra, makes a version of it. The result is embarrassing. He is trying to tell a story and there is no story to tell. I was also bowled over by 'Strawberry Fields Forever', although not sure what was going on, and 'Penny Lane' was a totally satisfying quirky little fantasy. These have a peculiar personal resonance for me because I was having the first satisfactory 'affair' of my life; one of the few times we went out dancing these two songs were played continually, and their euphoria characterized our relationship, something coming out of a younger generation that I could wallow in with total sincerity and excitement in the best of African drawing-rooms. They encouraged me to go beyond the joys of ballroom dancing to the wilder reaches of free expression.

Less personally but very sincerely I found *Sgt. Pepper's Lonely Hearts Club Band* a very satisfying LP. The music-hall type songs were warm and witty, and 'She's Leaving Home' was more serious and equally satisfying. When I was young the grown-ups and the children listened to the same songs and there was satisfying variety. This LP seemed to restore that happy situation. Rock music began with tearing up cinema seats and frightening the parents. *Sgt. Pepper* brought it all back to the parlour. And my mother could enjoy the intelligent cheekiness of John and perky Paul and homely Ringo. I don't think she would have enjoyed John's more pretentious nonsense, like 'Working Class Hero' ... neither did I.

JOHN STEPHENSON

AT LAST WE COULD HAVE our own unsupervised party: a 'Free House'. We drew the curtains, turned off all the lights, and clicked the levers on Joy Fox's Dad's turntable to 33 r.p.m. It was Booterstown, Dublin, 1965, we were fourteen, and the album that played over and over all night was the Beatles' *Rubber Soul*. For me, this first of the 'great' Beatles albums will always evoke an age of shame-ridden innocence in Ireland: nights when the sweaty hands of boys furtively explored the covered breasts and groins of coyly resistant girls. We were all in heat. Yet fear of sin, of parents, of the unknown realms of sexuality, kept our knickers in place. Ireland was emerging from generations of restrictive rural iso-lationism. We were the first post-de Valera generation, and our main aim was to get our rocks off, and theirs off our backs. No wonder that parents 'quite liked' the Beatles. Beautiful songs like 'Norwegian Wood', 'Michelle', 'I'm Looking Through You' and 'You Won't See Me', did nothing more harmful than intensi-fy our adolescent sense of unfulfilled love. Angst as wistfulness. So all our love stories and the Story of Life would forever be reflected in the canon of *Revolver*, *Sgt. Pepper's*, the White Album, *Abbey Road* and *Let it Be*. But for me it started with *Rubber Soul* and I'm glad now that it ended when it did, and that the Beatles never got back together again. There is only one Sistine Chapel.

But there are innumerable Rolling Stones. So when, also in 1965, my friend Paul Cronin in Deansgrange first played me the throbbing rhythm and blues of 'I'm a King Bee', I was catapulted on a parallel journey that whispered 'danger' and climaxed with the Stones' most underrated album: *Their Satanic Majesties Request*. The Beach Boys had *Pet Sounds*, the Beatles had *Sgt. Pepper's* and the Stones had *Satanic Majesties*. The latter was the most discordant and eerily decadent. 'Two Thousand Light Years from Home' and 'She's a Rainbow' were the forbidden fruit which I licked juicily in 1967. I had danced with mind and body as the Stones demanded Satisfaction and claimed our right to Do it in the Street. After *Satanic Majesties* I could lose my virginity with abandon. So I did, in Salthill, on the August Bank Holiday Weekend. No wonder that parents 'hated' the Stones. By now I was shifting from the Mod precision, dictated by *Rave* magazine's seminal male fashion page, to a more personal androgynous style, reflective of my own sexuality. The atmosphere of *Satanic Majesties*, and the look of the Stones at that time, affirmed my choices. Only Lou Reed's 1973 *Transformer* was ever to come that close again. *Satanic Majesties* was the album I needed also to integrate my search for sexual liberation with my search for social justice, human dignity, poetry and truth which had begun earlier with the purchase of my first album by that other giant of the time.

I had to go without a few pleasures to afford the thirty bob (£1.50) required to buy *The Freewheelin' Bob Dylan* from the small basement record desk of Switzers in Grafton Street in 1965. So started my collection of the conscience of the era. Paul collected the Stones. Me, Dylan. Everyone had the Beatles. We all despised G.I. Elvis, not to mention Cliff. We taped for one another on my Dad's reel-to-reel tapes, then state-of-the-art. I would listen for hours, days and weeks on end to Mr Zimmerman; and he changed my life. Dylan's *Freewheelin'* was a lucky choice for my first album purchase. I entered the teen consumer market and left it at the same moment. This was the voice of revolution. As the Americans began their rearguard action in Vietnam against the power and integrity of indigenous peoples, as the censorious Victorian Catholic establishment of the Irish State began their rearguard action against the anarchic spirit and enquiring mind of this island people, as the last vestiges of the British Empire began its tragic and tortuous rearguard action in defence of the archaic, along came a voice that provided a complex vision of a future which we are still deciphering. I followed Dylan's journey faithfully through the magnificent *Bringing It All Back Home*, *Blonde on Blonde*, *John Wesley Harding* and *Nashville Skyline*. But I lost touch with him as he lost touch with himself, and *Blood on the Tracks* seemed like a last, great howl from the man who helped me to stand up against the conservative authoritarianism of my father, my schools, my Church, my government, and any manifestation of oppression I have ever encountered.

I only realize now why it is that Miles Davis's 1960 *Sketches of Spain* has remained inside me since Bill Graham first played it for me in the rooms that we shared in Trinity College from 1971 to 1973, before I became President of the Students Council. (God Reward You, Bill, for all the music you found and propagated in your life.) By the seventies I had become a dialectical materialist. I had forgotten all Dylan's sublime love songs, and Lennon's. I was fighting mad. The spirituality implicit in *John Wesley Harding* had been put to one side. But after each day of shouting and roaring at my fellow students, or hectoring them in interminable pamphlets and articles, I would return to what had become a hippie squat in New Square and let Miles transport my soul. *Sketches of Spain* is music at its most sublime, and Davis was an elemental force. He too may have done greater albums, but, as Dylan, Jagger, Richards, Lennon, McCartney and the whole world seemed to be foundering in the retreat of the ill-formed sixties dream, Miles was keeping his note pure, and I found that note in *Sketches*.

Yet this revelation was signalled to me in another form, in 1969, in Hanover, Germany, just after the '68 Revolution. I was between school and college, a *Gastarbeiter aus Irland*, living in an urban commune. A psychology professor offered me some LSD and put on Pink Floyd's *The Piper at the Gates of Dawn*. No words can describe my first 'trip'. Suffice it to say that I went to heaven and hell and back, on my way taking in the meaning of life and all of her mysteries and molecular structures. If music is colour, then Floyd's first album was the most beautiful pattern ever made. But then it was my first acid trip, and they don't make acid like they used to. I still get a synaptic buzz when I hear *Piper at the Gates of Dawn*, and I owe my subsequent four-year psychedelic journey through West Coast music to this very English record. Zappa, Jefferson Airplane, Vanilla Fudge, the Doors, Santana, Quicksilver Messenger Service, all seem now like one blurred golden era in my life. Of course I stayed with Floyd too, especially *Ummagumma* and *Atom Heart Mother*. Then I got bored by them. Or maybe I was just easing up on the acid. One way or another, I hold *Gates of Dawn*, and Floyd, responsible for opening my eyes and heart to the essential beauty of life itself, and all of her cosmic manifestations.

By 1974 I was in the safe hands of the feminists. Now there's a LIFE's journey! Carole King's *Tapestry* will surely reckon in every woman's list. Lucky that I'm a sissy. This wasn't a woman trying to rock like a man. This was woman as woman. This was sisterhood writ large. *Tapestry* will always evoke memories of long days and nights in the company of strong women, building mutual respect. It led me in 1976 into the arms of a feisty feminist beauty called Mary Donohoe, with whom I was to spend the next seven years of my life. She was twenty-one when we met, and about to graduate as Ireland's youngest-ever architect. I was twenty-five, and running the Project Arts Centre. She was a woman. I was still a boy. It is odd how young men have an instinctive need to undermine their women, and how young women can be so complicit in this. It is only now that I hear the wisdom of *Tapestry*. In the seventies I was posing, as Nell McCafferty can verify. No, as Mary can testify. Anyway, by the early 1980s I had all but destroyed our relationship, and Mary was repossessing herself.

Then along came Grace Jones, and cocaine, and champagne and Dublin night-clubs. *Island Life* became my self-destructive theme album as Thatcher and Reagan took over the world, and as I reeled from the scragging which was the only reward I got for the Sense of Ireland Festival in London in 1980. *Island Life* was power raunch. It was like a drug. I wanted it to keep on pulsing through me. It made my blood boil. Slave to her rhythm, I wanted Grace to 'Strip me, whip me and fuck me'. I suppose my self-esteem must have been pretty low. For me this was *Satanic Majesties* on cocaine and poppers: from idealistic androgyne to hell-cat hermaphrodite. Even Bowie was wearing suits now, and cruising like a corporate mogul. But *Island Life* was not just great music. It was clever and funny too. Grace Jones taught me a sense of humour, and irony. Finally, I began to loosen up. I wouldn't have enjoyed U2's *Zooropa* as much as I did if the wit of *Island Life* wasn't still coursing through my veins. A totally disruptive sense of humour became my core defence against a world that seemed to have turned its back on all that was good. So most strangers, and not a few acquaintances, women in particular, find my 'onslaught manner' hard to take. I blame Grace. It takes a lot of courage to make a holy show of yourself, to be outrageous. So I still love both dancing and making love to Grace's grand guignole. I'm just a little less feverish now.

By the time I had calmed down, evil white powders out of the system, I was in London working in the cottage enterprise that passes for a British Film Industry. Though I was responsible at various stages for producing about twenty music videos, and for co-ordinating the soundtrack to a ropey Pogues feature film, and so found myself dealing every day in new albums and artists, none of these caught my fancy as much as a quirky outfit called the Penguin Café Orchestra, with whom I had no dealings whatsoever. I shall always view my six years studying and working as a film producer in London through the prism of the Penguin Café Orchestra's 1984 *Broadcasting From Home* album. The almost hypnotic quality of this very sophisticated composition was just what my breast and head needed at that time. Penguin Café Orchestra soothed the one and excited the other. But *Broadcasting From Home* gave me more than lasting pleasure. It provided me with the base for my only solo creative work, apart from ham-fisted poetry. I made a film of my own. It was a simple three-minute exercise, shot and edited to a track from the album. It was good. The only version is now lost, except to me. Penguin Café Orchestra gave me the confidence of my own creativity. What value was set on creativity by the parents and teachers of my generation in Ireland? So little, I believe, that it has been our destiny to lead the fight for it. Now all is changed, changed utterly: artistry abounds. The Ireland I grew up in had a fundamental antipathy to artists and their associates. I had to wage a war so that my dear, departed kid brother, Karl, could grow up to be an artist in Ireland. Thank you England, and the Penguin Café Orchestra, for giving me my own break.

The struggle of my generation in Ireland to take possession of our space continues to be dogged by one niggling, but important thing. The men won't dance. Too many of my male peers are 'up their bums' about dancing. *Gravitas schmavitas*. I love dancing. As I can't nominate a Tamla Motown compilation, or an Abba compilation, or an Elvis compilation (yes, I've seen the light since), or a Stones again, my dancing feet are tempted to go to James Brown, or Bob Marley, or Cameo, or Madonna, or Jackson, or Prince, or Soul II Soul, or De La Soul, or House of Pain, or even my arms to Led Zeppelin. God, the list is endless. But no! With so many great numbers, the winner has to be the glorious, silly, delightful *Saturday Night Fever*. Straight white male strut, *par excellence*: Dork as diva. This is the perfect dance album for Irish men of a certain age to get up on their own in front of the gals and strut their stuff. Shake those moneymakers. So Get Down!, Dick Spring, John Bruton, Michael McDowell, Proinsias de Rossa, Pat Rabbitte, Peter Cassells, Adrian Munnelly, Paul McGuinness, Michael D., and all you male movers and shakers who won't move and shake. Close your eyes and think of *Riverdance*, and the liberation of the Irish dancing body: the final liberation.

Which brings me to the album that will probably mean most to me as I journey though this new Ireland of the 1990s: *Planxty*. Made in 1972 by Dónal Lunny, Christy Moore, Andy Irvine and Liam Óg Ó Floinn, this wonderful, seminal, transformation of Irish music took everything I knew about our traditional music, from my father's beloved sean-nós to the towering work of the Chieftains, and punched a hole into the future with the entire kit and caboodle. While Van the God-as-Man was recreating our urban idiom, Dónal and the lads were reworking the land and the sea. I experienced Planxty first live, and rushed out to buy their eponymous first album. This was Irish music I could dance to, even though I hadn't a 'proper' step on me. I still don't. But sure who cares? As I listen now to Planxty, I realize that my generation in Ireland was destined to face the ultimate rock challenge: how to plug in to the rest of the world while staying true to yourself. Now that we've made the big connection, can we hold our own special thing together? Maybe it's time I learned those Irish dance steps, *agus a lán eile.*

COLM TÓIBÍN

I PASSED BY YOUR STREET YESTERDAY, and looked out of the minicab window as though I were a ghost spirited back to a place which was important for me in the time when I was alive. This was where I came with so much hope in January 1988. You know how I remember or think I remember everything – dates, times of the day, moments, who else was in the room, what book I was writing; and you remember nothing – remembering like this does not interest you. You will shake your head and smile when I remind you that I arrived in London in January 1989 at about seven o'clock on a Monday evening, and I had three or four bags including a suit-bag which had burst open because I had put clothes and books into it. I had caught the train from Luton to King's Cross, and I stood there with my stuff all around me and phoned you and the phone was engaged and when I got through you told me that I should get a taxi and you gave me precise instructions – what to say to the driver – so I could get to your street.

If I had that time back again, if I could get the remote control and press a button, I would change everything. There are things which I bitterly regret. I thought that moving in with you, or staying with you for a while, would be easy. Or I thought nothing. Or I do not know what I thought. The house was very grand and I was surprised by that, I did not realize that only the façade was grand; the apartments were small. You came down to the door and we tried, despite your bad back, to carry all of the luggage upstairs. We must have kissed and embraced. I imagine now – I cannot remember everything – that in one of those moments on the stairs or in the hallway when I was close to you, I felt a desire to resist you which was stronger than the desire to be with you, and I was frightened by this.

So it was done. I was in London now. The gas fire was on; the room was warm. The table was set. I probably brought wine and gin. The bed was made. And you were ready for this, for an evening which would set the tone for the near future, or for the rest of our lives. But I wanted to be anywhere except here in a room with you. I would have loved if you had said that a friend was coming around, or we were going out to dinner, or to the theatre or a movie. I wanted you – I had not come here under false pretences; and, also, I did not want you, I was not able for all the raw emotion that was in your room in that street in Pimlico that night. Nothing had prepared me for it. I wanted to escape, and I felt guilty because I could never have told you that. You would, I suppose – am

I wrong about this? – have wanted me to leave now, go back to Dublin, or Barcelona, or wherever, and I could not have done this, because all of my hopes for the future were bound up with you. I hope you understand that I meant you no harm. For reasons which I will try to explain I could not bear the idea that someone wanted me, but I did not feel this until I was sitting in that room with you, and I was shocked at how strongly I wanted to keep you at arm's length.

In one of those nights just after Christmas in a friend's house in Dublin we had kept the whole table awake with songs. I loved your voice. We must have had the same Joan Baez record in our houses when we were kids – you knew the words of every song: 'All My Trials', 'Matty Groves', 'Mary Hamilton', 'A Silver Dagger'. And I knew from the way you sang them that you had listened to that record over and over, letting the songs stand for the emotions you could not easily express in the city of Derry – nor I in Wexford – at that time. I remember bottle after bottle of red wine, and your head thrown back and your curly hair and your eyes closed. All my trials, Lord, soon be over.

That night when I came to London I asked if there was a pub around here that you went to. No, you said there was a pub just across the road, but you never went there. Could we go to a pub, I asked. I don't know why I want to go to a pub, I said. I just do. Maybe it's being in a strange city: I still can't believe that I'm here. Maybe I just need to establish that I'm here, that I have arrived, I said. You smiled, you were puzzled, but I think that you thought it was not important.

We went to the pub across the road, one of those lonely pubs in London, part of a chain, but run by Irish people. We had two pints, maybe three, or maybe I had three and you had two, and we talked, but all the intimacy had gone; we could have been colleagues, work-mates, old friends from college, former lovers, cousins. Neither of us was comfortable with this – it was not what I had come to London for.

When we went to bed that night I told you that I wanted to sleep. I pushed myself as hard as I could to want you, to put my arms around you and kiss you and run my hands down your back, but the other feeling – the urge to turn away from you – was too strong. It is not true to say that I gave in to it. I did not give in to it. I had no choice. I turned away from you, and when I woke in the morning you were sleeping on a mattress on the floor of the living-room, and I had to convince you to come to bed with me and lie with me. I had done the damage: I wanted you now, having not wanted you. I had made it clear that there would be a distance between us. I knew that what I was doing was wrong.

You could not handle this mixture of love and distance, although you too had your own ways of keeping me at bay, but I feel now that they were subtler than mine because they were not as strong. And now I forget something that is important. I forget where we were when you asked me to tell you what was wrong and I said that sometimes I felt cold and there was nothing I could do about it. It was in London, it was dark, the early evening. We were in a bar or a restaurant or even a party and I started to talk and you realized that we needed to be alone together so we left and went home and lay in the bed in the dark and

I told you things which I did not think were important before.

I was twelve when my father died; you knew that much. Like others whose parents are still alive, you do not understand what that means, how much you love your parents and depend on them when you are that age without knowing you love them and depend on them. When my father died half the world collapsed, but I did not know that this had happened. I worked – perhaps from the very moment I realized that he might be dead – at pretending it was nothing. It was as though half my face was blown away and I kept talking and smiling and eating my dinner thinking it had not happened, or it would grow back.

Some of this is private and belongs to other people as well as me. But I told you how I came home every day from school in the years after he died to an empty house, to an atmosphere full of everyone's absence. I had no friends – later, I had friends in the town, but in that year I had no friends. And suddenly now – in that year, 1967 – the radio, especially BBC Radio 1 but also Radio Luxembourg, became the new presence in the house, and some of the DJs' voices became more real for me than some of the things which were happening around me. I remember when the schedule was changed and the DJs redeployed, I felt their absence more deeply than I felt anything else. And all those songs about lost love and longing – Marvin Gaye, Stevie Wonder, Diana Ross, Roy Orbison – gave me feelings which I could not afford to have about what had just happened to my life. I searched and searched in a record shop in Wexford for old Roy Orbison singles about grief and loss.

I began to follow the top twenty, and I began to buy LPs. I would take the record player from the back room into the front room and sit all evening listening to Leonard Cohen, whose songs I first heard on an album by the Johnstons called *Give A Damn*. I remember that voice, Adrienne or Lucy Johnston's, or later Leonard Cohen's, or the Bob Dylan of *John Wesley Harding*, as the only thing that occurred in those years which made any difference to me. In that vast upheaval in my family, parts of me froze, the parts which allowed me to be close to someone, to depend on someone, and I did not know how to deal with this. I did not even know it was happening: it was only during the long afternoons and evenings in the winters in that town when I listened to certain songs I felt close to it and vaguely understood its implications.

We lay in the dark and I explained this to you. I cannot remember but I must have held you, I'm sure I held your hand or gripped your arm as I told you this, and maybe I tried to make you feel that once I had said all of this, worked it out for both of us in the darkness of your bedroom in London, that it would go away, or would be seen as an excuse, something which I could not help, and it would all be easier for us in the future. And maybe it was easier, maybe saying it helped, but it was, as you know, not enough.

[CHAPTER FOUR: 'MUSIC'. FROM A NOVEL IN PROGRESS]

NIALL TONER

RAGGED BUT RIGHT
THE GREENBRIAR BOYS

In 1960, at the Galax old-time fiddlers' contest in Virginia, there was a competition for string bands with a small cash prize and rosettes for the runners-up.
Most of the competing bands were made up of elderly men from the hills and
hollows of rural Virginia and Tennessee, and it was more than just slightly
unusual when the judges found out that one of the groups taking part in the contest comprised three Jewish teenagers from New York City. They were Ralph
Rinzler, John Herald and Bob Yellin, and they called themselves the Greenbriar
Boys. With their amazing instrumental prowess on mandolin, guitar and banjo,
and superb vocal harmonies, they went on to win the competition by a huge
margin and made music history in doing so as the first young revivalist band
from a city, rather than a rural background, to do so. Their great triumph at
Galax led to interest from record companies and later that same year they
recorded their début album in New York, with the addition of Eric Weissburg on
string bass. Incidentally, Weissburg was to find fame and fortune in later life as
the man who tutored the young boy banjo player in *Deliverance* for John
Boorman, and caused a major lawsuit against the filmmakers by wrongly laying
claim to the tune 'Duelling Banjos', actually composed by Don Reno and Arthur
Smith. Anyway I came across the Greenbriar Boys' *Ragged But Right* album, with
its copious sleeve notes, sometime in early 1962 in one of the Murray's record
shops in Dublin, and it has stayed on my turntable ever since. I know every
nuance and twist and vocal foible on this disc, and still, almost thirty-five years
later, it stands as a brilliant example of just how exciting these traditional
American songs can be when played with such panache by three young enthusiasts from New York.

MOANING THE BLUES
HANK WILLIAMS

At least four of the singers who have made a major impression on my life were
introduced to me by the same person. We lived in Harolds Cross in Dublin, and
one of my childhood pals was Fran O'Donnell who lived on the same street.
Fran's mother was a teacher who worked for half the year in Grantham in

Lincolnshire, and as a result Fran spent a considerable part of his young life in England where he was exposed to a wider range of experiences, including music, than his more sheltered contemporaries in Dublin. During the late fifties, I was tuning into Radio Luxembourg and had just discovered some of the early Lonnie Donegan and Elvis Presley. Fran happened to be home on summer holidays and we got talking about music. When he saw that I was keen to hear more, he invited me into his house where he played me a whole variety of amazing stuff, including Hank Williams, and I was hooked. For quite some time I borrowed as many records as Fran would let me have, and spent endless hours at home, absorbing the songs of Hank Williams and others, all the time scrimping and saving my pocket money. I finally had enough to order my own first album in Pigotts of Wexford Street, which was next door to the De Luxe Cinema, now Ricardo's snooker hall. Fifteen and six was the price of Hank Williams's *Moaning the Blues*, about seventy-eight pence in today's money but a fortune in 1957. It was cash well spent. 'Mind Your Own Business', 'Hey Goodlookin'', 'Your Cheatin' Heart' and 'Moanin' the Blues' all went on to be classics which are still sung and widely recorded today – though I'm not quite sure how Hank would have reacted to his 'Hey Goodlookin'' being used in a TV advertisement for a fad diet food.

RY COODER
RY COODER

In 1971 I was working in an all-night petrol station in Inchicore. One of the great advantages of that kind of work is that there's not really much doing between midnight and 8 a.m., it's just that you have to be there. I rather liked the arrangement: it gave me time to practise my mandolin and listen to the radio. This was long before the days of late-night radio and, as in the fifties, I would tune into Radio Luxembourg until 2 a.m. and after that to various continental stations. One night Pete Murray was doing an interview with George Harrison, live on air, during which they discussed Harrison's influences and tastes in music. Pete had also asked George to bring along some pieces of contemporary stuff that appealed to him, and one of those was an old blues standard, 'Going to Brownesville', given an amazing injection of new energy by an unknown Californian singer/instrumentalist called Ry Cooder. I was so impressed by his sound that I spent the next couple of weeks hunting around Dublin for his record. As had happened on so many other occasions, nobody had ever heard of Ry Cooder, and it took a sustained campaign of pestering Pat Egan's cellar to obtain my copy of that Cooder début. I think that what impressed me most about this album was that despite the fact that all of the songs, with the exception of one short instrumental, 'Available Space', were covers of old blues, country and music-hall pieces, Cooder managed to stamp them with a musical postmark that was distinctively his own. I went on to follow Cooder's recording career with *Boomer's Story*, *Into the Purple Valley* and so on into his success in film music, but nothing he has done since has quite had the same effect on me as 'Going to Brownesville' from his début album.

GP AND GRIEVOUS ANGEL
GRAM PARSONS

The Sackville String Band was a loose amalgam of musicians that I was involved with in the early seventies, and we played a wide range of what could be termed American traditional music. At various times the band would number anything from three to six musicians, including banjo players, guitarists, bassists and fiddlers. One of the most talented and intriguing characters ever to have played in the group was the late Imor Byrne from Dundalk, a great fiddle player and a gifted raconteur and songwriter. Imor had gained his initial fiddling experience in Irish traditional music around his hometown, and had spent considerable time in America and Holland, all the time being exposed to many and varied musical styles. He was one of the most relaxed people I have ever known, and his catch phrase was 'Close up the Honkytonks', a title from a Gram Parsons record, although I didn't know it at the time. Imor made several attempts to interest me in the music of Gram Parsons but I believed then that Bill Monroe and Hank Williams and Jimmie Rodgers said it all for me, and I didn't have much time for the West Coast electric approach. Sadly, it wasn't until after Imor Byrne's untimely passing that I took another listen to the music of the late Gram Parsons, and became an instant convert. The Parsons recordings with Emmylou Harris also gave me a wonderful insight into the talent of this lady of country music who was in later years to forge such a successful solo career for herself. Every time I hear Gram Parsons sing 'Close up the Honkytonks', I remember Imor Byrne.

BEGGARS BANQUET
THE ROLLING STONES

I spent much of the sixties living in Cork city where I was involved with music and musicians, and also managed to do about a hundred different things to scrape a living. I fished for eels on Inniscara Reservoir, I sold homebrew beer and breathalyzers, drove trucks and vans and at one time ran a 'Head Shop' à la San Francisco called Paraphernalia. One night at the shop I was tuned into BP Fallon on Radio Éireann and he was presenting one of the most interesting radio programmes of all times, called *Like It Is*, in a style similar to John Peel or Dave Fanning today. BP played two songs, 'No Expectations' and 'Dear Doctor', without saying who the performers were, and while I was listening I thought to myself, 'There's two great country songs!' When BP then announced that both numbers were written by Jagger and Richards from their current album, I dashed out the next day and bought *Beggars Banquet*, and it remains a firm favourite. There were also a couple of odd coincidences about this record which I did not know about until years afterwards. Apparently the young Ry Cooder had made a very strong contribution to the inital recordings with his slide guitar-playing but his tracks were overdubbed by Keith, and the reason for some of the songs having more than a strong country flavour was that Gram Parsons was hanging out with Mick, and especially Keith, and playing fun sessions with them during this period. It's also interesting to note that 'No Expectations' went on to be a country and bluegrass standard and has been recorded by Tom T. Hall, Bill Keith and Jim Rooney, the Bluegrass Cardinals and Willie Nelson.

BILL MONROE AND HIS BLUEGRASS BOYS
BILL MONROE

One of my earliest memories of a song that grabbed me by the neck was Elvis Presley singing 'Blue Moon of Kentucky'. It was probably Scotty Moore on guitar and Bill Black on string bass, and the song just seemed to boogie along in perfect rhythm and rhyme. Once again, it was my Harolds Cross pal Fran O'Donnell to the rescue when he said, 'Wait till you hear the original!' The original turned out to be Bill Monroe from Kentucky, who had written and recorded the song four years earlier. 'It's an ill wind ...', as they say, but Presley's hit version of 'Blue Moon of Kentucky', while generating a substantial amount of royalties for Bill Monroe, signalled the unstoppable era of rock'n'roll, while at the same time putting bands like the Bluegrass Boys out of work. I eventually obtained the Bill Monroe album containing 'Blue Moon' and it remains one of my favourite recordings. When you bear in mind that there were five stringed instruments, a lead vocal and three-part harmonies on the choruses, and that his recordings were made around 1949, with the band gathered around one microphone in the Camden studios in Knoxsville, it's still hard to beat for sheer drive and clarity and it's a distinctive sound which has often been copied but never equalled.

THE SINGING BRAKEMAN
JIMMIE RODGERS

In January 1994 I got a telephone call from a friend of mine who said he was doing some work for Van Morrison, who was looking for a couple of Jimmie Rodgers songs to record on some sort of tribute album. He was asking me because he knew I was a Rodgers fan, and he had heard that I had the complete Jimmie Rodgers collection. The only problem, my friend said, was that Van Morrison did not yodel and therefore required songs without yodelling bits. This proved to be a stumbling-block as almost all of of Jimmie Rodgers songs depend very much on this particular element. And so, up to the time of going to press, Van has not recorded a Jimmie Rodgers song, yet. I had first heard of Jimmie from my father, himself a keen musician, who told me about this prolific songwriting brakeman who had died of TB in the thirties. I went in search of his music in the early sixties but was met with the usual blank stares in record shops from so-called experts. Then, on a visit to London, I came across my first Jimmie Rodgers

LP in Dobells' record shop. 'TB Blues', 'Travellin' Blues' and 'Blue Yodel No. 9' became firm favourites and almost any of his songs still bring a lump to my throat. I'm happy to say that as part of their fiftieth anniversary celebrations, Peer Music made the entire Jimmie Rodgers repertoire available on an eight-CD set and I was even happier to be presented with that set by Rannock Donald, on behalf of Ralph Peer III – whose grandfather, Ralph Peer, had originally discovered Rodgers.

DOC AND MERLE
DOC AND MERLE WATSON

Hearing Doc Watson for the first time can have two effects on the aspiring student guitarist. You either want to give up altogether or lock yourself away for forty years in the vain hope that you might some day be as good. I was one of the lucky ones who thought that I could never aspire to anything even like a poor imitation, and I just got along with enjoying Doc's music. I first discovered Doc Watson's music not long after he himself had been 'discovered' by Ralph Rinzler, who had travelled to Deep Gap in North Carolina to record Tom Clarence Ashley and his band for Folkways Records. As it happened, Tom's regular guitar player was ill and his place was taken by Arthel 'Doc' Watson, a local blind guitarist who made his living playing with a 'wedding band'. When Rinzler heard Watson's impeccable flowing guitar lines, he knew he was onto something special, and the rest, as they say, is history. Doc Watson went on to record about twenty-six of the most influential guitar albums of all time. Sadly, his son Merle Watson, who was playing back-up guitar on the first album that I procured, died tragically in a tractor accident near his home. I had the honour to bring Doc and Merle to Ireland for the first time in 1977. They shared a meal with us at the house and although Doc was a small eater, Merle managed to polish off most of the fresh salmon all by himself. R.I.P.

SONGS OF THE MOUNTAINS
THE CARTER FAMILY

I'm not sure about the nineties, but anyone starting out to learn to play guitar in the fifties, sixties, seventies or even the eighties, would very often find themselves learning some of the basics to a song called 'The Worried Man Blues':

It takes a worried man, to sing a worried song (x2)
I'm worried now, but I won't be worried long.

With the three basic chords for that song you were already starting to sound like a real musician, and the utter simplicity of it really appealed to me. Enquiries as to where the song came from fell on deaf ears until I bumped into a guitar player in London in the sixties who just happened to be playing the odd gig with a guy called Rod the Mod (later to be better known as Rod Stewart). The guitar player was Denny Lane and not only did he show me how to play a proper Carter lick on the guitar but he introduced me to the Carter Family world of music. A.P. Carter, Sarah Carter and Mother Maybelle Carter wrote and recorded over three hundred songs between 1927 and 1933, and in so doing became one of the most influential groups in the history of country music.

'Worried Man Blues', 'Will the Circle Be Unbroken', 'Wreck of the Old 97', 'Wildwood Flower', the list goes on. There's hardly a country band in the world without at least one Carter song in their repertoire and every country guitar player features the occasional 'Carter lick'. My first Carter Family long-playing record, bought for a pound, still has pride of place on the record shelf.

OLD TIME SONGS
THE NEW LOST CITY RAMBLERS

If there was one group of musicians who did just about everything I wanted to do, who played every instrument I wanted to play and sang every song I wanted to sing, then these guys had to be it. It was as though they had been listening to everything that I had been chasing for years, and they probably had. I loved everything about them. Their album sleeves were always designed in black and white or sepia tones and would feature a photo on the front cover depicting the boys in 1930s style, complete with hats and boots and suits and vintage instruments. Like the Greenbriar Boys, the New Lost City Ramblers comprised three Jewish boys from New York. Not perhaps the sort of place you would expect to find a hotbed of traditional American music, but the square in Greenwich Village was a melting-pot meeting place for musicians in the fifties and early sixties. Woody Guthrie had been there, Bob Dylan was to come out of there and a thousand other bands and groups started there. Mike Seeger, John Cohen and Tom Paley (later replaced by Tracey Swartz) found that they had a common interest in, and curiosity about, the huge body of traditional and commercial country music that had been recorded and forgotten between the early 1920s and 1960. They made field trips to the Appalachian and Blue Ridge mountains and searched for old record collections and manuscripts and built up a massive collection of songs and tunes that might otherwise have been forgotten. Folkways Records under the tutelage of Moses Ash had the foresight to see the potential for a massive archive. Folkways recorded and released as much material as the NLCR could record and in the process produced about thirty fine albums which are collectors' pieces today. The first album of theirs that I managed to get had a blues, a traditional fiddle tune, two banjo breakdowns, a mandolin tour-de-force, one ballad sung a cappella, two Charlie Poole songs, a Carter Family song and a cowboy murder ballad! A truly amazing mixed bag.

The New Lost City Ramblers were responsible for introducing thousands, if not millions, to the rich and varied musical heritage of rural America.

BRIAN TRENCH

I DON'T HAVE A DOG-EARED COPY of *St Dominic's Preview* whose vinyl bears the scratches of a thousand playings on auto-change BSR turntables. I don't have a yellowing copy of *Bringing It All Back Home* whose sleeve shows the scars of its use as a surface for rolling up. I don't have a first edition of *Sgt. Pepper's Lonely Hearts Club Band* whose artwork still makes me drool.

I laugh at the surprises of improvisation and at the joy of a big band in full flight. I cry for release from the intense emotion which a brass band or a crowd singing can stir. Music was important to me in those days of 'beat' and R&B. It's a vital accompaniment to life now. But the intervening years, or even the longer period from that first skiffle band or the shock of 'Rock Around the Clock', are not marked along the way by milestone albums. Among the many hundred albums I possess there are none with particularly strong resonances of life lived with greater abandon. Commercial popular music is tied to its context. It carries evocations of style and attitude that are bound to an epoch. In rock terms, that's a few months, a year or, at best, a couple of years. When those styles and attitudes no longer appeal, the music loses much of its validity or changes its meaning.

John McLaughlin's seventies' work with the Mahavishnu Orchestra reflected some of the spirit of the time, not least in its dedication to the leader's guru, but it speaks very faintly across the years. Less visible but much more important was McLaughlin's earlier participation in the Miles Davis band that recorded *Bitches Brew* in 1969. As well as charting new paths for jazz, that album opened up possibilities in fusion that reached into the main streams of rock.

Hearing McLaughlin now with a drummer and organist whose combined ages are less than his fifty-three years demonstrates that it is those with the capacity to renew their music who really span the generations. John McLaughlin, ex-Mahavishnu, ex-Shakti, ex-One Truth Band, ex-Trio of Doom, occasional member of Three Great Guitars (with Paco de Lucia and Larry Coryell/Al di Meola), achieves new authority by synthesizing, within a jazz embrace, the diverse musical styles he has adopted over the years.

By contrast, when McLaughlin's contemporary Mick Jagger performs today we marvel at the physical agility and at the capacity to recreate the formula. There is no substantial new invention. Indeed, there cannot be, for that would defeat the purpose. A remarkable number of those who started making waves in the mid-to-late-sixties are still musically active. But the Kinks cause cringes when they sing 'Waterloo Sunset' again. Eric Clapton regresses steadily. Joe Cocker has merely added some seasonings over the years. Exceptionally, Van Morrison continues to re-invent himself and his music.

These are 'my generation'. I share a year of birth with Clapton and Morrison. But Clapton and Morrison were already major international stars before I acquired a record-player. In fact I didn't start accumulating any of their albums, or the Rolling Stones', until well into the seventies. As it happens, Morrison's 1977 release, *Wavelength*, took on special importance because I had it and played it repeatedly at a time when I was largely house-bound.

In the sixties records were largely a source of material to be plagiarized. The BV5, based in Drogheda, did Beatles, Stones (no conflict there; I don't recall the irreconcilable difference between Beatles-persons and Stones-persons which legend has constructed), Animals, Hollies. We opened for the showbands in the Abbey Ballroom, when the early arrivals had room to link up in a line across the floor and dance in formation. When the floor was sufficiently crowded we made way for the Pacific or the Hoedowners. Individual songs mattered much more than albums. Singles were, in any case, the common currency of the time. Frequent radio airplay often gave us, and particularly our singer-drummer, Jon Ledingham, later Jonathan Kelly, enough clues to reconstruct the song.

One album from that period to which I occasionally return is a blues compendium released in 1963 and featuring Muddy Waters, Howlin' Wolf, Willie Dixon, Sonny Boy Williamson, Buddy Guy and others. Importantly, it includes a version of Waters's classic, 'Got My Mojo Workin'', which we attempted to get working for the patrons of the Abbey. The album has additional personal significance: I heard Dixon and Howlin' Wolf close-up in a small Wiesbaden club in 1962 or 1963. They were in one of the first blues 'packages' to tour Europe. I can still see T. Bone Walker's distinctive stance with the guitar held at right angles to his hip and hear John Lee Hooker's skipped beats. I am fairly certain they played Willie Dixon's 'Little Red Rooster' that night, but like most of this music it reached us mainly through the mediation of the Rolling Stones, Spencer Davis, the Animals and others.

The borrowings from these groups continued, though to a lesser degree, with the Boomerangs, based in Dublin. Jonathan Kelly was our singer, guitarist and songwriter. We played the TV Club and recorded two Kelly originals as a double-sided single in 1966, recently dug out of the vaults for inclusion in an Irish 'beat' compilation. We also provided backing for Tolka Row's Jim Bartley in his bid for pop stardom.

What we were now listening to was Dylan. He played his first-ever concert in Europe with electric band in the Adelphi cinema about this time. But what we were playing was rather less challenging. Jonathan Kelly moved to London, secured the non-Bee Gee Gibb brother as manager, and recorded several albums, mainly of his own songs. On one of these, Eric Clapton was a backing musician, who thus followed in my trail in being chosen to record with Jonathan Kelly. He got in ahead of me in appearing with Jimi Hendrix, but let that wait for a second.

I graduated from keyboards to washboard in the House of David Jug Band. A couple of albums by Bob Muldaur, probably belonging to fellow-Trinity College student Trevor Crozier, were the inspiration for this short-lived line-up. We played support to South African folk singer Nadia Cattouse and, in Belfast, to Alexis Korner, the gravelly-voiced pioneer of blues and R&B in England. (By some strange tragic twist, as I was recalling those events and Trevor Crozier for the first time in very many years, news reached me that Trevor was killed in a road accident in Malawi in November 1994.)

As a student in Berlin in 1966 I helped form the Ones. We – that is, myself on keyboards and Volker, the saxophonist – recruited Charlie, a singer who strutted his stuff in a reasonable pastiche of Jagger, and Edgar, a guitarist, whom we met on a break from his job painting ads on the sides of buses. Our six-piece group played an R&B- and soul-inflected programme. Georgie Fame's minor hit 'Sunny' was one of the stronger numbers. We were selected to support the Jimi Hendrix Band when they played Berlin in spring 1967, just after he had first gigged with Clapton and Cream in London.

I miscalculated the time it would take to explore the outer reaches of the West Berlin tram network and arrived late for our spot. The band had to pull me up on to the stage from among the crowd and straight into the first number. The crowd seemed to think it was part of the act. None of this, nor anything else happening around him that day, made much impression on Hendrix, who remained in apparent stupor at the side of the stage. Kicked into action later by the boilerhouse team of Noel Redding and Mitch Mitchell, he delivered a teeth-tingling performance. Up close, it was the constant stoking of the fires from Redding and Mitchell which impressed. Down among the crowd, Hendrix galvanized all the attention as he helped boost the Fender share price with another assault on their products.

Despite my Jimi Hendrix experience I never acquired a Hendrix album. Nor did the exposure fundamentally influence the Ones. Our guitarist Edgar Froese took his guitar-playing as far from Hendrix as could be imagined, going on to form Tangerine Dream and make a series of increasingly soporific albums.

Back in Dublin, I joined the still-emerging Dr Strangely Strange. In the following months we played alongside Sweeney's Men in a Stephen's Green pub, support to Thin Lizzy in a Parnell Square club and curtain-raiser for our most immediate inspiration, the Incredible String Band, in Liberty Hall. We appeared on the *Late Late Show* and did a gig in Carlow attended by Joe Boyd of Island Records. (It was fourteen years later that Eric Clapton, then a tax-exile resident of Co. Kildare, got to play Carlow ...) The fruits of courting Joe Boyd came after I had left the group and the old standard, 'Sweet Lorraine', and a mild protest about Dublin Corporation's neglect of Dublin's historic building were dropped from the programme. Band member Tim Booth told *Melody Maker* that I went to France to make revolution and walked through a glass door. I went to Bordeaux four months after the 'events' of May 1968. The glass door was in Torquay.

After Strangely Strange I stopped playing. I had played rock and folk music because I could. The music which meant more was beyond my capabilities. Hearing Gerry Mulligan albums in my brother's flat in the early sixties had begun tuning my ears to modern jazz. Whatever urge the music-making satisfied was sublimated in listening and in the platonic performance of reviewing.

The accumulated music of the past twenty-five years is marked by live music experiences as much as by recordings: alto saxophonist Phil Woods with the European Rhythm Machine in Bordeaux in 1969; multi-saxophonist Roland Kirk in University of Warwick; Duke Ellington in the Berlin Philharmonic Hall; Art Blakey and his Jazz Messengers in Dublin and Cork; the John Abercrombie Quartet just off a plane in Lisbon; Elvin Jones, Dizzy Gillespie, the Cuban band Irakere and others in Ronnie Scott's; 80/81, with Pat Metheny, Charlie Haden and Dewey Redman, at the Cascais festival; Mike Westbrook's quintet in Belfast; Branford Marsalis in Dublin; Wynton Marsalis in Cork; Kenny Garrett in the astonishing icing-sugar Congress Hall of Warsaw, John McLaughlin in Paris and Perugia. The locations are imprinted with the music in the memory. Even outstanding performances by Van Morrison, Paul Brady, Rickie Lee Jones, Moving Hearts, Paul Simon, David Byrne, Ry Cooder, and others who triumphed over the limitations of the National Stadium, Point or RDS have not registered on the same scale.

Bassist Charlie Haden's Liberation Music Orchestra, which contains stirring references to the Spanish Civil War and the only genuinely moving treatment of the sixties anthem 'We Shall Overcome', was one foundation stone for a jazz collection which continues to grow eclectically. Having 'discovered' alto saxophonist Arthur Blythe and his eccentric band, with cello and tuba, I have acquired a small set of Blythe albums, first LPs, now CDs. The latest purchase will always get repeated playings until it becomes part of the musical furniture. There are small but significant slices too of the work of Haden's erstwhile collaborator Carla Bley, of vibraphonist Gary Burton (though I would be much less inclined to listen to him now), of Lester Bowie, and that's just touching the letter B. The acquisitions have also taken me back to early Ellington, Basie in the swing era, Lester Young, Charlie Parker, John Coltrane. But the demands of reviewing, as well as curiosity in hearing how jazz continuously renews itself, have encouraged a tendency to move on, which may also explain the paucity of permanent favourites.

Rock musicians who command continuing respect include: Frank Zappa, whose talent was debased by his own and others' too-frequent references to his genius; Randy Newman, who produced a remarkable series of albums through the seventies; Steely Dan, who shared a sense of irony with Zappa and Newman; and Joni Mitchell, who doesn't, but who emerged from the chrysalis of her folk days as a musician of mature sensibility and versatility. From more recent times, I miss Joe Jackson as an eccentric presence and confess, as I gather one must, to enjoying the global ramblings of Sting and Paul Simon.

Earth, Wind and Fire seemed much more exciting at the time than they do in retrospect. Stevie Wonder's output was and is uneven, but a half-dozen albums from the early and mid-seventies have proven durable. The Crusaders and, later, Weather Report were sought out for their straddling of the styles. My interest in soul was under-represented – a couple of James Brown's albums, and a great Etta James LP, which was lost to a loan. So too were the early Bob Marley releases on Island, also much-played. Youssou N'Dour has filled something of that gap.

This may seem a pluralist mush. I envy others the experience of pieces of music lived intensely, loved in their detail, appreciated for their place in the artist's total work. I admire the dedication of those who seek out the never-reissued vinyl release in order to complete a set. I may have missed something but, for me, moving with the music means enjoying diversity and discovery.

PAOLO TULLIO

I'M GOING TO PUT MY NECK ON THE BLOCK and make a prediction. What this book will turn out to be is a history of an era that is coming to an end. The music that we define as Classic Rock is fast approaching its best-before date.

Consider this: if My *Generation* had been compiled in the fifties we would all have been writing about our favourite big bands: Glenn Miller, Tommy Dorsey and the hundreds of others who smiled at the audience over their shoulder while waving a little stick. That was the way music was presented. Big bands were on the radio, infant TV, and on film: it was how popular music was understood.

Bill Haley and His Comets put paid to all that with 'Rock Around the Clock'. I vaguely remember looking out of my bedroom window in Salisbury watching the ABC cinema emptying across the street – people were dancing on the pavements. As a five- or six-year-old I watched the start of a revolution. What had been minority music was suddenly white and mainstream. The music industry would never be the same again; the old order slowly died away and a new one took over. Instead of a big band with brass, woodwind and strings, rock-'n'roll gave us three guitars and a drum kit and it's been with us ever since.

Believing as I do that all things have a beginning, a middle and an end, it follows that this musical format must also have an end. It's getting harder and harder to be original within the framework. An analogy: to us one big band sounds pretty much like another – at the time, of course, they were all thought to be unique and distinctive.

I'm not clever enough to predict what will come next; but the format of the last forty years has run its course. So my list is not just a personal odyssey through the haze of drugs and rock, but a finished listing. I won't be adding another rock record to it, even if I live a whole lot longer.

And so to the first album, the first I ever bought for myself: Elvis's *Jailhouse Rock*. Thank you, Colonel Parker, for getting rock'n'roll out into the marketplace for the white boys, and thanks to Carole King and Gerry Goffin for writing a rake of them. This was my first inkling that there was a world of music out there that was not controlled and directed by Tin Pan Alley. It took me years to find out that we never heard the originals in the fifties and sixties; we got British cover versions, just as the Americans got white cover versions of black music. It's hard to believe today what a rough ride Buddy Holly got for playing 'nigger music' and hard to believe how long it took Chuck Berry to break through.

Please Please Me was a milestone. The Beatles did something new: they wrote their own material. They were the first globally known hyphenates – singer-songwriters. The music industry had some difficulty adjusting to this: people who wrote and performed their own material had more control than the industry was used to giving to artists. The artist was becoming more important than the song. My first tentative kissings and fondlings were to the sounds of the Beatles, while I wore a black polo-neck in deference and let my hair grow. I listened to it recently, and still the memories of slobbering and inept French kisses are there to haunt me.

Later teens brought the first big shift in my view of music. An English public school gave me plenty to rebel against. I don't remember who introduced me to him, but Jimi Hendrix represented all the rebellion that I felt. I fell in love with 'Purple Haze', and bought *Are You Experienced?* This was the real beginning: Hendrix and and my first blast of the killer weed – a heady and potent mix that has been hard to shift since. The two became inextricably linked.

The next two years, which involved the freedom of a first university year, evoke a dim memory of psychotropic experimentation. Two albums still register through the miasma of separate realities: *Free* and *Led Zeppelin*. I bought *Free* in Barcelona and *Led Zeppelin* in Paris, so all sorts of memories come with that baggage – the powerful stimulants of youth, holidays and blonde girls called Ulrike. 'All Right Now' still makes my feet move.

Sitting on the floor of a bedsit one night my man Niall put some headphones on me. Very, very stoned I listened to Lou Reed and Nico on the Andy-Warhol-produced Velvet Underground album. 'Venus in Furs' and 'Waiting for the Man' sound good even now. This was music and drugs entwined as I had never heard it before. I liked it. So, of course, did thousands of others who found in the lyrics of this kind of music signposts to help them navigate the drug-induced wastelands of their souls. False gurus and crap music rode successfully on this bandwagon for years. It seemed the more stoned you got the more the idols had feet of clay – no one really knew the way through this new world of altered states.

Psychotropic investigation led me to Dr John, the Night Tripper. Strong jou-jou. If anyone reading this has my copy of Dr John, give it back, I want to relive my youth. When the same Niall who turned me on to Lou Reed went semi-permanently into another reality, I slowed up on this particular line of investigation. Sod the smart-arse druggy lyrics, I thought, I want to dance.

Motown made me feel good, but I can't think of an album that I liked the whole way through and I don't really think of it as Classic Rock. Creedence Clearwater Revival were great, but Lowell George was better. His solo album after Little Feat, *thanks, I'll eat it here*, is still a favourite – best version of 'Can't Stand the Rain' that I know.

Just like me, my favourite rockers are ageing. We grew up side by side, checked out substances at the same time, chased sex together. I've been faithful to my era, to my generation: as my heroes grew older I followed their musical trek. It's a form of laziness: it's easier to go on buying old favourites than to find new ones, just as it's easier to be with old friends. I like and listen to a lot of today's bands, mainly of my son's choosing; but obviously they weren't formative for me. The Mothers, Big Brother, Sly and the Family Stone and the Rolling Stones set the patterns of my particular likes and dislikes.

When I'm not indulging in nostalgia, Ryland P. Cooder and J.J. Cale rock me. I play Cooder's *Bop Till You Drop* more than most, so I'll include that as number nine. Every time I drive over the Wicklow Gap I just can't help it; I start singing 'Down in Hollywood'.

Looking over this list there seems to be nothing gentle. This is not representative of my music collection, so to be fair, balanced and impartial, James Taylor's *Sweet Baby James* fills the number-ten slot. No hard-edged acid rock this, just a little gentle blow. The very thing for balmy, bucolic summer afternoons now that the long trip through sex, drugs and rock'n'roll is slowing up.

Which is where the trip has left me – a committed culchie living in the sticks, far from the techno-rave. Perhaps that's what's given me this strange notion that Classic Rock is nearly over. Maybe it's me that is.

Two favourite album covers stand out, both for their artwork. Big Brother's *Cheap Thrills* – a Robert Crumb classic – and the Mothers' *Weasels Ripped My Flesh* by Neon Park, whoever he may be.

MARK VENNER

GRIS-GRIS
DR JOHN, THE NIGHT TRIPPER

Mac Rebennack as full-blown psychedelic high priest of the voodoun. A year after *Sgt. Pepper*, the *gris-gris* man rises from those dark Louisiana bayous with a concoction the likes of which had never been heard before (or since!). My mother wondered what on earth it was, but I loved it. Together with musical witch-doctor Harold Battiste, the good doctor led me through the swamps to Professor Longhair, Huey Meaux, Zydeco and good old Nathan Abshire.

ONCE UPON A TIME IN THE WEST
ENNIO MORRICONE

The silent railroad station in the desert. A fly buzzes and Jack Elam twitches; water drips onto Woody Strode's filthy stetson. And then the train; it pulls away and through the swirling dust a figure; the Man with the Harmonica. And as the dust still swirls so comes the music, a breathtaking hybrid ... Rodrigo crossed with Duane Eddy: Morricone.

RONNIE LANE'S SLIM CHANCE
RONNIE LANE

Songs of the open road. On the sleeve notes Ronnie tells us not to adjust our sets, the rumble is wind in the microphone. And we're off with his merry band. Fiddles and rusty guitar strings and Ronnie's cracked voice. Smoke in the lanes, the rumble of the Burton wagons, the yelp of a lurcher, roll your own cigs, hedgehog pie and Kushty Rye ... God bless you, Ronnie.

FIVE THOUSAND SPIRITS OF THE LAYERS OF THE ONION
THE INCREDIBLE STRING BAND

Some listened to *Deep Purple in Rock*, but others knew. 'The First Girl I Loved', Robin Williamson's delirious epic of adolescence recalled. Out of the Edinburgh folk scene they came, flowing hair and bottle-green velvets, carrying with them the blues, Celtic reels, Sufi legends, sitars and steam organs, shambolic and whimsically strange ... never to be forgotten.

FIVE LEAVES LEFT
NICK DRAKE

On the sleeve he gazes through the broken attic windows of a derelict cottage. This handsome, gentle, sad minstrel with his impossibly bleak songs: the arrangements as spare and delicate as the lyrics. He made Leonard Cohen sound positively jubilant. One had to be alone to listen to Nick Drake, and this still holds true.

LIEGE AND LIEF
FAIRPORT CONVENTION

Nineteen sixty-nine and folk-rock truly comes of age. Dave Swarbrick, demon fiddler; Richard Thompson, the only guitar hero I've ever had; Ashley Hutchings, guiding light of the entire movement; and then Sandy ... she sings of madness and magic on 'Tam Lin', of the ill-fated soldier boy in 'The Deserter', and yet more magic in Thompson's haunting ballad 'Crazy Man Michael'. A beautiful and unique collection that now brings a tear to my eye.

BLIND FAITH
BLIND FAITH

They were hailed as the first supergroup, but we didn't give a shit about that: it was the music, a vast swirling canvas for the ears. Windwood giving us Buddy Holly, Ginger Baker's work-out on 'Do What You Like', and of course, Clapton's spine-tingling hymn 'Presence of the Lord'. I can still remember the effect his solo had on me when I first heard it.

BACK TO THE CHICKEN SHACK
JIMMY SMITH

My best friend's elder brother turned me on to 'the cat', I was fifteen and hooked ... that sound! The Hammond, the whirring Leslie speaker, tonic mohair suits and Dexedrine, Sta-prest white Levis and lambrettas, expresso bars, Ben Shermans and the Marquee, Stanley Turrentine, Kenny Burrell and Jimmy Smith. Real cool.

THE RED-HEADED STRANGER
WILLIE NELSON

Barrelhouse piano, bull fiddle and Willie's idiosyncratic nylon string guitar. Forget *Tommy* and other overwrought concept albums of the mid-seventies. Here was a story told in song that was as bleak and chilling as a Peckinpah movie, with Willie's nasal whine cutting through you like a buzz-saw.

VEEDON FLEECE
VAN MORRISON

The Man's overlooked masterpiece. On the sleeve with Irish wolfhounds he is as ill at ease as only Van can be. But in the grooves he soars with double bass, acoustic guitar and flute: it's reminiscent of *Astral Weeks* ... organic, flowing songs that tell of mystics and murderers and gypsies riding with their hearts on fire. A strange and difficult album that stays with me.

DICK WARNER

THE MAIN PROBLEM POSED BY THE SIXTIES is trying to decide whether it was a wonderfully exciting renaissance of creativity or whether it was just that we were all young. In Ireland the sixties started somewhere around 1965 or 1966 and ended abruptly in 1973.

In 1965 I walked through the Front Gate of Trinity College, Dublin as a nineteen-year-old undergraduate wearing a sports jacket and grey flannel trousers with turn-ups, a short-back-and-sides and a bald chin. Musically I was already tiring of the Beatles (I enjoy them more today), committed to a life-long adoration of the Rolling Stones, had discovered John Lee Hooker and was about to have my young mind blown by James Brown. The twenty-three-year-old who walked out through that Gate in 1969 with a second-class honours degree was a very different person. He had shoulder-length hair and a beard and wore a long black cloak with a gold lining over knee-length black leather boots. The previous year he had married a Californian hippie at a flower-power ceremony. He was listening to Janis Joplin, Country Joe and the Fish, Frank Zappa, the Velvet Underground, Procul Harum, Pink Floyd and ... still the Rolling Stones. His most important baggage was a collection of ideas and values that were to last into the nineties. He was almost completely a sixties product.

Much more than music happened in those four years. But music was always there – background music, foreground music, music as the primary artic-ulation of a generation that was changing things and was quite aware of the fact that it was changing things. Music was there when Daniel Cohn-Bendit manned the barricades in Paris, when Bernadette Devlin led Civil Rights marches, when we stood outside the American Embassy getting our pictures taken by CIA agents as we chanted 'Hey, hey, LBJ ... How many kids you kill today?' Music was there when we drank our pints and smoked our joints, when we debated Marxist theory, made love with our girlfriends on mattresses on the floor, when we woke up and when we went to sleep – even when we meditated.

It wasn't only rock music. Joan Baez sang one night in the Trinity Folk Club and Joe Heaney was a regular, his musical grace opening a new door to an old style. At lunchtime we ate sandwiches of cold beef and brown sauce in O'Donohue's of Merrion Row and listened to the Dubliners live – for free.

I have chosen just one album (it seems to me we still called them LPs in those days) to remind me of my presence on the fringes of the folk music revival.

Christy Moore's *Prosperous* is legendary. It spawned Planxty and launched Christy on a career which is still ascending. It also has personal connections for me. It was recorded in the basement of Downings House, which is a couple of miles from where I live and which I know well. The house belongs to my friend Andrew Rynne, who played a key role in getting the musicians together for the session – and who still knows how to throw a party.

We were permeated by music and by the conviction that we were the counter-culture. I'm still convinced of this – but today there is a difference of stress. At the time the stress was on 'counter', today it's on 'culture'. Hindsight sees the most remarkable thing about the sixties as the fact that it was a culture. The music, the politics, the clothes, Stewart Brand and his Whole Earth Catalog, the poetry of Allen Ginsberg, experiments in free love and communal living, Susan Sontag and Andy Warhol and the mini-skirt – they all integrated into something new and something whole. And the dynamo at the centre threw out an endless series of blue sparks, some of which grew to be serious brush fires. Like the Women's Movement, the exploration of space, the Green Movement, Black Power and the information super-highway – the sixties invented them all. And the very naiveté that was at the heart of it was also its strength.

It was also a healthy time in which hedonism was balanced by idealism and pomposity punctured by humour. There was a counter-counter-culture – a habit of satire that innoculated objectivity into the madness. This is why my list of ten albums – and reducing it to ten was very hard – includes Frank Zappa, consummate musician and piss-taker, and the Bonzo Dog Band. This band was originally called the Bonzo Dog Dada Band, then the Bonzo Dog Doo-Dah Band, then the Bonzo Dog Band. The progression is important. They were a bunch of English art students impressed by Dadaism. They embraced Dada's anarchic humour, applied it to what was going on around them and produced, on the album I have chosen, a seminal track – 'Can Blue Men Sing the Whites?' The counter to the counter-culture.

Of course it all ended with the first oil crisis of 1973 and the sound of bubbles bursting. I have two albums from before the real sixties – a John Lee Hooker and a James Brown – and just one post-bellum album from the Boomtown Rats.

Bob Geldof's neo-punk group again has personal significance above and beyond its musical achievements. The sixties is something I'm always trying to revisit. It's an uncomfortable thing to do – like trying to sleep in the bed in which you once lost your virginity. I made an attempt sometime in the seventies by attending the Trinity Ball. I was wandering rather sadly round the campus, watching all the straight young people in their evening dress, when I heard sounds coming out of the Dining Hall. An unknown group was playing there and stirring up some of of the old adrenalin. I stayed a good while – as excited as an old soldier getting a whiff of cordite – and shouted at somebody to tell me the name of the group as I was leaving. The Boomtown Rats, of course.

It's been an interesting experience, writing this and listening to the music again. Looking back, my main impression of the sixties is of a narrow beam of light which illuminated the century between the greyness of post-war austerity and the greyness of post-oil-crisis recession.

John Lee Hooker Plays & Sings the Blues	John Lee Hooker
James Brown Live at the Apollo	James Brown
We're Only in it for The Money	The Mothers of Invention
I Feel Like I'm Fixing to Die	Country Joe and the Fish
The Doughnut in Granny's Greenhouse	The Bonzo Dog Band
I Got Dem Ol' Kozmic Blues Again Mama!	Janis Joplin
Let It Bleed	The Rolling Stones
Prosperous	Christy Moore
Dark Side of the Moon	Pink Floyd
A Tonic for the Troops	The Boomtown Rats

IAN WHITCOMB

THE FIRST RECORDS I KNEW were thick black 78s and I played them over and over on a portable wind-up gramophone. They were my mother's records from the age of the flapper: chirpy dance bands bouncing, carefree and gay in constant foxtrot, relieved by a 'vocal refrain' in which a high-voiced, natty man praised Kentucky or Carolina, yearning with all his heart to be there in the morning. I desperately wanted to be there too – anywhere in that glorious, gorgeous freedom country of America; anywhere away from the sexless, kirby-gripped, grey-bagged Britain of the early fifties.

I reckoned that beyond the horn, deep inside the gramophone, were lots of little bright bandsmen ready to lead me to the land of pop dreams ... a delicate magic they wrought ... the records snapped very easily and then nothing but tears ... There was a lot of crying in the songs too, ballads of love and marriage and babies. It was all foreign to me, though I liked the music, especially when a novelty number turned up like 'The Naughty Lady of Shady Lane'. I sang that *a capella* to the boys in my dormitory and they were attentive, laughing at the punchline which reveals that the sexy lady is really a baby of nine days. Yes, they laughed, and that stopped them from punching.

Then came rock'n'roll to save us all.

ROCK AROUND THE CLOCK
BILL HALEY AND HIS COMETS

I was the first at Bryanston School to display this anthem album of rock'n'roll. These were the days when even the very term rock'n'roll spelled danger; you saw it scrawled on ancient shire halls and rusty stations; I wrote it in the snow in front of the grand neo-Georgian country house that was Bryanston.

There was no photo of good old Bill on the LP cover – maybe he wasn't handsome enough. On a red backing 'Rock' was spelled in a fancy shoe, a smiling clock, knitted fingers, a sock and a ruler. Not very stimulating but OK because the staff didn't want to encourage masturbation.

Of course, the music on the heavy vinyl cake was terrific. Every track rattled and raced with the characteristic snapped bass, the single rim shots, the kittenish ping of the steel guitar, and the brazen honk of the sax. And riding this kitchen clatter was the genial, almost avuncular, call of Bill Haley. He was like a square-dance caller, welcoming us to the exciting new world of R-O-C-K.

I played this record to death, to the delight of our dormitory. Even the housemaster considered Haley and his merry men to be harmless fun. 'You'll soon graduate to Gilbert & Sullivan and Bach!' he smirked. But the school jazz buffs, a deadly and spotty bunch, couldn't stand the stuff. 'It doesn't swing and it's downright vulgar,' sniffed the secretary who, naturally, wore glasses.

Even today I still thrill to the railway swing and sway of Bill Haley and His Comets. Bill may have died barmy in a Southern caravan site but I can remember fondly the night I gripped his hand in a Hollywood club. The hideous bell-bottomed seventies were in full drag and Bill was grabbing the gigs whenever he could. He seemed so surprised when I expressed my debt to him. I had to tell Bill, the family man from Chester in Pennsylvania, how much he meant to me and how his music had set me on a journey into American pop from which I've never recovered.

MEMORIES
AL JOLSON WITH ORCHESTRA

I still have the ten-inch 'long-playing flexible micro-groove record' of Jolson that I bought at the same time as the Bill Haley. To me there was no generational chasm between Jolie and Bill, between the chestnuts of yesterday and the hot stuff of 'today' – at least not when the irrepressible Al forced his way into my heart, into my whole body. The urgency of his voice – 'Come on and love me! The world is yours if you just follow me!' – promised a rich and sexy world and, like Haley's, I knew it was across the sea somewhere. 'That blubbering masquerader,' sneered one British critic, and I knew that my schoolboy jazz intellectuals hated Al for his squareness and his blacking up. Yes, he was indefensible, but the rallying call was a siren song and I responded to Al's sobbing for Mammy, for lost boys, for lost Dixie paradises, for lost childhood – and for the hint that someday we'll find what we're looking for because, as Al cried, 'You ain't heard nothing yet!'

HISTORIC RECORDINGS OF THE FIRST RECORDED JAZZ MUSIC
ORIGINAL DIXIELAND JAZZ BAND

At this stage the reader might well ask what these records have to do with classic rock. As a classic rocker, sometimes known as 'The Father of Irish Rock', I retort that rock'n'roll didn't just spring out of America parentless: Elvis Presley and Jerry Lee Lewis were big Jolson fans, and his jazz band is a model for the controlled chaos that went to make the best of rock instrumental groups. These five boys from New Orleans combined a wild weaving of tunes with the juicy harmonies of nineteenth-century Europe spiced with blue notes, smears and tom-tomming Africa. The result was pure American pop, and they promoted themselves with a Barnum-like zeal. Showbiz hype plus youth music – the very essence of rock'n'roll. In fact, the ragtime rhythms of this band have a lot more in common with early classic rock (the true fifties variety) than the sludgy beat of the big bands that preceded the rock explosion.

'We are the assassinators of melody' claimed the Dixieland Band's leader, with true rock posturing offensiveness. And, of course, once again my schoolboy contemporaries stuck up their noses at the barnyard cries of the little band from Dixie. 'It doesn't swing,' they again pronounced. 'Thank God for that,' I answered and returned to my Haley, my Jolson, and my popularity among the younger boys.

JIMMY YANCEY
JIMMY YANCEY

Now we reach the nitty-gritty. I soon discovered that rock piano is no more (and often much less) than boogie-woogie piano. And the primitive master of such boogie – the Rousseau – was Jimmy Yancey. His playing is so deceptively simple, the same idiosyncratic phrases in title after title; even though this one's called 'At the Window' and that one's 'Boodlin', these little jewels, these miniatures, could just as well be numbered works, like a Chopin opus. Of course, Yancey, a black Chicagoan who made his living as a baseball-park groundsman, was technically limited – he was certainly no Art Tatum and thank God for that. Because, to my mind, artists without the full palette avoid the pitfall of glibness and pyrotechnics. Every note can become a treasure. Yancey's lightly rocking bass riff became the fundament of New Orleans rock'n'roll as any Fats Domino record tells you.

For ages I sat at our mini-piano in the family flat on Putney Heath trying to kidnap the Yancey licks, playing the record at a slower speed so as to fathom exactly what the master was doing. At Trinity College, Dublin, in the early sixties I demonstrated my new boogie skills to the Jazz Club, throwing in a few crushed notes for good measure. 'Yeah,' they shouted, like true blue jazzers. Soon I was the TCD blues expert. When it came time for rhythm and blues my piano bashing was just the job. And from R&B to R&R was but a short step with the same style – except that the delicacies, the subtle nuances of the reflective Yancey, were thrown away. This beat music, as played by my Dublin band Bluesville, needed a more naggingly percussive sound, and this I found in the gut-bucket bottom of Champion Jack Dupree.

BLUES FROM THE GUTTER
CHAMPION JACK DUPREE

The Champion's parents were burned up in a New Orleans fire and he went to an orphanage but later took to the streets where he learned rudimentary barrel-house piano from a fellow called Drive 'Em Down. 'Frankie & Johnny' and 'Stack-O-Lee' served him well till work dried up in the 1930s. That's when he took to boxing and became the Champ. A pianist who boxed! Those precious fingers! Of course this colourful stuff was strong brew for me as a kid who saw America as the only real country, where everyone was on the road and Beat, and only the blacks knew the answers to life. Champion Jack's 'lyrics' (what a pre-cious word!) concerned the taking of drugs and of lives and I should have got a romantic charge out of this, but it was his thundering and repetitive piano play-ing that hit me: I knew I could easily copy it and stick it inside our band so that such an insistent banging might be heard even among the clangour of the elec-tric guitars. Yes, I stole the Champ's style but I left him his soul and his experi-ences. As a British public schoolboy I'd had my share of discomfort but nothing compared to Champion Jack, and so I tempered my shouts of pain with a little humour. Maybe I should have gone the whole black hog like Mick Jagger but I'm really not into blackface minstrelsy.

WILLIE'S BLUES
WILLIE DIXON WITH MEMPHIS SLIM

With this record I became a thief of the blues. But then who invented the blues scale, the blues chord progression, the blues form? Whoever it was should have rightfully reaped millions in royalties! However – I did steal: the very name 'Bluesville' I got from this album's label (Prestige/Bluesville) and the first track was a low-down, nasty, sexy song called 'Nervous' in which the brawny, much-used-and-abused Willie Dixon stuttered his nervousness to a lady with the dev-ilish powers of male arousal.

I adapted this to my persona – which was easy because I have a stutter – and fitted some new words. Here at last was a black blues which spoke of my life's burden, my experience. No longer would I be a mere copycat! I was a fellow suf-ferer! When Bluesville and I performed the song at Dublin blood-and-thunder dance halls and cellars the girls screamed and moaned and I felt that delicious sex wave wrap all over me. I knew I could be a star.

'N-E-R-V-O-U-S!' my version of Dixon's song, was released as a follow-up to my Top Ten hit, 'You Turn Me On', and climbed into the Top Fifty in late 1965. And now trouble began: Mr Dixon's publishers demanded full ownership, my publishers disagreed, the record sank, and we eventually agreed to split the royalties. Later Willie Dixon and I met up and there was no fighting. We all get the blues from somewhere, as I said earlier.

Mind you, I was furious when, playing a Dublin visit after a successful American tour with the Rolling Stones and the Kinks, I witnessed a perfor-mance by Bluesville: the singer who'd been substituting for me had the nerve to copy my stuttering right down to a T-t-t-t-t-t-T. So, naturally, I dashed onto the stage and walloped him with my rolled-up copy of *Billboard*. He was making fun of my disability, he was stealing my rightful angst.

THE GREATEST SHOW ON EARTH
JERRY LEE LEWIS

I have never heard any record that matches the excitement created by Jerry Lee, the demon king of rock'n'roll, at this performance, this sermon, this crazed, semi-religious speaking-in-tongues, witnessed by fifteen thousand Alabamans at the Birmingham Municipal Auditorium. I could see him raking the keys, stalking the piano top, screaming blue murder in a Baptist manner. I knew that here was unrestricted personality, madness even, on the loose. And when he struck up an old riff on 'Memphis' I realized that this was the riff for me. So I used it on my smash hit, 'You Turn Me On', when Bluesville and I had some extra studio time at the end of our first album session in Eamonn Andrew's studio in Henry Street, Dublin. At the end of the song we all had a good laugh – and us, serious blues lovers! Little did we suspect that as 'The Turn On Song' and then as 'You Turn Me On' this novelty trifle would sail me into worldwide fame, would be recorded by Sandy Nelson, the Surfaris, Mae West, and would become a standard in Brazil. My Top Ten status was taken into account when I sat for my finals in Modern History. I was awarded a decent degree and praised by my tutor. The Provost offered me a lectureship but, like Pilate, did not stay for an answer. Later I met and performed with Jerry Lee. He gave me a much too hearty slap on the back.

THE BEST OF MUDDY WATERS
MUDDY WATERS

'I got a black cat bone, I got a mojo tooth/ I got the John the Conqueroo, I'm gonna mess with you!' After careful study of these lyrics (or leer-ics), I proceeded to perform them at Trinity College parties, astounding the undergraduates and attracting certain women. This was the raw and heady brew of lumpen proletariat America, with the added attraction of negritude and voodoo. What a romantic and intoxicating mixture! And so very safe and unthreatening on an LP record, spun over many nights near an oil heater in the snugness of my Merrion Square digs, and then transmogrified by me and a few mates at these parties where Fiona heaved her bosom thrillingly and Jeremy pronounced the performance to be jolly authentic.

I still love Muddy Waters and all those other rough bluesmen. But I now recognize, as a responsible citizen of Los Angeles, that the street life of the underclass is not for me and my family. It is a threat, it represents the horde of barbarians at my gate. Except that my front gate is hidden by exotic desert trees, and those old Muddy Water records, rampant with hoochie coochie men and rolling stones and razors, are stacked away in distant cupboards.

WITH MY UKELELE
GEORGE FORMBY

At the same time that Bluesville and I were the toast of Dublin's beat cities my ukelele was not gathering dust. I'd had one since my Junior Freshman days and many's the time I'd entertained my friends on car trips to the Wicklow hills or going beagling. Simple and toothy-faced George Formby, the Lancashire lad with the saucy-seaside postcard songs and a skilful syncopated banjo-ukulele strum, provided me with grand material on these trips. Formby and other stalwarts of the Music Hall were the British equivalent of American blues and country music. I suppose I really should have taken my inspiration from those nearer my own class – from Noël Coward and Sandy Wilson – but somehow there wasn't anything one could do to their music. It was self-contained, even self-satisfied. And anyway, beyond the picture of fat women and underwear and Mr Wu, there was the euphoric lift of the Formby uke strum and the smiling music, always upbeat and major key. No damned sophistication, which I've always associated with adulteration and a general world-weariness.

How I managed to combine my rock performances with the Formby-like strumming and sentiments is another story – and is told in my book, *Rock Odyssey* (where circumstances lead me to an acid-rock festival in which my uke song is greeted with fury by the stoned-out audience and I have to be rescued from the stage by members of the local police golf club). Nowadays I accompany myself much more on the uke than on the piano and I'm rarely to be seen playing rock. Rock is a little unseemly for a man of my years. Funnily enough, Formby remained a pixie to the end of his life, whereas Mick Jagger looks like an ancient devil.

SURFIN' USA
THE BEACH BOYS

In 1963/64, when I made my first trips to America, it was the West Coast which most attracted me, particularly the beaches of Southern California. Here at last I saw the physical ideals that hitherto I'd only seen on the movie screen or in comic books. Pneumatic girls and boys with washboard stomachs, all milkshake-and-burger fed. Aryans of the Golden West! There was a music to accompany these super boys and girls, called 'Surf'. It certainly sounded just right – chocolate chords and swishing guitars and peanut butter-smooth voices. But I was a bit surprised when I saw pictures of the most popular of the surf kings: the Beach Boys were rather plump and homely. However, I took the best of the surf spirit back with me to Dublin and in wintry, foggy basement clubs I showed off my striped t-shirts and my baseball boots and the dance movements I'd learned in those glorious hedonist summers. From out of my demonstration of 'The Swim' came 'You Turn Me On'. And all the while I was longing to get out of this damp and dreary corner of Europe and return to my sexy Eden on the West Coast of America.

Now I live on the site of Nirvana. But it all evaporated years ago, if it ever existed. Fires, floods, riots and earthquakes have wiped my picture-slate clean. I'm left with only a dream – which is all I started with, and which is probably where I came from.

KATHLEEN WILLIAMSON

IT WAS THE BRONX, 1957, by the fire-escape window in the bedroom I shared with my two sisters in the four-storey walk-up in an Irish-going-Black neighbourhood. A pile of 45s – often provided by the jukebox man at my mother's waitress job – and a portable Victrola provided a kinetic audio mandala. The mantras would come in a few more years. I fantasized of travelling into the future and heard the unborn bleeps, blaps and blips of Morton Subotnik's 'Golden Apples of the Sun', the first recordings of the Moog synthesizer. Mom, a winter-of-'47 emigrant, would tell me hurried stories about childhood in Mayo, about berry-picking and wild donkeys.

In 1960 there was less money, no Victrola, no television, and another sister. We were one of a few 'white' families in Brooklyn's Puerto Rican Park Slope. Boys on the stoops drummed out hypnotic poly-Latin rhythms on the tops of metal garbage cans. By 1961 we had moved to Boro Park, where resident fundamentalist Hasidim didn't share music with 'goyim'. We had two televisions for a brief time then – one for the parents and a very old big box with a tiny tube for us girls. It didn't always work and we habitually tested and replaced the tubes. When the Beatles first appeared on the *Ed Sullivan Show*, my wicked stepfather banished us to the old box. We frantically banged, turned, adjusted, and prayed Hail Marys to it and caught the performance. To borrow from Lennon's sentiments about Elvis, before the Beatles 'there was nothing'. Lennon walked into the marrow of my soul. A new sentience began.

The future came closer. In 1965 'Satisfaction' blared from our open bedroom windows over the streets of parading, conservative, Sabbath-observing Hasidim. I would sing every hit to seduce my girlfriends with a $25 pawned dreadnought. The purchases and experiences of new 45s and albums, from the Mamas and the Papas to the Jefferson Airplane, and matching chord music books defined the passing years. Street corners became the venue and rock'n'roll the religious worldview.

During the second half of the sixties, we lived in Brooklyn's Bensonhurst. The girls' bathroom at high school was crowded and dense with cigarette and pot smoke. I would stand on the radiator and do early Elvis imitations, and the black girls would impersonate hysterical white female fans. Bell-bottoms, black armbands, Little Red Books, Afros, double barrels of sunshine, and moratoriums against the war in Viet Nam. TV became pictures accompanied by the Mothers of Invention's *Freak Out*. I was a neighbourhood guitar-player in a basement rock band. Younger boys would giggle at the way my right breast rested on the curve of my Japanese Strat. On the avenue below a bedroom window above De Palo's Salumeria, you could hear the Fender Twin Reverb that broadcast my twelve-string harmony with the Bill Lawrence pick-up. This sixteen-year-old girl was supposed to be mindlessly riding around in a car driven by some guitar-pluckin' boy instead of woodshedding – a 'queer' gender disruption amongst the Bensonhurst bimbos and bimbettes. A mother for whom I babysat reasoned that her younger sister was too boy-crazy and that I was too mad for art and music. The woman's scheme was that we'd have a good influence on each other. So we did. We became lovers. Her mafia father threatened to carve my heart out. Incense, linseed oil and turpentine, painting easels and guitar stands, lava lamps, hot tribalism, the long play of 'She's So Heavy', black lights and the *art du jour* day-glo posters of psychedelic Hendrix filled my room.

In Manhattan, my mother was waitressing lunch shifts near Roosevelt Hospital, where John Lennon would one day be delivered and pronounced dead. We were ever the descendants of Mayo every year down Fifth Avenue at the St Paddy's Day Parade. The beginning of the seventies brought an unprecedented mixed bag: superstars, high-heeled low sparks, more intellect and protest. Jazz, soul and rock intensified their mediations. This rebel had long ago torn her dress ... and burned her bra. The Electric Circus, Fillmore East and the Stonewall Riots marked the Village. Being a flexible hippie lezbo, I used to spin 'disco' in a mafia-owned queer bar on Flatbush Avenue. It was the pre-Bee Gee disco world of what came from soul and Motown: Marvin Gaye, Al Green, Aretha Franklin, Funkadelic, Isaac Hayes ... yowza! The music in those early discos helped a lot of rock straights become gay-friendly, as they found gay clubs stylish, avant-garde and jumpin' with great non-stop creaming dance music.

Cultures, ethnic communities, ideological blocs and individuals are various. We are a Bakhtinian kaleidoscope, cacophonies of ideals and agendas. In the years of Woodstock, we sang of love, peace and happiness but abortion was illegal and unaddressed. 'My generation' was as conservative as any other on the politics of homosexuality. Rock'n'roll brought with it 'unisex' clothing but also defined itself with pumping phallocentrism, patriarchal capitalism, and obligatory heterosexuality like the institutional windows and halls that the changing times had promised to shake and rattle.

The unsuccessful portion of our revolution was embodied at Sinéad O'Connor's performance at the celebration of the thirtieth anniversary of Bob Dylan's first CBS album at Madison Square Garden. She entered the stage prepared to perform a Dylan tune. I heard comradely female cheers, delighted alto and soprano choruses. Then, a slow pianissimo of bass and baritone-pitched booing infected the crowd and crescendoed to the force of a lemming stampede. I was aghast. Well, well, well ... strange bedfellows indeed ... masculinist hegemony waving its freak flag, choosing papist photographs over women's rights to body and expression. An Irish woman has full licence to rip up the bloody Pope:

'slaves of slaves' as Connolly described her and further reduced in the post-revolutionary Irish-Catholic state. When iconoclast Lenny Bruce comically slandered the Pope thirty-some years earlier, he was sanctified by the male subcultural élite. And *Saturday Night Live*, the show on which she had unexpectedly committed the unforgivable sin of papal rejection, had always been sacrilegious in its humour. No solidarity for Sinéad came from the stage. Dylan was a wimpdick lying bag o' shit for not marching out with Sinéad and daring that audience to boo them both off the stage. If you want honest poetry go to Michelle Shocked.

For me, even in the shadow of Lennon's passing, that was one of the nights that the music died and, like any religious movement, the so-called counterculture had to face its own disbeliefs and ironies. I had to finally verbalize the nagging reality that Dylan and the boys never raised their guitar pikes in favour of gender equality. They wear and discuss women like pornographic accessories. The Italian Riviera resort mayor who would ban fat or 'ugly' women in bathing suits from his seaside jurisdiction could have easily gleaned his sentiments from MTV. The species of rock'n'roll is desperate for an evolution, rather than a revolution, from our own gender hypocrisies and dependence on social and environmental parasitism. That's a tall order in these times when marketing doublespeak labels a performance from satellite to our big-screen televisions 'Unplugged'. One faith-restoring event was when k.d. lang won the Grammy for best vocalist. I felt an unprecedented quality of pride for her accomplishment and our social progress.

Nevertheless, despite all of its problems and contradictions, I am a rock-garden devotee. A friend asked me, 'If you were exiled on an island with ten albums, what would they be?' The choices reveal the contradictory matrices of my Dionysian and Apollonian sides, my penis and Venus envies. Impossible choices, but sitting here writing this article in Mayo, thousands of miles from my massive collection of vinyls and CDs, it's easier to pick out the ones I thrive on in my memories. These are albums that free me, that incite divine hysteria, glee, sensuality and psychic nitty-gritty, the kinds of happiness and liberty that makes 'enlightened' rationale irrelevant.

The first that comes to mind is *Electric Ladyland* by Hendrix, 'Have you ever been, not only experienced, but to electric ladyland?' 'Voodoo Chile' in all its medley variations on the theme is, ooooh, *duende*. 'Crosstown Traffic', well, even on car radio that album makes a happening, in the sense of Dali, in the most mundane hot and humid traffic jam. Nobody ever did or ever will do for guitar what Hendrix did, pure fucking genius is an understatement.

Essential in the collection would be the Beatles, but picking from the albums between *Sgt. Pepper's* to the last one is torture. 'Within You and Without You' is a great early third-world borrowing for levitating through life. I do believe it's true ... an island ethic. The Beatles hippified *agape*. Lust/love, philosophy, social commentary and spiritual messages are woven throughout. Beatles music soothed the savage beast and racist provincial turf-gang Italian boys in Bensonhurst. Lennon's 'Woman is the Nigger of the World' is one rare 'rock' art song that speaks to the gender inequality issue. Lennon really loved women and had the balls to express it. And on academic discourses such as nation-formation, he was an uncredited trendsetter. For example, 'Imagine' preceded Benedict Anderson's *Imagined Communities*, with its subsequent nearly biblical referential value, by about ten years. The Beatles, along with albums such as the Moody Blues' *Tuesday Afternoon*, and the rock opera *Tommy*, added orchestral beauty to the rock tundra.

Of the Who albums, *Live at Leeds* compiles some of their best materials in a great live recording. The exhumed version of 'Magic Bus' is especially percussive and well arranged. Townshend is always a maestro extraordinaire. Even at forty-something, we keep singing 'I hope I die before I get old', celebrating in lugubrious fashion our de, de, degeneration. Caught in the liminal and living in rock, the ironies of ageism beset us. The energy of the album is irresistible: I can clean the whole house in one spin of it AND dance. The *Tommy* opera is probably the closest thing to male rock'n'roll's pre-Jeannette Wintersonian deconstruction of heroification and holiness. I'll miss it badly in favouring *Leeds*, but there are enough cuts from the opera to sustain me.

Put me in a car for four days driving in the mountains of Arizona with one tape and it would have to be *Avalon* by Roxy Music. Scenic cruising music can't be improved beyond this album, especially the uplifting carefree affirmation that 'More than this there's nothing'. The tracks are self-propelling. The hooks rest on dynamite arrangements and theatre. For example, 'I was blind, can't you see?' isn't the most clever or profound writing, but with the music attached you feel like you can be redeemed by any past lover. My sisters and I have shared many whirling Lughnasa frenzies in the kitchen with that album.

k.d. lang's *Ingenue* is a recent victory for misfits like myself. The lyrics allow a wide variety of people to identify with the first person, but for a lesbian here is a rare empowering opportunity to hear popular media that actually speaks to her life. Lang's voice, the style, phrasing, dynamic power and theatrics, is awesome and polished. She is soooo cool. Turn it up. Someone always marching brave, here beneath my skin ... soaring ... constant craving.

No island collection would be complete without the double album of James Brown and the Blue Flames' *Live at the Apollo Theater*, to put you in a 'cold sweat'. I can relive many a New York apartment grungy get-downer dance marathon with that album.

An atypical bopper, which would have to be available for constant replay, is John McLaughlin's first Shakti album, with the series of live cuts on one side – 'What Need Have I for This? What Need Have I for That?', 'I am Dancing at the Feet of my Lord', 'All Is Bliss, All Is Bliss'. Recorded live somewhere in New York, it thrives on the fringes of Hindu-classical-rock-jazz fusion. The violinist, Shankar, and the tabla player set the standards for 'tight'. The Mahuvishna man was always like a bumble bee looking for somewhere to land and in Shakti he found his element. I remember that album on the turntable for the first time and dancing around my baby niece's crib in Brooklyn back in 1978. She slumbered, already accustomed to loud rock'n'roll blasting in the apartment. What a great dance-around-an-angel that was.

It would be hard to pick from the Yoko Ono stuff, the queen mother of punk and new wave, and her collaboration with Lennon. Although *Double Fantasy* is a favourite, it carries too many associations of the days around his murder. So, I'd pick the one that features her best song compositions performed by other great artists such as the B-52s and Elvis Costello. I think she was multimedia cutting edge. To hell with all the jealous petty misogynist and xenophobic cranial-anal inversions who demonized her. From 'Fly' to 'Thin Ice' and 'Every Man Has a Woman Who Loves Him' to 'Beautiful Boy' she has proven herself as a conceptualist, songwriter and producer. No doubt, himself would agree.

Big Brother and the Holding Company's *Cheap Thrills* is the rock-blues album of the century. When Janis sings the blues, she makes even Billie Holiday sound like Shirley Temple. Her voice on *Cheap* is more guttural than the Gyoto Monks and I swear you can hear split notes and multiple intonations in those woahs, wails and whimpers. Was it Southern Comfort or Buddha that made her say 'It's all the same fuckin' day, man'? No matter, each time I hear that album I merge with the performance. A lot of people say Big Brother wasn't such a hot band, but for that magic moment they were perfect. Gershwin, Mama Thornton, Bessie Smith – she brought together American blues in one fatal sweep. I often thought Robert Plant was a Joplin wannabee.

For number ten, I'll have to settle on Blind Faith, the supergroup, and one of the best albums to live by: 'Doooo ... Whaaaat ... Yooooou Like', 'Sea of Joy' 'Presence of the Lord' and Buddy Holly's 'Well Alright'. Awesome grooves, great hooks, and tight jams, brilliant audio heaven, the perfect accompanying nourishment for trials, tests, tribulations and celebrations. It blends the best work of the best musicians of the best rock'n'roll genre – the raw and cool vocals of Winwood, the chops of Clapton – with a genealogy deep in jazz, black and British music, and the Baker bass drum spine and anarchic ordering.

I'm ready for the island now, in the Bronx, Tucson, or Mayo. 'It's just a foolish dream that you dream, in the nights when lights are low.' Rock is as strong a force as ever, and just when you think it's had its day, a good new group comes out or an old group releases a great new album. It is ever-evolving, and there's room for everybody; 'and in the end, the love you take is equal to the love ... you make'. Rock'n'roll is dead, long live rock'n'roll.

RON WOOD

WHEN I WAS A KID MY PARENTS' HOUSE used to rock every weekend. My dad would be on harmonica or piano and his pals – scrap-metal dealers, pig-bin men, various types bordering on the gypsy strain, and lots of his Paddy friends as he called them – would play accordions, kazoos, the banjo, mandolin, penny-whistle or comb-and-paper, basically anything that made a noise. Lots of these guys are still around. My son Jesse plays guitar in a band and I recently met some of the old-timers at a gig he was playing. They remembered taking me up and putting me to bed while the parties were in full swing downstairs.

I still must have been in short trousers when my older brothers Art and Ted started taking me to gigs; to the Marquee, the 100 Club or the Railway Hotel in Harrow Wealdstone – that was the rockingest club. Cyril Davis and his band brought the whole R&B scene into the pubs and clubs of England: with Alexis Korner and Long John Baldry, blues was played properly for the first time this side of the Atlantic. There were some great musicians; Nicky Hopkins on piano, Dick Heckstall-Smith on sax, this great guitar player called Strawberry, and on drums either Graham Burbage, who also played with Chris Barber's jazz band, or Carlo Little, who had the first leopard-skin drum kit and played with Screamin' Lord Such. Carlo used to drop off copies of the latest hot American 45s. My brother Ted sang with this line-up, so it was the best introduction to live music a kid could have had. A bit later on I remember seeing the Who – then the High Numbers – live for the first time. A really hard-hitting, mind-blowing experience. The Move were another fantastic live band. There seemed to be so many new directions in music at that time.

COUNT BASIE
COUNT BASIE

One of the first records I walked out and bought on my own; I thought I did pretty well and it impressed my brothers, particularly Ted who was a jazzer and pretty advanced. I really got off on this record and it stands the test of time.

JERRY LEE LEWIS
JERRY LEE LEWIS

I vividly remember my brothers coming home with *Great Balls of Fire*, and this, Jerry Lee's first album on Sun Records, is a classic with great tracks like

'Goodnight Irene', 'Ubangi Stomp' and 'Matchbox'.

Jerry Lee has been a pal for a long time and we've played together often. Things are never quiet around The Killer. One time we were using a Winnebago camper-van as a dressing-room before a show and the make-up girl came in, splashed a bit of aftershave on Jerry Lee, and left. Then the hairdresser arrived. She leaned over him and sniffed. 'Mmmm, Jerry Lee,' she says, 'you smell great. What've you got on?' And Jerry Lee replies, 'I've got a hard-on, baby, but I didn't know you could smell it.'

MUSIC FROM BIG PINK
THE BAND

When I lived in Lower Sloane Street above Perry Preston's The Estate Agent – at the time when Davis Bowie, wearing his floppy hat and pushing a pram, lived down the road – I had this Geordie pal called Lee, who played with the Nice. He brought *Music from Big Pink*. This really turned me around.

DELANEY AND BONNIE AND FRIENDS
DELANEY AND BONNIE

This was another album that opened up new musical directions. Little did we know that when we met the band their sax player Bobby Keyes would become such a part of the Stones sound. They also had Marcy Levy on backing vocals. She was part of Shakespears Sister most recently, but I remember Marcy back then with great delight!

LIVE AT NEWPORT
MUDDY WATERS

One of our mentors. Every time I met him before I joined the Stones he always thought that I was already a member of the band. 'My MAAAN from the ROLLING Stones,' he'd say and I'd reply, 'Not yet, Muddy, not yet.' I was still with the Jeff Beck Group at the time.

Muddy is the real thing. My brother Art always used to sing 'Got My Mojo Working' and 'Hoochie Coochie Man' with his band the Artwoods, but when I first heard this album it made me realize just what it was that Art was trying to get to. Those songs – 'I'm a Man', 'Mannish Boy' and so on – still ring true. It doesn't matter how many groups covered them – and cover them they did, believe me, to the extent that they got a bit corny – but the originals never die.

ELECTRIC WOLF
HOWLIN' WOLF

'Smokestack Lightning' was huge when I was growing up. It still is and Howlin' Wolf, like Muddy, has made music that will last for ever.

FACT OF LIFE
BOBBY WOMACK

Bobby is all heart. Being the Sam Cooke band graduate that he was, Bobby took over Sam's wife after Sam was killed. 'OK, you're going to marry me now, you're going to look after me,' she said to Bobby. He was a bit of a young whipper-snapper at the time, but he's got a heart of gold, so Bobby went along with it and married her. There are songs like 'I'm Through' and 'You're Welcome, Stop on By' on this album that are just beautiful.

Bobby came to stay with us once in Wimbledon. It was firework night and we had people over and a big bonfire. 'What's all this bangin' going on?' he asked when he came out and didn't understand what was happening. He warmed his hands by the fire, had a quick look and went back in. But in the meantime a friend had brought over a big Alsatian, a huge dog, which had crept up under Bobby's bed to get away from the fireworks.

Bobby goes back to bed, turns over, puts his hand under the bed and feels this massive carpet-like thing which moves. He was so frightened he leapt out of bed and came running downstairs in a panic, just at the very moment a kid had thrown a Jumping Jack Flash, which was now going bang-bang-bang under Bobby's feet. He started to do this crazy dance about the place – the freaked-out Soul Man in England on the fifth of November.

Bobby has seen and done so much, going right back to his times in the Soul Stirrers and the Five Blind Boys of Alabama – he's not blind, of course, but he said that that didn't seem to matter. I'm not sure that there weren't seven of them anyway.

THE MIGHTY MAYTONES
THE MIGHTY MAYTONES

A fantastic album, very hard to get hold of. It's still somewhere, either in my collection or in Keith's. Songs are memories and a lot of the times when I first hung out with Keith come back to me when I hear this. The soundtrack to *The Harder They Come* also brings back special memories from that time, too.

When I first hung out with Mick he turned me on to *Black Snake Blues* by Clifton Chenier. Just the most fantastic accordion and washboard stuff by Clifton and his brother Cleveland Chenier. I've never seen it since.

PAT GARRETT AND BILLY THE KID
BOB DYLAN

I love that era that Bob went through. That's where he's rooted, I think. There's a little bit of Mexico in every Jew, or indeed in each of us! There's a little bit of the old cowboy, it's lovely.

Bob's musical range is limitless. We did some recording together in the late summer of this year and at the end of the evening's session I said, 'Bob, do you realize we have gone from the Palomino Lounge (a country-and-western club in the San Fernando Valley) to Ronnie Scott's Jazz Club to the early days of the Round House in London, ending up with music which reminded me so much of the early days with the Faces?' We went from rough to smooth, crossed over, and crossed back over again.

I've played a lot with Bob, since the time of *Knocked Out Loaded*, when I was living in L.A. When people say, 'You've really got some weird friends, Woody, I can't get a word out of him,' they don't understand. Underneath that hooded figure there's just a little Gemini trying to get out. We're both Geminis and that's why I understand him.

TERRY WOODS

SINCE BEING ASKED TO CONTRIBUTE a piece for this book, I've gone around the houses trying to find an easy way into it, to no avail. The only way is to go back to the beginning.

As I grew up in the working-class Dublin of the fifties, I was more a child of the wireless than of records. I don't think I bought a record until I was already involved in playing music. I went to school at St James's CBS and, unlike some who seem to have had a wonderful and happy time, I had a miserable and unhappy time. These good, holy and Irish men ('send him to the Brothers, they'll put manners on him') unfortunately had a negative effect on me where Irish culture was concerned. It took me years to get over it. In consequence my abiding interests were soccer and the pictures. I must have driven my mother mad cadging money for The Lyric on James Street, especially if there was a cowboy picture on and in particular if John Wayne was in it. In those days once you'd paid your tanner in you could sit there all day, and mostly I did. When my interest in music was awakened it was directed towards America. I had a natural feel for it and shouldn't have been at all surprised.

In the fifties Irish radio was still insular. There wasn't much American music to be heard, so my older sister and I used to listen to AFN (American Forces Network in Germany) and suddenly my ears pricked up. Ricky Nelson, Buddy Holly, the Everly Brothers and a pair of Levi jeans sent from America. I'd arrived. In the early sixties the folk revival began, and again my sister led the way. I found myself not only listening to but playing mainly American music. I still hadn't bought a record-player as the records I wanted weren't available in Dublin at that time, so I invested in a tape-recorder to tape what some of my better-informed friends had and to scan the airwaves for the likes of Ewan McColl and Peggy Seeger and the BBC folk programmes. Then Bob Dylan's first album arrived and I was knocked sideways. This was where I wanted to go. There was nothing else for it – a record-player was called for at last and a lot of vinyl has gone under the bridge since.

Being the awkward bastard that I am, trying to make the selection has been a trial, but here they are:

BRINGING IT ALL BACK HOME
BOB DYLAN

This album was inspirational. I loved everything about it and still do. 'It's Alright Ma', 'Gates of Eden', 'Maggie's Farm'. Back then it changed the way I looked at music. It opened up so many possibilities. I got introduced to Dylan in Dublin afterwards and he just grunted. Years later, when the Pogues toured the West Coast of America with him, I was introduced to him again and guess what?

TIM HARDIN 1
TIM HARDIN

The late Tim Hardin, one of my favourite writers and singers in the early sixties, wrote 'If I Was a Carpenter' and 'Reason to Believe'. He was a man I would love to have met, who never achieved the commercial success he deserved. The way he sang and played was so different.

TURBULENT INDIGO
JONI MITCHELL

From her first album, *Song to a Seagull*, which I bought in Breen's Record Shop in Liffey Street by sheer chance not long after its release, right along the line she's made some stunning records. She has a way with lyrics that has always grabbed my attention. In the winter of 1994, not long after the Baltic Sea ferry disaster, I found myself shitting bricks on an overnight ferry trip between Stockholm and Helsinki. Everyone else went to the bar while I, having been alcohol-free for the last few years, retired to my bunk, knees knocking, with my books and walkman. It was a long night, but Joni soothed me through the darkest hours. The two songs that stand out for me are 'The Magdalene Laundries' and 'The Sire of Sorrows'.

THE BAND
THE BAND

This was like a tap on the head with a sledgehammer. They were doing with traditional American themes what I wanted to do with Irish music. I still get off on it.

SURREALISTIC PILLOW
THE JEFFERSON AIRPLANE

Dublin 1967/68, The Strip, The Neptune Rowing Club's Pigs Cheek Suppers, New Amsterdam Coffee House, The Bailey. It was a great time, 'Somebody to Love', 'White Rabbit', a time of great awakening and possibly some chemical confusion.

HAVE MOICY
MICHAEL HURLEY/ THE UNHOLY MODAL ROUNDERS/ JEFFREY FREDERICKS & THE CLAMTONES

A great friend, Jack Galloway, an actor with whom I'd lived, drank, fought, died, woke up, drank again and generally caroused about London from the early seventies onwards, turned me on to Michael Hurley, a man after my own heart. Him, Boone, and Jocko do their own thing and what about the begrudgers? This album is a combined effort and has some very witty songs on it. Always brings back a lot of mad memories.

SWORD FISH TROMBONES
TOM WAITS

Pogue time in Europe, and there was a lot of it. Up and down the Berlin corridor (before German unity), P.V.'s missing passport, Russian vodka, The Vopos, insanity but very funny – and all the time Waits growling in my ear. I told him (Waits) about it afterwards on another mad outing in Chicago, but that's another story.

THE PLAYBOY OF THE WESTERN WORLD
SEÁN Ó RIADA AGUS CEOLTÓIRÍ CHUALANN

After all my experiences of the Christian Brothers it was hearing Ó Riada, and in particular this record, that rehabilitated my interest in Irish traditional music and got it going again. Very much a favourite record.

ZUMA
NEIL YOUNG

He is one man who, love him or hate him, never lost the plot. From Buffalo Springfield onwards he has made some great records. He is a regular on my walkman or car machine. *Zuma* evokes particular musical memories for me of the mid-seventies – Loughcrew, Frank Murray and Philip Lynott, Sound Techniques Studio, the pub across the road.

BOOMER'S STORY
RY COODER

There is not a lot left to say about Mr Cooder. He has it. Whatever the fuck it is, he just has it. There had to be one in here and this is it. This record has given me and continues to give me so much pleasure, blah, blah, blah, blah ...

Sin a bhfuil.

NOTES ON CONTRIBUTORS

BOLGER, DERMOT
Poet, writer, publisher and Northsider, whose best novel, *The Journey Home*, was published in 1990.

BOOTH, TIM
Born in 1943, educated Trinity College, Dublin, worked in advertising before leaving to play music with Dr Strangely Strange. Two albums recorded, *Kip of the Serenes* (1968) and *Heavy Petting* (1970). Band split up, but get together for special events. Third album in gestation – *the difficult third album*. These days, a film-maker, artist and designer, lurking on the northern edge of the Wicklow hills, or some place like Clonakilty. Dangerous when roused.

BRADY, PAUL
Singer-songwriter and early member of the traditional group, Planxty. His first rock album, *Hard Station*, appeared in 1981. Bob Dylan said of him, 'People get famous too fast these days and it destroys them. Some guys got it down – Leonard Cohen, Paul Brady, Lou Reed, secret heroes.' His songs have been recorded by Bonnie Raitt, Tina Turner and Cher, among others. Most recent album, *Spirits Colliding*, 1995.

CASEY, PHILIP
Born to Irish parents in London in 1950 and raised in Co.Wexford, he lived in Barcelona from 1974 to1977 and has travelled widely in Israel and Europe. His publications include *The Year of the Knife*, *Poems 1980-1990* (1991), a play, *Cardinal*, and a novel, *The Fabulists* (1994), which won the Listowel Writers' Prize in 1995. Is currently completing a novel called 'The Water Star'.

CASSIDY, LAURENCE
Born in 1950, he is director of the 'Ireland and Its Diaspora' Festival at the Frankfurt Book Fair 1996, and also of the Dublin International Writers' Festival. He has worked as literature and community arts officer of the Arts Council/An Chomhairle Ealaíon.

CHARLES, PAUL
Born in Magherafelt, Co. Derry. First record bought was 'Luke the Drifter' by Hank Williams. Managed a Co. Derry group, Blues by Five, at fifteen. Moved to London where he managed the Belfast band, Fruuup. Now runs Asgard, Europe's oldest contemporary music agency, with Paul Fenn.

CORDELL, DENNY
Left school and became road manager to Chet Baker. The 1960s hit records he produced included 'A Whiter Shade of Pale' by Procol Harum, 'Go Now' by the Moody Blues, 'Flowers in the Rain' by the Move and 'Get Away' by Georgie Fame. Moving to the US he formed Shelter Records and produced best-selling albums by Joe Cocker (*With a Little Help from My Friends*), Tom Petty and the Heartbreakers, Freddie King, J.J. Cale, Leon Russell and Phoebe Snow. He sold his company in 1979 and moved to Co. Carlow, where he bred and trained greyhounds and racehorses, including Baba Karam, the Champion Irish two-year-old colt. In 1991 he joined Island Records in New York and signed the multi-million-selling Limerick band, the Cranberries. Died in February 1996.

MARY COUGHLAN
Galway-born singer and songwriter. Her albums include *Under the Influence* (1990), *Sentimental Killer* (1992) and *Live in Galway* (1996). Currently lives in Bray, Co. Wicklow.

JEANANNE CROWLEY
Dublin-born actress and writer.

CUNNINGHAM, PETER
Born in 1947 and grew up in Waterford. He held a succession of jobs until 1985, when he began to write modern thrillers before turning to contemporary fiction. His most recent novel, *Tapes of the River Delta*, has been published in the United Kingdom, the United States and in Germany.

CURTIS, P.J.
Born in Kilnaboy, the Burren, Co. Clare, in 1944. He has worked as a broadcaster since 1980 on RTÉ Radio 1, 2FM, BBC Radio Ulster and Clare FM. Has produced thirty-five albums for artists and groups such as Altan, Freddie White, Stocktons Wing, Maura O'Connell, Dolores Keane and Mary Black. He has also written several novels, short stories and poems, and has contributed to *Hot Press*, the *Irish Times* and the *Sunday Tribune* over the years.

DEVLIN, BARRY
Born and raised in Co. Tyrone, he moved south in the late sixties and started Horslips in 1971. After ten years of Touring Which Wasn't Actually Hell, he and the other members split and got on with part two. Part two consists, these days, of screenwriting and spending a lot of time with his wife, Caroline, and his monosyllables, Paul, Jack and Kate.

DONALD, KEITH
Session musician and saxophonist with Moving Hearts, Mary Black and Mary Coughlan, among others. Now a director of Music Base in Dublin's Temple Bar.

DONOVAN
Born in Glasgow in May 1946. Having dropped out of art school, he learned the acoustic guitar and started writing his own songs, which were influenced by blues, jazz and folk. He had a string of hits in the sixties, including 'Sunshine Superman' and 'Catch the Wind'. In 1990 he moved to Ireland with his wife Linda. He is currently working on a new album.

DORGAN, THEO
Born in Cork in 1953 and educated in University College Cork. He edited, with Gene Lambert, 'The Great Book of Ireland', with Máirín Ní Dhonnachadha, *Revising the Rising* (1991), and *Irish Poetry Since Kavanagh* (1990). A director of *Poetry Ireland*, his recent collection, *Rosa Mundi*, appeared in 1995.

DOYLE, RODDY
The author of five novels: *The Commitments* (1987), *The Snapper* (1990), *The Van* (1991), *Paddy Clarke Ha Ha Ha* (1993) – for which he won the Booker Prize – and *The Woman Who Walked into Doors* (1996). He has written two plays, *Brownbread* (1987), and *War* (1989). He co-wrote the screenplay of *The Commitments* (1991) and scripted the screenplays of *The Snapper* (1993), *Family* (1994) and *The Van* (1996).

DUNNE, JOHN
Fiction critic for *Books Ireland*. His stories have appeared in a wide variety of magazines and a novel, *Purtock*, was published in 1992. His radio dramas have been broadcast by RTÉ. In 1996 he won the Listowel Writers' Week Short Story Award.

ENRIGHT, ANNE
Born in 1962 in Dublin, where she now lives and works. She went to school there and in Vancouver and attended Trinity College, Dublin. Has worked as an actress and producer; she has also written *The Portable Virgin* (1991) and *The Wig My Father Wore* (1995).

FAITHFULL, MARIANNE
Songwriter, singer and actress, she had her first hit record in 1964 and played Irina in Chekhov's *The Three Sisters* at the Royal Court Theatre, London, in 1967. After a mid-career struggle with addiction, she came to live in Co. Kildare. Played Pirate Jenny in Frank McGuinness's translation of *The Threepenny Opera* at the Gate Theatre and has most recently toured the world with her 'Weimar Cabaret' one-woman show.

FALLON, BP
A true renaissance man, BP Fallon is a writer, photographer, mime artist, tv presenter, deejay, record producer, songwriter, manager and media guru – among his clients have been Traffic, T. Rex and Led Zeppelin. Joined U2 on their Zoo TV tour as viber and disc jockey. Lives in Ireland and hopes to go to heaven one day.

FALLON, PETER
Born 1951, educated Glenstal Abbey and Trinity College, Dublin, founded Gallery Press in 1970. Poetry collections include *The Speaking Stones* (1978), *Winter Work* (1983), *The News and Weather* (1987) and *Eye to Eye* (1992). Lives with his family on a sheep farm in Loughcrew, Co. Meath.

FINN, ALEC
Born in Yorkshire of Irish parents, where he went to art school, dropped out and was sent to his aunt in Roscommon. He discovered how wonderful Ireland was and never went back. He lived in Dublin for seven years before moving to Galway with his bouzouki and falcons. In 1974 in Spiddal he met Mary Bergin and Frankie Gavin and formed Dé Dannan. He has made music ever since.

FOSTER, AISLING
Grew up in Terenure, Dublin, and finished school aged sixteen. She attended the National College of Art before graduating in Arts from University College Dublin. As well as work in advertising and journalism she has written plays for BBC Radio 4, 'The First Time', a story for teenagers, and a novel, *Safe in the Kitchen* (1993). Lives in London with her husband and two children.

FOSTER, JOHN WILSON
Born in Belfast, and is professor of English at the University of British Columbia, Vancouver. Author of a number of books including *Forces and Themes in Ulster Fiction* (1974), *Colonial Consequences* (1991) and *The Achievement of Seamus Heaney* (1995).

GALE, MARTIN
Born in Worcester, England, in 1949. Moved to Ireland in 1950. Educated at Newbridge College and Blackrock Academy (Willie Martin's). Studied painting in the National College of Art and Design. Has exhibited widely in Ireland and other countries. Became a member of Aosdána in 1982.

GÉBLER, CARLO
Born in Dublin, raised in London and now lives in Enniskillen, Co. Fermanagh. He is the author of a number of novels, including *The Eleventh Summer*, *The Cure* and a collection of short stories, *W.9 & Other Lives*. An occasional director of films, such as the BBC 2 series, *Plain Tales from Northern Ireland*, and more recently for Channel 4, *Baseball in Irish History*. He is married to Tyga; they have four children.

GILFILLAN, KATHY
A long time ago in Bethlehem she started life as a junior copywriter in advertising, serving her time for fifteen years. She intends to spend the next fifteen years writing film scripts and plays more in the style of Ernie Wise than Harold Pinter. Is married to Paul McGuinness and has two children.

GILLESPIE, ELGY
Dublin-born author of a book on the Liberties, and former editor of *San Francisco Review of Books*. Freelance writer for British and Irish magazines. Lives in California with various cats and roommates.

GOULDING, TIM
Born in Dublin 1945. Self-taught artist, first one-man show at Hendrik's Gallery, Dublin, 1969, exhibiting since in Ireland, London, Paris, Cagnes-sur-Mer, Mannheim, Washington and New York. In the late sixties, with Tim Booth and Ivan Pawle, played with the psychedelic lounge band, Dr Strangely Strange, and spawned two albums, *Kip of the Serenes* (Island) and *Heavy Petting* (Vertigo). Since 1980 Strange Lee Strange, now de-doctored, have made some fitful thrusts into the soft underbelly of the Irish Musical Public and are currently working on a third and definitive album with the working title of *Strictly Rubato*. Has lived in Allihies, West Cork, since 1968. Member of Aosdána.

GRAHAM, BILL
A cultured polymath and co-founder of *Hot Press* in 1977, he maintained a prodigious output of well-informed articles on a variety of topics until his death in May 1996. Graham's influence on the development of recent Irish music was profound. A friend and adviser to many artists, he was the first to appreciate the potential of U2, whose early success owed much to his assistance.

HAMILTON, HUGO
Born in Dublin of German-Irish parents. His novels include *Surrogate City*, *The Last Shot* and *The Love Test*. His collection of short stories, *Dublin Where the Palm Trees Grow*, appeared in 1996.

HANLY, MICK
Singer-songwriter, formed Monroe in 1973 with Mícheál Ó Domhnnaill and recorded *Celtic Folkweave* with several members of the Bothy Band. Wrote and performed with Moving Hearts in the 1980s before going solo. Albums include *Still Not Cured* and *all i remember*. Mary Black, Christy Moore, Dolores Keane and Hal Ketchum, among others, have covered his songs.

HEALY, DERMOT
Born in 1947 in Co.Westmeath and is author of *Banished Misfortune* (1982), *Fighting with Shadows* (1984), *A Goat's Song* (1995) and *The Bend for Home* (1996). He has been active in writing workshops and community writing projects. He is a member of Aosdána.

HOGAN, DESMOND
Born in east Galway, he has had four novels published, three volumes of stories and a collection of non-fiction, *The Edge of the City* (1993). He now lives in west Limerick after many years abroad.

HUTCHINSON, JOHN
Has worked at the National Gallery of Ireland, at RTÉ, and as lecturer at the National College of Art and Design. During the 1980s he was a freelance journalist, writing about the visual arts and rock music (his first interview was with Eric Clapton, his last with U2). Since 1991 he has been director of the Douglas Hyde Gallery.

KENNY, MARY
Dublin-born, London-based columnist with the *Sunday Telegraph*. Discovered Elvis Presley in January 1995.

LINDSAY-HOGG, MICHAEL

Has directed television, theatre and films, and, in keeping with the idea of favourites, lists some of the productions he thinks he got somewhat right: *Do You Know the Milky Way?* – 1964 Dublin Theatre Festival; *Paint it Black* – the Rolling Stones on *Ready, Steady, Go!*; *Through the Night* – a TV play by Trevor Griffiths; *Professional Foul* – a TV play by Tom Stoppard; *Whose Life is it Anyway?* with Tom Conti in London; *Agnes of God* – Broadway, New York; *The Normal Heart* – New York Public Theatre; *Graceland* – Paul Simon; *The Object of Beauty* with John Malkovich and Andie MacDowell. He lives in Ireland as much as possible.

MACGOWAN, SHANE

Singer and songwriter with, first, the Pogues and currently the Popes. He lives in London.

MCCABE, PATRICK

Born in Clones 1955. Educated Venice Café, Luxor Cinema, Clones. Novels include *Carn*, *The Butcher Boy*, *The Dead School*. Moved to get into Lillies' Bordello one night but was chased.

MCCAFFERTY, NELL

Born in Derry in 1944, was a founding member of the Irishwomen's Liberation Movement and took part in the Contraceptive Train ride from Dublin to Belfast in 1971.

MCGINLEY, CIARAN

Born in the mid-fifties in Ballinasloe, Co. Galway, co-founded *In Dublin* in 1976, and has worked with many musicians over the years as a promoter. A decade later he co-founded the woodland organization Crann. Since submitting his contribution, he has left his beloved Cabra in Dublin 7 to live in the paradise island of Sri Lanka, where he is completing a novel.

MCGRATH, PATRICK

Living in New York and London, he is author of five books of fiction, most recently *Asylum* (1996), and is editor of the anthology *The New Gothic*. Wrote the screenplay adaptation of his first novel, *The Grotesque*. The film was released in June 1996, starring Sting.

MC GUINNESS, FRANK

A playwright.

MCGUINNESS, PAUL

Born in 1951 on an RAF base in Germany. His father was from Liverpool and his mother was from Kerry. He went to Clongowes and Trinity College, Dublin. He has managed U2 since 1978. Is joint owner of Ardmore Film Studios and has been a member of the Arts Council since 1988.

PADDY MOLONEY

Uilleann piper, tin-whistle player and member of the Chieftains.

MORRISON, DANNY

Born in Belfast, January 1953. Former editor of *An Phoblacht/Republican News* and National Director of Publicity, Sinn Féin. Elected to the Northern Ireland Assembly for Mid-Ulster 1982-86. Wrote *West Belfast* (1989), served five and a half years in jail (1990-95) in connection with the abduction of a police informer, and wrote *On the Back of the Swallow* (1994). His third novel will be published in April 1997.

MOYLAN, TERRY

Started learning the pipes with Leo Rowsome in 1968 and became a member of Na Piobairí Uilleann the same year. Has published *Ceol an Phiobaire* (1981), his edition of tunes notated from the playing of pipers, and three collections of set-dances collected from traditional sources, *Irish Dances* (1984),

The Pipers' Set & Other Dances (1985) and *The Quadrilles & Other Sets* (1988). In 1994 his edition of Kerry box-player Johnny O'Leary's repertoire appeared, and in 1996 he published a CD collection of O'Leary's music and co-edited an anthology of the writings of Breandan Breathnach.

MULDOON, PAUL
Born in Co. Armagh in 1951. He read English at Queen's University, Belfast, and while he was at university his first collection of poems was published. His most recent collection, *The Annals of Chile* (1994), won the T.S. Eliot Prize and was a Poetry Book Choice. In 1987 he moved to the United States, and is now a professor at Princeton University.

MYERS, KEVIN
Born in Leicester, England, in 1947. Educated at Ratcliffe and University College Dublin. He worked for RTÉ in the early seventies and as a freelance journalist in Belfast from 1973-78. He joined the *Irish Times* in 1980 and has written 'An Irishman's Diary' since 1981.

NAPER, CHARLES
Born in 1951. Moved to Loughcrew, Co. Meath, in 1953. Educated at Headfort (Ireland), Wellington College (England), Trinity College, Dublin (briefly), Polytechnic of South Bank, London. Presently working as telemanagement salesman, ostrich farmer, B&B manager and chef.

O'BRIEN, GEORGE
Born in 1945, was raised in Lismore, Co. Waterford. He is an associate professor at Georgetown University, Washington DC, and is the author of an autobiographical trilogy, *The Village of Longing* (1987), *Dancehall Days* (1988) and *Out of Our Minds* (1994).

O'CONNOR, JOSEPH
Born in Dublin in 1963. His books include *Cowboys and Indians*, *True Believers*, *Desperadoes*, *Even the Olives Are Bleeding*, *The Secret World of the Irish Male*, *The Irish Male at Home and Abroad* and *Sweet Liberty: Travels in Irish America*. Scripted *A Stone of the Heart*, *The Long Way Home* and *Ailsa*, and the acclaimed stage play *Red Roses and Petrol*. He contributes a weekly column to the *Sunday Tribune*.

O'GRADY, TIMOTHY
Raised in the United States, and has lived in Ireland and in London where he now works. He is the co-author, with Kenneth Griffith, of *Curious Journey, An Oral History of Ireland's Unfinished Revolution* (1982), and *Motherland* (1989).

O'TOOLE, FINTAN
Born in Dublin in 1958, and now works as a columnist and critic for the *Irish Times*. He has broadcast widely in Ireland and Britain. His most recent books are *Black Hole, Green Card* and *Meanwhile Back at the Ranch*. Currently working on a biography of Richard Brinsley Sheridan.

PAISLEY, RHONDA
Born in 1959 in Belfast where she now lives, she is an artist and part-time lecturer in Art and Design in Lisburn College. She has written three books.

REDDING, NOEL
Born on 25 December 1945 in Folkestone, Kent. He took up guitar at thirteen, started his first group at fifteen, and went professional at seventeen with the Burnettes. In September 1966 met and joined what became the Jimi Hendrix Experience – now playing bass instead of guitar. Left the Experience in June 1969 to form the Fat Mattress. After meeting Carol Appleby, moved to West Cork in 1972. Formed the Noel Redding Band, making two albums for RCA. In '77/78 toured Europe with Eric Bell and Les Sampson. In 1980 toured Italy and USA playing acoustic guitar with Carol, on vocals, for ten years, until her death in June 1990 in a car crash. Is presently writing film scripts.

ROWSON, MARTIN
A freelance cartoonist whose work appears in the *New Statesman*, *Guardian*, *Independent*, *Today* and *Sunday Tribune*. He has also done graphic versions of *The Waste Land*, adapted for opera in 1994, and *The Life* and *Opinions of Tristram Shandy, Gentleman* (1996).

SHERIDAN, JIM
Worked in theatre in Ireland and New York before co-writing and directing his first feature film, *My Left Foot*, in 1989. Wrote and directed *The Field* (1990) and *In the Name of the Father* (1993). His film *Some Mother's Son (1996)* won awards at the Edinburgh and San Sebastian film festivals.

SHERIDAN, PETER
Involved in Dublin theatre since his teens. Plays include *Mother of All the Behans*, *The Liberty Suit* and *Diary of a Hunger Strike*. Is working on a number of film projects, including a life of Brendan Behan.

SHORT, PETE
Pete Short is part of Dublin's city-centre streetscape, and has sold *In Dublin* and *Hot Press* outside Bewley's in Grafton Street for as long as we can remember. He is also a father, poet and writer, with an encyclopaedic knowledge and love of music.

SIMMONS, JAMES
Poet and song-writer. Born Derry, educated at Campbell College and Leeds University. He founded *The Honest Ulsterman* in 1969 and in 1990 established the Poets' House at Islandmagee with his third wife. His collections include *Constantly Singing* (1980) and *From the Irish* (1985), as well as three albums of his own songs.

STEPHENSON, JOHN
Born in Dublin 1951 and educated at Trinity College, Dublin, he has worked as producer and provocature in the arts for over twenty years. Ran the Project Arts Centre in the 1970s and directed 'A Sense of Ireland' in London in 1980. Has been commissioned by the Department of Arts & Culture to draw up plans for Ireland's celebrations for the year 2000. His first novel, 'The Virgin', is to be published in 1996.

TÓIBÍN, COLM
Born Wexford 1955; journalist and novelist, now living in Dublin. He is author of *The South* (1990), *The Heather Blazing* (1992) and *The Story of the Night* (1996).

TONER, NIALL
Born in Dublin and got his first guitar at the age of fourteen. He founded the Lee Valley String Band and the Sackville String Band and has played with Doc Watson and Johnny Cash. In 1990, after a series of gigs in New York City with Hank Halfhead and the Rambling Turkeys, he began writing songs and released his début CD in autumn 1996.

TRENCH, BRIAN
Journalist, lecturer, keen cook and father of two. An early member of Dr Strangely Strange, he worked with *Hibernia* magazine, the *Sunday Tribune* and the *Sunday Business Post*, among others, before joining Dublin City University. He lives in Dublin.

TULLIO, PAOLO
Has held a reefer, but never inhaled the smoke.

VENNER, MARK
Has lived in Ireland since 1977. Having worked in the music business for many years, he formed his own band, the Wilf Brothers, in the mid-eighties. They helped popularize Cajun music in Ireland

and continue to play, attracting the likes of Ronnie Wood to perform with them. Also works in television and has recently completed a movie script, *Banshee*.

WARNER, DICK
Born of Anglo-Irish parents, travelled a lot as a child and received little formal secondary education. In the early sixties he went to Trinity College, Dublin, and in the seventies joined RTÉ as a radio producer, living for a while on a boat on the Grand Canal. He currently lives in Co. Kildare with his wife Geraldine, two sons, Luke and Sam, three cats, a dog, nine hens, a cock and three sheep. He is best known for the award-winning television documentary series, *Waterways*.

WHITCOMB, IAN
Born in England in 1941 and educated at Bryanston and Trinity College, Dublin. While supposedly studying, he played piano and sang in various Dublin bands including Bluesville, the first Irish rock band and the first to get into the American Hit Parade, touring that summer in the U.S. with the Beach Boys, the Rolling Stones, etc. Has never managed to throw off the shackles of a One-Hit-Wonder (although he's proud to be the Father of Irish Rock) despite writing nine books on popular music, including *After the Ball: Pop Music from Rag to Rock* (1972). He is married to Regina and lives in Altadena, near Pasadena, southern California, with Rudy Vallée's aged dog.

WILLIAMSON, KATHLEEN
A dual Irish/American citizen, musician/songwriter, anthropologist, judge, and adjunct professor of law. She resides in Arizona and can be reached through the Lilliput Press.

WOOD, RON
Member of the Rolling Stones, now living in Ireland.

WOODS, TERRY
Born Dublin 1947. Musician ... still.

INDEX